PARALLEL COMBINATORIAL OPTIMIZATION

Parallel and Distributed Simulation Systems / Richard Fujimoto

Mobile Processing in Distributed and Open Environments / Peter Sapaty

Introduction to Parallel Algorithms / C. Xavier and S.S. Iyengar

Solutions to Parallel and Distributed Computing Problems: Lessons from Biological Sciences / Albert Y. Zomaya, Fikret Ercal, and Stephan Olariu (Editors)

Parallel and Distributed Computing: A Survey of Models, Paradigms, and Approaches / Claudia Leopold

Fundamentals of Distributed Object Systems: A CORBA Perspective / Zahir Tari and Omran Bukhres

Pipelined Processor Farms: Structured Design for Embedded Parallel Systems / Martin Fleury and Andrew Downton

Handbook of Wireless Networks and Mobile Computing / Ivan Stojmenovic (Editor)

Internet-Based Workflow Management: Toward a Semantic Web / Dan C. Marinescu

Paralled Computing on Heterogeneous Networks / Alexey L. Lastovetsky

Performance Evaluation and Characterization of Parallel and Distributed Computing Tools / Salim Hariri and Manish Parashar

Distributed Computing: Fundamentals, Simulations, and Advanced Topics, 2nd Edition / Hagit Attiya and Jennifer Welch

Smart Environments: Technology, Protocols, and Applications / Diane Cook and Sajal Das

Fundamentals of Computer Organization and Architecture / Mostafa Abd-El-Barr and Hesham El-Rewini

Advanced Computer Architecture and Parallel Processing / Hesham El-Rewini and Mostafa Abd-El-Barr

UPC: Distributed Shared Memory Programming / Tarek El-Ghazawi

Ruling Distributed Dynamic Worlds / Peter Sapaty

Parallel Metaheuristics: A New Class of Algorithms / Enrique Alba (Editor)

Handbook of Sensor Networks: Algorithms and Architectures / Ivan Stojmenovic (Editor)

Dependable Computing: Paradigms, Performance Issues, and Applications / Hassan B. Diab & Albert Y. Zomaya (Editors)

High Performance Computing: Paradigm and Infrastructure / Laurence T. Yang & Minyi Guo (Editors)

Parallel Combinatorial Optimization / El-Ghazali Talbi (Editor)

PARALLEL COMBINATORIAL OPTIMIZATION

Edited by

El-Ghazali Talbi
University of Lille
Villeneuve d'Ascq, France

A JOHN WILEY & SONS, INC., PUBLICATION

Published by John Wiley & Sons, Inc., Hoboken, New Jersey
Published simultaneously in Canada

For general information on our other products and services or for technical support, please
contact our Customer Care Department within the United States at (800) 762-2974, outside the
United States at (317) 572-3993 or fax (317) 572-4002.

Wiley also publishes its books in a variety of electronic formats. Some content that appears in
print may not be available in electronic formats. For more information about Wiley products,
visit our web site at www.wiley.com.

Library of Congress Cataloging-in-Publication Data:

Parallel combinatorial optimization / edited by El-Ghazali Talbi.
   p.   cm.—(Wiley series on parallel and distributed computing)
   Includes index.
   ISBN-10 0-471-72101-8 (cloth)
   ISBN-13 978-0-471-72101-7
   1. Parallel processing (Electronic computers)   2. Electronic data processing—Distributed
processing.   3. Combinatorial optimization.   I. Talbi, El-Ghazali, 1965–   II. Series.
   QA76.58.P3754   2006
   004′.35—dc22   2006007169

10 9 8 7 6 5 4 3 2 1

To my daughter Besma, you are my sweet little girl with an impressive intelligence.
To my mother Zehour for her infinite sacrifice.
To my father Ammar who continues to support me in my academic research.

Combinatorial optimization is a branch of optimization in applied mathematics and computer science, related to operations research, algorithm theory and computational complexity theory that sits at the intersection of several fields, including artificial intelligence, mathematics, and software engineering.

Combinatorial optimization algorithms (exact algorithms and metaheuristics) solve instances of problems that are believed to be hard in general, by exploring the usually large solution search space of these instances. These algorithms achieve this by reducing the effective size of the space, and by exploring that space efficiently.

Parallel combinatorial optimization algorithms are raising significant interest in science and technology since they are able to solve complex problems in different domains (telecommunications, genomics, logistics and transportation, environment, engineering design, etc.).

The need of parallel computing technologies has three main purposes: (1) solving problems faster; (2) solving larger problems; and (3) obtaining robust algorithms.

This book focuses on different parallel optimization algorithms:

- Exact algorithms: branch and bound, dynamic programming, branch and cut, semidefinite programming, constraint programming.
- Metaheuristics: local search, tabu search, simulated annealing, scatter search, GRASP, VNS (variable neighborhood search), ant colonies, genetic programming, evolution strategies, genetic algorithms.
- Hybrid approaches combining exact algorithms and/or metaheuristics.
- Multiobjective optimization algorithms.

This book presents not only parallel algorithms and applications, but also frameworks and libraries that integrate parallel algorithms for combinatorial optimization. Many researchers in this field are not aware of the existence of those frameworks. This will encourage the reusing of existing programs with a high level of transparency regarding the target parallel architecture.

The intended audience consists mainly of the research, development, and engineering fields. For research and development, many domains are concerned: algorithmics and complexity, computer science, mathematics, and operations research. Many engineers are also dealing with optimization in their problem solving (scheduling, routing, network design, etc.). Moreover, the application audience of the book will deal with many important and strategic domains, such as genomics, wireless telecommunication, engineering design, data mining and machine learning.

Many undergraduate courses on optimization throughout the world would be interested in the contents thanks to the introductory part of each chapter, and the additional information on internet resources for the topic. In addition, the doctoral courses related to optimization and complex problem solving will be a direct target of the book.

The purpose of this book is also to serve as a single up-to-date source of reference concerning parallel and distributed issues to the combinatorial optimization community. The contents will provide details on modern and ongoing research on parallel algorithms and applications for combinatorial optimization.

The book is organized following three different issues: (*1*) parallel algorithms; (*2*) parallel frameworks; and (*3*) parallel applications.

For the first issue (parallel algorithms), some chapters present a state of the art of parallel strategies, plus a part devoted to background on sequential algorithms. Each chapter will compare the most important issues featured by the parallel models against the sequential cases.

The second issue presents the well-known parallel and distributed frameworks for combinatorial optimization (COIN, PARADISEO, BOB++, MW, SDPARA, etc.).

For the third issue, some chapters deal with complex and NP-hard problems from different domains, such as telecommunications, genomics, and satisfiability problems.

LIFL Laboratory   EL-GHAZALI TALBI
USTL—INRIA—CNRS

ACKNOWLEDGMENTS

Thanks to all contributors of this book for their cooperation in bringing this book to completion. Thanks to Albert Zomaya who encourage me to go ahead with the idea of editing a book on parallel combinatorial optimization. Thanks also go to all members of my research team OPAC and the INRIA DOLPHIN project: V. Bachelet, J-C. Boisson, M. Basseur, S. Cahon, C. Dhaenens, Z. Hafidi, L. Jourdan, N. Jozefowiez, M. Khabzaoui, D. Kebbal, J. Lemesre, N. Melab, H. Meunier, N. Mezmaz, F. Seynhaeve, A. Tantar, E. Tantar, B. Weinberg. Finally I should like to thank the team at John Wiley & Sons who gave me excellent support throughout this project, and especially for their patience.

■ CONTRIBUTORS

E. Alba, Departamento de Lenguajes y Ciencias de la Computacion
E.T.S.I Informatica, Campus Teatinos, 29071 Malaga (Spain)
eat@lcc.uma.es

F. Almeida, Dpto. Estadistica, I. O. y Computacion
Universidad de La Laguna, 38271 La Laguna Tenerife (Spain)
falmeida@ull.es

M. Basseur, LIFL—University of Lille—INRIA—CNRS
Bat.M3 Cité Scientifique 59655 Villeneuve d'Ascq (France)
basseur@lifl.fr

S. J. Benson, Mathematics and Computer Science Division
Argonne National Laboratory
Argonne, IL 60439 (USA)
benson@mcs.anl.gov

S. Cahon, LIFL—University of Lille—INRIA—CNRS
Bat.M3 Cité Scientifique 59655 Villeneuve d'Ascq (France)
cahon@lifl.fr

T. Crainic, Département Management et Technologie
Université du Québec
315, rue Sainte-Catherine est, local R-2380
Montréal QC H2X 3X2 (Canada)
theo@crt.umontreal.ca

C. Dhaenens, LIFL—University of Lille—INRIA—CNRS
Bat.M3 Cité Scientifique 59655 Villeneuve d'Ascq (France)
dhaenens@lifl.fr

K. Fujisawa, Department of Mathematical sciences
Tokyo Denki University
Ishizaka, Hatoyama, Saitama, 350-0394 (Japan)
fujisawa@r.dendai.ac.jp

M. Fukuda, Department of Mathematical and Computing Sciences
Tokyo Institute of Technology
2-12-1-W8-29 Oh-okayama, Meguro-ku, Tokyo 152-8552 (Japan)
mituhiro@is.titech.ac.jp

W. Glankwamdee, Lehigh University
Dept. of Ind. & Systems Eng., 200 W. Packer Avenue,
Bethlehem PA 18015 (USA)
wag3@lehigh.edu

D. Gonzalez, Dpto. Estadistica, I. O. y Computacion
Universidad de La Laguna, 38271 La Laguna Tenerife (Spain)
dgonzalez@ull.es

L. Jourdan, LIFL—University of Lille—INRIA—CNRS
Bat.M3 Cité Scientifique 59655 Villeneuve d'Ascq (France)
jourdan@lifl.fr

M. Kojima, Department of Mathematical and Computing Sciences
Tokyo Institute of Technology
2-12-1-W8-29 Oh-okayama, Meguro-ku, Tokyo 152-8552 (Japan)
kojima@is.titech.ac.jp

B. Lecun, Prism—Université de Versailles
45, Avenue des Etats-Unis 78035 Versailles (France)
Bertrand.Lecun@prism.uvsq.fr

J. Lemesre, LIFL—University of Lille—INRIA—CNRS
Bat.M3 Cité Scientifique 59655 Villeneuve d'Ascq (France)
lemesre@lifl.fr

T. Linderoth, Lehigh University
Dept. of Ind. & Systems Eng., 200 W. Packer Avenue,
Bethlehem PA 18015 (USA)
jtl3@lehigh.edu

G. Luque, Departamento de Lenguajes y Ciencias de la Computacion
E.T.S.I Informatica, Campus Teatinos, 29071 Malaga (Spain)
gabriel@lcc.uma.es

S. L. Martins, Departamento de Ciencia da Computacao
Universidade Federal Fluminense
Niteroi, RJ 22410 (Brazil)
simone@dcc.ic.uff.br

N. Melab, LIFL—University of Lille—INRIA—CNRS
Bat.M3 Cité Scientifique 59655 Villeneuve d'Ascq (France)
melab@lifl.fr

M. Mezmaz, LIFL—University of Lille—INRIA—CNRS
Bat.M3 Cité Scientifique 59655 Villeneuve d'Ascq (France)
mezmaz@lifl.fr

K. Nakata, Department of Industrial Engineering and Management
Tokyo Institute of Technology
2-12-1-W8-29 Oh-okayama, Meguro-ku, Tokyo 152-8552 (Japan)
knakata@me.titech.ac.jp

I. Pelaez, Dpto. Estadistica, I. O. y Computacion
Universidad de La Laguna, 38271 La Laguna Tenerife (Spain)
ipelaez@ull.es

I. Rosseti, Departamento de Ciencia da Computacao
Universidade Federal Fluminense
Niteroi, RJ 22410 (Brazil)
rosseti@dcc.jc.uff.br

C. Roucairol, Prism—Université de Versailles
45, Avenue des Etats-Unis 78035 Versailles (France)
Catherine.Roucairol@prism.uvsq.fr

T. Ralphs, Industrial and Systems Engineering
Lehigh University
200 W. Packer Ave.
Bethlehem, PA 18015-1583 (USA)
tkralphs@lehigh.edu

C. C. Ribeiro, Departamento de Ciencia da Computacao
Universidade Federal Fluminense
Niteroi, RJ 22410 (Brazil)
celso@inf.puc-rio.br

I. Sakellariou, Department of Informatics, Aristotle University
54124 Thessaloniki (Greece)
iliass@csd.auth.gr

D. Singer, LITA—Université de Metz—Faculté des Sciences
Ile de Saulcy 57045 Metz Cedex (France)
daniel.singer@sciences.univ-metz.fr

E-G. Talbi, LIFL—University of Lille—INRIA—CNRS
Bat.M3 Cité Scientifique 59655 Villeneuve d'Ascq (France)
talbi@lifl.fr

I. Vlahavas, Department of Informatics, Aristotle University
54124 Thessaloniki (Greece)
vlahavas@csd.auth.gr

M. Yamashita, Shindow Laboratory—Department of Industrial Management
and Science
Kanagawa University (Japan)
Makoto.Yamashita@ie.kanagawa-u.ac.jp

CHAPTER 1

Parallel Branch-and-Bound Algorithms

TEODOR GABRIEL CRAINIC

Département de management et technologie École des Sciences de la Gestion Université du Québec à Montréal and CIRRELT, Canada

BERTRAND LE CUN and CATHERINE ROUCAIROL

Laboratoire PR*i*SM, Université de Versailles (France)

1.1. INTRODUCTION

In the beginning of the twenty-first century, large unsolved combinatorial optimization problems have been solved exactly.

Two impressive cases should be mentioned. First are two instances of the famous Symmetric Traveling Salesman problem (TSP) with >10,000 cities (respectively, 13,509 and 15,112 cities; instances usa13509, d15112) by Applegate *et al.* (1). Second are instances of the Quadratic Assignment Problem (QAP) up to size 32, Nugent 30 (900 variables) and Krarup 32 (1024 variables) by Anstreicher, Brixius, Goux, and Linderoth (2,3). The results on the instance Nugent 30 have been announced in American (Chicago Tribune, Chicago Sun Times, HPCWire, WNCSA Access Magazine) and French (InfoScience, Le Monde, Transfert) newspapers. This impressive media frenzy reflected the impact of the achievement, which was deemed of the same order of magnitude as the victory of IBMs parallel computer DeepBlue over the chess world champion Kasparov.

Several factors combined to bring on these achievements. A first reason is the scientific progress in Operations Research, in particular regarding the quality of the lower bounds for these problems (cutting plane techniques for the TSP and convex quadratic programming for the QAP). The computation of these new bounds is very time consuming, however. Moreover, the bounds are computed at each node of a tree whose size is huge (several billions of nodes). The progress in processor computing power certainly contributed.

Parallel Combinatorial Optimization, edited by El-Ghazali Talbi
Copyright © 2006 by John Wiley & Sons, Inc.

These two reasons would not have been sufficient, however. The utilization of *parallel branch-and-bound* (B&B) strategies on large computer clusters and grids with advanced programming tools, including multithreading and fault tolerance functionalities, is the third factor of success. Indeed, the TSP instance usa13509 required 48 workstations (DECAlpha, Pentium II, Pentium Pro, and Ultrasparc) that explored in parallel a tree of 9539 nodes. The instance Nugent 30 (30 firms to be assigned to 30 sites) needed the exploration of a tree with 11,892,208,412 nodes and a network of 2510 heterogeneous machines with an average number of 700 working machines (Pc, Sun, and SGI Origin2000). These machines were distributed in two national laboratories (Argonne, NCSA), five American universities (Wisconsin, Georgia tech, New Mexico, Colombia, Northwestern), and was connected to the Italian network INFN. The time spent was ~1 week! But, the equivalent sequential time on a HP-C3000, for example, was estimated at 218,823,577 s or 7 years!

The resolution of these problems by using parallel B&B illustrates the interest of this methodology. Not all NP-hard combinatorial optimization problems or problem instances may be equally well addressed, however. An honest analysis of the above results shows that these performances are also due to some characteristics of the problems, particularly the existence of very good upper bounds. Moreover, the tree search strategy used was equivalent to a brute force exploration of the tree. In most cases, bounds are less tight and more advanced parallel tree exploration strategies must be used. The goal of this chapter is to discuss some of these challenges and present some of the parallel B&B strategies that may be used to address them. We will show how parallelism could help to fight against the combinatorial burst and to address efficiently (linear speed up) and accurately (optimal solutions) combinatorial optimization problems of considerable size. A general review of parallel B&B methodology and literature may be found in Gendron and Crainic (4).

The chapter is organized as follows. Section 1.2 briefly recalls the sequential B&B algorithm. Section 1.3 presents the different sources of parallelism that can be exploited in a B&B algorithm. Section 1.4 discusses the performances that can be obtained from a theoretical and experimental point of view. Section 1.5 presents different parallelization strategies, with their respective advantages, issues, and limits. Section 1.6 briefly reviews B&B libraries proposed to help the user to implement the different parallelization strategies and to benefit from advanced programming tools, including multithreading and fault tolerance functionalities. To illustrate these concepts, the application of parallel B&B to the QAP is presented in Section 1.7. Section 1.8 contains concluding remarks.

1.2. SEQUENTIAL B&B

Let us briefly recall the main components of a B&B algorithm. Suppose the following combinatorial optimization problem is to be solved: Given a finite discrete set X, a function $F: X \to \mathbb{R}$, and a set S, where $S \subseteq X$, and an *optimal* solution $x^* \in S$, such that $f(x^*) = \min\{f(x)|\forall x \in S\}$. The set S is usually a set of constraints and is called feasible domain, all elements $x \in S$ being *feasible* solutions. We assume that S is finite or empty.

A **branch-and-bound** (B&B) solution method consists in implicitly enumerating S by examining a subset of feasible solutions only. The other solutions are eliminated when they cannot lead to a feasible or an optimal solution.

Enumerating the solutions of a problem consists in building a B&B tree whose nodes are subsets of solutions of the considered problem. The size of the tree, that is, the number of generated nodes, is directly linked to the strategy used to build it.

Synthetically, the B&B paradigm could be summed up as follows:

Building the Search Tree

- A *branching scheme* splits X into smaller and smaller subsets, in order to end up with problems we know how to solve; the B&B nodes represent the subsets, while the B&B edges represent the relationship linking a parent-subset to its child-subsets created by branching.
- A *search* or *exploration strategy* selects one node among all pending nodes according to priorities defined *a priori*. The priority of a node or set S_i, $h(S_i)$, is usually based either on the depth of the node in the B&B tree, which leads to a depth-first tree-exploration strategy, or on its presumed capacity to yield good solutions, leading to a best-first strategy.

Pruning Branches

- A *bounding function* υ gives a *lower bound* for the value of the best solution belonging to each node or set S_i created by branching.
- The *exploration interval* restricts the size of the tree to be built: Only nodes whose evaluations belong to this interval are explored, other nodes are eliminated. The smallest value associated to a pending node in a current tree, the upper bound UB, belongs to this interval and may be provided at the outset by a known feasible solution to the problem, or given by a heuristic. The upper bound is constantly updated, every time a new feasible solution is found (value of the best known solution, also called the *incumbent*).
- *Dominance relationships* may be established in certain applications between subsets S_i, which will also lead to discard nondominant nodes.

A Termination Condition

This condition states when the problem is solved and the optimal solution is found. It happens when all subproblems have been either explored or eliminated.

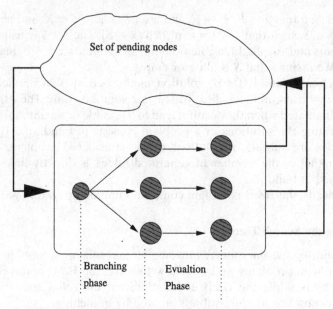

Fig. 1.1. Graphical view of a sequential B&B algorithm.

From an algorithmic point of view, illustrated in Fig. 1.1, a B&B algorithm consists in carrying out a series of basic operations on a pool of nodes (set of nodes of varying or identical priority), usually implemented as a priority queue: *deletemin* (select and delete the highest priority element), *insert* (insert a new element with predefined priority), *deletegreater* (delete elements with higher priority than a given value).

1.3. SOURCES OF PARALLELISM

Two basic, by now classic, approaches are known to accelerate the B&B search:

1. *Node*-based strategies that aim to accelerate a particular operation, mainly at the node level: Computation in parallel of lower or upper bound, evaluation in parallel of sons, and so on.
2. *Tree*-based strategies that aim to build and explore the B&B tree in parallel.

Node-based strategies aim to accelerate the search by executing in parallel a particular operation. These operations are mainly associated to the sub-problem, or node, evaluation, bounding, and branching, and range from "simple" numerical tasks (e.g., matrix inversion), to the decomposition of computing intensive tasks (e.g., the generation of cuts), to parallel mathematical programming (e.g., simplex, Lagrangean relaxation, capacitated multicommodity network flow) and meta-heuristic (e.g., tabu search) methods used to compute lower bounds and to derive feasible solutions. This class of strategies has also been identified as *low-level* (or *type 1*) parallelization, because they do not aim to modify the search trajectory, neither the dimension of the B&B tree nor its exploration. Speeding it up is the only objective. It is noteworthy, however, that some node-based approaches may modify the search trajectory. Typical examples are the utilization of parallel Lagrangean relaxation or parallel simplex, particularly when multiple optima exist or the basis is transmitted by the nodes generated by the branching operation.

Other strategies, for example, *domain decomposition* (decompose the feasible domain and use B&B to address the problem on each of the components of the partition) and *multisearch* (several different B&B explore the same solution domain in parallel with or without communications), hold great promise for particular problem settings, but have not yet been studied in any particular depth. Note that these strategies are not mutually incompatible. Indeed, when problem instances are particularly hard and large, several strategies may be combined into a comprehensive algorithmic design. Thus, for example, node-based strategies could initiate the search and rapidly generate interesting subproblems, followed by a parallel exploration of the tree. Or, a multisearch approach may be set up, where each B&B search is using one or more parallel strategies. Tree-based strategies have been the object of a broad and most comprehensive research effort. Therefore, in this chapter, the focus is on tree-based strategies.

Tree-based parallelization strategies yield *irregular algorithms* and the corresponding difficulties have been well identified [e.g., Authié *et al.* (5) and the STRATAGEMME project (6)]:

- Tasks are created dynamically in the course of the algorithm.
- The structure of the tree to explore is not known beforehand.
- The dependency graph between tasks is unpredictable: no part of the graph may be estimated at compilation or runtime.
- The assignment of tasks to processors must be done dynamically.
- Algorithmic aspects, such as sharing and balancing the workload or transmitting information between processes, must be taken into account at run time in order to avoid overheads due to load balancing or communication.

Furthermore, parallelism can create tasks that are redundant or unnecessary for the work to be carried out (*research overhead*), or which degrade performances, the so-called *speedup anomalies*. Some of these issues are examined in the next section.

1.4. CRITICAL B&B TREE AND SPEEDUP ANOMALIES

The success of the parallelization of a B&B algorithm may be measured experimentally by the **absolute speedup** obtained with p processors, defined as the

```
Node root; // the root node.
PriorityQueue set; // the priority queue that  stores the
                   // set of pendings nodes
Node incumbent; // the Incubent.

  set.Ins(root);
  while (! set.empty() ) {
    Node n = set.deletemin();
    foreach ( Node s son of n) { // Branching
      s.Evaluate(); // Evaluation of the node s
      if ( s.IsSolution() && incumbent.Cost()>s.Cost() ){
          incumbent= son;
      pq.Deletegreater(incumbent.Cost());
      }
      else if ( s.Feasible() && incumbent.Cost()>s.Eval() )
          set.Insert(s);
    }
  }
```

Fig. 1.2. Pseudo-code of a sequential B&B algorithm.

ratio of the time taken by the best serial algorithm over that obtained with a parallel algorithm using p processors, for one instance of a problem. For the sake of simplicity, **a relative speed-up** is often used, defined as the ratio of the time taken by a serial algorithm implemented on one processor over the time required by parallelizing the same algorithm and implementing it on p processors. *Efficiency* is a related measure computed as the speedup divided by the number of processors.

For parallel tree-based B&B, one would expect results that show almost linear speedup, close to p (efficiency close to 100%). Yet, the relative speedup obtained by a parallel B&B algorithm may sometimes be quite spectacular, $>p$, while at other times, a total or partial failure (much $<p$) may be observed. These behavioral anomalies, both positive and negative, may seem surprising at first (7). They are mainly due to the combination of the speedup definitions and the properties of the B&B tree where priorities, or the bounding function, may only be recognized *a posteriori*, once the exploration is completed. These issues have been the subject of a great deal of research in the 1980s (we would like to quote Refs 8, 9 and refer to Ref. 6 for a more comprehensive literature review).

In fact, the time taken by a serial B&B is related to the number of nodes in the fully developed tree. The size of the B&B tree—where the branching rule, the bounding function v, and the node-processing priority h have been defined *a priori* (prior to execution)—depends on the search strategy and the properties of v.

Four different types of nodes may be defined in a B&B tree (6,7), illustrated in Section 1.3:

1. Critical nodes, set C, representing incomplete solutions with a value strictly smaller than the optimum solution f^*.
2. Undecidable nodes, set M, which are nonterminal, incomplete, solutions with a value equal to f^*.
3. Optimal nodes, set O, with the value f^*.
4. Eliminated nodes, set E, with a value strictly $>f^*$.

As a B&B algorithm is executed according to a *best-first* strategy, it develops all the critical nodes, some undecidable nodes, and one optimal node. Certain nodes belonging to E can be explored when using other strategies. Any strategy will always develop the set of critical nodes, also called the **critical tree**. Several executions may correspond to the same developed B&B tree, according to the choices made by the strategy between nodes of equal priority, which may be very numerous.

The **minimal tree** is defined as the tree which, regardless of the exploration strategy, must be built to prove the optimality of a feasible solution and that has the minimal number of nodes. Notice that the critical tree (critical node) is included in the minimal tree. In parallel processing, p processors must explore all nodes in the minimal tree. In serial processing, speedup is always linear (lower than or equal to p) if the minimal tree has been built. Therefore, the serial time is that of the *best* possible serial algorithm.

The fact that it is not always possible to define *a priori* the search strategy to construct the minimal tree shows that speedups may be favorable (the serial tree is very large) or unfavorable, and therefore proves the existence of these anomalies. It is interesting to note that parallelism may have a corrective effect in serial cases, where the minimal tree has not been built.

In a theoretical synchronous context, where one iteration corresponds to the exploration of p nodes in parallel by p processors between two synchronizations, a suitable condition for avoiding detrimental anomalies is h to be discriminating (9). One necessary condition for the existence of favorable anomalies is that h should not be completely *consistent* with υ (strictly higher priority means a lower or equal value). This is the case of the breadth and depth-first strategies.

The *best-first* strategy constructs the minimal tree if (sufficient condition) there are no undecidable nodes ($M = \emptyset$), and if the bounding function is *discriminating*, which means that υ is such that no nodes have equal priority. The best-first strategy has proved to be very *robust* (10). The speedup it produces varies within a small interval around p. It avoids detrimental anomalies if υ is discriminating, as we have already seen, or if it is consistent (at least one node of the serial tree is explored at each iteration) (11).

Rules for selecting between equal priority nodes have been studied (11), with the aim of avoiding unfavorable anomalies in best-first B&B algorithms, thus eliminating processing overheads or memory occupation, which is not the case with the other proposals (12). Three policies, based on the order in which nodes are created in the tree, have been compared: (*1*) newest (the most

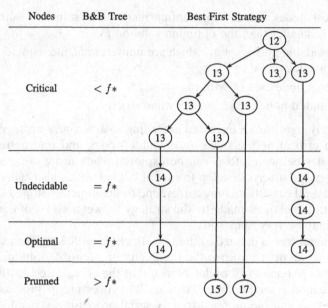

Fig. 1.3. Example of nodes classification of a B&B tree.

recently generated node); (2) leftmost (the leftmost node in the search tree); and (3) oldest (the least recently generated node).

Bounds calculated on expected speedups show that the "oldest" rule is least likely to produce anomalies. It is therefore interesting to study the data structures which, unlike the well-known heaps, can implement the "oldest" rule. As similar results (condition of existence of anomalies) may be demonstrated when the number of processors is increased (growth anomalies or non-monotonous increases in speed up), some researchers worked on defining a measurement, the isoefficiency function $iso(p)$ (13), based on general results on the "scalability" of parallel algorithms: in order to maintain an efficiency of e with p processors, the size of the problem processed should grow according to a function $iso(p)$.

Despite the obvious advantage of keeping acceleration anomalies possible, the interest in avoiding detrimental anomalies has been emphasized. In this context, Li and Wah (9) presented a special condition on the nodes with same priority that is sufficient to avoid degradation. Their method is attractive for depth-first search strategies where anomalous behavior is quite usual, and has been improved technically by Kalé and Saletore (12).

An example of anomaly with best-first strategy is given in Fig. 1.4. Since the cost of unfavorable anomalies needs to be compared with the price to forbid them, it may be worthwhile to consider the design and analysis of basic best-first search strategies, which deal with active nodes of same priority (same value), without either processing or memory overhead due to the removal of unfavorable anomalies.

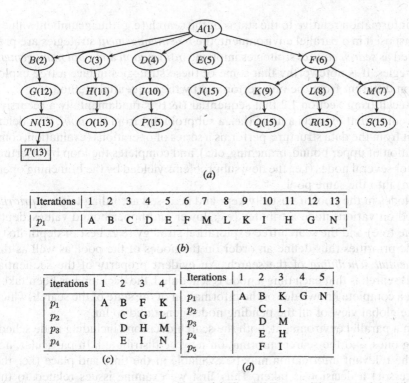

Fig. 1.4. Example of Anomaly on a B&B. (*a*) The B&B tree. (*b*) Sequential scheduling with best-first search. (*c*) Parallel scheduling with 4 processors. (*d*) Parallel scheduling with five processors.

However, it is very important during the design process of a B&B algorithm to be able to define different priorities for subproblems (nodes) to be explored and to deal with nodes of equal priorities.

1.5. STRATEGIES FOR PARALLELIZATION

Most parallel B&B algorithms implement some form or another of tree exploration in parallel. The fundamental idea is that in most applications of interest the size of the B&B enumeration tree grows, possibly rapidly, to unmanageable proportions. So, if the exploration of the search tree is done more quickly by several processes, the faster acquisition of knowledge during the search (communication between processes) will allow for pruning more nodes or for eliminating more branches of the tree.

To describe the possible strategies, we start from a representation of the sequential B&B where a number of operations are performed on the data structure containing the work to be done (e.g., nodes in various states) and the information relative to the status of the search (e.g., the incumbent value). Transposed in a parallel environment, the *tree management* strategies are presented as *search control* strategies implying *information* and *pool management* strategies. It is noteworthy that some of these strategies induce a tree exploration different from the one performed by the sequential method.

Recall from Section 1.2 that sequential B&B is fundamentally a recursive procedure that extracts a node (i.e., a subproblem) from the *pool*, thus deleting it from the data structure, performs a series of operations (evaluation, computation of upper bound, branching, etc.), and completes the loop by inserting one or several nodes (i.e., the new subproblems yielded by the branching operation) into the same pool.

Nodes in the pool are usually kept and accessed according to their *priority* based on various node attributes (e.g., lower and upper bound values, depth in the tree) and the search tree exploration strategy (e.g., best or depth-first). Node priorities thus define an order on the nodes of the pool, as well as the *sequential scheduling* of the search. An evident property of the sequential B&B search is that each time a node is scheduled, the decision has been taken with a complete knowledge of the information of the state of the search, which is the global view of all the pending nodes generated so far.

In a parallel environment, both the search decisions, including node scheduling ones, and the search information may be distributed. In particular, not all the relevant information may be available at the time and place (i.e., the processor) a decision is taken. Thus, first we examine issues related to the storage and availability of information in a parallel exploration of a B&B tree. We then turn to the role processors may play in such an exploration. The combination of various alternatives for these two components yield the basic strategies for parallel B&B algorithm design.

Two issues have to be addressed when examining the search information in a parallel context: (*1*) how is this information stored; (*2*) what information is available at decision time.

The bulk of the search information is made up of the pool of nodes, and *pool management* strategies address the first issue with respect to it: if and how to decompose the pool of nodes. A *centralized* strategy keeps all the nodes in a central pool. This implies that this unique pool serves, in one form or another, all processors involved in the parallel computation. Alternatively, in a *distributed* strategy, the pool is partitioned, each subset being stored by one processor. Other relevant information (e.g., global status variables like the value of the incumbent) is of limited size. Consequently, the issue is not whether it is distributed or not, but rather whether it is available in an up-to-date form when decisions are taken.

In a parallel B&B algorithm, more than one processor may decide, more or less simultaneously, to process a node. Their collective action corresponds to the *parallel scheduling* of the search, that is, to the management of the entire, but often distributed, pool and the corresponding distribution of work among processors.

The scheduling of nodes is based on the node priorities, defined as before in the sequential context. We define as *search knowledge*, the pool of nodes with their priorities, plus the incumbent value and the other global status variables of the search. The search knowledge may be *complete* or *partial*. If the search knowledge is complete, the resulting scheduling is very close to the sequential scheduling. Indeed, when at each step, the processor that has to make up a scheduling decision has an exact and complete knowledge of all the pending nodes to process, its decision is almost the same as in the sequential case. When only partial information is known to a processor, the scheduling could be really different compared to the sequential one.

When information is distributed, parallel scheduling must also include specific provisions to address a number of particular issues:

- The definition of a parallel initialization phase and of the initial work allocation among processors.
- The updating of the global status variables (e.g., the value of the incumbent).
- The termination of the search.
- The minimization of the idle time.
- The maximization of the meaningful work.

Search control strategies specify the role of each processor in performing the parallel search, that is, decisions relative to the extraction and insertion of nodes into the pool(s), the exploration strategy, the work to perform (e.g., total or partial evaluation, branching, offspring evaluation), the communications to undertake to manage the different pools, and the associated search knowledge.

From a search control point of view, we distinguish between two basic, but fundamental, types of processes: *master*, or *control*, and *slave* processes. Master processes execute the complete range of tasks. They specify the work that slave processes must do and fully engage in communications with the other master processes to implement the parallel scheduling of the nodes, control the exchange of information, and determine the termination of the search. Slave processes communicate exclusively with their assigned master process and execute the prespecified tasks on the subproblem they receive. Slave processes do not engage in scheduling activities.

The classical *master-slaves*, or *centralized control*, strategy makes use of these two types in a two-layer processor architecture, one master process and a number of slave processors (Fig. 1.5). This strategy is generally combined to a centralized pool management strategy. Thus, the master process maintains global knowledge and controls the entire search, while slave processes perform the B&B operations nodes received from the master processor and return the result to the master.

At the other end of the spectrum, one finds the *distributed control* strategy combined to a distributed pool management approach. In this case, sometimes also called *collegial* and illustrated in Fig. 1.6, several master processes

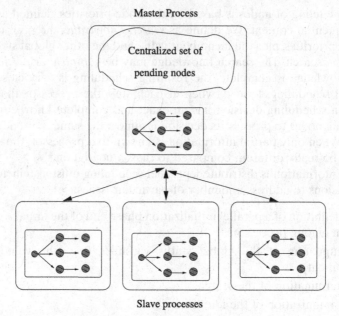

Fig. 1.5. Master-slave B&B algorithm.

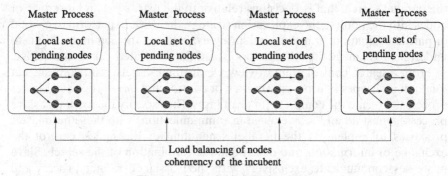

Fig. 1.6. Collegial B&B algorithm.

collegially control the search and the associated information. In this basic approach, there are no slave processes. Each master process is associated to one of the local pools that stores a subsets of the currently existing nodes (there is no sharing of local pools among several masters). It then performs the B&B operations on its local pool based on this partial node information, as well as on information transmitted by the other processes. The all-master processes combined activities thus makes up the partial-knowledge parallel scheduling.

The pool distribution and thus the search information distribution often results in uneven workloads for the various processes during the search. A *load balancing* strategy must then be implemented to indicate how the information relative to the processor workloads circulates and how the corresponding load balancing decisions are taken. Information updating the global status variables (incumbent value, termination status, etc.) must also be exchanged. This communication policies set enforces the global control over the search. From a control point of view, two approaches are again available: either the decision is collegially distributed among the processes or it is (more or less) centralized. Thus, in the basic collegial strategy introduced above, all master processes may exchange messages (according to various communication topologies and policies) and decide collectively on how to equilibrate loads. Alternatively, one of the processors acts as load balancing master. It collects the load information and decides on the data exchanges to perform.

These strategies and types of processes are the basic building blocks that may be combined to construct more complex, hierarchical parallel strategies, with more than one level of information (pool) distribution, search control, and load balancing. Thus, for example, a processor could depend on another for its own load balancing, while controlling the load balancing for a group of lower level master processes, as well as the work of a number of slave processes.

1.6. BRANCH-AND-BOUND SOFTWARE

The range of purpose for B&B software is quite large, so it stands to reason that the numbers of problem types, user interface types, parallelization types, and machine types are also large.

This chapter focuses on software for which there exists an interface to implement Basic B&B, which means that one can use this type of library to implement one's own bounding procedure and one's own branching procedure. Several Libraries or applications exist, which are dedicated to one type of problems, commercial linear solvers like CPLEX, XPress-MP, or Open Source Software like GLPK (14) or lp_Solve are dedicated to solve Mixed Integer Linear program, but the B&B part is hidden in a "Black-Box". It could not be customized to implement an efficient parallel one.

However, these solvers could be used using a callable library. An application that implements a Parallel Basic B&B could use this kind of Solvers to compute the Bound. In this case, only the linear solver is used, the B&B part is ignored.

We first explain the designing tips used to develop this kind of software. Then we try to discuss the different Frameworks in terms of User algorithms they provide, the proposed Parallelization strategies, and finally the target machines.

1.6.1. Designing of a B&B FrameWork

When we consider the really basic form of B&B, *framework* is the only possible form of software. A Framework in this context is an implementation of a B&B, with hooks that allow the user to provide custom implementations of certains aspects of the algorithm. For example, the user may wish to provide a custom branching rule, or custom bounding function. The customization is generally accomplished either through the use of C language callback functions or through a C++ interface in which the user must derive certain base classes and override default implementations for the desired function. In most cases, base classes and default implementations are abstract. The main algorithm, for example, the B&B loop, is written as a *skeleton* of algorithm. A skeléton uses abstract classes or abstract functions that must be redefined to obtain a concrete application.

In a Basic B&B, the abstractions are the following: node type, which includes the data in order to compute the bound of the subproblem and also stores the partial solution of the subproblem; solution type, which includes the value and the solution itself (the value of the variables), sometimes the type could be the same for the solution and for the subproblem; a function to evaluate the node, which according to the data stored in the node computes the evaluation of the partial solution, or the cost of a complete solution; a function used for branching, which must implement the method by which a subproblem is divided into subproblems according to the problem; a function to generate the root subproblem; and a function to generate the initial solution.

The Framework generally offers the following functionalities: the priority of a node that decides the order in which the subproblems will be explored. The choice of the node priority defines the search strategy; the management of the pending nodes, which is generally made using priority queues. As said in Section 1.5 about the parallelization strategy, the framework could store one or several priority queues, the managing of the pending nodes is then centralized or distributed; the management of the incumbent when a process finds a better solution, the framework must update it automatically in the other processes; and the main B&B loop that is executed by each process.

Let us present a modified version of Fig. 1.2 in order to present the data or function that must must be redefined by the user and the parts that are provided by the Framework. This design is not the unique possible design for a Framework. Authors of such a framework surely present theirs in a different way. But we believe that this design is what correponds more to reality.

The type Node represents a subproblem. As already mentioned, it must be defined by the user, in a Object Oriented Framework (written in C++, e.g.), the user defines its own type by derivating the type offered by the Framework.

Here, the type of the Solution (incumbent) is the same as the type of a subproblem; as said before, some Frameworks defined different types for the solution and for the nodes.

The type ParaPriorityQueue is provided by the Framework. It is used by the main loop to obtain a new node to be explored and to insert a new generated nodes.

```
// User Defined
procedure Branch(Node current, ParaPriorityQueue set) {
    foreach ( Node s son of current) { // Branching
        ... // fill the data of s according to the problem
        Evaluate(s); // Evaluation of the node s
                     // Redefined by the user
        if ( s.IsSolution() && incumbent.Cost()>s.Cost() ){
            incumbent= son;
            Update(incumbent); // FrameWork defined
        }
        else if ( s.Feasible() \&\& incumbent.Cost()>s.Eval() )
            set.Insert(s); // Framework defined
    }
}


// Framework defined
procedure MainLoop() {
    Node root;              // the root node.
    ParaPriorityQueue set;  // the priority queue that  stores the
                            // set of pendings nodes
    Node incumbent;         // the Incubent.

    // Only executed by one processor
    if ( I am Master processor ) {
        Initialize(Root)  // User Defined
        set.Ins(root);  // Framework defined
    }
    // The main loop
    while (! set.empty() ) { // Framework defined
        Node n =  set.deletemin();// Framework defined
        Branch(n,set); // User defined
    }
}
```

Fig. 1.7. Skeleton of a parallel B&B algorithm.

According to the parallelisation strategy, this type could have different implementations. First, in a centralized strategy, it is just an interface to receive or send nodes from and to the master process. Second, in a distributed strategy the ParaPriorityQueue stores a local priority queue, and also executes a load balancing procedure in order to ensure that each process has enough interesting nodes. This Data structure, or more generally this interface, could be seen as a high level communication tool. The main loop does not know where the nodes are really stored, but it just knows that this tool could be used to obtain and to insert nodes. The IsEmtpty method or function of the ParaPriorityQueue interface will be true only if no more Nodes exist in the entire application. In a distributed parallel machine like a cluster, for example, this interface will use a message passing library, like MPI or PVM, to transmit Nodes from one process to another.

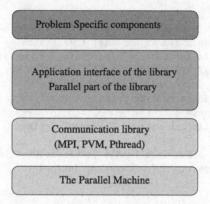

Fig. 1.8. Graphical view of a Framework and its interactions.

The Update function or method is used to broadcast to each process, the value or the new best solution found. The same communication library as the ParaPriorityQueue will be used. The management of the incumbent could be merged with the management of the Pending nodes.

Then we could see the Framework as a composition of different levels as presented in the Fig. 1.8. On the higher level, the user defines types and functions. On the low level the target machine.

There are many Frameworks for parallel B&B including:

1. PUBB (Univ. of Tokyo) (15).
2. BOB++ (Univ. of Versailles) (16).
3. PPBB-Lib (Univ. of Paderborn) (17).
4. PICO (Sandia Lab. & Rutgers University) (18).
5. FATCOP (University of Wisconsin) (19).
6. MallBa (Consortium of Spanish universities) (20).
7. ZRAM (Eth Zürich) (21).
8. BCP (CoinOR) (22).
9. ALPS/BiCePS (Leghih University, IBM, Clemson University) (22,23).
10. MW Framework (Leghih University) (24).
11. Symphony (Rice Univ.) (22,25,26).

They differ by the type of B&B they are able to solve, by the type of parallelization they propose, and then by the cibling machine.

Some of them propose a C interface [Bob (27), PPBB-Lib, MallBa, ZRAM, PUBB], although the other ones propose a C++ interface (Bob++, ALPS/BiCePS, PICO, MW).

1.6.2. User Algorithms

As already discussed, there exist a large variety of B&B: Basic B&B with a huge set of bounding procedures, Branch and Price, Branch and Cut. One could also consider that a simple divide and conquer algorithm is a base for a B&B algorithm.

With this multiplcity of methods, to make Framework easy to maintain, easy to use, and as flexible as possible, a possible design is a multilayered class library, in which the only assumptions made in each layer about the algorithm being implemented are those needed for implementing specific functionnality efficiently. Each of the proposed frameworks proposes a subset of these layers in core.

1.6.2.1. The Low-Level Algorithm: The Divide and Conquer. From a design point of view, a Simple tree search procedure like Divide and Conquer could be a base for a B&B procedure. Both are tree search procedures, but the B&B has additional functionalities, like prunning where the evaluation of the subproblem is used to discard a branch of the tree. For the parallelism, the differences of these two algorithms do not imply many modifications. If a parallel B&B is implemented, a parallel Divide and Conquer could also be implemented without a big overcost. For example, ZRAM, Bob++, ALPS, PUBB and MallBa implement simple tree search algorithms like backtracking. ZRAMand MallBA proposes Divide and Conquer and B&B has two different methods. Although, Bob++, ALPS, and PUBB, try to modelize Divide and Conquer as a base class of a B&B.

1.6.2.2. The Basic B&B. Bob, Bob++, PUBB, PPBB, ZRAM, PICO, MallBa, ALPS, BCP, and MW, propose an interface for a basic B&B. The interface are quite similar, and correspond to the design we presented in the previous section.

1.6.2.3. Mixed-Integer Linear Programming. A Mixed-Integer Linear Program could be solved using a B&B where the bounding operation is performed using tools from linear programming and polyhedral theory. Since Linear Programming does not accommodate the designation of integral variables, the integrality constraints are relaxed to obtain a linear programming relaxation. Most of time, this formulation is augmented with additional constraints or cutting planes, that is, inequalities valid for the convex hull of solutions to the original problem. In this way, the hope is to obtain an integral (and hence feasible) solution.

Each Framework that proposes a Basic B&B could also be used to solve Integer Linear Programs. The evaluation function and the Branching function could be written using a linear solver. The Coin Open Solver Interface (OSI) is very usefull for that. The OSI consists of a C++ base class with containers for storing instance data, as well as a standard set of problem import, export modification, solution, and query routines. Each supported solver has a corresponding derived class that implements the methods of the base class. A nonexhaustive list of supported solver is CPLEX, XpressMP, lp_solve, GLPK, CLP.

However, an important feature that must be included in Frameworks to solve such problems efficiently, is a way to globally store the set of already generated cutting planes. One cutting plane that has been generated for one subproblem could be valid for another subproblem. Then, to avoid redundant computation, cutting planes should be stored in a "global data structure", from which processes could obtain an already generated cutting plane without regenerating it. The ALPS/BiCePS, PICO, SYMPHONY, and BCP Frameworks propose such data structure. The ALPS framework introduces the notion of Knowledge Base (KB).

1.6.2.4. Branch and Price and Cut.

The Frameworks that propose a native interface for Branch and Price and Cut are Symphony and ALPS/BiCePS. As SYMPHONY is written in C, its user interface consists in implementing callback funtions including cutting-planes, generation, management of cut pool, management of the LP relaxation, search and dividing strategies, and so on.

ALPS/BiCePs, which seems to be the Symphony replacement should also propose an interface for Branch, Price, and Cut. Unlike Symphony, ALPS/BiCeps is layered allowing the resolution of sevral types of B&B. Symphony seems to be only for Branch and Cut.

1.6.2.5. Other User Methods.

Another very interesting method that could also be offered by this kind of Framework is a graph search procedure. Bob++, ZRAM and MallBa propose an interface to develop Dynamic Programming application. In this kind of method, the difficulty is the parallel management of the state space. In a parallel environment the state space must be global, thus an algorithm to maintain the coherency of the state space between all the processes must be proposed.

1.6.3. Parallelization Strategies

Symphony and MW, use the master-worker paradigm (see Section 1.5) to parallelize the application. The nodes management is thus centralized. One process, the master, controls all the aspects of the search. In the other processes, the workers do the work (an exploration of one or several nodes) provided by the master. But as the task unity is the subtree and not the subproblem, each worker performs a search on a subtree, thus it could be considered that the worker controls its search. Hence, the control of the search is distributed. MW (24) has an interesting feature in a sense that it is based on a Fault Tolerant communication library Condor (28). As said before, this strategy works well for a small number of processors, but does not scale well, as the central pool inevitably becomes a computational and communications bottleneck.

ALPS (23) and PICO (18) propose to use the Master-Hub-Worker paradigm, to overcome the drawbacks of the master-Worker approach. A layer of middle management is inserted between the master and worker process. In this scheme, "a cluster" consists of a hub, which is responsible for managing a fixed number of workers. As the number of processes increases, more hubs and cluster of workers are simply added. This decentralized approach maintains many advantages of global decision making while reducing overhead and moving some computational burden from the master process to the hubs.

The other libraries propose one or several distributed strategies. Some of them have used PVM (29) (PUBB, Bob, PPBB-Lib, ZRAM), but the modern ones use MPI (Bob++, ALPS, PICO, MallBa). PPBB-Lib proposes a fully distributed parallel B&B, where each process stores a local pool of subproblems. Several Load balancing strategies were proposed in order to ensure that each local pool has enough work.

In the vast majority of these frameworks, there is no easy way to extend the parallel feature. Only one parallel algorithm and one communication layer are proposed. As its ancestor Bob, Bob++ also proposes an interface to extend the parallel part of the library. Master–Slave, fully distributed, or mixed strategy could be implemented using this interface. Master–Slave, distributed versions of parallelisations exist for the Bob Library.

1.6.4. The Target Machines

According to the accessibility of the authors to specific machine, Frameworks have been ported to various types of machines. For example, Bob has been ported on PVM (29), MPI, PM^2 (30), Charm++ (31), Athapascan (32), POSIX threads, using shared memory machines, and then using distributed machines. The recent architecture being clusters of shared memory machines (SMP) or grid-computers, the current frameworks have proposed versions for these machines. MallBA, PICO, and ALPS use MPI as their message passing library. Bob||, MallBa, PICO, and ALPS run very well on a massively parallel distributed memory system. Bob++ (Athapascan based version) could also run on a cluster of SMPs, where a multithreading programming paradigm is used on each SMP node. Bob++ has been succesfully tested on a Grid (see Section 1.7).

As far as we know, only Bob++, MW, PICO, ALPS, MallBa, and Symphony are still being maintained.

1.7. ILLUSTRATIONS

Parallel B&B algorithms have been developped for many important applications, such as the Symmetric Traveling Salesman problem [Applegate, Bixby,

Chvatal, and Cook (1)], the Vehicle Routing problem [Ralphs (33), Ralphs, Ladány, and Saltzman (34)], and the multicommodity location and network design [Gendron and Crainic (35), Bourbeau, Gendron, and Crainic (36)], to name but a few. In this section, we illustrate the parallel B&B concepts introduced previously by using the case of the Quadratic Assignment Problem. The description follows the work of (37).

The Quadratic Assignment Problem (QAP) consists to assign n units to n sites in order to minimize the quadratic cost of this assignment, which depends on both the distances between the sites and the flows between the units. It can be formulated as follows:

Given two $(n \times n)$ matrices,

$F = (f_{ij})$ where f_{ij} is the flow between units i and j,

$D = (d_{kl})$ where d_{kl} is the distance between sites k and l

find a permutation p of the set $N = \{1, 2, \cdots, n\}$, which minimizes the global cost function:

$$Cost(p) = \sum_{i=1}^{n} \sum_{j=1}^{n} f_{ij} d_{p(i)p(j)}$$

Although the QAP can be used to formulate a variety of interesting problems in location, manufacturing, data analysis, and so on, it is a NP–hard combinatorial problem, however, and, in practice, extraordinarily difficult to solve even for what may seem "small" instances. This is very different compared to other NP–hard combinatorial optimization problems, for example, the Traveling Salesman problem, for which, in practice, very large instances have been successfully solved to optimality in recent years. To illustrate this difficulty, the B&B for QAP develops huge critical trees. Thus, for example, the tree for Nugent24 has 48,455,496 nodes with bounds for values in [3488, 3490], while for Nugent30, the tree has 12,000,000,000 nodes for 677 values in interval [5448, 6124]. This extreme difficulty in addressing the QAP has resulted in the development of exact solution methods to be implemented on high-performance computers (7,38–43).

The parallel B&B presented in this section is based on the serial algorithm of Mautor and Roucairol (11) and uses the lower bound procedure (DP) of Hahn-and-Grant (44). This lower bound is based upon a new linear formulation for the QAP called "level_1 formulation RLT". A new variable is defined $y_{ijkl} = x_{ij}x_{kl}$ and the formulation becomes

$$(QAP:) Min \sum_{i=1}^{n} \sum_{j=1}^{n} \sum_{k=1 k \neq i}^{n} \sum_{l=1 l \neq j}^{n} C_{ijkl} y_{ijkl} + \sum_{i=1}^{n} \sum_{j=1}^{n} c_{ij} x_{ij}$$

$$\sum_{k=1 k\neq i}^{n} y_{ijkl} = x_{ij} = 0,1 \qquad \forall (i,j), l \neq j \tag{1.1}$$

$$\sum_{l=1 l\neq j}^{n} y_{ijkl} = x_{ij} = 0,1 \qquad \forall (i,j), k \neq i \tag{1.2}$$

$$y_{ijkl} = y_{klij} \qquad \forall (i,j), k \neq i, l \neq j \tag{1.3}$$

$$\sum_{j=1}^{n} x_{ij} = 1 \qquad \forall i = 1, \ldots, n \tag{1.4}$$

$$\sum_{i=1}^{n} x_{ij} = 1 \qquad \forall j = 1, \ldots, n \tag{1.5}$$

$$y_{ijkl} \geq 0 \qquad \forall (i,j,k,l), k \neq i, l \neq j \tag{1.6}$$

The Linear programming relaxation of this program provides a lower bound to the QAP. But, as the number of variables and constraints is huge, it cannot be computed by commercial softwares. Hahn-and-Grant proposed a procedure called DP based on a successive dual decomposition of the problem (44). The DP bound is obtained iteratively by solving $\tilde{n}2 + 1$ linear assignment problems (using the Hungarian method), instead of solving the large linear program given above.

A "polytomic" branching strategy is used (45). This strategy extends a node by creating all assignments of an unassigned facility to unassigned locations based upon the counting of *forbidden* locations. A forbidden location is a location where the addition of the corresponding leader element would increase the lower bound beyond the upper bound. At a given unfathomed node, we generate children according to one of the following schemes

- *Row Branching*. Fix $i \in I$. Generate a child problem for each $j \in J$ for which the problem with $X_{ij} = 1$ cannot be eliminated;
- *Column Branching*. Fix $j \in J$. Generate a child problem for each $i \in I$ for which the problem with $X_{ij} = 1$ cannot be eliminated.

Several different branching strategies to choose the candidate for next generation i (row) or j (column) have been considered:

1. SLC: Choose row i or column j, which maximizes the sum of leaders.

$$Max(\sum C_{ijij})$$

2. SLC_v2: Add the nonlinear elements of each submatrix to the associated leader and choose row or column with maximal sum.

$$Max\left(C_{ijij} + \sum_{k=1}^{n} \sum_{l=1}^{n} C_{ijkl} \right)$$

3. SLC_v3: Choose a row or column with a maximal sum of elements in their associated submatrices.

The implementation of the B&B algorithm is made with Bob++ framework (16) on top of the Athapascan environment. Athapascan is a macrodata-flow application programming interface (API) for asynchronous parallel programming. The API permits to define the concurrency between computational tasks that make synchronization from their accesses to objects into a global distributed memory. The parallelism is explicit, and functional, the detection of the synchronization is implicit. The semantics is sequential and an Athapascan program is independent from the target parallel architecture (cluster or grid). The execution of the program relies on an interpretation step that builds a macrodata-flow graph. The graph is direct and acyclic (DAG) and it encodes the computation and the data depencies (read and write). It is used by the runtime support and the scheduling algorithm to compute a schedule of tasks and a mapping of data onto the architecture. The implementation is based on using a light-weight process (thread) and one-side communication (active message).

In the context of B&B, an Athapascan task is a subproblem. The execution of the task yields to the exploration of a subtree of the B&B tree. The set of ready tasks (the subproblems) is distributed on the processors. Each processor stores a list of ready tasks locally. As Athapascan performs load balancing on the lists to insure maximal efficiency, each processor has a subproblem to work on. Each Athapascan's list of ready tasks is equivalent to a local priority queue that stores a subproblem in a parallel B&B. Then, according to the strategies listed in Section 1.5, the Bob++/Athapascan Framework proposes a fully distributed strategy.

First, we present results on a small cluster (named COCTEAU, located at the PRiSM laboratory, University of Versailles): 7 DELL workstations (Xeon bi-proc, 2.4 GHz, 2 GB RAM, 5 Go memory, Red Hat 7.3). The cluster was not dedicated, but was very steady. Table 1.1 displays the results.

TABLE 1.1. Runtime of Parallel QAP on COCTEAU Cluster of Size 10

Instance	Cocteau Cluster, SLC		
	Sequential Time, min	Parallel Time, min	Efficiency
Nug18	23.31	2.43	0.959
Nug20	246.98	24.83	0.994
Nug21	548.31	54.86	0.999
Nug22	402.43	44.23	0.909
Nug24	10764.2	1100.56	0.978

Performances are very good, as the efficiency is close to 1. The performance decreases slightly as the size increases up to 24. To show that the results are not machine dependant, we display the results of experiments with the same number of processors on a larger cluster (located in Grenoble and named I-cluster 2): 104 HP nodes (bi-Itanium-2900 MHz, 3 GB RAM, Intel icc 8 Compiler) interconnected by a Myrinet network. As displayed in Table 1.2, with 14 processors, the performances are similar, while for two problems, Nugent 18 and 20, favorable anomalies appear with a speedup >14.

Tables 1.1 and 1.2 show the results with the SLC Branching strategy presented above. We compare different branching strategies (SLC, SLC_v2 SLC_v3) using the small cluster (14 processors) implementation. Results are displayed in Table 1.3. The total number of explored nodes is comparable with a small advantage to strategy SLC_v3. Notice that the optimal solution is known for Nugent problems of size up to 30, and thus the upper bound is initialized to this value plus one unit. The parallel branch and bound algorithm developed the critical tree (critical nodes C representing incomplete solutions with a value strictly smaller than the optimum solution f^*) and explored some nodes in the set of undecidable nodes M, nonterminal or incomplete solutions with a value equal to f^*, and one node in O (optimal nodes with value f^*). Indeed, the set E of eliminated nodes (with a value strictly $>f^*$) is empty. But

TABLE 1.2. Performance of Parallel QAP on I-Cluster 2 of Size 14

Instance	Running time, min			Performances	
	Sequential	Parallel(7CPUs)	Parallel(14CPUs)	Speedup	Efficiency
Nugent18	54.24	7.54	3.39	16	114.28
Nugent20	588.46	84.29	41.96	14.02	100.17
Nugent21	1208.9	173.53	87.14	13.87	99.09
Nugent22	959.7	138.14	69.45	13.81	98.7

TABLE 1.3. Comparison of Branching Strategies

Instance	SLC_v2		SLC_v3	
	Nodes	Time	Nodes	Time
Nug12	11	01.01	10	01.03
Nug14	121	04.04	122	04.04
Nug15	248	14.16	239	10.13
Nug17	1,653	173.74	1,674	107.07
Nug18	4,775	593.90	4,744	369.70
Nug20	42,223	5,248.15	42,232	4,892.72
Nug22	47,312	7,235.75	47,168	7,447.54
Nug24	266,575	73,821	265,687	69,365

TABLE 1.4. Runtime of Parallel B&B for QAP on a Large Cluster with 80 Processors

Instance	I-Cluster2, SLC				
	1CPU	20CPUs	40CPUs	50CPUs	80CPUsb
Nug18	11.07	1.07	1.6	0.53	n.a
Nug20	149.06	5.78	4.56	3.38	4.46
Nug21	61.28	2.41	2.11	1.55	2.98
Nug22	214.7	8.26	5.81	4.56	6.01
Nug24	n.a	82.18	44.35	37.25	27.96

the set M could be very large and, according to the branching strategy, the size of the explorated tree could be very close to the size of the minimal tree. For Nugent 24, at the root node, the search interval is very thin in comparison with the number of explored nodes, while, later, many nodes have equal evaluation.

In addition, tests have been conducted on a higher number of processors, on the I-cluster 2. Table 1.4 shows that the results for the problem Nugent 24 up to 80 processors are very good. The other problems are too small to have the time to use all the 80 processors. This is the reason why the times with 80 processors is slightly higher than those with 50 processors.

To complete this illustration, we discus the implementation of the parallel B&B algorithm for the QAP using *Grid Computing*. Grid computing (or meta-computing or using a computational grid) is the application of the resources of many geographically distributed, network-linked, heterogeneous computing resources to a single problem at the same time. The main features of meta-computing are

- Dynamically available computing resources: Machines may join the computation at any time.
- Unreliability: Machines may leave without warning due to reboot, machine failure, network failure, and so on.
- Loosely coupling: Huge network, "low" communication speed, communication latency are highly variable and unpredictable.
- Heterogeneous resources: Many different machines (shared workstations, nodes of PC clusters, supercomputers) and characteristics (memory, processors, OS, network latency, and so on.

Programs should therefore be self-adaptable and fault tolerant. Grid computing requires the use of software based upon resource management tools provided by projects like Globus (46), Legion (47), and Condor (28). The goal of these tools is to assign processors to a parallel application. These software do not perform load balancing between the processes, however.

The advantage of such a platform compared to a traditional multiprocessor machine is that a large number of CPUs may be assembled very inexpensively. The disadvantage is that the availability of individual machines is variable and communication between processors may be very slow.

We experimented our parallel QAP algorithm, using the Athpascan environment, on a French grid initiative, called e-Toile, where six locations with clusters or supercomputers were linked by a very high-speed network. The middleware used was the e-Toile Middleware that was an evolution of the Globus middleware. We obtained and proved the optimal solution to the Nugent 20 instance in a time of 1648 secondes (>4h), using a cluster of 20 machines (AMD MP, 1800+) at one location, while only 499s (8,31 min) were required with the following 84 machines located in different sites:

- 7*bi-Xeons 2.4 GHz, 2 Go (Laboratory PriSM-Versailles).
- 10*bi-AMD MP 1800, 1 Go (CEA-Saclay).
- 10*bi-Xeons, 2.2 GHz, 2 Go (EDF-Clamart).
- 15*bi-PIII, 1.4 GHz, 1 Go (ENS-Lyon).

A relative speedup of $T_{20}/T_{84} = 3.1$ was thus achieved.

1.8. CONCLUSION

We have presented a summary of basic concepts for parallel B&B methodology applied to hard combinatorial optimization problems. This methodology is achieving very impressive results and is increasinly "accessible" given the continuously decrease in the costs of computers, networks, and communication devices.

We have also presented several software tools that help to implement Parallel B&B algorithms. These tools offer a large variety of interfaces and tools that allow the user to implement algorithms from the basic B&B to the most sophisticated branch and cut. However, a lot of work has to be done to include fault-tolerance, self-adaptibility, multiapplication, heterogeneity in these tools.

We also present the resolution of the Quadratic assignement problem, for which the parallelism is really a great feature to solve Instances that could never been approach before.

REFERENCES

1. D. Applegate, R.E. Bixby, V. Chvatal, and W. Cook. On the solution of traveling salesman problem. *Doc. Math.*, **ICM**(III):645–656 (1998).
2. K.M. Anstreicher and N.W. Brixius. A new bound for the quadratic assignment problem based on convex quadratic programming. *Math. Prog.*, **89**(3):341–357 (2001).
3. J.P. Goux, K.M. Anstreicher, N.W. Brixius, and J. Linderoth. Solving large quadratic assignment problems on computational grids. *Math. Prog.*, **91**(3):563–588 (2002).

4. B. Gendron and T.G. Crainic. Parallel Branch-and-Bound Algorithms: Survey and Synthesis. *Oper. Res.*, **42**(6):1042–1066 (1994).

5. G. Authié *et al. Parallélisme et Applications Irrégulières.* Hermès, 1995.

6. C. Roucairol. A parallel branch and bound algorithm for the quadratic assignment problem. *Discrete Appl. Math.*, **18**:211–225 (1987).

7. B. Mans, T. Mautor, and C. Roucairol. A parallel depth first search branch and bound algorithm for the quadratic assignment problem. *Eur. J. Oper. Res. (Else-vier)*, **3**(81):617–628 (1995).

8. T.-H. Lai and S. Sahni. Anomalies in parallel branch-and-bound algorithms. *Communication A.C.M.*, **27**:594–602 (June 1984).

9. G. Li and B.W. Wah. Coping with anomalies in parallel branch-and-bound. *IEEE Trans. Comp.*, **C-35**(6):568–573 (June 1986).

10. C. Roucairol. Recherche arborescente en parallèle. RR M.A.S.I. 90.4, Institut Blaise Pascal—Paris VI, 1990. In French.

11. B. Mans and C. Roucairol. Theoretical comparisons of parallel best-first search branch and bound algorithms. In H. France, Y. Paker, and I. Lavallée, eds., *OPOPAC, International Workshop on Principles of Parallel Computing*, Lacanau, France, November 1993.

12. L.V. Kalé and Vikram A. Saletore. Parallel state-space search for a first solution with consistent linear speedups. *Inter. J. Parallel Prog.*, **19**(4):251–293 (1990).

13. Anshul Gupta and Vipin Kumar. Scalability of parallel algorithms for matrix multiplication. *Proceedings of the 1993 International Conference on Parallel Processing*, Vol. III—Algorithms & Applications, CRC Press, Boca Raton, FL, 1993, pp. III-115–III-123.

14. Andrew Makhorin. Glpk (gnu linear programming kit). Available at http://www.gnu.org/software/glpk/glpk.html.

15. Y. Shinano, M. Higaki, and R. Hirabayashi. A generalized utility for parallel branch and bound algorithms. *Proceedings of the 7nd IEEE Symposium on Parallel and Distributed Processing (SPDP '95)*, 1995, pp. 858–865. Available at http://al.ei.tuat.ac.jp/yshinano/pubb/.

16. B. Le Cun. Bob++ framework: User's guide and API. Available at http://www.prism.uvsq.fr/blec/Research/BOBO/.

17. S. Tschoke and T. Polzer. Portable parallel branch-and-bound library user manuel, library version 2.0. Technical Report, University of Paderborn, 1998.

18. J. Eckstein, C.A. Phillips, and W.E. Hart. Pico: An object-oriented framework for parallel branch-and-bound. Technical Report 40-2000, RUTCOR Research Report, 2000.

19. Q. Chen and M.C. Ferris. FATCOP: A fault tolerant condor-PVM mixed integer program solver. Technical Report, University of Madison, Madison, w1, 1999.

20. E. Alba *et al.* Mallba: A library of skeletons for combinatorial optimisation. In B. Monien and R. Feldman, eds., *Euro-Par 2002 Parallel Processing*, Vol. 2400 of *Lecture Notes in Computer Science*, Springer-Verlag, Berlin Heidelberg, 2002, pp. 927–932.

21. A. Brunnger, A. Marzetta, K. Fukuda, and J. Nievergelt. The parallel search bench zram and its applications. *Ann. Oper. Res.*, **90**:45–63 (1999).

22. The COIN-OR Team. The coin-or organization. http://www.coinor.org/.

23. Y. Xu, T.K. Ralphs, L. Ladányi, and M.J. Saltzman. Alps: A framework for implementing parallel search algorithms. *The Proceedings of the Ninth INFORMS Computing Society Conference* (2005).

24. J. Goux, J. Linderoth, and M. Yoder. Metacomputing and the master-worker paradigm, Technical Report, Angcnne National Laboratory. 1999.

25. T.K. Ralphs and M. Guzelsoy. The symphony callable library for mixed integer programming. *The Proceedings of the Ninth INFORMS Computing Society Conference*, San Francisco, USA, (2005).

26. T.K. Ralphs. Symphony 3.0.1 user's manual. http://www.branchandcut.org/.

27. M. Benaichouche *et al.* Bob: une plateforme unifiée de développement pour les algorithmes de type branch-and-bound. RR 95/12, Laboratoire PRiSM, Université de Versailles—Saint Quentin en Yvelines, May 1995. In french.

28. M. Litzkow, M. Livny, and M.W. Mutka. Condor—a hunter of idle workstations. *Proceedings of the 8th International Conference of Distributed Computing Systems (ICDCS '88)*, 1988, pp. 104–111.

29. V.S. Sunderam. PVM: a framework for parallel distributed computing. *Concurrency, Practice and Experience*, **2**(4):315–340 (1990).

30. J.F. Mehaut and R. Namyst. *PM²: Parallel Multithreaded Machine. A multithreaded environment on top of PVM. Proceedings of EuroPVM'95*, Lyon, September 1995.

31. L.V. Kale and Sanjeev Krishnan. Charm++: Parallel Programming with Message-Driven Objects. In Gregory V. Wilson and Paul Lu, eds., *Parallel Programming using C++*, MIT Press, 1996, pp. 175–213. Boston, MA.

32. T. Gautier, R. Revire, and J.L. Roch. Athapascan: an api for asynchronous parallel programming. Technical Report, INRIA RT-0276, 2003.

33. T.K. Ralphs. Parallel Branch and Cut for Capacitated Vehicle Routing. *Parallel Comp.*, **29**:607–629 (2003).

34. T.K. Ralphs, L. Ladány, and M.J. Saltzman. Parallel Branch, Cut, and Price for Large-Scale Discrete Optimization. *Math. Prog.*, **98**(13):253–280 (2003).

35. B. Gendron and T.G. Crainic. A Parallel Branch-and-Bound Algorithm for Multicommodity Location with Balancing Requirements. *Comp. Oper. Res.*, **24**(9):829–847 (1997).

36. B. Bourbeau, B. Gendron, and T.G. Crainic. Branch-and-Bound Parallelization Strategies Applied to a Depot Location and Container Fleet Management Problem. *Parallel Comp.*, **26**(1):27–46 (2000).

37. A. Djerrah, V.D. Cung, and C. Roucairol. Solving large quadratic assignment problems, on clusters and grid with bob++/athapascan. *Fourth International Workshop of the PAREO Working Group on Parallel Processing in Operation Research*, Mont-Tremblant, Montreal, Canada, January 2005.

38. J. Crouse and P. Pardalos. A parallel algorithm for the quadratic assignment problem. *Proceedings of Supercomputing 89*, ACM, 1989, pp. 351–360.

39. A. Brüngger, A. Marzetta, J. Clausen, and M. Perregaard. Solving large-scale QAP problems in parallel with the search library ZRAM. *J. Parallel Distributed Comp.*, **50**(1–2):157–169 (1998).

40. V-D. Cung, S. Dowaji, Cun B. Le T. Mautor, and C. Roucairol. Concurrent data structures and load balancing strategies for parallel branch-and-bound/a*

algorithms. *III Annual Implementation Challenge Workshop, DIMACS*, New Brunswick NJ, October 1994.

41. B. Le cun and C. Roucairol. Concurrent data structures for tree search algorithms. In J. Rolim A. Ferreira, ed., *IFIP WG 10.3, IRREGULAR94: Parallel Algorithms for Irregular Structured Problems*, Kluwer Academic, Gereva, Swizterland, September 1994, pp. 135–155.

42. Y. Denneulin, B. Lecun, T. Mautor, and J.F. Mehaut. Distributed branch and bound algorithms for large quadratic assignment problems. *5th Computer Science Technical Section on Computer Science and Operations Research*, Dallas, TX, 1996.

43. Y. Denneulin and T. Mautor. Techniques de régulation de charge—applications en optimisation combinatoire. *ICaRE'97, Conception et mise en oeuvre d'applications parallèles irrégulières de grande taille*, Aussois, 1997, pp. 215–228.

44. P. Hahn and T. Grant. Lower bounds for the quadratic assignment problem based upon a dual formulation. *Oper. Res.*, **46**:912–922 (1998).

45. T. Mautor and C. Roucairol. A new exact algorithm for the solution of quadratic assignment problems. *Discrete Appl. Math.*, **55**:281–293 (1994).

46. Ian Foster and Carl Kesselman. Globus: A metacomputing infrastructure toolkit. *Inter. J. Supercomp. Appl. High Performance Compu.*, **11**(2):115–128 (Summer 1997).

47. A. Natrajan *et al.* The legion grid portal. *Grid Computing Environments 2001, Concurrency and Computation: Practice and Experience*, 2002. Vol. 14 No 13–15 pp. 1365–1394.

████ **CHAPTER 2**

Parallel Dynamic Programming

F. ALMEIDA, D. GONZÁLEZ, and I. PELÁEZ

Dpto. Estadística, I. O. y Computación
Universidad de La Laguna
Spain

2.1. INTRODUCTION

Dynamic programming (DP) is an important problem-solving technique that has been widely used in various fields, such as control theory, operations research, biology, and computer science. The method is commonly included in the exact enumerative resolution methods. The DP technique is frequently used when the solution to a problem can be viewed as the result of a sequence of decisions. Many of these problems need a complete enumeration of the decision sequences from which the best is picked. Dynamic Programming often drastically reduces the amount of enumeration by avoiding consideration of some decision sequences that cannot possibly be optimal. In DP an optimal sequence of decisions is arrived at by making explicit appeal to the principle of optimality. Although Section 2.2 briefly summarizes some of the elements of the DP technique, in this chapter we will assume that the sequential technique is familiar to the reader. The intension is to illustrate different approaches to parallelize DP programs and how these concepts can be implemented into algorithmic skeletons.

After an analysis of the basic literature on the topic, we find out several difficulties, there is an evident gap between the theoretical concepts introduced by the technique and the algorithm to be derived that finally will be implemented. This is, for example, a fact observed with the recursive formula associated to DP, that is usually presented as a "magic" formula. Although generic procedures are available for most of the exact and heuristic techniques, that is not the case for the DP method. While many DP algorithms for

Parallel Combinatorial Optimization, edited by El-Ghazali Talbi
Copyright © 2006 by John Wiley & Sons, Inc.

specific problems have been implemented, the literature about general procedures and libraries is scarce.

In introductory courses on algorithm design, dynamic programming is usually taught by example. Students are presented with a number of typical applications, and given an informal statement of the principle of optimality. By doing a number of similar examples in exercises, they then acquire the skill to apply dynamic programming to other problems. This is the approach followed for example by Ref. 1, where a deep discussion on the topic of sensitivity analysis in DP problems is also found, and by some other well-known text books as (2–5) and many others. This fact is not a handicap to generate sequential and parallel algorithms for new problems by itself, but it constitutes a grate disadvantage to approach the technique from a generic perspective. Generic tools (like algorithmic skeletons) are usually supported by general procedures describing the algorithmic technique to be implemented.

Since the method was first presented by Bellman in the 1950s, numerous formalizations of DP have been presented stating with the principle of optimality as a monotonicity condition, for example (6,7). These works do, however, stop short of presenting a single, generic program that solves all applications of their formalization at one stroke. The construction of such a generic program, and the appropriate means for expressing it, have been the subject in Refs. 8 and 9. While in Ref. 8 general DP programs are viewed as multistage finite automatons, with a certain superimposed cost structure, in Ref. 9 the aim is achieved following the functional programming paradigm. The important class of polyadic recurrences seen in Refs. 10 and 11 are out of the scope of this chapter in both former approaches. In some other cases (12), the problem formulation is devoted to nonserial polyadic problems while multistage serial problems are assumed to be obtained as particular cases (see Section 2.2 for a classification of DP problems). Although this is true from the theoretical point of view, in practice, to be efficient each class of DP problem must be considered as an individual case.

In conclusion, generic approaches are limited to classes of problems or they are not suitable to be assumed by a software component. It is worth mentioning that another source of difficulties is from the fact that the notation used changes substantially from one formalization to the other, and in most cases, the sensitivity analysis is not considered at all.

A similar situation has been found in the parallel case. Again, parallelizations for specific DP problems have been presented by many authors for various architectures including clusters of heterogeneous systems (13–22) and general parallel procedures are restricted to limited classes of recurrences. All of these cases suggest, however, parallel algorithms for problems on the same class. A unified parallel general approach was presented in Ref. 23 as an extension to the work of Ref. 8, but the strong theoretical effort introduced in the polyadic case dissuades us from using it as a model to follow.

Two main difficulties must be stressed when parallelizing DP problems. The first difficulty arises with the data dependencies associated with the functional equation to be evaluated. Several data dependency patterns can be found and no general sequence order of evaluation can be provided. Figure 2.1 shows the data dependency for the 0/1 Knapsack Problem, a paradigmatic example of multistage problem, where each row of the table depends on the immediate preceding row. In Fig. 2.2, we can see the data dependency for the Matrix Multiplication Parenthesization Problem. In this case, the upper half of a matrix with nonuniform dependencies must be computed. In both former cases, the matrices could be computed by performing parallel evaluations of the rows, columns, or even diagonals. Each one of the parallelizations involves

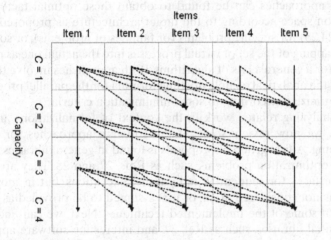

Fig. 2.1. Data dependency for 0/1 Knapsack Problem.

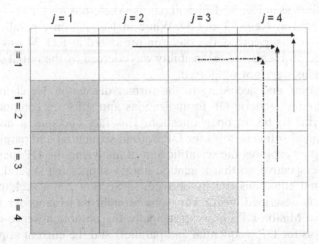

Fig. 2.2. Data dependency for the Matrix Multiplication Parenthesization Problem.

advantages and disadvantages according to the computation–communication pattern involved.

The second problem to face is that usually DP algorithms show an optimal behavior when they are just considered from the theoretical point of view in which as many processors as the numbers of inputs are available. However, most of them run poorly when they are executed on current architectures. The implementation of these algorithms on a target architecture is strongly conditioned by the actual assignment of virtual processes to the physical processors and their simulation, the granularity of the architecture, and the instance of the problem to be executed. To preserve the optimality of the algorithm, a proper combination of these factors must be considered.

Several approaches can be found to obtain these optimal factors. Tiling the iteration space according to the target architecture as proposed in Refs. (16,19,20,24,25) for specific problems (or families of problems), or solving the optimal mapping of the set of virtual processes into the actual one as proposed in Ref. 26 for a general class of algorithms. Both approaches involve the development of the analytical complexity time formula for the parallel program and then to optimize it according to some minimization criteria.

After analyzing related work in the context of formalizations and parallelizations, we now review some of the software approaches for dynamic programming. A first group of proposals is found in general libraries for combinatorial optimization problems, such as Refs. 27 and 28. They are used to supply interfaces for sequential and parallel executions, but in most of the cases DP is not considered at all, or it is assumed to be provided as a particular case of some of the implemented techniques. Next, we can find specific DP sequential libraries, such as Ref. 29, and interesting software approaches derived from laboratories that apply solvers like LINGO (30) to DP problems, following particular methodologies. No parallelizations are provided in these cases. Scientific libraries, such as GSL (31), are open to improvement by including DP routines as in Ref. 32. Efficient parallel skeletons for DP problems have been presented at Refs. 33 and 34. While in Ref. 33, only parallel pipeline approaches were supported, the skeleton presented in Ref. 34 was restricted to multistage problems, the extensibility was coerced by the initial design and new paradigms were not supported.

At this point, and according to the former discussion, we claim that the subject of finding generic DP formalizations and software components as a whole remains to be an open question. This fact becomes a handicap to develop general software tools for DP, both in sequential and parallel.

This chapter explores the scientific aim of analyzing the DP method from a generic perspective, so that a generic library supporting several classes of DP functional equations can be derived. In Section 2.3, a skeleton library, Mallba-DP, is described. Several reasons brought us to consider the actual design of the Mallba-DP library; principally, the notable absence of general software tools for DP (sequential and parallel) and the current apparent gap among general methods and DP applications. We propose to cover this gap by trying to minimize the user effort to manage the tool while keeping standard methodologies at the same time. The skeleton presented is portable, efficient, and can be easily applied to many applications. Various parallel paradigms and architectures are provided and the parallelism is hidden to the users. The computational results confirm the advantages of the design methodology.

2.2. THE DYNAMIC PROGRAMMING TECHNIQUE

2.2.1. The Method

We found a starting point for our methodology in Ref. 35, where sequential and parallel dynamic programming formulations are presented by cases of study, and each case represents a general class of recurrences. When a new problem is presented, any of the former examples could be used as a guide. These samples suggest parallel algorithms for other problems in the same class. Note, however, that not all DP problems can be parallelized following these examples.

Next, DP concepts needed to use the tool to be presented in Section 2.3 are summarized. The notation commonly used in most of the formalizations is used.

Dynamic programming represents the solution to an optimization problem as a recursive equation whose left side is an unknown quantity and whose right side is a minimization (or maximization) expression. Such an equation is called the functional equation or recurrence equation for DP. These DP problems may be classified in terms of the functional equation. A functional equation that contains a single recursive term yields a *monadic* DP formulation. The DP formulations whose cost functions contain multiple recursive terms are called *polyadic* formulations. The functional equations provide the mechanism to obtain optimal solutions to subproblems. The dependencies between subproblems in a DP formulation can be represented by a directed graph. Each node in the graph represents a subproblem. Nodes of the graph are usually referred to as states. A directed edge from state i to state j indicates that the solution to the subproblem represented by state i is used to compute the solution represented by state j. The edges of the graph are commonly known as decisions. The optimal solution for a subproblem is obtained as a sequence of decisions (a policy) starting from the initial state. Usually, the states of the graph are arranged in a bidimensional matrix (the DP table) holding the information relevant to evaluate the functional equation and the optimal policy. The DP table is necessary to store precomputed states. Once the table has been computed, a reverse traversing of the table allows us to obtain the optimal policy. Thus, solving a DP problem consist of obtaining the functional equation, evaluating the DP table, and returning the optimal policy if necessary. Usually, the sensitivity analysis (What if $\cdots$?) is also required information that can be derived from the study of the table. If the graph is acyclic,

TABLE 2.1. Examples of DP Recurrences

Problem	Recurrence	DP Category
0/1 Knapsack	$f_{kc} = \max\{f_{k-1c}, f_{k-1c-wk} + p_k\}$	Serial monadic
Longest common subsequence	$f_{ij} = f_{i-1j-1} + 1$ if $x_i = y_j$; or $f_{ij} = \max\{f_{ij-1}, f_{i-1j}\}$ if $x_i \neq y_j$	Nonserial monadic
Floyd's all-pairs shortest paths	$d_{ij}^k = \min\{d_{ij}^{k-1}, d_{ik}^{k-1} + d_{kj}^{k-1}\}$	Serial polyadic
Optimal matrix parenthesization	$c_{ij} = \min\{c_{ik} + c_{k+1j} + r_{i-1}r_k r_j\}$	Nonserial polyadic

then the states of the graph can be organized into levels or stages such that subproblems at a particular level depend only on subproblems at previous stages. In this case, the DP formulation can be categorized as follows. If subproblems at all levels depend only on the results at the immediate preceding levels, the formulation is called a *serial* or *multistage* DP formulation; otherwise, it is called a *nonserial* DP formulation. Based on the preceding classification criteria, four classes of DP recurrences can be defined: *serial monadic*, *serial polyadic*, *nonserial monadic*, and *nonserial polyadic*. These classes are not exhaustive; some DP formulations cannot be classified into any of these categories. Even then, our methodology may also be applicable and the skeleton may be easily extended if required. Table 2.1 show examples of DP problems on each one of the classes. These examples will be used as test problems in Sections 2.3 and 2.4. See Ref. 35 for a detailed description of these problems and formulations.

2.2.2. Parallel Approaches for Dynamic Programming

In general, the resolution of DP problems can be viewed as the evaluation of a set of cells on a matrix, the states of the DP table. This evaluation is conditioned by the dependencies of the functional equation, what finally means dependencies among cells of the matrix. The sequential computation of the table only involves the decision of sequence order of evaluation avoiding the violation of such dependencies. However, in the parallel case the data allocation strategy and the processor synchronization method are also elements to be considered. These elements may vary according to the architecture of the target and to the problem itself. The target architecture is an important factor as long as it imposes some important constraints, ignoring the impact derived from cache effects, the number of actual processors, the ratio computation–communication, can be mentioned as well as other features. On the other hand, the problem fixes the dependencies among the cells by itself and according to it, the traversing mode for the matrix as well.

Two main approaches can be found for parallelizing DP algorithms. The first method uses the set of processors in parallel to evaluate stages in sequence following a SPMD programming model. A computation step is followed by a synchronization for data exchange among the processors. This synchronization step in many cases involves a collective operation. Stages comprise sets of cells depending only on cells computed in previous iterations. Typically, serial problems stages represent rows on the DP table while in non-serial problems the diagonals are good candidates to group the cells into the stages. Rows or diagonals are then computed in parallel. They will be referred to as parallelizations by rows or by diagonals, respectively. Obviously, the performance will be conditioned by the computation/communication ratio. The second strategy allocates cells to processors to be computed in parallel. The matrix is split into different pieces composed of one or several cells, and the evaluation of these pieces is assigned to different processors. Synchronizations are performed by demand through point-to-point communications among the processors involved. This is the technique applied, for example, when assigning the computation of a row of the table to a different processor and the columns are processed in parallel under a pipeline scheme. Synchronizations are carried out only among consecutive processors. In this second approach, tiling techniques are usually exploited to improve the performance.

Figure 2.1 shows the dependency matrix for the 0/1 Knapsack Problem problem. Dependencies appear only among consecutive rows (the stages). Assuming as many processors as elements on the row, according to the first method, a cell of the row is assigned to a processor and rows are computed in sequence starting from row $C = 1$. A synchronization step follows the evaluation of each row. Since in practice the number of actual processors is lower than the number of cells per row, the elements of the row must be assigned to the processors following block, cyclic, or block-cyclic mappings. Figure 2.3 depicts a cyclic mapping of stages composed of eight elements using four processors. The shadowed areas correspond to stages.

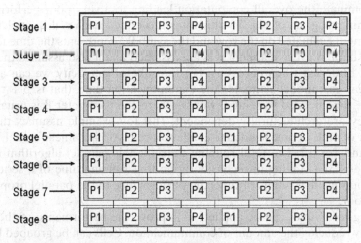

Fig. 2.3. Evaluation of a 0/1 Knapsack Problem by rows.

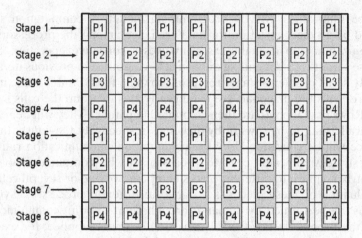

Fig. 2.4. Evaluation of a 0/1 Knapsack Problem by columns.

The second parallelization approach is illustrated in Fig. 2.4. Each row of the matrix is assigned to one processor so columns are computed in parallel. Shadowed areas represent parallel evaluations that, in this case, do not correspond to stages. Data dependencies force the execution following a pipeline scheme, processors receive evaluated cells from the left in the pipeline, compute new cells, and send them to the right in the pipeline. In this case, a latency caused for the data dependency is introduced. The latency on a cell consists of the time to compute the data needed by the cell plus the time to send these data (Fig. 2.5).

According to the dependency pattern, a communication is needed each time a processor computes a cell. The communication overhead introduced may dominate the overall computation leading to a very poor performance. The timing diagram of Fig. 2.5 illustrates this effect. Each cell is labeled with the element evaluated on the row and the symbol S represents the time needed to send data. A cyclic mapping is again assumed and it also assumes the presence of buffering when necessary. For the sake of simplicity, we can assume the linear cost model estimates the communication time, that is, $\beta + \tau$. Here L is the time needed to send L words, where the parameter β is usually $> \tau$ and they are architecturally dependent. This toy example assumes that the number of units of time needed to evaluate a cell is 0.5 in a linear model, where $\beta = 1$ and $\tau = 0.2$. The total running time for this parallel algorithm in this example is 31.1. Taking into consideration that running time of a sequential evaluation needs 32 units of time, the performance of the parallel proposal is quite poor.

Tiling techniques can be applied to improve the performance of the algorithm by reducing the amount of communication. Cells can be grouped before being sent into a single packet. The technique, reduces the time invested in

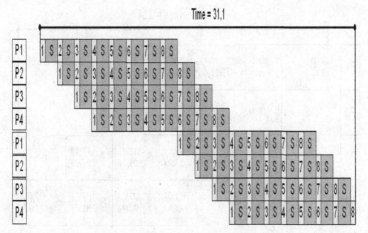

Fig. 2.5. Cyclic mapping of one row to one processor. The time to evaluate a state is 0.5, $\beta = 1$ and $\tau = 0.2$. States are sent as soon as they are evaluated.

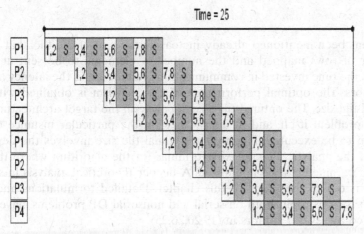

Fig. 2.6. Cyclic mapping one row to one processor. The time to evaluate a state is 0.5, $\beta = 1$ and $\tau = 0.2$. States are packed before being sent.

communications, but increases the latency among processors. Following the example shown in Fig. 2.5, we can see, in Section 2.6, the timing diagram for the problem by evaluating two cells at a time on each processor. A total running time of 25 units is now obtained. The performance can be further improved by increasing the size of the block in the cycle, that is, assigning more rows per processor. In the example in Fig. 2.7, a pure block mapping is obtained by mapping two rows per processor. However, in general, mixed block-cyclic strategies can be obtained. This mapping leads to a running time of 22.4 units of time.

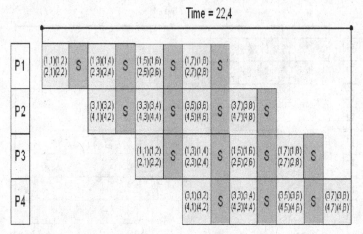

Fig. 2.7. Block-Cyclic mapping of rows processors. The time to evaluate a state is 0.5 $\beta = 1$ and $\tau = 0.2$. States are packed before be sent. Data exchange is reduced but latency is increased.

As has been mentioned already, increasing the size of the tile, that is, the number of rows mapped and the number of elements to be sent at once, reduces the time invested in communications, but increases the latency among processors. The optimal performance of the algorism is obtained with the optimal tile size. The optimal tile size depends on the target architecture and on the problem itself, and in many cases on the particular instance of the problem to be executed. Finding the optimal tile size involves the development of the analytical complexity formulas for the algorithm where the tile size is a parameter to be minimized. A deeper theoretical analysis in such a subject is out of the scope of this chapter. Detailed formulations and nice solution for this topic, both on serial and nonserial DP problems, have been presented by several authors in (19,20,26,25).

2.3. A DYNAMIC PROGRAMMING SKELETON

In general, the development of a software skeleton for a given technique involves identifying those elements in the technique that may be abstracted from particular cases and those elements that depend on the application. In the case of the DP method, we assume that the user has been able to obtain functional equations by themselves. The DP table may be abstracted as a table of states, assuming that the user supplies the structure of a state and its evaluation through functional equations. The skeleton may provide the table and several methods to traverse it during the evaluation of the states. These methods allow different traversing modes (by rows, by columns, by diagonals) and the user picks the best that does not violate the dependencies of the functional equations. Some recurrences admit several traversing modes in terms of dependencies, but the running time may vary from one mode to the other. In the sequential case, the traversing mode indicates that the states of the row (column or diagonal, respectively) will be processed in sequence, while in the parallel case, the semantic appeals to the evaluation of the row (column or diagonal, respectively) using the whole set of processors simultaneously. This approach allows introduction of any of the parallelization strategies designed for DP algorithms. The dimensions of the DP table depend on the instance and should be given at running time.

Both object oriented languages and functional languages provide the high levels of expressiveness required by this skeleton. Functional languages are sometimes critizied as being inefficient and far from most of the standards in development.

We enumerate important features that, in our opinion, should be covered by a software library oriented to the DP problem-solving paradigm:

- Coherence with a methodology. The tool should be close to the methodology used to derive the functional equations.
- Expressiveness to represent functional recurrences.
- Support for a wide range of problems in terms of classes of recurrences.
- Capability to deal with large problems.
- Flexibility to add new classes of recurrences or solving strategies.
- Facilities for every issue involved in the dynamic programming technique. The tool should be able to provide not only optimal solutions, but also optimal policies for any subproblem on the DP table.
- Ability to develop sensitivity analysis.
- Ease of use.
- Portability.
- Efficiency.
- Transparent use of parallel platforms for nonexpert users.
- Capability to deal with different parallelization strategies.

Among the object oriented languages, C++ has proved to achieve acceptable levels of expressiveness at low loss of efficiency. Parallelism can be easily introduced in C++ through the bindings provided by parallel standard libraries, such us MPI or OpenMP. Mallba-DP, and has been developed in C++, which makes it portable to most of the sequential and parallel platforms.

Mallba-DP provides support for the well-known classes of recurrences described in Section 2.2. The DP problems belonging to these classes can be implemented using a common interface for sequential and parallel executions. The design is flexible enough to deal with new DP problems.

The Mallba-DP skeleton follows the model of classes described in the Mallba library (34) and adds those particular elements related to DP, while

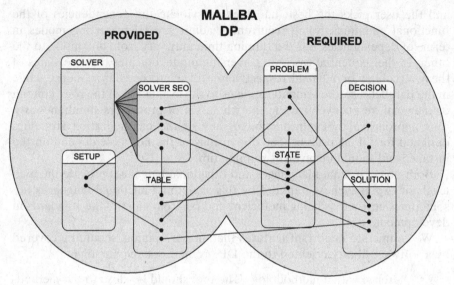

Fig. 2.8. The Mallba-DP class design.

keeping the features of efficiency and ease of use at the same time. It has been implemented in C++ and abstracts the concepts of State and Decision into required classes. The user describes the problem and the solution, and the methods to evaluate a state (the functional equation) and to obtain the optimal solution. The provided classes will allocate and evaluate the Dynamic Programming table supplying the necessary methods to return the solution. Implementation details are hidden from the user. Several solver engines are provided to manage sequential and parallel executions on shared, distributed, hybrid heterogeneous platforms. Each solver implements different traversing modes of the DP table. Figure 2.8 gives an overview of the required and provided classes in Mallba-DP.

We now illustrate the use of Mallba-DP through a case of study, the 0/1 knapsack problem.

2.3.1. The Classes Problem and Solution

The class Problem represents the specific problem to be solved and defines the data structures for the problem and the methods to manipulate them. For example, the knapsack problem can be defined by the number of objects N, the capacity of the knapsack C, and two integer vectors to store weights and profits, w and p, respectively. All the methods needed to manage a problem (constructors, getters, setters, etc.) should also be defined (see the code in Fig. 2.9).

```
requires class Problem {
    int N;        // Number of objects
    int C;        // Capacity
    int w[MAX_N]; // Weights
    int p[MAX_N]; // Profits

    public:
    // Methods to manage the class
    ....
};
```

Fig. 2.9. Defining the class Problem.

```
requires class Solution {
    State optimal_state;
    Decision *optimal_policy;
    int numdecisions;

    public:
    // Methods to manage the class
    ....
};
```

Fig. 2.10. Defining the class Solution.

The complexity of defining a problem may vary in terms of the features of the implemented problem, but in most cases studied it seems to be very simple.

The class Solution (Fig. 2.10) represents a solution to the problem. Again data structures and methods are required from the user. In our particular case, the maximum profit and the set of objects to be inserted need to be defined. An optimal state provides the value for the optimal profit, and an array holds the set of decisions for an optimal policy. Classes State and Decision are used in these definitions to represent DP states and decisions, respectively. These two classes will be described later.

2.3.2. The Classes State and Decision

Class State holds the information associated with a DP State. This class stores and computes the optimal value in the state and the decision associated to the optimal evaluation. The evaluation of a state involves access to the information of some other states in the DP table. Mallba–DP provides an object of

```
requires class State {
    const Problem &pbm;
    Solution &sol;
    int value;
    Decision d;
    Table &table;

    public:
    // Methods to manage the class
      ....
    // Evaluate the state: Functional equation
    void Evalua(int stage, int index);

    // Return decision leading to the optimal value in this state
    void former_decision(State st, int current_stage, int current_index,
             int &former_stage, int &former_index);

};
```

Fig. 2.11. Defining the class State.

the class Table hidden in each instance of the class Solver. The methods
GET_STATE(i,j) and PUT_STATE(i,j) of the Table allow it to get and
insert states in a table.

The code in Fig. 2.11 defines the class state for our example. It defines a
problem (pbm), a solution (sol), a decision (d), and the DP table (table).
These variables may be considered as generic variables since they should
appear in any problem to be solved. The variable value stores the optimal
profit. It is worth mentioning two particular methods in this class, the method
Evalua, that implements the functional equation, and the method used
for the reverse traversing of the table to obtain the optimal policy
(former_decision). Implementations of these methods are shown in Fig.
2.12. The method Evalua is assumed to receive the indices of a state in the
DP table; any of the recurrences of Table 2.1 can be expressed under this prototype. If the functional equation for a specific problem requires a different
prototype, the skeleton allows overloading, thus applying the polymorphism
inherent to C++.

The class Decision allows representation of the decision taken during the
evaluation of the states. In our example, this class consists of an integer value
to store *zero* or *one*, however, in other problems the decision could store a
more complex data structure. The code of Fig. 2.13 shows the definition of the
class.

```
void State::Evalua(int stage, int index){
  State st(pbm, sol, table);
  State tmp(pbm, sol, table);
  .....
  st = table.GET_STATE(stage-1, index);
  st.set_decision(0);
  if(index >= pbm.weight(stage)) {
    tmp = table.GET_STATE(stage-1, index-pbm.weight(stage));
    if (st.get_value() < (tmp.get_value() + pbm.profit(stage)) {
      st.set_value(tmp.get_value() + pbm.profit(stage));
      st.set_decision(1);
    }
  }
  table.PUT_STATE(st, stage, index);
  .....
}

void State::former_decision(State st, int current_stage, int current_index,
      int &former_stage, int &former_index) {
Decision current_decision = st.get_decision();
sol.set_optimal_policy(current_stage, current_decision);
former_index = current_index - ((pbm.weight(current_stage)) *
      current_decision.get_value());
former_stage = current_stage - 1;
}
```

Fig. 2.12. Implementation of the methods Evalua and former_decision of class State.

```
requires class Decision {
    int value;

    public:
    // Methods to manage the class
    ....
};
```

Fig. 2.13. Defining the class Decision.

2.3.3. The `Main()` Function

Once all required classes have been defined, they can be used to solve the problem and obtain the results. To achieve it, the `Main()` function should be implemented. The code in Fig. 2.14 illustrates an example of the implementation for this function. The library "`KP.hh`" is included. It holds the classes previously defined and the classes provided by the dynamic programming skeleton.

A provided class (`Setup`) stores the instance-dependent parameters that are needed by the solver engine, in our example, the number of stages and the number of states to allocate the DP table. An instance `solver` of the class `solver_seq` is created using as a parameter the instance to be solved. This object will be used as a solver for our problem through the method `run_byrows()`. When the method `run_byrows()` is invoked, the states of the DP table are automatically evaluated following the traversing mode by rows. A parallel execution in a shared memory machine could be performed using the class `solver_sharedmemory`, using the same method `run_byrows()` the parallel evaluation of the rows in the DP table is achieved. Note that the interface for the sequential and parallel execution is the same, only a different solver class is expected to be used.

In the example of Fig. 2.14, once the function `run_byrows()` has been executed, the DP table is shown at the standard output. Next, the optimal policy is calculated calling the method `get_policy()` provided with the object `solver` that seeks the optimal policy starting from the final state. Finally, the solution is printed to the standard output.

```
....
#include "KP.hh"
int Main (int argc, char** argv) {
  Problem pbm;
  Solution sol(pbm);
  Setup setup;
  ifstream f1(argv[1]);
  f1 >> setup;
  ifstream f2(argv[2]);
  f2 >> pbm;
  Solver_seq solver(pbm, setup);
  solver.run_byrows();
  solver.show_table();
  solver.get_policy(setup.get_Num_Stages() - 1, setup.get_Num_States());
  sol = solver.solution();
  cout << sol << endl;
}
```

Fig. 2.14. Implementation of the Main() function.

```
Stages: 5
States: 10

Objects: 5
Capacity: 10
Weights: 3 11 6 4 2
Profits: 2 20 9 3 5
 0(0)  0(0)  0(0)  2(1)  2(1)  2(1)  2(1)  2(1)  2(1)  2(1)  2(1)
 0(0)  0(0)  0(0)  2(0)  2(0)  2(0)  2(0)  2(0)  2(0)  2(0)  2(0)
 0(0)  0(0)  0(0)  2(0)  2(0)  2(0)  9(1)  9(1)  9(1)  11(1)  11(1)
 0(0)  0(0)  0(0)  2(0)  3(1)  3(1)  9(0)  9(0)  9(0)  11(0)  12(1)
 0(0)  0(0)  5(1)  5(1)  5(1)  7(1)  9(0)  9(0)  14(1)  14(1)  14(1)

Solution: 14
Optimal Policy: 0 0 1 0 1
Time: 2.3e-05
```

Fig. 2.15. Execution screen for a knapsack problem.

2.3.4. The Output

We now illustrate an example of execution of the former problem for an input knapsack instance with: $N = 5$, $C = 10$, $w = \{3, 11, 4, 6, 2\}$ and $p = \{2, 20, 9, 3, 5\}$. The output obtained is shown in Fig. 2.15. First, the data information associated with the problem under execution is presented: the setup parameters (number of stages and number of states) and the input problem data (number of objects, capacity of the knapsack), weights and profits. Once the solution is computed, the DP table will be presented. This table will provide the optimal profit and the set of objects to include into the knapsack. The DP table depicts for each state, the optimal value and the decision taken (parenthical), *zero* to exclude the object and *one* to insert it. After the DP table, the optimal solution and the optimal policy are presented.

2.3.5. Sensitivity Analysis

The DP table is a helpful instrument to perform the sensitivity analysis since it not only stores the optimal solution, but also all the subproblems evaluated during the computation. In our particular case, we may be interested in investigating the effect of increasing the capacity of the knapsack in the optimal solution. A knapsack with capacity equal to *10* provides a profit equal to *14*, the same profit obtained with capacities <*10*. Assuming that an increase of the capacity also involves a cost, a knapsack with capacity equal to *8* should be selected as the optimal solution in this case. Moreover (Fig. 2.16), if the capacity is increased to *11*, a greater profit would have been obtained (*20*). The function Main() can be easily transformed by the user to specify ranges where the capacity of the knapsack may vary, and then to obtain the best ratio benefit/cost. That makes the sensitivity analysis easier.

```
Stages: 5
States: 11

Objects: 5
Capacity: 11
Weights: 3 11 6 4 2
Profits: 2 20 9 3 5
 0(0)  0(0)  0(0)  2(1)  2(1)  2(1)  2(1)  2(1)  2(1)  2(1)  2(1)  2(1)
 0(0)  0(0)  0(0)  2(0)  2(0)  2(0)  2(0)  2(0)  2(0)  2(0)  2(0)  20(1)
 0(0)  0(0)  0(0)  2(0)  2(0)  2(0)  9(1)  9(1)  9(1)  11(1) 11(1) 20(0)
 0(0)  0(0)  0(0)  2(0)  3(1)  3(1)  9(0)  9(0)  9(0)  11(0) 12(1) 20(0)
 0(0)  0(0)  5(1)  5(1)  5(1)  7(1)  9(0)  9(0)  14(1) 14(1) 14(1) 20(0)

Solution: 20
Optimal Policy: 0 1 0 0 0
Time: 2.5e-05
```

Fig. 2.16. Sensitivity Analysis using the DP table.

2.3.6. The Class Solver

The class Solver provides solver engines for different platforms. This class contains the data structures and methods needed to perform a DP execution according to the specifications.

In practice, it is a virtual class and the solvers provided are defined as subclasses of this main class. Current design considers the following set of Solvers:

- `Solver_seq`. The sequential solver.
- `Solver_sharedmemory`. The solver for shared memory systems.
- `Solver_distributedmemory`. The solver for distributed memory machines.
- `Solver_hybrid`. The solver for hybrid platforms combining both of the former.
- `Solver_heterogen`. The solver on heterogeneous environments where the processing elements may have different computational capabilities, and the interconnection network may be different on any pair of processing units.
- `Solver_debug`. The solver to run under debug mode. It provides step-by-step executions and some other facilities. It can be used by the user to discover the traversing modes suitable for their application. The solver, automatically, can try different traversing modes and detect whether dependencies on the functional equation are being violated.
- `Solver_profile`. The solver to profile and tune the application in parallel platforms. The code required from the user can be automatically instrumented. The instrumented code can be profiled to feed analytical models and tune the application for optimal executions.

Figure 2.17 shows the class Solver_seq. When an object of this class is instantiated, the DP table is dynamically created according to the setup parameters. In Fig. 2.18, we can see how the DP table is traversed by the method run_byrows of the class Solver_sharedmemory. Rows are evaluated in sequence and the set of processors computes every row in parallel. Since the inner loop is parallelized, we use two OpenMP pragmas to avoid the

```
provides class Solver_seq: public Solver {
    // The Problem
    const Problem &pbm;
    // The Setup
    const Setup &setup;
    // The Solution */
    Solution sol;
    // The Dynamic Programming Table
    Table table;
    .....

    public:
        ...
        // Runs the Solver traversing the table by rows*/
        virtual void run_byrows();
        ...
}
```

Fig. 2.17. Defining a Sequential Solver.

```
void Solver_sharedmemory::run_byrows() {
    int i, j;
    int num_stages = setup.get_Num_Stages();
    int num_states = setup.get_Num_States();
    #pragma omp parallel private(i)
    {
        for (i = 0; i < num_stages; i++) {
                #pragma omp for private(j) firstprivate(i)
                for (j = 0; j < num_states; j++)
                        table.GET_STATE(i, j).Evalua(i, j);
        }
    }
}
```

Fig. 2.18. Implementation of the function run_byrows using OpenMP.

destruction of the parallel region on each iteration. The states are evaluated using the method `Evalua`. This method has been supplied by the user and implements the functional equation.

2.4. COMPUTATIONAL RESULTS

This section is devoted to validating the performance of parallelizations under the skeleton experimentally. Running times for sequential executions are compared with execution times provided by the `Solver_sharedmemory`. As test problems we consider the problems shown in Table 2.1, the 0/1 Knapsack Problem (KP), the Longest Common Subsequence Problem (LCS), the Floyd All-Pairs Shortest-Paths algorithm (FSP), and the Optimal Matrix Parenthesization Problem (MPP). They represent four different classes of recurrences and can be used as examples for many other DP problems. Three series of instances have been randomly generated for each problem. Since the KP and FSP problems are *serial* problems they have been solved using the traversing mode by rows, both in sequential and parallel. The *nonserial* property of the LCS and MMP problems impose the use of diagonal modes on the traversing. For the LCS, the diagonal mode starts the evaluation at the left upper corner of the DP table and for the MMP problem it begins the evaluation at the main diagonal and ends at the right upper corner.

The computational experiments have been carried out on an IBMRS-6000 SP with 8*16 Nighthawk Power3 @375 Mhz (192 Gflops/s) with 64 Gb RAM. The nodes are connected through an SP Switch2 operating at 500 MB/s. In our computational experiments, we used only one node of 16 processors. Codes have been compiled using the OpenMP native compiler.

Tables 2.2–2.5 show the running times and speedups obtained for the KP, LCS, FSP, and MPP, respectively. Running times are all expressed in seconds. The computational results demonstrate the advantages of design methodology. The tool shows a satisfactory performance in all the cases. As expected,

TABLE 2.2. Running Times and Speedups for Knapsack Problems[a]

No. Processors	Time			Speedup		
	KP1	KP2	KP3	KP1	KP2	KP3
1	2.379	9.531	18.975			
2	1.222	4.841	9.627	1.945	1.968	1.971
4	0.640	2.493	4.944	3.716	3.822	3.837
8	0.359	1.326	2.632	6.612	7.187	7.207
16	0.305	0.939	1.871	7.778	10.147	10.139

[a]N is the number of objects and C is the capacity of the Knapsack; KP1 ($N = 1600$ $C = 3200$), KP2 ($N = 3200$ $C = 6400$) and KP3($N = 6400$ $C = 6400$).

TABLE 2.3. Running Times and Speedups for Longest Common Subsequence Problems[a]

No. Processors	Time			Speedup		
	LCS1	LCS2	LCS3	LCS1	LCS2	LCS3
1	0.895	10.049	30.647			
2	0.477	4.761	13.379	1.876	2.110	2.290
4	0.255	2.289	6.391	3.511	4.390	4.795
8	0.148	1.233	3.336	6.050	8.148	9.186
16	0.137	0.786	2.084	6.493	12.770	14.700

[a]$N1$ and $N2$ are the lengths of the sequences; LCS1 ($N1 = 1000, N2 = 1000$), LCS2 ($N1 = 3000, N2 = 3000$) and LCS3 ($N1 = 5000, N2 = 5000$).

TABLE 2.4. Running Times and Speedups for Floyd All-Pairs Shortest-Paths Algorithms[a]

No. Processors	Time			Speedup		
	FSP1	FSP2	FSP3	FSP1	FSP2	FSP3
1	4.537	15.706	25.043			
2	2.316	7.823	12.454	1.958	2.007	2.010
4	1.169	3.917	6.371	3.880	4.009	3.930
8	0.611	1.973	3.197	7.421	7.959	7.832
16	0.345	1.026	1.644	13.133	15.296	15.226

[a]N is the number of vertices of the graph; FSP1 ($N = 200$), FSP2 ($N = 300$) and FSP3 ($N = 350$).

TABLE 2.5. Running Times and Speedups for Optimal Matrix Parenthesization Problems[a]

No. Processors	Time			Speedup		
	MPP1	MPP2	MPP3	MPP1	MPP2	MPP3
1	0.0314	6.189	72.826			
2	0.0185	3.080	33.529	1.700	2.009	2.172
4	0.0118	1.570	15.821	2.651	3.941	4.603
8	0.0102	0.823	7.8610	3.065	7.516	9.264
16	0.0117	0.462	4.0663	2.690	13.379	17.909

[a]N is the number of matrices; MPP1 ($N = 100$), MPP2 ($N = 500$) and MPP3($N = 1000$).

larger instances show better speedups. Superlinear speedup is observed for the MPP3 instance when using 8 and 16 processors, this is likely due to the better use of the caches on the parallel versions. A very poor speedup is observed for the smallest instance (MPP1).

2.5. ACKNOWLEDGMENTS

We acknowledge the European Center for Parallelism of Barcelona (CEPBA) for allowing us to use their machines. This work has been partially supported by EC (FEDER) and the Spanish MCyT (Plan Nacional I+D+I TIN2005-09037-C02).

REFERENCES

1. D.K. Smith. *Dynamic Programming. A practical Introduction.* Ellis Horwood, 1991.
2. A.V. Aho, J.E. Hopcroft, and J.D. Ullman. *Estructuras de Datos y Algoritmos.* Addison Wesley Iberoamericana, 1988.
3. E. Horowitz and S. Sahni. *Fundamentals of Computer Algorithms.* Computer Science Press, 1978.
4. G. Brassard and P. Bratley. *Fundamentals of Algorithmics.* Prentice Hall International editions, 1996.
5. T.H. Cormen, C.E. Leiserson, and R.L. Rivest. *Introduction to Algorithms.* The MIT Press and McGraw-Hill Book Company, Mungah, 1989.
6. P. Helman. A common schema for dynamic programming and branch and bound algorithms. *J. ACM*, **36**:97–128 (1989).
7. R.M. Karp and M. Held. Finite state process and dynamic programming. *SIAM J. Appl. Math.*, **15**:693–718 (1967).
8. T. Ibaraki. *Enumerative Approaches to Combinatorial Optimization, Part II. Ann. Oper. Res.*, **11**:1–4 (1988).
9. O. de Moor. Dynamic programming as a software component. In N. Mastorakis, editor, *Proceedings of the 3rd WSEAS International Conference on Circuits, Systems, Communications and Computers*, 1999.
10. G. Li and B. Wah. Parallel processing of serial dynamic programming programs. In *Proceedings of COMPSAC 85*, 1985, pp. 81–89.
11. B. Wah, G. Li, and C. Fen. Multiprocessing of combinatorial search problems. Vol. 18, 1985, pp. 93–108. 1°6, IEEE Computers.
12. A. Gibbons and W. Rytter. *Efficient parallel algorithms*, Chap. 3.6 now Efficient algorithms for dynamic programming. Cambridge University Press, 1988.
13. F. Bitz and H.T. Kung. Path planning on the warp computer using a linear systolic array in dynamic programming. *Int. J. Comput. Math.*, **25**:173–188 (1988).
14. Z. Galil and K. Park. Parallel algorithms for dynamic programming recurrences with more than o(1) dependency. *J. Parallel Distributed Comput.*, **21**:213–222 (1994).
15. B. Louka and M. Tchuente. Dynamic programming on two-dimensional systolic arrays. *Inform. Proc. Lett.*, **29**:97–104 (1988).
16. S. Miguet and Y. Robert. Dynamic programming on a ring of processors. *Hypercube and Distributed Computers*, 1989, pp. 19–33.
17. W. Rytter. On efficient parallel computations for some dynamic programming problems. *Theor. Comput. Sci.*, **59** (1988).

18. C. Rodríguez, D. González, F. Almeida, J. Roda, and F. García. Parallel algorithms for polyadic problems. *Proceedings of the 5th Euromicro Workshop on Parallel and Distributed Processing*, 1997, pp. 394–400.

19. R. Andonov, S. Balev, S. Rajopadhye, and N. Yanev. Optimal semi-oblique tiling and its application to sequence comparison. *13th ACM Symposium on Parallel Algorithms and Architectures (SPAA)*, 2001.

20. R. Andonov and S. Rajopadhye. Optimal Orthogonal Tiling of 2-D Iterations. *J. Parallel Distributed Comput.*, **45**:159–165 (Sept. 1997).

21. L.M. Moreno. Computación en paralelo y entornos heterogéneos (in spanish). Ph.D. thesis. Universidad de La Laguna.

22. J.P. Martínez, J. Cuenca, and D. Giménez. Heuristics for work distribution of a homogeneous parallel dynamic programming scheme on heterogeneous systems. *Parallel Computing*, 2005.

23. D. Morales *et al.* Parallel dynamic programming and automata theory. *Parallel Comput.*, 2000.

24. S. Miguet and Y. Robert. Path planning on a ring of processors. *Int. J. Comput. Math*, **32**:61–74 (1990).

25. F. Almeida *et al.* Optimal tiling for the rna base pairing problem. *SPAA*, 2002, pp. 173–182.

26. D. Gozález, F. Almeida, L. Moreno, and C. Rodríguez. Towards the automatic optimal mapping of pipeline algorithms. *Parallel Comput.*, **29**:241–254 (2003).

27. J. Eckstein, C.A. Phillips, and W.E. Hart. PICO: An object-oriented framework for parallel branch and bound. Technical report, RUTCOR, 2000.

28. B. Le Cun. Bob++ library illustrated by VRP. In *European Operational Research Conference (EURO'2001)*, Rotterdam, 2001, p. 157.

29. B.C. Lubow. SDP: Generalized software for solving stochastic dynamic optimization problems. *Wildlife Soc. Bull.*, **23**:738–742 (Sept. 1997).

30. P. Lohmander. Deterministic and stochastic dynamic programming. Available at www.sekon.slu.se/PLO/diskreto/dynp.htm.

31. M. Galassi *et al.* *GNU scientific library reference manual*, July 2002. ed. 1.2, for GSL Version 1.2.

32. J. Aliaga *et al.* Parallelization of gsl on clusters of symmetric multiprocessors. *Proceedings of the PARCO'05, Málaga, Spain, 2006. To be published.*

33. Daniel González-Morales *et al.* A skeleton for parallel dynamic programming. *Euro-Par '99: Proceedings of the 5th International Euro-Par Conference on Parallel Processing*, Springer-Verlag, London, 1999, pp. 877–887.

34. E. Alba *et al.* MALLBA: A library of skeletons for combinatorial optimisation (research note). *Proceedings of the 8th International Euro-Par Conference*, Vol. 2400 of *LNCS*, 2002, pp. 927–932.

35. V. Kumar, A. Grama, A. Gupta, and G. Karypis. *Introduction to Parallel Computing Design and Analysis of Algorithms*. The Benjamin / Cummings Publishing Company, Inc., 1994.

■■■■ **CHAPTER 3**

Parallel Branch and Cut

T.K. RALPHS

Department of Industrial and Systems Engineering, Lehigh University, Bethlehem, PA 18015

3.1. INTRODUCTION

This chapter discusses parallelization of the branch-and-cut algorithm for solving general mixed-integer linear programs (MILPs). Branch and cut is a specialization of the more general class of algorithms known as *branch and bound* and is currently the most effective and commonly used approach for solving difficult MILPs. Virtually all modern software packages for solving MILPs use a variant of the branch-and-cut approach. Despite vast improvements in implementation over the past two decades and recent quantum leaps in computing power, however, many MILPs arising in practice remain difficult to solve by branch and cut. The difficulty stems mainly from limitations in memory and processing power, so a natural approach to overcoming this difficulty is to consider the use of parallel computing platforms, which can deliver a pooled supply of computing power and memory that is virtually limitless.

Branch and cut is a divide-and-conquer algorithm that partitions the original solution space into a number of smaller subsets and then solves the resulting smaller MILPs in a recursive fashion. Such an approach appears easy to parallelize, but this appearance is deceiving. Although it is easy in principle to divide the original solution space into subsets, it is difficult to do this in such a way that the amount of effort required to solve each of the resulting smaller MILPs is approximately equal. If the work is not divided equally, then some processors will become idle long before the solution process has been completed, resulting in inefficiency. Even if this challenge is overcome, it might still be the case that the total amount of work required to solve the subproblems far exceeds the amount of work required to solve the original problem on a single processor.

Parallel Combinatorial Optimization, edited by El-Ghazali Talbi
Copyright © 2006 by John Wiley & Sons, Inc.

The challenge to be faced in parallelizing any algorithm is to use additional resources, that is, processors, as efficiently as possible. This consists not only of maximizing the number of processors that have work to do at any given time, but also ensuring that the work they are doing is "useful." In other words, the total amount of work performed in a parallel algorithm for solving a given problem should be as close as possible to the total amount of work performed using the best sequential algorithm. These two goals together mean that if we have p processors available and the time required to solve a given instance on one processor is S, we would ideally like to be able to solve the instance on p processors in time S/p. This is the yardstick against which parallel performance is generally measured.

The purpose of this chapter is not to present a single approach to parallelization of branch and cut, but to introduce the reader to a range of issues that arise in such parallelization. Defining a single "best" approach is not possible in general—an approach suited for one class of problems may fail miserably on another, as we demonstrate in Section 3.5. Achieving good parallel performance requires, first and foremost, efficient mechanisms for sharing information among the available processors. In fact, the way in which processors share information is the primary determinant of parallel efficiency. Because sharing information is usually costly, there is a fundamental tradeoff between the cost of this sharing and the loss of efficiency that can result from *not* sharing. It is this tradeoff that is examined in the remainder of the chapter.

This chapter is organized as follows. Section 3.2 reviews necessary background, including the branch-and-cut algorithm and basic concepts in parallel computing. Section 3.3 discusses in broad terms the issues involved in parallelizing branch and cut, including the types of information that must be shared and what specific tradeoffs must be considered in designing an efficient algorithm. Section 3.4 describes the implementational details of two software packages that can be used for solving MILPs in parallel, SYMPHONY and ALPS. The two packages take very different approaches to parallelization and they are used to illustrate the tradeoffs discussed in Section 3.3. Section 3.5 analyzes computational results obtained using SYMPHONY to solve instances from a number of representative problem classes. Finally, Section 3.6 concludes and summarizes the material presented in the rest of the chapter.

3.2. BACKGROUND

3.2.1. Mixed-Integer Linear Programming

3.2.1.1. Definitions. A mixed-integer linear program is the problem of optimizing a linear objective function over a polyhedral feasible region with the additional constraint that some of the variables are required to take on integer values. More formally, a MILP is a problem of the form

$$z_{IP} = \min_{x \in \mathcal{P} \cap (\mathbb{Z}^p \times \mathbb{R}^{n-p})} c^\top x \qquad (3.1)$$

where $\mathcal{P} = \{x \in \mathbb{R}^n \mid Ax = b, x \geq 0\}$ is a polyhedron defined by *constraint matrix* $A \in \mathbb{Q}^{m \times n}$ and *right-hand side vector* $b \in \mathbb{R}^m$, and $c \in \mathbb{R}^n$ is the *objective function vector*. For the remainder of the chapter, this standard notation will be used to refer to the data associated with a given MILP. Note that we have assumed without loss of generality that the variables indexed 1 through p are the *integer variables*, that is, those required to take on values in $\mathbb{Z}$. The variables indexed $p + 1$ through n are then the *continuous variables*. The case in which all variables are continuous ($p = 0$) is called a *linear program* (LP). Associated with each MILP is an LP, called the *LP relaxation*, with feasible region $\mathcal{P}$, obtained by relaxing the integrality restrictions. By convention, we set $z_{IP} = \infty$ if $\mathcal{P} \cap (\mathbb{Z}^p \times \mathbb{R}^{n-p}) = \emptyset$.

3.2.1.2. Branch and Bound

Overview. Branch and bound is the basic algorithmic approach taken by virtually all modern MILP solvers. The algorithm uses a divide and conquer strategy to partition the feasible set $\mathcal{F} = \mathcal{P} \cap (\mathbb{Z}^p \times \mathbb{R}^{n-p})$ into subsets and then optimizes over each resulting subset in a recursive fashion. The goal is to determine a least cost member of $\mathcal{F}$ (or prove $\mathcal{F} = \emptyset$), so we first attempt to find a "good" solution $\bar{x} \in \mathcal{F}$ (called the *incumbent*) by a heuristic procedure or otherwise. If we succeed, then $\bar{z} = c^\top \bar{x}$ serves as an initial upper bound on z_{IP}. If no such solution is found, then we set $\bar{z} = \infty$.

The *processing* or *bounding* operation is to solve a relaxation of the original problem, yielding a lower bound on the value of an optimal solution.[1] If solving the relaxation yields a member of $\mathcal{F}$, then such member is also optimal for the MILP itself and we are done. Otherwise, we identify k disjoint polyhedral subsets of $\mathcal{P}$, $\mathcal{P}_1, \cdots, \mathcal{P}_k$, such that $\cup_{i=1}^k \mathcal{P}_i \cap (\mathbb{Z}^p \times \mathbb{R}^{n-p}) = \mathcal{F}$. This is called the *branching* or *partitioning* operation. Each of these subsets defines a new MILP with the same objective function as the original, called a *subproblem*. Based on this partitioning of $\mathcal{F}$, we have

$$\min_{x \in \mathcal{F}} c^\top x = \min_{i \in 1..k} \left(\min_{x \in \mathcal{P}_i \cap (\mathbb{Z}^p \times \ell^{n-p})} c^\top x \right), \qquad (3.2)$$

so we have reduced solution of the original MILP to solution of a family of smaller MILPs. The subproblems associated with $\mathcal{P}_1, \cdots, \mathcal{P}_k$ are called the *children* of the original MILP, which is itself called the *root subproblem*, as well as the *parent* of each of its children.

---

[1]We assume the relaxation is bounded, or else the original MILP is itself unbounded.

After partitioning the root subproblem, we initialize C, the set of *candidate subproblems* (those that await processing or partitioning) with the children of the root subproblem and associate with each of these an initial lower bound computed during the partitioning procedure. The next step is to select a candidate subproblem i (with feasible region $\mathcal{P}_i \cap (\mathbb{Z}^p \times \mathbb{R}^{n-p})$), remove it from C, and process it. Processing results in a new lower bound z_i and (possibly) a relaxed solution $\hat{x}^i \in \mathbb{R}^n$. There are three possible outcomes:

1. If $\underline{z}_i \geq \overline{z}$, then the subproblem cannot have a solution with value strictly better than $\overline{x}$ and we may discard, or *fathom*, it. This includes the case where $\mathcal{P}_i \cap (\mathbb{Z}^p \times \mathbb{R}^{n-p}) = \emptyset$.
2. If $\hat{x}_i \in \mathcal{F}$ and $\underline{z}_i = c^\top \hat{x}_x^i < \overline{z}$, then $\hat{x}_x^i$ becomes the new incumbent. We set $\overline{z} \leftarrow c^\top \hat{x}_x^i$, $\overline{x} \leftarrow \hat{x}_x^i$, and again fathom the subproblem.
3. If none of the above three conditions hold, then the subproblem becomes a candidate for the partitioning operation.

If a subproblem becomes a candidate for partitioning, it can either be partitioned immediately, or placed back in the candidate list. Once partitioned, the children of a subproblem are added to the candidate list and the subproblem itself is discarded. The overall algorithm consists of continuing to select subproblems from the candidate list in a prescribed order (called the *search order*) and processing or partitioning them, as appropriate, until C is empty, at which point the current incumbent must be the optimal solution. If no incumbent exists at termination, then $\mathcal{F} = \emptyset$.

It is common to associate the set of subproblems with a tree, called the *search tree*, in which each node corresponds to a subproblem and is connected to both its children and its parent. We therefore use the term *search tree node*, or simply *node*, interchangeably with the term subproblem and refer to the original MILP as the *root node* or *root* of this tree.

Implementation. From the above description, it can be seen that any branch-and-bound algorithm consists of four essential elements:

- *Upper bounding method*: A method for determining an initial incumbent and corresponding upper bound $\overline{z}$ (optional).
- *Lower bounding method*: A method for processing a subproblem.
- *Branching method*: A method for partitioning a subproblem.
- *Search strategy*: A method for determining the search order.

By implementing these elements in various ways, one can derive a wide range of specialized versions of branch and bound.

The branch-and-bound procedure can be seen as an iterative method for improving the difference between the current upper bound (the objective function value of the current incumbent) and the current lower bound (the minimum of the lower bounds associated with the candidate subproblems). The difference between these two bounds is called the *optimality gap*. Typically, the goal of both the bounding and the branching operations is to improve the lower bound, while the search strategy can be focused on improving either the upper or the lower bound. Methods for bounding and branching are generally developed with a particular application or problem class in mind, but search strategies can be discussed in a more generic fashion. The possible strategies are numerous, but we summarize the most common approaches below.

Many search strategies employ a fixed rule for selecting the next subproblem to process. A common such method is *best-first search*, which chooses a candidate node with smallest lower bound. Because of the fathoming rule employed in branch and bound, a best-first search strategy ensures that no subproblem with a lower bound above the optimal solution value can ever be chosen for processing. Therefore, the best-first strategy tends to minimize the number of subproblems processed and to improve the lower bound quickly. However, this comes at the price of sacrificing incremental improvements to the upper bound, since the upper bound will generally become finite only when an optimal solution has been located. The lack of a good upper bound can also hurt overall efficiency by reducing the effectiveness of procedures both for fathoming and for tightening of variable bounds based on the size of the optimality gap.

At the other extreme, *depth-first search* chooses the next candidate to be a node at maximum depth in the tree, that is, a node whose path to the root node in the search tree is longest. Depth first is one of a class of strategies, called *diving strategies*, that may retain one or more children of the current subproblem for processing even when there exist candidates nodes with smaller lower bounds. In contrast to best-first search, which will produce few suboptimal solutions, diving strategies may produce many suboptimal solutions, typically early in the search process. This allows the upper bound to be improved quickly in the early phases of the algorithm, which can be advantageous if early termination is necessitated. Diving strategies also have the advantage that the change in the relaxation being solved from subproblem to subproblem may be very slight, so the relaxations may be solved more quickly than in best-first search.

Neither best-first search nor depth-first search attempt to select nodes that have a high probability of leading to improved feasible solutions. Estimate-based methods are improvements in this regard. The *best-projection* method (1,2) measures the overall "quality" of a node by combining its initial lower bound with the degree of infeasibility of a relaxed solution obtained either while processing the parent or during branching. Alternatively, the *best-estimate* (3) method combines a node's lower bound, degree of infeasibility, and an estimate of the value of an optimal solution to the subproblem.

Since we have two goals in node selection—finding improved feasible solutions (i.e., improving the upper bound) and proving that the current incumbent is itself a "good" solution (i.e., improving the lower bound)—it is natural to develop node selection strategies that switch from one goal to the other during the course of the algorithm. This results in a two-phase search strategy. In the first phase, we try to determine "good" feasible solutions, while in the second phase, we try to prove this goodness. Perhaps the simplest two-phase algorithm is to perform depth-first search until a feasible solution is found, then switch to best-first search.

Hybrid methods also combine two or more node selection methods, but in a different manner than in two-phase methods. In a typical hybrid method, the search tree is explored using a diving strategy until the lower bound of the child subproblem being explored rises above a prescribed level in comparison to the overall lower or upper bound. At this point, a new subproblem is selected by a different criterion (e.g., best-first or best-estimate), and the diving process is repeated. For an in-depth discussion of search strategies for mixed-integer linear programming, see the paper of Linderoth and Savelsbergh (4).

3.2.1.3. Branch and Cut.

3.2.1.3. Branch and Cut. When the relaxation used in the processing step is an LP relaxation, we obtain a general class of algorithms known as *LP-based branch and bound*. For many problem classes, the bound yielded by the initial LP relaxation is not strong enough to allow efficient solution of difficult instances, but we can improve the bound by dynamically generating valid inequalities that can than be added to the LP relaxation to strengthen it. Padberg and Rinaldi called this technique *branch and cut* (5).

More formally, an *inequality* is a pair (a, a_0) consisting of a *coefficient vector* $a \in \mathbb{R}^n$ and a *right-hand side* $a_0 \in \mathbb{R}$. Any member of the half-space $\{x \in \mathbb{R}^n \mid a^\top x \le a_0\}$ is said to *satisfy* the inequality and all other points are said to *violate* it. An inequality is *valid* for a given MILP if all members of the feasible set $\mathcal{F}$ satisfy it. A valid inequality (a, a_0) is called *improving* for the MILP if

$$\min_{x \in \mathbb{R}^n}\{c^\top x \mid x \in \mathcal{P}, ax \le a_0\} > \min_{x \in \mathbb{R}^n}\{c^\top x \mid x \in \mathcal{P}\}$$

A necessary and sufficient condition for an inequality to be improving is that it be violated by all optimal solutions to the LP relaxation, so violation of the *fractional solution* $\hat{x} \in \mathbb{R}^n$ generated by solving the LP relaxation is a necessary condition. Even if a given valid inequality violated by $\hat{x}$, also called a *cut*, is not improving, adding it to the current LP relaxation may still result in the generation of a new fractional solution and, in turn, additional candidate inequalities.

An important observation is that an inequality (a, a_0) is valid for $\mathcal{F}$ if and only if it is valid for the associated polyhedron $\text{conv}(\mathcal{F})$. Valid inequalities that are necessary to the description of $\text{conv}(\mathcal{F})$ are called *facet-defining inequalities* (see Ref. 6 for a precise definition). Because they provide the closest possible approximation of $\text{conv}(\mathcal{F})$, facet-defining inequalities are typically very effective at improving the lower bound. They are, however, difficult to generate in general. For an arbitrary vector $\hat{x} \in \mathbb{R}^n$ and polyhedron $\mathcal{R} \subseteq \mathbb{R}^n$, the problem of either generating a facet-defining inequality (a, a_0) violated by $\hat{x}$ or proving that $\hat{x} \in \mathcal{R}$ is called the *facet identification problem*. The facet identification problem for a given polyhedron is polynomially equivalent to optimization over the same polyhedron (7), so generating a facet-defining inequality violated by an arbitrary vector is in general as hard as solving the MILP itself. The problem of generating a valid inequality violated by a given fractional solution, whether facet defining or not, is called the *separation problem*.

A high-level description of the iterative bounding procedure used in branch and cut is shown in Fig. 3.1. Generally, the loop consists of an alternation between solution of the current LP relaxation and the generation of valid inequalities violated by the relaxed solution. Because the number of violated valid inequalities generated in each iteration can be quite large, they are first added to a local queue. Following the generation step, a limited number of violated inequalities are taken from the queue and added to the LP relaxation. It is important to note that not only are valid inequalities added to the relaxation each iteration, but both valid inequalities and variables are considered for deletion as well. For valid inequalities, this deletion is based on the values of each constraint's corresponding slack and dual variables. For variables, removal occurs when both the lower and upper bound for a variable are fixed to the same value through a procedure that compares each variable's reduced cost to the current optimality gap (for a description of this procedure, called *reduced cost fixing*, see Ref. 8).

Efficient management of the LP relaxation is critical to the efficiency of branch and cut, since both the memory required to store the search tree and the time required to process a node are highly dependent on the number of constraints and variables that are "active" in each subproblem. In practice, there are a number of extra steps that can be taken, such as logical preprocessing and execution of primal heuristics, to accelerate the overall performance of the algorithm, but these are ancillary to the topic of this paper. More details regarding the management of the LP relaxation in a typical MILP solver are provided in Ref. 9.

If the procedure in Fig. 3.1 fails to fathom the subproblem, then we are forced to branch. In branch and cut, the branching method should generally have three properties. First, the feasible region of the parent problem should be partitioned in such a way that the resulting subproblems are also MILPs.

Input: A subproblem defined by $\mathcal{P}_i \in \mathcal{C}$, an initial set of additional valid inequalities defining an auxiliary polyhedron $\mathcal{R}$ (possibly generated during processing of the parent subproblem), and the global upper bound $\bar{z}$.

Output: Either (1) a lower bound $\underline{z}_i$ on the optimal value of the subproblem, or (2) an indication that the subproblem can be fathomed.

1. Form the initial LP relaxation

$$\min_{x \in \mathcal{P}_i \cap \mathcal{R}} c^\top x \qquad (3.3)$$

   where $\mathcal{R}$ is the polyhedron representing additional valid inequalities.

2. Solve the current LP relaxation

$$z_i = \min_{x \in \mathcal{P}_i \cap \mathcal{R}} c^\top x \qquad (3.4)$$

   and let $\hat{x}$ be the resulting fractional solution.

3. If $\underline{z}_i \geq \bar{z}$, then subproblem i can be fathomed. STOP.

4. If $\hat{x} \in \mathcal{P}_i \cap (\mathbb{Z}^p \times \mathbb{R}^{n-p})$, then subproblem i can be fathomed. If $\underline{z}_i < \bar{z}$, then set $\bar{x} \to \hat{x}$ and $\bar{z} \to \underline{z}_i$. STOP.

5. Generate a set valid inequalities violated by $\hat{x}$ and add them to the local queue $\mathcal{L}$.

6. Remove variables that can be fixed from the relaxation.

7. Remove ineffective valid inequalities from the description of $\mathcal{R}$.

8. If $\mathcal{L} = \emptyset$, then subproblem i is a candidate for partitioning. STOP and output the lower bound $\underline{z}_i$.

9. Otherwise, add valid inequalities from $\mathcal{L}$ to the description of $\mathcal{R}$ and go to Step 2.

Fig. 3.1 The node processing loop in the branch-and-cut algorithm.

This means that the subproblems are usually defined by imposing additional linear inequalities. Second, the union of the feasible regions of the subproblems should contain at least one optimal solution to the parent problem. Finally, since the primary goal of branching is to improve the overall lower bound, the current fractional solution should not be contained in any of the members of the partition. Otherwise, the overall lower bound will not be improved.

Given a fractional solution $\hat{x} \in \mathbb{R}^n$ to the LP relaxation, an obvious way to fulfill the above requirements is to choose an index $j \leq p$ such that $\hat{x}_j \notin \mathbb{Z}$ (a *fractional variable*) and create two subproblems, one by imposing an upper bound of $\lfloor \hat{x}_j \rfloor$ on variable j and a second by imposing a lower bound of $\lceil \hat{x}_j \rceil$. This is a valid partitioning, since any feasible solution must satisfy one of these two linear inequalities. Furthermore, $\hat{x}$ is not feasible for either of the resulting subproblems. This partitioning procedure is known as *branching on a vari-*

able. More generally, one can branch on other disjunctions. For any vector a $\in \mathbb{Z}^n$ whose last $n - p$ entries are zero, we must have $a^\top x \in \mathbb{Z}$ for all $x \in \mathcal{F}$. Thus, if $a\hat{x} \notin \mathbb{Z}$, a can be used to produce a disjunction by imposing the inequality $a^\top x \leq \lfloor a^\top \hat{x} \rfloor$ in one subproblem and the inequality $a^\top x \geq \lceil a^\top \hat{x} \rceil$ in the other subproblem. This is known as *branching on a hyperplane.* Typically, branching on hyperplanes is a problem-specific method that exploits special structure, but it can be made generic by keeping a pool of inequalities that are slack in the current relaxation as branching candidates (10).

When branching on variables, there are usually many fractional variables, so we must have a method for deciding which one to choose. A primary goal of branching is to improve the lower bound of the resulting relaxations. The most straightforward branching methods choose a branching variable based solely on the set of fractional variables and do not use any auxiliary information. Branching on the variable with the fractional part closest to 5, the first variable (by index) that is fractional, or the last variable (by index) that is fractional are examples of such procedures. These rules tend to be too myopic to be effective, so many solvers use more sophisticated approaches. Such approaches fall into two general categories: *forward-looking methods* and *backward-looking methods.* Methods in each category attempt to choose the best partitioning by predicting, for a given candidate partitioning, how much the lower bound will actually be improved. Forward-looking methods generate this prediction based solely on locally generated information obtained by "presolving" candidate subproblems. The most common forward-looking branching method is *strong branching,* in which the solver explicitly performs a limited number of dual simplex pivots on the LP relaxations in each of the children resulting from branching on a given variable in order to estimate the change in bound that would occur from that choice of branching. Backward-looking methods take into account the results of previous partitionings to predict the effect of future ones. The most popular such methods depend on the computation of *pseudo-costs* (3,11), which are calculated based on a history of the effect of branching on each variable. Of course, as one might expect, there are also hybrids that combine these two basic approaches (12).

3.2.2. Parallel Computing Concepts

3.2.2.1. Architecture. The architecture of the parallel platform (defined as a specific combination of software and hardware) on which an algorithm will be deployed can be a significant factor in its design. In particular, the topology of the communications network determines which pairs of processors can communicate directly with each other (13). Although many specialized network topologies have been developed and studied, recent trends have favored the use of commodity hardware to construct so-called *Beowulf clusters* (14). In this chapter, a simplified parallel architecture similar to that of a typical Beowulf cluster is assumed. The main properties of such an architecture are listed below.

- The cluster is comprised of homogeneous *processing nodes*, each with a single central processing unit (or *processor*).
- The processing nodes are connected by a dedicated high-speed communication network that allows every processing node to communicate directly with every other processing node.
- There is no shared access memory (memory that can be accessed directly by multiple processors). Only local memory is available to each processor. No assumption is made regarding the local memory hierarchy.
- Communication between processing nodes is via a *message-passing* protocol. This means that information can only be passed from one processing node to another as a string of bits with an associated *message tag* indicating the structure of the information contained in the message. The two most common message-passing protocols are PVM (15) and MPI (16).

This cluster architecture and the algorithms we discuss are *asynchronous* by nature, meaning that the processors do not have a common clock by which to synchronize their calculations. Synchronization can only be accomplished through explicit communication. In our simplified model, the two main resources required for computation are memory and processing power, each of which can only be increased by adding *processing nodes* to the cluster. A processing node consists of both a processor and associated memory, but we will assume that each processing node has sufficient memory for required calculations and will refer to processing nodes simply as "processors."

3.2.2.2. Scalability.

As mentioned earlier, the primary goal of parallel computing is to take advantage of increased processing power to solve problems faster. The *scalability* of a parallel platform is the degree to which it is capable of efficiently utilizing increased computing resources (usually processors). Here, we focus on the effect of the algorithm design, and therefore compare the speed with which we can solve a particular problem instance using a given parallel algorithm to that with which we could solve it on a single processor. The *sequential running time* (S) is used as the basis for comparison and is usually taken to be the wall clock running time of the best available sequential algorithm. The *parallel running time* (T_p) is the wall clock running time of the parallel algorithm running on p processors. The *speedup* (S_p) is simply the ratio S/T_p. Finally, the efficiency (E_p) is the ratio S_p/p of speedup to number of processors. Note that all these quantities depend on p.

A parallel algorithm is considered scalable if it results in an efficiency close to one as the number of processors is increased. When a parallel algorithm maintains an efficiency ≥ 1, we say that it has achieved *linear speedup*. In theory, a parallel algorithm cannot have an efficiency strictly greater than one (this is called *superlinear speedup*), but in practice, such a situation can sometimes occur (see Refs. 17 and 18 for a treatment of this phenomenon). When an algorithm has an efficiency <1, the *parallel overhead* is $O_p = T_p(1 - E_p)$.

Conceptually, execution of a parallel algorithm can be divided into three phases. The *ramp-up phase* is the period during which work is initially partitioned and allocated to the available processors. This phase is loosely defined to last until all processors have been assigned at least one task (the exact definition can vary, depending on the application). The division of work that occurs during the ramp-up phase may be accomplished on a single processor or may itself be parallelized to the extent possible. The second phase is the *primary phase*, during which the algorithm operates in steady state. This is followed by the *ramp-down* phase, during which termination procedures are executed and final results are tabulated and reported. The ramp-down phase is loosely defined to start when the number of available tasks first falls below the number of available processors.

The division of the algorithm into phases is to highlight the fact that certain portions of every algorithm (e.g., the ramp-up and ramp-down phases) are inherently sequential. Amdahl was the first to point this out and called this part of the running time the *sequential fraction* (19). The inherently sequential portions of the algorithm can be significant contributors to parallel overhead. Determining the initial pool of tasks and allocating them to processors is an inherently sequential task, at least in part, and the efficiency with which this can be done is usually an important factor in determining the amount of parallel overhead. Because of this, if the problem size is kept constant, efficiency generally drops as the number of processors increases. If the number of processors is kept constant, however, then efficiency generally *increases* as problem size increases (20–22). This led Kumar and Rao to suggest a measure of scalability called the *iso-efficiency function* (23), which measures the rate at which the problem size has to be increased with respect to the number of processors in order to maintain a fixed efficiency.

3.2.2.3. Knowledge Management.

As mentioned in the introduction, achieving good parallel performance involves the design of a scheme for sharing information between processors as the algorithm progresses. Consider the following four main components of parallel overhead:

- *Communication Overhead.* Time spent sending and receiving information, including time spent inserting information into the send buffer and reading it from the receive buffer at the other end.
- *Idle Time (Ramp-Up/Ramp-Down).* Time spent waiting for initial tasks to be allocated or waiting for termination at the end of the algorithm.
- *Idle Time (Synchronization/Handshaking).* Time spent waiting for information requested from another processor or waiting for another processor to complete a task.
- *Performance of Redundant Work.* Time spent performing work (other than communication tasks) that would not have been performed in the sequential algorithm.

The first three sources of overhead are costs incurred in order to share information among the processors, whereas the last one is essentially the cost incurred by *not* sharing *enough* information. This highlights a fundamental tradeoff: to achieve high efficiency, we must limit the impact of the first three sources of overhead without increasing the impact of the fourth source.

We refer to information generated during the execution of the algorithm as *knowledge*. Trienekens and de Bruin introduced the notion that the efficiency of a parallel algorithm is inherently dependent on the strategy by which this knowledge is stored and shared among the processors (24). From this viewpoint, a parallel algorithm can be thought of roughly as a mechanism for coordinating a set of autonomous agents that are either *knowledge generators* (KGs) (responsible for producing new knowledge), *knowledge pools* (KPs) (responsible for storing previously generated knowledge), or both. Specifying such a coordination mechanism consists of specifying what knowledge is to be generated, how it is to be generated, and what is to be done with it after it is generated (stored, shared, discarded, or used for subsequent local computations).

In order to effectively manage and organize the potentially huge amount of information to be generated, knowledge is typically categorized by type, with each KP containing only knowledge of a particular type. In addition, KPs may be either *local* (only accessible locally) or *global* (available to share with other processors). Within each pool, knowledge is organized to make retrieval and management as easy as possible. Whenever the amount of knowledge generated could exceed the amount of storage capacity, each knowledge object can be assigned a numerical priority that reflects its perceived importance to the overall computation. This allows the KPs to be purged periodically to remove low-priority items.

3.2.2.4. Task Management.
Just as KPs can be divided by the type of knowledge they store, KGs may be divided either by the type of knowledge they generate or the method by which they generate it. In other words, processors may be assigned to perform only a particular task or set of tasks. If a single processor is assigned to perform multiple tasks simultaneously, a prioritization and time-sharing mechanism must be implemented to manage the computational efforts of the processor.

The *granularity* of an algorithm is the size of the smallest task that can be assigned to a processor. Choosing the proper granularity can be important to efficiency. Too fine a granularity can lead to excessive communication overhead, while too coarse a granularity can lead to excessive idle time and the performance of redundant work. We have assumed an asynchronous architecture, in which each processor is responsible for autonomously orchestrating local algorithm execution by prioritizing local computational tasks, managing locally generated knowledge, and communicating with other processors. Because each processor is autonomous, care must be taken to design the entire system so that *deadlocks*, in which a set of processors are all mutually waiting on one another for information, do not occur.

3.2.3. Previous Work

The branch and bound algorithm described in Section 3.2.1.2 was first suggested by Land and Doig in 1960 (25). In 1970, Mitten abstracted branch and bound into the theoretical framework we are familiar with today (26). However, it was another two decades before sophisticated software packages for solving MILPs began to be developed. Most of the software packages currently available implement some version of the branch-and-cut algorithm we have described. Available noncommercial generic MILP solvers include bonsaiG (27), CBC (28), GLPK (29), lp_solve (30), MINTO (31), and SYMPHONY (32,33). Commercial MIP solvers include ILOG's CPLEX and Dash's XPRESS. Generic frameworks that allow the user to take advantage of special structure by implementing specialized functionality, such as problem-specific cut generation, include SYMPHONY, COIN/BCP (34), ABACUS (35), and CBC. CONCORDE (36,37), a package for solving the traveling salesman problem, also deserves mention as the most sophisticated special-purpose code developed to date.

Numerous software packages implementing parallel branch and bound and parallel branch and cut have also been developed. The previously mentioned SYMPHONY, COIN/BCP, and CONCORDE all have parallel execution modes and can be run on networks of workstations. Other related software includes frameworks for implementing parallel branch and bound, such as PUBB (38), BoB (39), PPBBLib (40), and PICO (41). PARINO (42), and FATCOP (43) are parallel generic MILP solvers.

3.3. PARALLELIZING BRANCH AND CUT

3.3.1. Knowledge Management

In branch and cut, an optimal solution to a given problem instance can be thought of as a type of knowledge, which is typically the sole end product of the algorithm. Producing such a solution, however, requires production of a great deal of auxiliary knowledge during the course of the algorithm. This knowledge is typically discarded at termination, but may be retained in some cases for the purpose of providing a proof of optimality or performing sensitivity analysis. Below, we discuss the various types of knowledge that can be produced during branch and cut and the issues involved in sharing and storing each type.

Bounds. The bounds that must be shared in branch and cut consist of the single global upper and lower bounds associated with the subproblems that are candidates for processing. Knowledge of these bounds is important mainly for the avoidance of redundant work. In branch and cut, the primary source of redundant work is the processing of nodes whose initial lower bound exceeds the optimal solution value. In theory, the processing of such nodes is avoidable with the proper search strategy, but in practice, such redundant work may occur even in the sequential case if a search strategy other than pure best first is employed.

Although the final output of the algorithm is a single optimal solution, suboptimal solutions may be produced during the course of the algorithm. The primary importance of such solutions is that they may be the new incumbent at the time of their production, and hence may provide a new global upper bound. It is important that new global upper bounds be broadcast as quickly as possible to other processors, as this knowledge allows nodes whose lower bounds exceed this new upper bound to be fathomed, thus avoiding the performance of redundant work. Dissemination of upper bounds generally incurs low overhead and does not pose a serious scalability issue.

Knowledge of lower bounds is also important in avoiding the performance of redundant work. The distribution of lower bounds among the candidate subproblems is used to determine if work should continue on nodes that are locally available or if new nodes should be requested from a remote pool. This is part of the overall process of redistributing candidate nodes during the algorithm, called *load balancing* (see Section 3.3.3.2). Making knowledge of lower bounds available may be difficult to accomplish because the number of candidate nodes available globally can be extremely large and they may not be stored centrally.

Node Descriptions. Two computational tasks that arise naturally in branch and cut are the processing of a subproblem in the search tree (bounding) and the partitioning of a subproblem into a number of new subproblems (branching). These two tasks are generally, though not always, the smallest units of work assigned to a processor. For efficiency, the branching operation is frequently accomplished immediately following the processing operation.

In order to process a node, it is necessary to have a detailed description of it. The description of a search tree node consists primarily of descriptions of the valid inequalities and variables that are active in the node and a complete description of the current *basis* (assuming a simplex-based LP solver) or other information either inherited from the parent or computed during branching to allow a warm start to the bound computation (for the definition of a basis and its role in the solution of linear programs, see Refs. 44 or 8). Along with the set of active constraints and variables, we must also store the branching hyperplane(s) that led to generation of the node. Processing a node results in the generation of new knowledge in the form of bounds (described above) and (possibly) valid inequalities. Valid inequalities discovered during the processing of a node may also be shared, as described in the next section. If a node fails to be fathomed, then it becomes a candidate for branching.

The branching operation results in the generation of new node descriptions, which may be stored locally (in a *node pool*) or shared with other processors. An important question that arises is how to ensure that each processor assigned the task of processing search tree nodes has a constant supply of *high-priority* nodes in its local pool, where the priority of a node is determined by the search strategy being employed. We further discuss this and other topics related to load balancing in Section 3.3.3.2.

Cuts. One of the advantages of branch and cut over generic LP-based branch and bound is that the inequalities generated at each node of the search tree may be valid and useful in the processing of search tree nodes in other parts of the tree. Valid inequalities are usually categorized as either *globally valid* (valid for the convex hull of solutions to the original MILP, and hence for all other subproblems as well), or *locally valid* (valid only for the convex hull of solutions to a given subproblem). Because some classes of valid inequalities are difficult to generate, inequalities that prove effective in the current subproblem may be shared through the use of *cut pools* that contain lists of such inequalities for use during the processing of subsequent subproblems. The cut pools can thus be utilized as an auxiliary method of generating violated valid inequalities during the processing operation.

Because the number of cuts generated during execution of the branch-and-cut algorithm can be very large, careful management of these cuts is crucial. This includes not only periodic purging of duplicate, dominated, and "ineffective" cuts from the pool(s), but also the use of efficient data structures, called *representations*, for storing the cuts in a form that is independent of any LP relaxation or specific search tree node. A cut's representation is a compact description that contains information about how to add it to a particular LP relaxation and allows for the efficient calculation of the degree of violation with respect to a given fractional solution. Adding a cut to a given LP relaxation consists of constructing the row to be added to the constraint matrix and determining the corresponding right-hand side value, taking into account the current set of active variables. The representation is used not only to store each cut, but also to pass it from one processor to another when necessary. Prudent maintenance of the cut pools can provide a global picture of which cuts are the "most important," leading to significant improvements in the effectiveness of the algorithm.

In some implementations of branch and cut, it may be necessary or desirable to identify cuts or variables by assigning them unique global indices. The set of variables is static, so *a priori* assignment of global indices to each variable is easy. The set of potential valid inequalities on the other hand, is not generally known or may be too large to index. In such a case, global indices can be issued from a central bank to avoid conflict, or can be generated by hashing the representation. The first approach is simpler, but creates another potential bottleneck operations. This bottleneck may be reduced by issuing large blocks of indices to individual processors for future allocation to generated cuts.

Branching Information. If a backward-looking branching method, such as one based on pseudo-costs, is used, then the sharing of historical information regarding the effect of branching can be important to the implementation of the branching scheme. The information that needs to be shared and how it is shared depends on the specific scheme used. For an in-depth treatment of the issues surrounding pseudo-cost sharing in parallel, see Refs. 41 and 42.

3.3.2. Task Management

In branch and cut, there are a number of distinct tasks to be performed and these tasks can be assigned to processors in a number of ways. The main tasks to be performed are

- *Node Processing.* From the description of a candidate node, the processing procedure produces either an improved bound or a feasible solution to the original MILP.
- *Node Partitioning.* From the description of a processed node, the partitioning procedure is used to select a method of branching and subsequently produce a set of children to be added to the candidate list.
- *Cut Generation.* From a solution to a given LP relaxation produced during node processing, the cut generation procedure produces a violated valid inequality (either locally or globally valid).
- *Pool Maintenance.* Some processors may be assigned the task of managing either node or cut pools.
- *Load Balancing.* One or more processors may be assigned the task of collecting information about the distribution of candidate subproblems globally and coordinating their redistribution when necessary (see Section 3.3.3.2).

The way in which these tasks are grouped and assigned to processors partly determines the parallelization scheme of the algorithm and its scalability. In Section 3.4, we discuss the scheme for assigning tasks to processors and coordinating them in two different software packages and analyze the effectiveness of each. Next, we discuss the main scalability issues surrounding the parallelization scheme.

3.3.3. Scalability Issues

3.3.3.1. Ramp-Up Phase. In branch and cut, the ramp-up phase is usually defined to last roughly until there are enough candidate nodes available to occupy all available processors. The problem of reducing idle time during the ramp-up phase has long been recognized as a challenging one (41,45,46). For instances in which the processing time of a single node is large relative to the overall solution time, idle time during the ramp-up phase can be one of the biggest contributors to parallel overhead. This is due to the amount of time

required to generate a pool of candidate nodes sufficient to occupy all processors. There are two obvious strategies available for reducing idle time during this initial phase: accelerating the production of the initial pool of candidate nodes and occupying processors with auxiliary tasks that may help accelerate execution during the primary phase.

To occupy otherwise idle processors, two auxiliary tasks that can be undertaken during the ramp-up phase are calculation of an initial upper bound and various types of problem preprocessing. Determination of the initial upper bound involves execution of one or more heuristic solution generation procedures, which can themselves be parallelized. Preprocessing tasks can include the execution of traditional integer preprocessing algorithms, the processing of the root node, the computation of initial pseudo-costs, and the tightening of bounds on variable values by comparison of reduced cost to the optimality gap. These tasks may also be parallelized.

Although processors can be effectively occupied with auxiliary tasks, such as those described above, the contribution of these auxiliary tasks to reduction; in running time may not be large enough to justify their execution if the assigned processors could be occupied with the processing of candidate nodes. It is therefore still advantageous to keep the ramp-up phase as short as possible. Unfortunately, effective techniques for accelerating the generation of the initial pool of candidate nodes have proven elusive. Following processing of the root node, it is clear that generation of the remaining pool can be parallelized to a limited extent by distributing nodes as they are produced rather than waiting until a full complement is available. This will obviously help, but has limited effect if the processing of the first few nodes in the tree is time-consuming with respect to the overall solution time. Another obvious approach is to reduce the processing time of each node in the ramp-up phase, either by limiting cut generation or by branching more quickly than one would otherwise.

Forrest et al. (47) noted that effective branching is most important in the early phases of the algorithm when it has the biggest impact on the eventual size of the search tree. In a sequential algorithm, additional time spent making branching decisions, (e.g., exploring additional strong branching candidates), does result in an overall reduction in tree size, which can translate into a reduction in solution time (up to a point). From this perspective, one would be tempted to devote more time to branching during the ramp-up phase, not less. This creates another challenging tradeoff between limiting ramp-up time and making good branching decision early. This tradeoff is an important one, but one that has also proved difficult to analyze. Informal experiments aimed at limiting ramp-up time by forcing early termination of the node processing loop shown in Fig. 3.1 and thus allowing the branching step to be invoked more quickly failed to produce positive results. Likewise, efforts at limiting the time devoted to performing the branching operation (e.g., considering fewer strong branching candidates) have also failed. A promising approach that has not yet been tested is to devote *more* effort to branching near the top of the tree, but to parallelize the branching procedure itself. With a strong branching approach, this could easily be done by distributing the candidates for presolving to multiple processors. It might also be possible to employ a branching rule that generates more than the usual two children. Such a rule would presumably produce candidate nodes more quickly, but might also increase the size of the search tree. To our knowledge, little or no investigation of such branching rules has been undertaken.

3.3.3.2. Primary Phase. During the primary phase, the main issue that arises is how to most effectively generate and share the two main types of knowledge that arise in branch and cut: node descriptions and valid inequalities. Node generation and sharing involves effective strategies for searching, load balancing, and branching, while cut generation and sharing involves effective strategies for managing the extremely large number of valid inequalities that may be generated during the course of the algorithm. In each case, there is a difficult balance to be struck between the efficiencies gained by centralization of knowledge, which leads to a much clearer global picture, and decentralization of knowledge, which allows the tasks associated with knowledge management to be distributed among a larger number of processors.

Search Strategy. The choice of search strategy has a number of important implications in a parallel implementation that go beyond those already discussed in Section 3.2.1.2. Because their implementation often involves the existence of multiple node pools from which candidates can be drawn, parallel algorithms require us to view search strategies in an entirely new light. The lack of global information about available candidate subproblems, for example, renders the implementation of a pure best-first search strategy in parallel impractical and inefficient. Not only would it be difficult and time consuming to identify the candidate subproblem with the smallest lower bound globally at a given point in time, but the cost associated with moving such subproblems from their current locations to available processors would be prohibitive.

In general, executing a given search strategy in parallel exactly as it would be executed sequentially is difficult because of the additional movement of nodes between processors that may be required. Because of this movement of nodes, parallel search strategies are inextricably linked with methods for load balancing, discussed below. As in sequential branch and bound, there is a tradeoff between strategies that attempt to minimize the overall size of the search tree and strategies that emphasize the generation of feasible solutions. With the additional expense that may be incurred retrieving nodes from remote pools, however, parallel search strategies require consideration of a third dimension to this tradeoff—that between choosing nodes available locally for processing and choosing those that must be retrieved from a remote pool. Parallel search strategies may give a higher priority to nodes available locally when deciding what node to process next.

The specification of a search strategy in parallel thus has two distinct elements: a local strategy and a global strategy. The local strategy specifies what nodes are preferred among those available locally, whereas the global strategy, tied closely to the load balancing scheme, specifies how nodes should be shifted between processors in order to pursue a given global strategy. We next present an overview of load balancing strategies. In Section 3.4, the implementation of two very different search and load balancing strategies used in two software packages for solving MILPs in parallel are described.

Load Balancing. The tradeoff between centralization and decentralization of knowledge is most evident in the mechanism for sharing node descriptions among the processors. This is perhaps the most challenging aspect of implementing parallel branch and cut during the primary phase and has been studied by a number of authors (48–53). Effective load balancing methods reduce both idle time associated with task starvation and the performance of redundant work. In branch and cut, the goal is to ensure that "high-priority" nodes, that is, those favored by the search procedure (typically nodes with small lower bounds), are available locally on all processors that require them. This means moving node descriptions from processors with an excess of high-priority nodes to those with a deficit of such nodes. Without such movement of nodes during the algorithm, the node pools of some processors would degrade in quality or become empty, while the node pools of other processors would contain too many high-priority nodes to be processed locally.

Before nodes can be shared, the first challenge is to recognize that an imbalance exists. If the size of a local pool becomes too small, this is easy to identify, but determining if the *quality* of the pool is too low may be more difficult, since this requires knowledge of the quality of the node pools residing at other processors. Once a deficit has been identified, it must be repaired through an exchange process that moves nodes from pools with excesses to pools with deficits.

Any scheme for accomplishing the load balancing described above involves some degree of centralization of knowledge in the form of either bounds or node descriptions themselves. Such centralization can either be undertaken through the maintenance of permanent centralized knowledge pools or through a periodic knowledge gathering and redistribution process. In Section 3.4, two software packages are discussed, one of which takes the first approach and one of which takes the second.

Cut Sharing. Cut sharing, while not as challenging or as critical as the sharing of node descriptions, can be important for applications where effective structured classes of valid inequalities are known, but are difficult to generate. The well-known Traveling Salesman Problem (TSP) and the related Vehicle Routing Problem, discussed in Section 3.5, are good examples of such problems. A number of interesting and difficult questions arise in designing strategies for cut management. The first of these is how many cut pools to maintain and whether to restrict the contents of these pools by type, by validity (i.e., by subtree in which the cuts are valid), or by some other criterion. Other questions to be answered include:

- Which locally generated cuts should be shared globally?
- When should a remote request for cuts be made and to which pool or pools should it be sent (if there is more than one)?
- Which cuts should be returned in response to such a request?
- Which cuts should be retained retain and which discarded when memory becomes a limitation?

Unfortunately, the answers to most of these questions depend strongly on the application. We will discuss one implementation of cut sharing in Section 3.4.1. For an in-depth discussion of a wide range of options for sharing cuts, see (42).

3.3.3.3. Ramp-Down Phase. In the ramp-down phase, we may again face the problem of not having enough nodes globally to occupy all available processors, as in the ramp-up phase. This problem is not as well recognized or studied in the literature as the problem of reducing ramp-up time, but it can also pose a serious scalability issue in some cases, as we demonstrate in Section 3.5. The methods available for addressing the problem are similar to those employed during the ramp-up phase, but further study of this phase of the computation is merited.

3.3.3.4. Properties of Instances. In addition to properties of the algorithm, properties of the instance or instances to be solved can also have a dramatic effect on scalability. If such properties can be predicted or discovered in advance, modification of the algorithm may lead to improved efficiency. In the case of a MILP instance about which nothing is initially known, the situation is more difficult and efficiency can suffer, even with a well-designed algorithm.

The main properties that are relevant when considering solution of a particular problem class are

- The length of time it takes to process a search tree node relative to total solution time.
- The length of time it takes to process nodes shallow in the tree relative to the length of time it takes to process nodes at deeper levels.
- The effectiveness of the initial upper bounding method.

In the first two cases, if the length of time it takes to process a search tree node is short relative to solution time, then the number of nodes in the search tree may be very large and this could result in an excessive amount of time spent load balancing. On the other hand, if the processing time per node is long relative to solution time, especially near the top of the tree, then the ramp-up phase may rob the overall algorithm of efficiency.

The effect of the initial upper bounding method is somewhat less clear. If the initial upper bound is optimal (or close to optimal), then the goal of the algorithm becomes proving optimality of the known solution. In this case, the search order, and hence load balancing, is much less important, and scalability is generally easier to achieve. On the other hand, if the initial upper bound is not near optimal, the solution time depends to a much greater extent on when an optimal or near optimal solution is discovered during the search process. One may be fortunate and discover the optimal solution relatively early in the process when searching in parallel, while not discovering the solution until late in the sequential search. Such early discovery of the optimal solution can reduce the size of the search tree and make node processing more efficient by allowing the bounds on variables to be tightened based on the size of the reduced costs and the optimality gap.

3.4. ALGORITHMS

This section briefly reviews the implementation of two frameworks we have developed based on the concepts just described. The first is SYMPHONY, which is written in C and takes a very centralized approach to knowledge management. The second is ALPS, a C++ framework, which takes a completely decentralized approach to knowledge management.

3.4.1. SYMPHONY

SYMPHONY is both a "black-box" MILP solver with an associated callable library and a highly customizable framework for implementing branch-and-cut algorithms tailored to specific applications (32,33). SYMPHONY evolved from the COMPSys framework of Ralphs and Ladányi (10,54) and is now part of the Computational Infrastructure for Operations Research (COIN-OR) (55). The source code for packaged releases is available for download and is licensed under the open-source Common Public License (CPL) (52). The source code for the current development version is available from the COIN-OR source code repository (55). SYMPHONY is fully documented, with a complete set of examples and specialized solvers included with the distribution. The solver contains several advanced features not available in other MILP codes, such as the ability to solve multicriteria MILPs, the ability to warm start the solution procedure, and the ability to perform basic sensitivity analyses. The basic algorithm can be modified and customized solvers built by the user through the use of numerous parameters and callback functions.

3.4.1.1. Knowledge Management. SYMPHONY employs a highly centralized knowledge management scheme. In particular, the algorithm maintains a single central node pool from which nodes are distributed for processing. The use of a central node pool means that accurate global information about the tree is always available, but only from the central server. This simplifies certain aspects of the parallel implementation dramatically, but also limits scalability, as the central pool inevitably becomes a bottleneck when a large number of processors are dedicated to node processing. Cuts can be stored either in a single central pool or in multiple pools, each dedicated to a particular subtree. Using a single cut pool creates another potential bottleneck, but the use of multiple pools may decrease effectiveness by limiting the extent to which cuts are shared throughout the search tree. These tradeoffs are discussed in more detail in Section 3.4.1.3.

3.4.1.2. Task Management.

SYMPHONY is implemented in C using a modular design that enables easy and highly configurable parallelization. There are five independent modules, each responsible for a distinct set of tasks. The *master* module is responsible for overall execution, including input and output, and the creation of all other modules. Of the other four modules, the *node processing* (NP) and *cut generation* (CG) modules are responsible for generation of new knowledge (node descriptions, feasible solutions, and valid inequalities), while the *tree management* (TM) and *cut management* modules are responsible for storage and management of previously generated knowledge (node descriptions and valid inequalities). The current incumbent is stored and broadcast by the master module.

SYMPHONY can be built and run in three different modes: sequential, parallel with shared memory, and parallel with distributed memory. We concentrate here on the distributed memory implementation. As a distributed memory code, the modules can be combined in a number of different ways at compile-time in order to produce executables capable of performing multiple functions. The most typical configuration is to combine the master, tree management, and cut management modules into a single executable responsible for all knowledge storage functions, while combining the node processing and cut generation modules into a single executable responsible for all knowledge generation processes. This configuration is very efficient for small numbers of processors, but makes the central knowledge storage process an even more significant computational bottleneck. For larger numbers of processors, locating the cut manager(s) on separate processors can provide some relief from this. Separating the master and tree manager modules or the node processing and cut generation modules provides little advantage in most cases. Below, we provide some details of the purpose and implementation of each module.

The Master Module. The master module performs problem initialization and I/O, stores problem data, stores and reports the results of solution procedure calls, and provides the user interface. Data stored in the master module is persistent and is maintained between solution procedure calls. Such data include information for warm starting of the solution procedure and lists of cuts generated by previous solution procedure calls. Retention of these data can facilitate the solution of sequences of slightly modified instances, such as those that arise in decomposition algorithms, among others.

The master module is not heavily tasked once the computation has begun, but functions independently in order to monitor the status of the solution procedure. The specific functions performed by the master module include the following tasks:

- Read in the parameters from a data file.
- Read in the data for the problem instance.
- Compute an initial upper bound using heuristics (may also be done in parallel).
- Perform problem preprocessing and determine the problem core (see the description of the TM module below).
- Create the tree manager module and initialize the algorithm by sending start data (either a description of the root node or warm starting data) to the TM module.
- Collect the output during the solution procedure and pass it to the output device.
- Process requests for problem data from remote processors.
- Receive new solutions and store them.
- Ensure that all other modules are still functioning.
- Store and report results at algorithm termination.
- Store any persistent data, such as warm starting information, needed for future solution procedure calls.

The Tree Management Module. Each time SYMPHONY's solution procedure is invoked, a new TM module is created to control the overall execution of the algorithm. The main task of the TM module is to act as the central node pool, maintaining the search tree and distributing descriptions of the nodes to be processed to the NP modules. After each node is processed, the responsible NP module sends the results to the TM module and queries it for the next next node to be processed, which is either a child of the node whose processing was just completed (and hence available locally) or a new node from the list of candidates, depending on the search strategy being employed. Specific functions performed by the TM module are

- Receive start data and initialize the list of candidates for processing (typically just the root node).
- Handle requests from NP modules to determine the next subproblem for processing.
- Receive the results of node processing and partitioning, create the child nodes (if necessary), and add them to the list of candidate subproblems.
- Keep track of the global upper bound and notify all node processing modules when it changes.

- Write current state information out to disk periodically to allow a restart in the event of a system crash.
- Keep track of run data and send it to the master program at termination.

Because of the single-pool approach taken by SYMPHONY, the search tree can be stored very efficiently. The set of active inequalities and the description of the basis tend not to change much from parent to child, so all of these data can be stored as differences with respect to the parent when that description is smaller than the explicit one. This method of storing the entire tree is highly memory efficient. The list of nodes that are candidates for processing is stored in a heap ordered by a comparison function defined by the search strategy. This allows efficient generation of the next node to be processed.

The size of the node descriptions themselves is limited by allowing the user to specify a problem *core*, consisting of a set of variables and constraints that are to be active in every subproblem. The core normally consists of a set of variables and constraints that are considered "important" for the given instance, in the sense that there is a high probability that they will be needed to describe an optimal solution. The main importance of the core is that its description can be stored statically at each of the processors and need not be part of each individual node description. This saves on both node set-up costs and communication costs, as well as making storage of the search tree more efficient.

The Cut Management Module. The concept of a cut pool was first suggested by Padberg and Rinaldi (5), based on the observation that inequalities generated while processing a given node in the search tree may potentially be useful at other nodes. Since generation of cuts is sometimes a relatively expensive operation, the cut management module can maintain a list of the "best" or "strongest" cuts found in the tree thus far for use in processing future subproblems. The cut management modules are thus knowledge pools that can be queried by the NP modules for violated valid inequalities to be added to the current LP relaxation. As mentioned previously, multiple cut management modules can be used, in which case each one services a separate subtree. More explicitly, the functions of the cut management module are

- Receive cuts generated by other modules and store them.
- Receive a solution and return a set of cuts eligible to enter the current LP relaxation.
- Periodically purge "ineffective" and duplicate cuts to control the size of the pool.

The Node Processing Module. The NP modules are responsible both for processing and partitioning of search tree nodes. Each node is processed completely and partitioned before the results are sent to the TM module; there is no option for partial processing or processing without partitioning. These operations are, of course, central to the performance of the algorithm and comprise a large part of the "useful" work. Search tree nodes are processed in an iterative loop similar to that described in Fig. 3.1. First, the initial LP relaxation is solved, then cuts are generated based on that solution, the relaxation is augmented, and the cycle repeats. This continues until either no more new cuts can be generated or the bound improvement in each round becomes too small, at which point branching occurs. Branching is accomplished by choosing one or more cuts or variables and partitioning the range of allowable values by changing the associated bounds or right-hand side ranges. Functions performed by the NP module are

- Inform the TM module when a new subproblem is needed.
- Receive a subproblem and process it, in conjunction with the cut management module.
- Decide which cuts should be sent to the global pool to be made available to other NP modules.
- If necessary, choose a branching set and send its description back to the TM module.
- Perform the fathoming operation.

The Cut Generation Module. The CG module performs only one function—that of generating valid inequalities violated by the current LP solution and sending them back to the requesting NP module. The current implementation allows for only one dedicated CG module per NP module. The functions performed by the cut generator module are:

- Receive an LP solution and attempt to separate it from the convex hull of all solutions.
- Send generated valid inequalities back to the NP module.
- When finished processing a solution vector, inform the NP module not to expect any more cuts in case it is still waiting.

3.4.1.3. Scalability. The main computational task in SYMPHONY consists of the processing and (possible) partitioning of a single subproblem. After processing and partitioning a subproblem, the NP module must return the results to the TM module and query it to determine its next task. SYMPHONY uses global indices to identify cuts, so the NP modules must also query the TM module for the assignment of these indices, as well as querying the cut management modules(s) for violated valid inequalities. Because of these synchronization steps and the centralized approach to knowledge storage, load balancing is not an issue in SYMPHONY. The NP modules have no local node pools, so work distribution is simply a matter of sending the candidate node with the highest priority to each NP module at the time of its request or instructing it to continue working on one of the children of the node it just finished processing.

As with most implementations of parallel branch and bound, ramp-up time is a major contributor to parallel overhead. If desired, SYMPHONY can employ a "quick branching" strategy similar to the one described earlier, in which branching occurs after a fixed number of iterations in the NP module regardless of whether or not new cuts have been generated. This strategy is pursued until all processors have useful work to do, after which the usual algorithm is resumed. This strategy has shown little success, however. No other strategies for decreasing ramp-up time or otherwise employing processors during this phase are available in SYMPHONY.

The fact that all NP modules must frequently query the single TM module also leads to scalability issues during the primary phase. Almost all of the overhead in SYMPHONY during this phase is either communications overhead (time spent packing, sending, receiving, and unpacking messages) or time spent idle waiting for an answer to a query sent to a knowledge pool. The majority of this idle time is associated with communication between the TM and NP modules regarding node processing. Additional idle time may be incurred waiting for the cut pool to answer its queries. When either of these knowledge storage modules become overtasked, idle time can increase dramatically. For this reason, SYMPHONY cannot typically achieve good scalability beyond 32 processors, as we discuss in Section 3.5.

3.4.2. ALPS

The *Abstract Library for Parallel Search* (ALPS) (57, 58) is a C++ framework for implementing customized versions of parallel *tree search*. Tree search is an algorithmic paradigm in which the nodes of a directed, acyclic graph are systematically searched in order to locate one or more *goal nodes*. A wide variety of specialized algorithms, including branch and cut, can be classified as tree search algorithms. Because of its more general approach, ALPS supports the implementation of a wider variety of algorithms and applications than SYMPHONY. Like SYMPHONY, ALPS is part of the COIN-OR repository (55). The source code is licensed under the open-source Common Public License (CPL) and is available from the COIN-OR source code repository (55). The library of C++ classes that constitutes ALPS can be derived to implement specialized classes that define various tree search algorithms. Two libraries built on top of ALPS, called the *Branch, Constrain, and Prices Software* (BiCePS) and the BiCePS Linear Integer Solver (BLIS), implement the specialized methods required for branch and cut. Two prototype solvers built with ALPS, one for solving the well-known knapsack problem and one for solving generic MILPs, are also available for download.

3.4.2.1. Knowledge Management. In contrast to SYMPHONY, ALPS takes an almost completely decentralized approach to knowledge management. In (59), building on ideas in (60), we proposed a tree search methodology driven by the concepts of knowledge discovery and sharing discussed in

Section 3.2.2.3. This methodology is the basis for the class structure of ALPS. A central notion in ALPS is that all information generated during execution of the search is treated as knowledge and is represented by C++ objects derived from a single common base class described below.

The most fundamental knowledge objects generated during the search are the descriptions of the search tree nodes themselves, which are organized locally into subtrees. To avoid the bottlenecks associated with central storage of the entire candidate list, every processor responsible for node processing hosts its own local node pool from which the node processing task can draw new candidates. The local node pools collectively contain the global list of candidate nodes, which are shared through the load balancing procedure described in Section 3.4.2.3. To further avoid the introduction of bottlenecks, load balancing is performed using a three-level scheme we call the *master-hub-worker* paradigm, also discussed in Section 3.4.2.3.

The AlpsKnowledge class is the virtual base class for any type of information that must be shared or moved from one processor to another. AlpsEncoded is an associated class that contains an encoded or packed form of an Alpsnowledge object, which consists of a bit array containing the data needed to replicate the object. This representation takes less memory than the object itself and is appropriate both for storage of knowledge and for transmission of knowledge between processors. The packed form is also independent of type, which allows ALPS to deal effectively with user-defined knowledge types. To avoid the assignment of global indices, ALPS uses hashing of the packed form to identify duplicate objects. ALPS has the following four native knowledge types:

- *AlpsSolution*. Contains the description of a goal state or solution to the problem being solved.
- *AlpsTreeNode*. Contains the data and methods associated with a node in the search graph, including a node description (of type AlpsNodeDesc) and the definitions of the process and branch methods.
- *AlpsModel*. Contains the data describing the original problem.
- *AlpsSubTree*. Contains the description of a subtree, which is a hierarchy of AlpsTreeNode objects, along with the methods needed for performing a tree search.

The first three of these classes are virtual and must be defined by the user in the context of the problem being solved. The last class is generic and application.

The AlpsKnowledgePool class is the virtual base class for knowledge pools in ALPS. This base class can be derived to define a KP for a specific type of knowledge or multiple types. The native KP types are

- *AlpsSolutionPool*. The solution pools store AlpsSolution objects. These pools exist both at the worker level (for storing solutions discovered locally) and globally at the master level.

- `AlpsSubTreePool`. The subtree pools store `AlpsSubTree` objects. These pools exist at the hub level for storing subtrees that still contain unprocessed nodes.
- `AlpsNodePool`. The node pools store `AlpsTreeNode` objects. These pools contain the queues of candidate nodes associated with the subtrees as they are being searched.

None of these classes are virtual and their methods are implemented independent of any specific application.

3.4.2.2. Task Management. In ALPS, each processor hosts a single, multitasking executable controlled by a *knowledge broker* (KB). The KB is tasked with routing all knowledge to and from the processor and determining the priority of each task assigned to the processor. A crude version of threading allows the single executable to performs multiple tasks, which can include hosting multiple knowledge pools, processing candidate nodes, or generating application-specific knowledge (e.g., valid inequalities). Each specific type of knowledge, represented by a C++ class derived from `AlpsKnowledge`, must be registered at the inception of the algorithm so that the KB knows how to route it when it arrives and where to send requests for knowledge from other KBs. The KB associated with a particular KP may field two types of requests on its behalf: (1) new knowledge to be inserted into the KP, or (2) a request for relevant knowledge to be extracted from the KP, where "relevant" is defined for each category of knowledge with respect to data provided by the requesting process. A KP may also choose to "push" certain knowledge to another KP, even though no specific request has been made.

Derivatives of the `AlpsKnowledgeBroker` class implement the KB and encapsulate the desired communication protocol. Switching from a parallel application to a sequential one is simply a matter of constructing a different KB object. Currently, the protocols supported are a serial layer, implemented in `AlpsKnowledgeBrokerSerial`, and an MPI (16) layer, implemented in `AlpsKnowledgeBrokerMPI`.

3.4.2.3. Scalability. In contrast to SYMPHONY, the basic computational task in ALPS is to process all the nodes of a subtree with a given root node. Each worker is capable of processing an entire subtree autonomously and has access to all of the methods needed to manage a sequential tree search. The potential for increased granularity reduces idle time due to task starvation, but, without proper load balancing, may increase the performance of redundant work. Because the processing of a subtree can be an extremely lengthy and unpredictable procedure, the task can be interrupted at any time for the purpose of load balancing and may even be preempted if higher priority work is made available. By storing subtrees as a complete unit, it is possible to use a data structure based on the concept of differencing introduced earlier in Section 3.4.1.2. This may help to minimize memory requirements, which could potentially be increased by the decentralized node storage scheme.

To overcome the drawbacks of the master-worker approach employed by SYMPHONY, ALPS employs a *master-hub-worker* paradigm, in which a layer of "middle management" is inserted between the master process and the worker processes. In this scheme, a *cluster* consists of a *hub* and a fixed number of *workers*. Within a cluster, the hub manages the workers and supervises load balancing, while the master ensures the load is balanced globally. As the number of processors is increased, clusters can be added in order to keep the load of the hubs and workers relatively constant. The workload of the master process can be managed by controlling the frequency of global balancing operations. This scheme is similar to one implemented by Eckstein et al. in the PICO framework (41), except that PICO does not have the concept of a master. The decentralized approach maintains many of the advantages of global decision making while reducing overhead and moving much of the burden for load balancing and search management from the master to the hubs. This burden is then further shifted from the hubs to the workers by increasing the task granularity, as described below.

Because all processes are completely autonomous in ALPS, the biggest scalability issues are idle time during ramp-up and effective load balancing. In ALPS, each node has an associated priority that indicates the node's relative "quality," i.e., the probability that the node or one of its successors is a goal node. In assessing the distribution of work to the processors, we consider both *quantity* and *quality*. ALPS employs a three-tiered load balancing scheme, consisting of *static*, *intracluster dynamic*, and *intercluster dynamic* load balancing.

Static load balancing, or *mapping*, takes place during the ramp-up phase. The main task is to generate the initial pool of candidate nodes and distribute them to the workers to initialize their local node pools. ALPS uses a *two-level root initialization* scheme, a generalization of the *root initialization* scheme of (49). During static load balancing, the master creates and distributes a user-specified number of nodes to the hubs. The hubs in turn create and distribute a user-specified number of successors to their workers, after which the workers initialize their subtree pools and begin. Time spent performing static load balancing is the main source of ramp-up, which can be significant when node processing times are large.

Inside a cluster, the hub manages dynamic load balancing by periodically receiving workload reports from cluster members. If it is found that the qualities are unbalanced, the hub asks workers with a surplus of high-priority nodes to share them with workers that have fewer such nodes. Intracluster load balancing can also be initiated when an individual worker reports to the hub that its workload is below a given threshold. Upon receiving the request, the hub asks its most loaded worker to donate nodes to the requesting worker.

The master is responsible for balancing the workload among hubs, which periodically report their workload information to the master. The master has an approximate global view of the system load and the load of each cluster at all times. If either the quantity or quality of work is unbalanced among the clusters, the master identifies pairs of *donors* and *receivers*. Donors are clusters whose workloads are greater than the average workload of all clusters by a given factor. Receivers are clusters whose workloads are smaller than the average workload by a given factor. Donors and receivers are paired and each donor sends nodes to its paired receiver.

A unique aspect of the load balancing scheme in ALPS is that it takes account of the differencing scheme for storing subtrees. In order to allow efficient storage of search tree nodes using differencing, we try at all times to ensure that search tree nodes are shared in a way such that those sent and stored together locally constitute connected subtrees of the search tree. To accomplish this, groups of candidate nodes that constitute the leaves of a given subtree are shared as a single unit, rather than being shared as individual nodes. Each subtree is assigned a priority, defined as the average of the priorities of a given number of its best nodes. During load balancing, the donor chooses the best subtree in its subtree pool and sends it to the receiver. If a donor does not have any subtrees to share, it splits the subtree that it is currently exploring into two parts and sends one of them to the receiver. In this way, differencing can still be used effectively, even without centralized storage of the search tree.

3.5. COMPUTATION

To give the reader a better appreciation for the performance of the schemes we have just described and for the specific components of overhead that are most prevalent, we now present the results of computational studies involving the solution of MILP instances from three different problem classes using the currently available beta version of SYMPHONY 5.1 and associated solvers. The LP relaxations were solved with the most recent version of the COIN-OR LP solver (55), also available under the CPL. The problem classes here have been chosen because they illustrate the wide range of properties that problem instances can have and the scalability issues that arise because of them. All tests were performed on a Beowulf cluster with 60 1.8 GHz 64-bit AMD Opteron processors, each with 1 G local memory. In Section 3.5.1, we analyze the solution of generic MILP instances, a wide ranging class containing instances whose properties are generally difficult to predict in advance. We report results from instances that exhibited good scalability, as well as a few that did not. In Sections 3.5.2 and 3.5.3, we discuss the solution of two classical combinatorial optimization problems, the Vehicle Routing Problem (VRP) and the Set Partitioning Problem (SPP). In the case of the VRP, node processing times are short and scalability is relatively easy to achieve. In the case of the SPP, node processing times can be extremely long and achieving scalability is much more difficult.

For all runs, SYMPHONY was configured so that the master and TM modules ran as a single process, with multiple combined NP and CG modules performing the node processing and cut generations tasks. The number of NP/CG modules used ranged from 1 to 32. Except where noted, no global cut pools were used. For each set of runs, the number of NP/CG modules used in the computation is identified. In parallel branch and cut, the size of the search tree is subject to a good deal of random fluctuation due to the asynchronous nature of the search. To reduce the effect of these fluctuations on the analysis, we performed three identical runs of each experiment. The numbers that appear in the tables of results are averages over these runs. We also report the timing information on a "per node" basis, which separates the effect of fluctuations in the number of nodes from fluctuations in the time needed to process a node, resulting in a much more consistent view of the trends as the number of processors increases.

The results in the tables that appear here break the main sources of parallel overhead down into specific identifiable components that were significant to SYMPHONY's performance. In the tables, the column headers have the following interpretations:

- *Tree Size* is the number of nodes in the search tree. Observing the change in the size of the search tree as the number of processors is increased provides a rough measure of the amount of redundant work. Ideally, the total number of nodes explored stays constant as the number of processors is increased.

- *Ramp-up* and *Ramp-down* are the total accumulated idle time during periods before and after the primary phase when the queue did not contain enough nodes to keep all processors busy.

- *Node Pack* is the time spent by the TM module generating node descriptions. This can be significant because explicit descriptions need to be constructed from the differenced form in which they are stored. Note that this is technically not parallel overhead, since it must be incurred even in the sequential algorithm. However, it does represent computation required to support the differencing mechanism, which is needed in part because of SYMPHONY's centralized node scheme.

- *Idle Nodes* is the idle time spent by the NP module waiting for a new node description to be sent from the TM module.

- *Idle Cuts* is the idle time spent by the NP module waiting for valid inequalities to be sent from the cut management module (if applicable).

- *Idle Index* is the idle time spent by the NP module waiting for the TM module to assign indices to valid inequalities still active at the termination of processing of a search tree node or those being sent to the cut management module.

- *Idle Diving* is the idle time spent by the NP module waiting for instructions from the TM module regarding whether to continue processing one of the available children of the current node or wait for a new node from the global candidate list.

- *CPU sec* is the total CPU time used by all modules. Note that this does not include idle time and hence can be significantly different from wall-clock time, described below.
- *Wallclock* is the amount of real time used by the solution procedure from start to finish. By multiplying wallclock running time by the number of processors and subtracting CPU time, one can obtain a rough estimate of the idle time incurred by all processes as a whole.
- *Eff* is the parallel efficiency and is equal to p time the wall clock running time with 1 NP/CG module divided by the wall clock running time with p NP/CG modules. In other words, it is approximately the percentage of time spent by all processors of the parallel algorithm doing "useful work", where the amount of useful work to be done is measured by the running time for the sequential algorithm. Note that the statistic reported here is not precisely the parallel efficiency described in Section 3.2.2.2, since the experiments with 1 NP/CG module were done in parallel as well (the single NP/CG module was running in parallel with the TM module) and since we use the number of NP/CG modules (not the number of processors) as the baseline. However, the resulting numbers give a clear picture of the trends in efficiency and this should not cause confusion.

3.5.1. Generic MILP

The test problems discussed below were selected from MIPLIB 3 (61), MIPLIB 2003 [45], and a suite of instances available from the Computational Optimization Research at Lehigh (COR@L) Web site (63). For these tests, SYMPHONY was used as a black-box solver, with valid inequalities generated using subroutines from the Cut Generator Library, also part of the COIN-OR repository (55). Strong branching was used to make branching decisions and the search strategy was a hybrid diving strategy in which one of the children of a given node was retained as long as its bound was within a given percentage of the best available.

Table 3.1 in the Appendix shows the results of the first set of experiments, in which SYMPHONY was run with default settings and no *a priori* upper bound. Detailed results are shown for each instance in the test set for the runs with a single NP/CG module and summary results only for all other runs. Table 3.2 shows the detailed results for the run with 32 NP/CG modules. For most of these instances, the time needed to process a search tree node is small in comparison with the overall running time, which tends to lead to good scalability. The results reflect this to a large extent, but as expected, overhead increases across the board as the number of NP/CG modules is increased. The increase from 16 to 32 NP/CG modules results in a much more significant amount of parallel overhead and a corresponding drop in efficiency. It is evident from these results that SYMPHONY will probably not scale well beyond approximately 32 NP/CG modules for instances with properties similar to these.

Examining each components of overhead in detail, we see that both ramp-up and ramp-down time grow significantly as the number of NP/CG modules is increased. This overhead is predictable, but difficult to eradicate. Time spent by the tree manager constructing node descriptions (*Node Pack*) remains relatively constant, as expected, and is not a scalability issue. The three columns representing idle time spent by the NP/CG modules waiting for various queries to be answered by the TM module are the most significant and addressable sources of inefficiency for SYMPHONY. The contention associated with the distribution of new node descriptions (*Idle Node*) is the most significant, but would be difficult to address without completely abandoning SYMPHONYs master-worker architecture. The idle time spent waiting for global indices to be assigned to cuts (*Idle Index*) and for decisions regarding whether to retain one of the children of the current node for processing (*Idle Dive*), however, might be reduced with a redesign of SYMPHONY's methodology. Preassigning blocks of indices to each NP/CG module could help alleviate the first of these bottlenecks, while more autonomy with respect to deciding whether or not to dive could help alleviate the second one. These improvements would significantly improve SYMPHONY's scalability, but contention at the TM module could not be eliminated entirely without moving away from SYMPHONY's master–worker architecture.

To assess the degree of performance of redundant work, we examine the trends in the total number of nodes in the search tree. For these experiments, as the number of NP/CG modules is increased, the number of nodes in the search tree actually drops slightly, accounting for the superlinear speedup observed with four and eight NP/CG modules. This drop is presumably due to the fact that feasible solutions are difficult to find for some instances and are discovered earlier in the search process during the parallel runs, resulting in smaller search trees. Overall, there is no evidence of additional redundant work being performed in the presence of parallelism.

To test the effect of having a good *a priori* upper bound, we performed a similar set of experiments in which the optimal solution value was provided *a priori*, so that the goal was simply to prove optimality of a known solution. The results (with a slightly smaller test set) are shown in Table 3.3. In this case, it is advantageous to follow an unconditional diving strategy in which the child of the current node is always preferred when there is one. This eliminates redundant work, but the results still exhibit a very slight increase in the number of search nodes as the number of NP/CG modules is increased. This hurts the parallel efficiency, but the provision of an *a priori* upper bound still improves solution times across the board in comparison to those in Table 3.1. Note that the total amount of overhead, especially the ramp down and the idle time spent waiting for new node descriptions to be sent from the TM module are very significantly reduced for these runs over the runs with default settings. The reason is because the depth-first strategy employed requires far fewer new candidate nodes to be sent from the TM module to the NP/CG modules. Despite this, the calculated efficiencies are similar because the basis of comparison in each case is itself a parallel run with a single NP/CG module. Because the baseline run with the depth-first strategy exhibits a much lower level of overhead to begin with than the baseline run with the default strategy, the relative efficiencies calculated are similar. Despite this, the depth-first approach is clearly superior in terms of the absolute level of overhead if an priori bound close to optimal is known.

To illustrate how variations in individual instances can effect scalability, Tables 3.4–3.6 show the scalability of three instances not included in the larger test set. Instance pk1 has a large search tree and relatively short node processing times, but still exhibits poor scalability, with all categories of overhead higher than expected. The large amount of ramp-down time is particularly intriguing for this instance. Instance p2756 exhibits very significant increases in the size of its search tree (indicating the performance of redundant work) as the number of NP/CG modules increases, resulting in increased overall running times beyond two NP/CG modules. Finally, instance nw04 is a set partitioning instance for which node processing times are extremely lengthy. Although initially exhibiting superlinear speedup (presumably due to earlier location of the optimal solution) and a drop in search tree size, the efficiency is eventually wiped out by significant increases in ramp-up time.

3.5.2. Vehicle Routing Problem

Next, we consider solution of instances of the well-known Vehicle Routing Problem introduced by Dantzig and Ramser (64). In the VRP, a fleet of k vehicles with uniform capacity C must service known customer demands for a single commodity from a common depot at minimum cost. Let $V = \{1, \ldots, |V|\}$ index the set of customers and let the depot have index 0. Associated with each customer $i \in V$ is a demand d_i. The cost of travel from customer i to j is denoted c_{ij}. We assume that $c_{ij} = c_{ji} > 0 \ \forall i, j \in V \cup \{0\}, i \neq j$ and that $c_{ii} = 0 \ \forall i \in V \cup \{0\}$. By constructing an associated complete undirected graph G with vertex set $V \cup \{0\}$ and edge set E, we can formulate the VRP as an integer program.

The instances in the test set were selected from a test set maintained by the author (65) and were solved with an application written by the author using SYMPHONY. Both the instances and the solver are available for download (66). The solver has previously been described in (67) and (54). The VRP is an ideal candidate for parallelization, since node processing times are consistently small relative to overall solution times and good a priori upper bounds are easy to generate. Table 3.7 in the Appendix shows the results of the first set of experiments in which the solver was run with default settings using an upper bound determined heuristically (not necessarily optimal) before starting the solution procedure. Detailed results are shown for each instance in the test set for the runs with 1 NP/CG module and summary results only for all other runs. Table 3.8 shows detailed results for the run with 32 NP/CG modules. In terms of efficiency, the results are similar to those for the generic MILP instances in Section 3.5.1, but the levels of overhead are much smaller. As in the case of the generic MILP instances, because the baseline levels of overhead are small to begin with, the efficiencies are similar in each case.

Table 3.9 shows results of a slightly smaller set of instances with no *a priori* upper bounds given. Here, the running times are longer and the search trees are bigger, but in terms of efficiency, the results are similar to those in Table 3.7. Finally, Table 3.10 shows the results with the same set of instances using a global cut pool. The use of the global pool decreases the size of the search tree, but introduces another source of idle time during node processing: time spent waiting for the global pool to return a set of violated valid inequalities. Overall, the additional overhead is worthwhile and is offset by a decrease in the number of search tree nodes. It is interesting to note, however, that the use of the global cut pool does cause a loss in efficiency. We conjecture that this is because the effect of the pool is lessened as the number of NP/CG modules is increased since effective inequalities have less time be shared after being discovered and therefore have a smaller effect. The difference in running times is relatively large for the runs with 1 NP/CG module, but there is almost no difference in the running times for the 32 NP/CG module runs, resulting in the observed relative loss of efficiency.

3.5.3. The Set Partitioning Problem

Finally, we consider the well-known Set Partitioning Problem. Given a ground set S of m objects and a collection $G = \{S_1, \cdots, S_n\}$ of subsets of S with associated costs c_j, $1 \le j \le n$, the SPP is to select a subset of G of minimum (or maximum) total cost such that the selected members are disjoint and their union is equal to S. In other words, the problem is to choose a minimum (or maximum) cost partitioning of the ground set from among the members of G. In contrast to the VRP, set partitioning problems are exceptionally difficult to solve in parallel because the time required to process a node can be extremely long. This is both because the LP relaxations are extremely difficult to solve and because it takes a significant amount of preprocessing, as well as a number of rounds of cut generation, to process each node. For this reason, most instances that can be solved in a reasonable time produce very small trees. This means that for most instances, the ramp-up phase dominates the total running time.

For our tests, we used the SPP solver originally implemented by Esö and described in Ref. 68. The solver, which includes its own custom cut generator and other application-specific methodology, was updated to work with the current version of SYMPHONY by the author and is available for download (69). The instances reported on here are from a test set also described in Ref.

68 and compiled from a number of different sources, including major airlines. In preliminary testing, most of the instances exhibited very poor scalability; it was not difficult to find instances for which the root node itself took several hours to process. The results in the tables are for five instances selected from those in Ref. 68 that exhibit the most reasonable scalability with SYMPHONY "out of the box." The small cardinality of this test set should serve to emphasize that these instances are the exception to the rule.

As in the previous section, Table 3.11 shows summary results obtained when solving these five instances with different numbers of NP/CG modules. Detailed results are shown only for the case with 1 NP/CG module. Table 3.12 shows results for the runs with 32 NP/CG modules. As could be expected, the results show that the node processing times are an order of magnitude larger than for the instances in Sections 3.5.1 and 3.5.2, so overhead is dominated very substantially by ramp-up and ramp-down time. Even for these relatively well-behaved instances, the efficiency that can be obtained with a straightforward implementation, such as we have described here is very low. In Refs. 70 and 68, it was shown that achieving high efficiency when solving the SPP can be achieved only if other parts of the algorithm, such as cut generation, execution of primal heuristics, and preprocessing, are also parallelized.

3.6. CONCLUSIONS AND FUTURE WORK

In this chapter, we have introduced the basic concepts and methodology required for parallelization of the branch-and-cut algorithm. Parallelizing branch and cut in a scalable fashion is a challenge that involves careful analysis of the costs and benefits of synchronization and the sharing of knowledge during the algorithm. Because this analysis can yield different results for different problem classes, it is not possible in general to develop a single ideal approach that will be effective across all problem classes. The synchronous approach taken by SYMPHONY is very effective for small numbers of processors, but is not scalable beyond 32 processors, even under ideal conditions. Large-scale parallelism requires an asynchronous approach, such as that taken by ALPS, that avoids creating bottlenecks in communication. In future work, we plan to continue developing ALPS, with the goal of correcting SYMPHONYs deficiencies and achieving the scalability needed to run on much larger computational platforms.

TABLE 3.1. Solving Generic MILPs with SYMPHONY[a]

Instance	Tree Size	Ramp Up	Ramp Down	Node Pack	Idle Node	Idle Index	Idle Dive	CPU sec	Wallclock	Eff
23588	591	0.00	0.00	0.02	0.09	0.02	0.09	52.56	53.52	
aligninq	761	0.00	0.00	0.07	0.43	0.02	0.09	225.42	229.14	
bell3a	24,957	0.00	0.00	1.48	4.16	0.22	4.08	171.96	191.45	
blend2	2,105	0.00	0.00	0.13	0.56	0.26	0.37	84.84	89.46	
enigma	3,046	0.00	0.00	0.03	0.08	0.19	0.56	35.05	38.21	
fixnet6	1,438	0.00	0.00	0.18	1.38	0.13	0.24	106.55	111.87	
gesa2	4,634	0.00	0.00	0.97	6.79	0.74	1.06	950.50	1001.08	
geas2_o	662	0.00	0.00	0.12	0.93	0.09	0.12	128.66	135.04	
l152lav	1,326	0.00	0.00	0.19	1.32	0.26	0.21	322.27	329.44	
misc07	12,606	0.00	0.00	1.24	3.83	0.76	1.77	1,186.99	1,241.22	
mod008	1,618	0.00	0.00	0.25	2.40	0.70	0.23	2,124.19	2,189.79	
pg	1,868	0.00	0.00	0.07	0.40	0.30	0.45	402.43	418.29	
pp08a	46,385	0.00	0.00	44.76	69.44	8.15	44.31	2,186.69	2,360.81	
pp08aCUTS	68,093	0.00	0.00	108.32	137.13	11.96	114.16	4,023.62	4,373.30	
rgn	1,284	0.00	0.00	0.05	0.42	0.08	0.15	10.92	12.00	
roy	346	0.00	0.00	0.01	0.08	0.06	0.05	12.53	13.18	
stein27	1,589	0.00	0.00	0.05	0.48	0.31	0.14	57.38	60.06	
stein45	12,108	0.00	0.00	1.44	8.82	4.37	1.68	2,281.73	2,324.85	
vpm1	10,012	0.00	0.00	0.65	4.33	0.86	1.19	245.64	257.89	
vpm2	11,444	0.00	0.00	1.51	7.66	1.39	1.56	459.96	477.37	
bienst1	13,372	0.00	0.00	1.88	7.11	1.53	2.14	3,180.44	3,229.25	
p0282	538	0.00	0.00	0.03	0.28	0.09	0.09	30.37	36.70	
1 NP	220,846	0.00	0.00	163.45	258.09	32.49	174.74	18,280.70	19,173.94	1.00
Per Node		0.0000	0.0000	0.0007	0.0012	0.0001	0.0008	0.0828	0.0868	
2 NPs	224,266	18.41	0.01	166.45	271.57	35.99	177.14	18,357.87	9,697.61	0.99
Per Node		0.0001	0.0000	0.0007	0.0012	0.0002	0.0008	0.0819	0.0865	
4 NPs	222,446	60.29	2.46	161.70	306.21	45.02	178.13	17,822.92	4,737.28	1.02
Per Node		0.0003	0.0000	0.0007	0.0014	0.0002	0.0008	0.0801	0.0852	
8 NPs	213,954	163.26	127.87	139.33	378.45	59.06	171.20	17,433.65	2,395.28	1.01
Per Node		0.0008	0.0006	0.0007	0.0018	0.0003	0.0008	0.0815	0.0896	
16 NPs	215,597	393.70	605.28	128.37	617.01	123.56	265.65	17,127.50	1,277.09	0.94
Per Node		0.0018	0.0028	0.0006	0.0029	0.0006	0.0012	0.0794	0.0948	
32 NPs	212,672	911.73	2,282.12	148.22	2,506.58	693.08	1,035.35	16,723.89	794.87	0.75
Per Node		0.0043	0.0107	0.0007	0.0118	0.0033	0.0049	0.0786	0.1196	

[a]Default settings and no *a priori* upper bound (summary).

TABLE 3.2. Solving Generic MILPs with SYMPHONY[a]

Instance	Tree Size	Ramp Up	Ramp Down	Node Pack	Idle Node	Idle Index	Idle Dive	CPU sec	Wallclock
23588	582	27.60	0.00	0.03	0.07	0.02	0.09	56.29	2.76
aligninq	1,139	98.19	0.00	0.14	0.67	0.02	0.13	362.38	14.90
bell3a	24,128	2.46	10.39	2.43	33.77	1.13	16.10	172.69	7.54
blend2	2,104	6.03	0.25	0.13	0.72	0.81	1.32	81.27	3.25
enigma	292	3.09	0.00	0.00	0.07	0.01	0.06	2.64	0.23
fixnet6	1,705	12.59	0.00	0.23	1.27	0.19	0.34	119.65	4.44
gesa2	5,324	148.49	0.21	1.33	8.50	1.12	2.27	1,008.88	38.41
geas2_o	1,123	44.27	0.00	0.18	1.04	0.11	0.23	184.86	8.06
l152lav	891	78.02	0.00	0.14	0.66	0.18	0.12	204.12	9.20
misc07	8,989	33.60	0.78	0.96	4.84	0.95	2.15	809.08	27.42
mod008	1,711	1.97	1,294.42	0.29	50.88	1.12	0.64	1,043.72	125.00
pg	1,231	306.90	7.44	0.06	0.89	0.56	0.64	286.77	22.86
pp08a	41,223	25.72	230.78	38.40	593.43	174.32	280.19	1,825.54	92.44
pp08aCUTS	62,529	22.22	707.14	93.64	1,753.50	490.87	709.92	3,766.79	214.47
rgn	1,357	5.98	0.66	0.07	0.66	0.17	0.32	11.41	0.69
roy	555	4.26	11.69	0.02	0.97	0.08	0.09	17.35	1.51
stein27	1,576	7.33	0.01	0.07	0.51	0.36	0.18	58.11	2.24
stein45	11,972	28.68	3.92	2.39	13.27	7.87	4.93	2,218.94	72.16
vpm1	14,123	11.55	3.42	1.44	9.06	1.80	2.70	337.21	11.88
vpm2	13,797	15.23	3.01	3.77	19.99	4.83	6.59	571.51	19.96
bienst1	14,183	15.93	7.99	2.31	10.91	6.38	5.86	3,522.96	112.94
p0282	2,132	11.63	0.02	0.16	0.91	0.21	0.46	61.71	2.50
32 NPs	212,672	911.73	2,282.13	148.22	2,506.58	693.08	1,035.35	16,723.89	794.87
Per Node		0.0043	0.0107	0.0007	0.0118	0.0033	0.0049	0.0786	0.1196

[a]Default settings and no *a priori* upper bound (32 NPs).

Instance	Tree Size	Ramp Up	Ramp Down	Node Pack	Idle Node	Idle Index	Idle Dive	CPU sec	Wallclock	Eff
23588	259	0.00	0.00	0.00	0.01	0.01	0.02	21.86	22.25	
aligninq	1,892	0.00	0.00	0.08	0.51	0.04	0.15	443.80	496.96	
bell3a	23,048	0.00	0.00	0.44	1.35	0.52	2.98	174.86	191.40	
blend2	1,099	0.00	0.00	0.01	0.01	0.04	0.06	30.78	32.12	
enigma	1	0.00	0.00	0.00	0.00	0.00	0.00	0.00	0.01	
fixnet6	529	0.00	0.00	0.02	0.12	0.03	0.06	29.66	30.97	
gesa2	1,707	0.00	0.00	0.10	0.76	0.18	0.17	396.93	419.19	
geas2_o	2,410	0.00	0.00	0.18	0.15	0.07	0.12	362.61	377.38	
1152lav	1,553	0.00	0.00	0.09	0.54	0.22	0.16	289.20	295.78	
misc07	7,795	0.00	0.00	0.22	0.78	0.37	0.87	648.57	665.83	
mod008	1,979	0.00	0.00	0.04	0.25	0.20	0.20	98.27	150.59	
pg	793	0.00	0.00	0.10	0.58	0.06	0.11	202.40	208.07	
pp08a	26,090	0.00	0.00	2.05	11.29	3.12	4.29	1,099.47	1,151.15	
rgn	1,466	0.00	0.00	0.02	0.18	0.08	0.15	11.59	12.81	
roy	588	0.00	0.00	0.01	0.05	0.05	0.05	17.92	18.46	
stein27	1,630	0.00	0.00	0.03	0.18	0.24	0.12	51.12	53.34	
stein45	12,179	0.00	0.00	0.65	3.66	3.43	1.22	2,071.94	2,102.30	
bienst1	9,721	0.00	0.00	0.79	0.21	0.18	0.24	1,801.06	1,824.56	
p0282	613	0.00	0.00	0.01	0.11	0.06	0.06	29.37	30.10	
1 NP	95,352	0.00	0.00	4.84	20.74	8.91	11.03	7,781.41	8,083.28	1.00
Per Node		0.0000	0.0002	0.0001	0.0002	0.0001	0.0001	0.0816	0.0848	
2 NPs	96,569	19.95	0.00	3.99	15.88	8.29	10.23	8,011.45	4,127.76	0.98
Per Node		0.0002	0.0000	0.0000	0.0002	0.0001	0.0001	0.0830	0.0855	
4 NPs	96,006	72.39	0.00	4.11	21.79	9.75	11.74	7,794.86	2,212.54	0.91
Per Node		0.0008	0.0000	0.0000	0.0002	0.0001	0.0001	0.0812	0.0922	
8 NPs	97,104	189.71	1.35	3.99	23.24	10.19	12.38	7,752.63	1,173.96	0.86
Per Node		0.0020	0.0000	0.0000	0.0002	0.0001	0.0001	0.0798	0.0967	
16 NPs	98,960	470.38	18.91	4.37	27.61	11.35	13.67	7,953.20	638.36	0.79
Per Node		0.0048	0.0002	0.0000	0.0003	0.0001	0.0001	0.0804	0.1032	
32 NPs	98,223	1,080.33	301.06	4.86	70.31	15.18	25.38	7,793.92	349.24	0.72
Per Node		0.0110	0.0031	0.0000	0.0007	0.0002	0.0003	0.0793	0.1138	

TABLE 3.4. Scalability of pk1 with SYMPHONY (Unconditional Diving)

NPs	Tree Size	Ramp Up	Ramp Down	Node Pack	Idle Node	Idle Index	Idle Dive	CPU sec	Wallclock	Eff
1	239,313	0.00	0.00	258.20	279.60	16.20	378.15	3,775.52	4,533.70	1.00
2	239,461	0.01	0.36	256.94	302.26	28.24	404.23	3,776.76	2,296.48	0.99
4	238,633	0.05	13.24	240.17	358.89	54.90	431.11	3,751.31	1,170.62	0.97
8	238,588	0.19	197.95	236.39	930.87	163.85	652.97	3,747.77	697.49	0.81
16	240,238	0.58	966.25	248.13	3,429.10	782.94	1,933.32	3,798.91	626.75	0.45
32	238,795	1.53	2,881.87	231.07	8,725.32	1,681.38	3,701.61	3,761.61	561.19	0.25

TABLE 3.5. Scalability of p2756 with SYMPHONY (Default Settings)

NPs	Tree Size	Ramp Up	Ramp Down	Node Pack	Idle Node	Idle Index	Idle Dive	CPU sec	Wallclock	Eff
1	353	0.00	0.00	0.17	1.02	0.04	0.05	100.41	130.37	1.00
2	619	0.42	0.00	0.28	1.66	0.07	0.11	161.51	84.29	0.77
4	11,244	1.65	0.00	6.76	28.13	0.97	2.08	2,195.41	571.95	0.05
8	19,502	2.93	0.03	14.51	57.67	1.35	3.95	3,906.41	507.37	0.03

TABLE 3.6. Scalability of nw04 with SYMPHONY (Default Settings)

NPs	Tree Size	Ramp Up	Ramp Down	Node Pack	Idle Node	Idle Index	Idle Dive	CPU sec	Wallclock	Eff
1	198	0.00	0.00	1.28	4.94	0.00	0.04	1075.76	1138.38	1.00
2	85	27.29	0.00	0.33	1.21	0.00	0.02	439.92	246.35	2.32
4	84	101.21	61.65	0.17	107.40	0.00	0.01	463.87	181.29	1.58
8	87	941.67	0.00	0.20	220.33	0.00	0.02	473.78	181.56	0.78
16	86	2283.04	0.00	0.17	225.41	0.00	0.02	468.53	182.60	0.39
32	87	4954.92	0.00	0.20	220.20	0.06	0.06	474.64	185.75	0.19

TABLE 3.7. Solving VRP Instances with SYMPHONY[a]

Instance	Tree Size	Ramp Up	Ramp Down	Node Pack	Idle Node	Idle Index	Idle Diving	CPU sec	Wallclock	Eff
hk48–n48–k4	110	0.00	0.00	0.00	0.03	0.01	0.01	16.77	17.35	
att–n48–k4	384	0.00	0.00	0.01	0.05	0.04	0.05	36.61	37.77	
E–n51–k5	41	0.00	0.00	0.00	0.01	0.01	0.01	14.86	15.49	
A–n39–k5	1,307	0.00	0.00	0.04	0.23	0.18	0.15	242.33	251.04	
A–n39–k6	328	0.00	0.00	0.01	0.07	0.04	0.03	31.95	32.66	
A–n45–k6	631	0.00	0.00	0.02	0.13	0.08	0.07	175.12	181.64	
A–n46–k7	43	0.00	0.00	0.00	0.01	0.01	0.00	15.03	15.71	
B–n34–k5	795	0.00	0.00	0.01	0.10	0.08	0.09	29.99	31.08	
B–n43–k6	288	0.00	0.00	0.01	0.05	0.04	0.03	38.24	39.67	
B–n45–k5	133	0.00	0.00	0.00	0.02	0.02	0.02	15.69	16.21	
B–n51–k7	367	0.00	0.00	0.01	0.12	0.05	0.05	53.50	55.37	
B–n64–k9	152	0.00	0.00	0.00	0.03	0.02	0.02	44.00	46.12	
A–n53–k7	3,056	0.00	0.00	0.17	1.16	0.39	0.33	1,295.06	1,362.33	
A–n37–k6	5,873	0.00	0.00	0.21	1.36	0.73	0.67	832.46	857.40	
A–n44–k6	5,963	0.00	0.00	0.31	1.95	0.80	0.67	1,677.44	1,741.78	
B–n45–k6	2,039	0.00	0.00	0.07	0.46	0.28	0.23	379.23	394.49	
B–n57–k7	3,205	0.00	0.00	0.17	1.11	0.42	0.41	976.52	1,036.09	
1 NP	24,715	0.00	0.00	1.03	6.89	3.20	2.86	5,874.80	6,132.22	1.00
Per Node		0.0000	0.0000	0.0000	0.0003	0.0001	0.0001	0.2377	0.2481	
2 NPs	24,680	19.48	0.00	1.01	6.65	3.18	2.91	5,832.25	3,054.99	1.01
Per Node		0.0008	0.0000	0.0000	0.0003	0.0001	0.0001	0.2363	0.2476	
4 NPs	23,930	74.77	0.00	0.96	7.03	3.05	2.73	5,620.94	1,488.74	1.03
Per Node		0.0031	0.0000	0.0000	0.0003	0.0001	0.0001	0.2349	0.2488	
8 NPs	24,366	221.67	3.56	0.97	8.41	3.36	3.00	5,701.00	774.99	0.99
Per Node		0.0091	0.0001	0.0000	0.0003	0.0001	0.0001	0.2340	0.2544	
16 NPs	25,668	572.93	11.83	0.98	11.52	3.75	3.51	6,090.37	437.66	0.87
Per Node		0.0223	0.0005	0.0000	0.0004	0.0001	0.0001	0.2373	0.2728	
32 NPs	25,516	1,416.55	60.98	3.02	113.66	121.30	110.45	5,998.93	257.71	0.74
Per Node		0.0555	0.0024	0.0001	0.0045	0.0048	0.0043	0.2351	0.3232	

[a]Default settings and heuristic upper bound (summary).

TABLE 3.8. Solving VRP Instances with SYMPHONY[a]

Instance	Tree Size	Ramp Up	Ramp Down	Node Pack	Idle Node	Idle Index	Idle Diving	CPU sec	Wallclock
hk48-n48-k4	178	59.11	2.78	0.01	0.46	1.20	0.91	26.11	3.06
att-n48-k4	349	34.03	0.04	0.01	0.75	1.51	1.29	32.45	2.53
E-n51-k5	37	74.11	0.00	0.00	0.05	0.05	0.06	13.82	3.24
A-n39-k5	1,228	99.86	0.04	0.06	4.11	6.57	5.99	232.97	11.36
A-n39-k6	328	35.52	9.34	0.01	0.99	1.23	0.98	32.02	2.75
A-n45-k6	727	105.07	0.08	0.06	2.71	3.38	2.64	215.34	10.96
A-n46-k7	36	157.81	0.00	0.00	1.19	0.04	0.03	13.93	5.53
B-n34-k5	859	10.77	0.01	0.02	1.34	1.69	2.34	32.36	1.68
B-n43-k6	296	65.73	6.82	0.02	3.32	1.16	0.94	37.50	3.68
B-n45-k5	179	72.23	7.21	0.01	1.75	0.50	0.48	20.82	3.72
B-n51-k7	365	41.01	12.07	0.02	2.05	1.66	1.39	52.84	3.79
B-n64-k9	136	158.05	0.00	0.04	3.51	0.85	0.70	36.11	6.59
A-n53-k7	3,012	178.18	0.53	0.45	14.87	12.61	11.52	1,278.10	49.22
A-n37-k6	5,999	54.78	12.96	0.51	23.60	27.99	24.62	849.45	32.03
A-n44-k6	5,916	115.84	1.03	0.79	28.99	30.29	27.20	1,667.73	60.78
B-n45-k6	1,991	74.93	0.32	0.26	8.53	11.16	9.86	372.13	16.08
B-n57-k7	3,877	79.51	7.76	0.73	15.44	19.40	19.49	1,085.24	40.73
32 NPs	25,516	1,416.55	60.98	3.02	113.66	121.30	110.45	5,998.93	257.71
Per Node		0.0555	0.0024	0.0001	0.0045	0.0048	0.0043	0.2351	0.3232

[a]Default settings and heuristic upper bound (32 NPs).

Instance	Tree Size	Ramp Up	Ramp Down	Node Pack	Idle Node	Idle Index	Idle Diving	CPU sec	Wallclock	Eff
hk48–n48–k4	110	0.00	0.00	0.00	0.02	0.01	0.01	17.88	18.46	
att–n48–k4	292	0.00	0.00	0.00	0.05	0.03	0.04	29.37	30.34	
E–n51–k5	38	0.00	0.00	0.00	0.01	0.01	0.00	13.29	13.88	
A–n39–k5	1,139	0.00	0.00	0.03	0.13	0.14	0.12	218.66	226.46	
A–n39–k6	273	0.00	0.00	0.00	0.04	0.03	0.03	26.88	27.53	
A–n45–k6	807	0.00	0.00	0.02	0.14	0.13	0.10	247.97	257.05	
A–n46–k7	83	0.00	0.00	0.00	0.01	0.02	0.01	45.01	47.51	
B–n34–k5	1,101	0.00	0.00	0.02	0.10	0.10	0.11	41.66	43.15	
B–n43–k6	197	0.00	0.00	0.01	0.04	0.03	0.02	27.52	28.54	
B–n45–k5	126	0.00	0.00	0.00	0.02	0.02	0.02	17.92	18.48	
B–n51–k7	327	0.00	0.00	0.01	0.09	0.05	0.05	47.01	48.75	
B–n64–k9	137	0.00	0.00	0.01	0.03	0.02	0.02	39.41	40.83	
A–n53–k7	1,682	0.00	0.00	0.08	0.63	0.21	0.17	698.52	735.62	
A–n44–k6	5,233	0.00	0.00	0.20	1.13	0.79	0.73	1,471.47	1,523.40	
B–n45–k6	5,413	0.00	0.00	0.18	0.95	0.82	0.81	1,115.43	1,157.26	
1 NP	16,958	0.00	0.00	0.56	3.40	2.40	2.26	4,058.00	4,217.26	1.00
Per Node		(0.0000)	0.0000	0.0000	0.0002	0.0001	0.0001	0.2393	0.2487	
2 NPs	16,918	16.61	0.00	0.55	3.73	2.54	2.36	4,051.79	2,115.68	1.00
Per Node		0.0013	0.0000	0.0000	0.0002	0.0001	0.0001	0.2395	0.2501	
4 NPs	16,933	68.54	0.00	0.54	4.02	2.41	2.25	4,030.29	1,066.63	0.99
Per Node		0.0040	0.0000	0.0000	0.0002	0.0001	0.0001	0.2380	0.2520	
8 NPs	16,891	199.20	1.02	0.54	4.27	2.56	2.40	4,031.21	551.15	0.96
Per Node		0.0113	0.0001	0.0000	0.0003	0.0002	0.0001	0.2387	0.2610	
16 NPs	18,715	513.93	29.95	0.58	7.29	2.97	2.84	4,520.36	330.86	0.80
Per Node		0.0275	0.0016	0.0000	0.0004	0.0002	0.0002	0.2415	0.2829	
32 NPs	16,160	1,249.31	75.52	1.42	60.44	81.97	78.37	3,781.30	176.54	0.75
Per Node		0.0773	0.0047	0.0001	0.0037	0.0051	0.0048	0.2340	0.3496	

[a]Default settings and no *a priori* upper bound (summary).

TABLE 3.10. Solving VRP Instances with SYMPHONY[a]

Instance	Tree Size	Ramp Up	Ramp Down	Node Pack	Idle Node	Idle Cuts	Idle Index	Idle Diving	CPU sec	Wallclock	Eff
hk48–n48–k4	101	0.00	0.00	0.00	0.02	0.04	0.01	0.01	16.56	17.25	
att–n48–k4	384	0.00	0.00	0.01	0.07	0.13	0.06	0.05	37.76	39.11	
E–n51–k5	53	0.00	0.00	0.00	0.01	0.09	0.01	0.01	18.64	19.46	
A–n39–k5	390	0.00	0.00	0.01	0.07	0.58	0.07	0.04	74.36	77.22	
A–n39–k6	315	0.00	0.00	0.01	0.05	0.15	0.05	0.03	29.70	30.48	
A–n45–k6	851	0.00	0.00	0.02	0.15	1.22	0.15	0.10	236.26	244.64	
A–n46–k7	24	0.00	0.00	0.00	0.01	0.08	0.00	0.00	12.90	13.64	
B–n34–k5	1,032	0.00	0.00	0.02	0.15	0.45	0.14	0.11	36.92	38.61	
B–n43–k6	746	0.00	0.00	0.02	0.14	0.42	0.12	0.08	80.08	83.17	
B–n45–k5	45	0.00	0.00	0.00	0.01	0.02	0.01	0.01	8.27	8.59	
B–n51–k7	897	0.00	0.00	0.03	0.23	0.47	0.14	0.10	125.30	130.27	
B–n64–k9	99	0.00	0.00	0.00	0.04	0.05	0.02	0.01	23.93	24.90	
A–n53–k7	1,358	0.00	0.00	0.06	0.50	4.21	0.21	0.14	515.92	539.48	
A–n37–k6	5,115	0.00	0.00	0.18	1.16	4.11	0.86	0.59	721.11	741.37	
A–n44–k6	3,633	0.00	0.00	0.14	1.09	4.97	0.59	0.39	889.40	920.67	
B–n45–k6	3,829	0.00	0.00	0.13	0.86	2.90	0.71	0.48	734.27	760.16	
B–n57–k7	2,345	0.00	0.00	0.09	0.65	1.94	0.35	0.32	508.84	536.20	
1 NP	21,217	0.00	0.00	0.70	5.22	21.82	3.49	2.48	4,070.21	4,225.21	1.00
Per Node		0.0000	0.0000	0.0000	0.0002	0.0010	0.0002	0.0001	0.1918	0.1991	
2 NPs	23,446	19.28	0.00	0.75	5.28	23.80	3.72	2.81	4,622.35	2,411.40	0.87
Per Node		0.0008	0.0000	0.0000	0.0002	0.0010	0.0002	0.0001	0.1971	0.2057	
4 NPs	23,424	74.96	2.18	0.77	6.83	26.20	3.79	2.69	4,611.47	1,217.96	0.86
Per Node		0.0032	0.0001	0.0000	0.0003	0.0011	0.0002	0.0001	0.1969	0.2080	
8 NPs	22,062	233.71	3.17	0.70	8.36	26.21	3.74	2.64	4,463.30	611.69	0.86
Per Node		0.0106	0.0001	0.0000	0.0004	0.0012	0.0002	0.0001	0.2023	0.2218	
16 NPs	22,756	597.00	31.30	0.71	10.59	30.20	4.17	3.08	4,626.46	343.32	0.76
Per Node		0.0262	0.0014	0.0000	0.0005	0.0013	0.0002	0.0001	0.2033	0.2414	
32 NPs	24,669	1,455.51	29.88	2.27	93.70	71.22	112.91	110.86	5,108.75	229.53	0.75
Per Node		0.0590	0.0012	0.0001	0.0038	0.0029	0.0046	0.0045	0.2071	0.2977	

[a]Default settings with heuristic upper bounds and global cut pool (summary).

Instance	Tree Size	Ramp Up	Ramp Down	Node Pack	Idle Node	Idle Index	Idle Dive	CPU sec	Wallclock	Eff
aa01	758	0.00	0.00	0.63	7.03	0.10	0.09	23,626.58	24,216.30	
aa04	1,153	0.00	0.00	0.48	6.21	0.10	0.15	12,746.12	13,063.71	
kl02	184	0.00	0.00	0.25	2.58	0.01	0.03	1,255.83	1,408.35	
v0415	191	0.00	0.00	0.06	0.49	0.03	0.03	94.39	140.57	
v1622	200	0.00	0.00	0.09	0.79	0.01	0.02	143.06	215.30	
1 NP	2,486	0.00	0.00	1.51	17.11	0.24	0.32	37,865.98	39,044.22	1.00
Per Node		0.0000	0.0000	0.0006	0.0069	0.0001	0.0001	15.2317	15.7056	
2 NPs	2,159	419.68	0.00	1.32	13.67	0.21	0.27	31,932.62	16,809.16	1.16
Per Node		0.1944	0.0000	0.0006	0.0063	0.0001	0.0001	14.7905	15.5712	
4 NPs	2,097	1,575.82	0.00	1.23	10.32	0.17	0.25	29,667.74	8,198.46	1.20
Per Node		0.7515	0.0000	0.0006	0.0049	0.0001	0.0001	14.1477	15.6385	
8 NPs	2,601	4,524.93	1,087.81	1.48	773.35	0.23	0.42	37,868.39	5,724.06	0.85
Per Node		1.7397	0.4182	0.0006	0.2973	0.0001	0.0002	14.5592	17.6057	
16 NPs	2,478	11,348.97	8,125.87	1.87	1,626.52	0.26	0.71	35,603.94	3,702.59	0.66
Per Node		4.5880	3.2792	0.0008	0.6564	0.0001	0.0003	14.3680	23.9070	
32 NPs	1,971	30,144.80	34,072.61	1.27	3,328.57	0.18	0.59	28,660.28	3,142.59	0.38
Per Node		15.2903	17.2826	0.0006	1.6883	0.0001	0.0003	14.5373	51.0083	

[a]Default settings and no *a priori* upper bound (summary).

TABLE 3.12. Solving SPP Instances with SYMPHONY[a]

Instance	Tree Size	Ramp Up	Ramp Down	Node Pack	Idle Node	Idle Index	Idle Dive	CPU sec	Wallclock
aa01	566	18,191.06	31,069.37	0.51	2,910.02	0.08	0.21	16,525.35	2,208.65
aa04	1,044	7,174.27	3,003.24	0.44	74.22	0.08	0.16	11,119.85	722.99
kl02	143	4,118.31	0.00	0.23	-208.02	0.01	0.11	865.38	181.49
v0415	218	661.16	0.00	0.10	136.31	0.02	0.10	149.71	29.46
v1622	222	487.67	0.00	0.12	11.29	0.00	0.08	173.08	24.61
32 NPs	1,971	30,144.80	34,072.61	1.27	3,328.57	0.18	0.59	28,660.28	3,142.59
Per Node		15.2903	17.2826	0.0006	1.6883	0.0001	0.0003	14.5373	51.0083

[a]Default settings and no *a priori* upper bound (32 NPs).

REFERENCES

1. J.J.H. Forrest, J.P.H. Hirst, and J.A. Tomlin. Practical solution of large scale mixed integer programming problems with UMPIRE. *Manag. Sci.*, **20**:736–773 (1974).

2. G. Mitra. Investigation of some branch and bound strategies for the solution of mixed integer linear programs. *Math. Prog.*, **4**:155–170 (1973).

3. M. Bénichou et al. Experiments in mixed-integer linear programming. *Math. Prog.* **1**:76–94 (1971).

4. J.T. Linderoth and M.W.P. Savelsbergh. A computational study of search strategies in mixed integer programming. *INFORMS J. Comput.*, **11**:173–187 (1999).

5. M. Padberg and G. Rinaldi. A Branch-and-Cut Algorithm for the Resolution of Large-Scale Traveling Salesman Problems. *SIAM Rev.*, **33**:60+ (1991).

6. G.L. Nemhauser and L.A. Wolsey. *Integer and Combinatorial Optimization*, John Wiley & Sons, Inc., New York, 1988.

7. M. Grötschel, L. Lovász, and A. Schrijver. The ellipsoid method and its consequences in combinatorial optimization. *Combinatorica*, **1**:169–197 (1981).

8. G.L. Nemhauser and L.A. Wolsey. *Integer and Combinatorial Optimization*. 1st ed. John Wiley & Sons, Inc., 1988.

9. T.K. Ralphs. SYMPHONY Version 4.0 User's Manual. Technical Report 03T-006, Lehigh University Industrial and Systems Engineering, 2003.

10. L. Ladányi. *Parallel Branch and Cut and Its Application to the Traveling Salesman Problem*. Ph.D. thesis, Cornell University, May 1996.

11. J.M. Gauthier and G. Ribière. Experiments in mixed-integer linear programming using pseudocosts. *Math. Prog.*, **12**:26–47 (1977).

12. T. Achterberg, T. Koch, and A. Martin. Branching rules revisited. *Oper. Res. Lett.*, **33**:42–54 (2004).

13. M. Cosnard and D. Trystram. *Parallel Algorithms and Arcitectures*. International Thomson Computer Press, Boston, MA, 1995.

14. R.G. Brown. Engineering a beowulf-style compute cluster. Available at http://www.phy.duke.edu/~rgb/Beowulf/Beowulf_book/Beowulf_book/,2004.

15. A. Geist et al. *PVM: Parallel Virtual Machine*. The MIT Press, Cambridge, MA, 1994.

16. W. Gropp, E. Lusk, and A. Skjellum. *Using MPI*. 2nd ed., MIT Press, Cambridge, MA, 1999.

17. A. de Bruin, G.A.P. Kindervater, and H.W.J.M. Trienekens. Asynchronous parallel branch and bound and anomolies. Report EUR-CS-95-05, Erasmus University, Rotterdam, 1995.

18. T.H. Lai and S. Sahni. Anomalies in parallel branch and bound algorithms. *Proceedings of the 1983 International Conference on Parallel Processing*, 1983, pp. 183–190.

19. G.M. Amdahl. Validity of the single-processor approach to achieving large-scale computing capabilities. *AFIPS Conference Proceedings*, AFIPS Press, 1967, pp. 483–485.

20. V. Kumar and A. Gupta. Analyzing scalability of parallel algorithms and architectures. *J. Parallel Distributed Comput.*, **22**:379–391 (Sept. 1994).

21. A.Y. Grama and V. Kumar. Parallel search algorithms for discrete optimization problems. *ORSA J. Comput.*, **7**:365–385 (1995).

22. J.L. Gustafson. Reevaluating Amdahl's Law. *Commun. ACM*, **31**:532–533 (1988).

23. V. Kumar and V.N. Rao. Parallel depth-first search, part II: Analysis. *Int. J. Parallel Prog.*, **16**:501–519 (1987).

24. H.W.J.M. Trienekens and A. de Bruin. Towards a taxonomy of parallel branch and bound algorithms. Technical Report EUR-CS-92-01, Department of Computer Science, Erasmus University, 1992.

25. A.H. Land and A.G. Doig. An automatic method for solving discrete programming problems. *Econometrica*, **28**:497–520 (1960).

26. L.G. Mitten. Branch-and-bound methods: General formulation and properties. *Oper. Res.*, **18**:24–34 (1970).

27. L. Hafer. bonsaiG 2.8, 2004. Available at http://www.cs.sfu.ca/~lou/BonsaiG/dwnldreq.html.

28. J. Forrest. CBC, 2004. Available at http://www.coin-or.org/.

29. A. Makhorin. GLPK 4.2, 2004. Available at htpp://www.gnu.org/software/glpk/glpk.htmol.

30. M. Berkelaar. lp_solve 5.1, 2004. Available at http://groups.yahoo.com/group/lp_solve/.

31. G.L. Nemhauser, M.W.P. Savelsbergh, and G.S. Sigismondi. MINTO, a Mixed INTeger Optimizer. *Oper. Res. Lett.*, **15**:47–58 (1994).

32. T.K. Ralphs. SYMPHONY Version 5.0 user's manual. Technical Report 04-T011, Lehigh University Industrial and Systems Engineering, 2004.

33. T.K. Ralphs and M. Guzelsoy. The SYMPHONY callable library for mixed-integer linear programming. *Proceedings of the Ninth INFORMS Computing Society Conference*, 2005, pp. 61–76.

34. T.K. Ralphs and L. Ladányi. *COIN/BCP User's Manual*, 2001. Available at http://www.coin-or.org.

35. M. Jünger and S. Thienel. The ABACUS system for branch and cut and price algorithms in integer programming and combinatorial optimization. *Software Practice Exp.*, **30**:1325–1352 (2001).

36. D. Applegate, R. Bixby, V. Chvátal, and W. Cook. On the solution of traveling salesman problems. *Documenta Mathematica*, Extra Volume Proceedings ICM III (1998) 1998, pp. 645–656.

37. D. Applegate, R. Bixby, V. Chvátal, and W. Cook. CONCORDE TSP solver. Available at http://www.tsp.gatech.edu/concorde.html.

38. Y. Shinano, K. Harada, and R. Hirabayashi. A generalized utility for parallel branch and bound algorithms. *Proceedings of the 1995 Seventh Symposium on Parallel and Distributed Processing*, IEEE Computer Society Press, Los Alamitos, CA, 1995, pp. 392–401.

39. M. Benchouche et al. Building a parallel branch and bound library. *In Solving Combinatorial Optimization Problems in Parallel, Lecture Notes in Computer Science* 1054, Springer, Berlin, 1996, p. 201.

40. S. Tschoke and T. Polzer. *Portable Parallel Branch and Bound Library User Manual: Library Version 2.0.* Department of Computer Science, University of Paderborn.

41. J. Eckstein, C.A. Phillips, and W.E. Hart. PICO: An object-oriented framework for parallel branch and bound. Technical Report RRR 40-2000, Rutgers University, 2000.

42. J. Linderoth. *Topics in Parallel Integer Optimization*. Ph.D. thesis, School of Industrial and Systems Engineering, Georgia Institute of Technology, Atlanta, GA, 1998.

43. Q. Chen and M. Ferris. Fatcop: A fault tolerant condor-pvm mixed integer programming solver. *SIAM J. Opn.*, **11**(4):1019–1036 (2001).

44. V. Chvátal. *Linear Programming*. W.H. Freeman and Company, New York, 1983.

45. B. Gendron and T.G. Crainic. Parallel branch and bound algorithms: Survey and synthesis. *Oper. Res.*, **42**:1042–1066 (1994).

46. B. Borbeau, T.G. Crainic, and B. Gendron. Branch-and-bound parallelization strategies applied to a depot location and container fleet management problem. *Parallel Comput.*, **26**:27–46 (2000).

47. J.J.H. Forrest, J.P.H. Hirst, and J.A. Tomlin. Practical solution of large scale mixed integer programming pr oblems with UMPIRE. *Manag. Sci.*, **20**:736–773 (1974).

48. C. Fonlupt, P. Marquet, and J. Dekeyser. Data-parallel load balancing strategies. *Parallel Comput.*, **24**(11):1665–1684 (1998).

49. D. Henrich. Initialization of parallel branch-and-bound algorithms. In *Second International Workshop on Parallel Processing for Artificial Intelligence (PPAI-93)*, August, 1993.

50. V. Kumar, A.Y. Grama, and Nageshwara Rao Vempaty. Scalable load balancing techniques for parallel computers. *J. Parallel Distributed Comput.*, **22**(1):60–79 (1994).

51. P.S. Laursen. Can parallel branch and bound without communication be effective? *SIAM J. Op.*, **4**:33–33 (May, 1994).

52. P. Sanders. Tree shaped computations as a model for parallel applications, 1998. In ALV198 workshop on afflication balancing pp. 123–123.

53. A. Sinha and L.V. Kalé. A load balancing strategy for prioritized execution of tasks. *Seventh International Parallel Processing Symposium*, Newport Beach, CA., April 1993, pp. 230–237.

54. T.K. Ralphs. *Parallel Branch and Cut for Vehicle Routing*. Ph.D. thesis, Cornell University, 1995.

55. COIN-OR: Computational Infrastructure for Operations Research, 2004. Available at http://www.coin-or.org.

56. T.K. Ralphs. SYMPHONY 5.0, 2004. Available at http://www.branchandcut.org/SYMPHONY/.

57. T.K. Ralphs, L. Ladányi, and M.J. Saltzman. A library hierarchy for implementing scalable parallel search algorithms. *J. Supercomput.*, **28**:215–234 (2004).

58. Y. Xu, T.K. Ralphs, L. Ladányi, and M.J. Saltzman. ALPS: A framework for implementing parallel search algorithms. *Proceedings of the Ninth INFORMS Computing Society Conference*, 2005, pp. 319–334.

59. T.K. Ralphs, L. Ladányi, and M.J. Saltzman. A library hierarchy for implementing scalable parallel search algorithms. *J. Supercomput.*, **28**:215–234 (2004).

60. H.W.J.M. Trienekens and A. de Bruin. Towards a taxonomy of parallel branch and bound algorithms. Report EUR-CS-92-01, Erasmus University, Rotterdam, 1992.

61. R.E. Bixby, S. Ceria, C.M. McZeal, and M.W.P. Savelsbergh. An updated mixed integer programming library: MIPLIB 3.0. *Optima*, **58**:12–15 (1998).

62. A. Martin, T. Achterberg, and T. Koch. MIPLIB 2003. Avaiable at http://miplib.zib.de.

63. J.T. Linderoth. MIP instances, 2004. Available at http://coral.ie.Lehigh.edu/mip-instances.

64. G.B. Danzig and R.H. Ramser. The truck dispatching problem. *Manag. Sci.*, **6**:80–91 (1959).

65. T.K. Ralphs. Library of vehicle routing problem instances. Available at http://branchandcut.org/VRP/data.

66. T.K. Ralphs. Symphony vehicle routing problem solver. Available at http://branchandcut.org/vap/

67. T.K. Ralphs. Parallel branch and cut for capacitated vehicle routing. *Parallel Comput.*, **29**:607–629 (2003).

68. M. Esö. *Parallel Branch and Cut for Set Partitioning*. Ph.D. thesis, Department of Operations Research and Industrial Engineering, Cornell University, 1999.

69. M. Esö and T.K. Ralphs. Symphony set partitioning problem solver. Available at http://branchandcut.org/spp/

70. J.T. Linderoth. *Topics in Parallel Integer Optimization*. Ph.D. thesis, Georgia Institute of Technology, 1998.

████████ CHAPTER 4

Parallel Semidefinite Programming and Combinatorial Optimization

STEVEN J. BENSON

Mathematics and Computer Science Division
Argonne National Laboratory
Argonne, IL 60439

4.1. INTRODUCTION

The use of semidefinite programming in combinatorial optimization continues to grow. This growth can be attributed to at least three factors: (*1*) new semidefinite relaxations that provide tractable bounds to hard combinatorial problems, (*2*) algorithmic advances in the solution of semidefinite programs (SDP), (*3*) and the emergence of parallel computing.

Solution techniques for minimizing combinatorial problems often involve approximating the convex hull of the solution set and establishing lower bounds on the solution. Polyhedral approximations that use linear programming (LP) methodologies have been successful for many combinatorial problems, but they have not been as successful for problems such as maximum cut and maximum stable set. The semidefinite approximation for the stable set problem was proposed by Grötschel *et al.* (1) and further developed by Alizadeh (2), Polijak *et al.* (3), and many other authors. The Lovász number (4) is the solution of an SDP that provides an upper bound to the maximum clique of a graph and a lower bound to its chromatic number. Tractable bounds have also been provided for MAX-CUT (5), graph bisection (6), MAX k-CUT (7,8), graph coloring (9), and the quadratic assignment problem (10). Many more combinatorial problems can be relaxed into a semidefinite program, and some of these relaxations offer a projection back to a feasible solution that is guaranteed to be within a specified fraction of optimality. These combinatorial problems are NP-hard in the general case, so even approximate solutions are difficult to find. Most polyhedral relaxations do not offer a performance

Parallel Combinatorial Optimization, edited by El-Ghazali Talbi
Copyright © 2006 by John Wiley & Sons, Inc.

guarantee, but Geomans and Williamson (5), in a now classic result, also proved a polynomial-time approximation algorithm for the MAX-CUT problems with strong performance guarantees. Other theoretical results on the effectiveness of semidefinite relaxation have been developed for MAX-SAT (11,12), MAX-2-SAT (11), MAX-(2+p)-SAT (14), and MAX k-CUT (7), and graph coloring (15). See Laurent and Rendl (16) for additional relationships between combinatorial optimization and semidefinite programming.

In semidefinite programming, the variable is not a vector but a symmetric matrix. Semidefinite problems minimize a linear function of the matrix subject to linear constraints and the essential constraint that the matrix be positive semidefinite. The last constraint is nonlinear and nonsmooth but convex, so semidefinite programs are convex optimization problems. Many of the algorithmic ideas for optimizing over a polyhedral set have been extending to semidefinite optimization. Interior-point solvers, in particular, have polynomial complexity and have been used to solve broad classes of SDP (17–21). Other methods, such as a generalized penalty method (22), the low-rank factorization method (23), and the spectral bundle method (24), have also proven effective for combinatorial problems. Surveys by Todd (25) and Wolkowicz (26) present many examples of SDP and the algorithms most frequently used for solving them.

Although interior-point methods have proven reliable on small and medium-sized semidefinite programs, the computational and storage demands of these methods can easily exhaust the resources of most computers and limit the size of problems that can be solved. Although they are "polynomially" solvable, semidefinite programs with dimension greater than 10,000 have been extremely hard to solve in practice. Graphs with more vertices and edges routinely arise in VLSI design and other applications. Much of the research in this field focuses on solving medium-scale problems more quickly and on solving large-scale problems by any means possible. High-performance computers have become more common, and the additional memory and processing power have alleviated some of the bottlenecks in large-scale semidefinite programs. The MPI (27) standard for passing messages between processors has facilitated software development on these platforms. Parallel linear solvers (28,29) and nonlinear solvers (30,31) have been developed using MPI. At least five parallel solvers for semidefinite optimization have also been written for high-performance architectures (18,32–35). This chapter will use one of those solvers, PDSDP, for its computations. All computations in this chapter used multiple processors on a cluster of 360, 2.4-GHz Pentium Xeon processors. Each processor had at least 1 GB of RAM, and they were connected by a Myrinet 2000 network.

4.2. MAXIMUM-CUT PROBLEMS

Let there be an undirected and connected graph $G = (V,E)$, where $V = \{1, \cdots , n\}$ and $E \subset \{(i,j): 1 \le i < j \le n\}$. Let the edge weights $w_{i,j} = w_{j,i}$ be given such that $w_{i,j} = 0$ for $(i,j) \notin E$, and in particular, let $w_{i,i} = 0$. The maximum cut problem (MAX-CUT) is to find a partition (V_1, V_2) of V so that the sum of the edge weights between V_1 and V_2 is maximized. It is well known that MAX-CUT can be formulated as

$$\text{maximize} \quad \frac{1}{2} \sum_{i<j} w_{i,j}(1 - v_i v_j) \quad \text{subject to} \quad v_i \in \{-1, 1\} \quad i = 1, \cdots, n$$

Defining

$$C_{i,j} = \begin{cases} -\dfrac{1}{4} w_{i,j} & \text{if } i \neq j \\ \dfrac{1}{4} \sum_{k=1}^{n} w_{i,k} & \text{if } i = j \end{cases}$$

one can rewrite as

$$\text{maximize} \quad \sum_{i,j} C_{i,j} v_i v_j \quad \text{subject to} \quad v_i v_i = 1 \quad i = 1, \cdots, n$$

If we introduce a matrix X from the set of symmetric $n \times n$ matrices, denoted $\mathbb{S}^n$, the combinatorial problem can be relaxed to

$$\text{maximize} \quad \sum_{i,j} C_{i,j} X_{i,j} \quad \text{subject to} \quad X_{i,i} = 1, \quad i = 1, \cdots, n \quad X \succeq 0 \quad (MC)$$

The notation $X \succeq 0$ means that $X \in \mathbb{S}$ and positive semidefinite. The formulation (MC) is equivalent to MAX-CUT when X has the form $X_{i,j} = v_i v_j$, but the semidefinite relaxation ignores this symmetric rank-one constraint on the matrix. The objective function and equality constraints in (MC) are both a linear function of X, and the feasible set is convex.

The work of Geomans and Williamson replaced the scalars v_i with unit vectors $v_i \in \mathbb{R}^n$ and scalar products $v_i v_j$ with vector inner products $\bar{v}_i^T \bar{v}_j$. A solution $(\bar{v}_1, \cdots, \bar{v}_n)$ consists of n points on the surface of the unit sphere in $\mathbb{R}^n$, each representing a node in the graph. After solving (MC), their algorithm partitions the unit sphere into two half-spheres using a random vector from the same sphere. The algorithm forms a partition consisting of the $\bar{v}_i$ in each half-sphere. Furthermore, Goemans and Williamson established the celebrated result that if all the weights are nonnegative, the expected value of such randomly generated cuts is at least 0.878 times the maximum cut value. This result gives a strong performance guarantee not available from polyhedral relaxations.

Similar problems impose additional constraints on the feasible set. For example, vertices s and t may be forced in different subsets by relaxing the constraint that $v_s + v_t = 0$ into $X_{s,s} + X_{s,t} + X_{t,s} + X_{t,t} = 0$. The minimum bisection problem partitions the vertices such that the V_1 and V_2 have the same cardinality. The semidefinite relaxation of the constraint that $|\sum v_i| = 0$ is $\sum X_{ij} = 0$. Randomized procedures for the $s - t$ cut problem and minimum bisection problem have also been effective (36).

4.3. COLORS, CLIQUES, AND STABLE SETS

Given an undirected graph $G = (V, E)$, a *clique* of graph G is a subset set of vertices such that every pair of vertices is adjacent. We denote the cardinality of the largest clique in a graph as $C(G)$. A *vertex coloring* of a graph is an assignment of colors to the vertices V such that no two adjacent vertices receive the same color. A graph is *k-colorable* if it can be colored with k colors or fewer. The smallest number of colors needed for this coloring is called the *chromatic number* of G, which we denote as $X(G)$.

Aside from its theoretical interest, the maximum clique problem arises in applications in information retrieval, experimental design, signal transmission, and computer vision (37). Graph coloring arises when finite differences are used to approximate sparse Hessian matrices, and well as in applications in computer register allocation (38–40), timetable scheduling (41–43), and electronic bandwidth allocation (44).

These classic problems in combinatorial optimization are well known to be NP-hard (45). The maximum clique problem and minimum coloring problem can be solved by using polynomial-time algorithms for special classes of graphs, such as perfect graphs and t-perfect graphs, circle graphs and their complements, circular arc graphs and their complements, claw-free graphs, and graphs with long odd cycles (46), but the existence of a polynomial time algorithm for arbitrary graphs seems unlikely.

Since the coloring of every vertex in a clique must be different, the cardinality of any clique in G is a lower bound on the chromatic number of G. The inequality $C(G) \leq X(G)$ is true for all graphs. When a graph (and every node induced subgraph) has a chromatic number that equals the cardinality of the largest clique, it is known as a *perfect graph*. For this special class of graphs, the maximum clique and vertex coloring problems can be solved to optimality by using a polynomial algorithm.

For a graph with n vertices, the Lovász number, $\vartheta(G)$, is the solution to a semidefinite program whose variable X is a symmetric $n \times n$ matrix. The SDP is

$$\text{maximize} \quad \sum_{i,j} X_{i,j}$$

$$(LOV)$$

$$\text{subject to} \quad X_{i,j} = X_{j,i} = 0, \quad \forall (i,j) \notin E$$
$$\text{trace} \ (X) = 1, \quad X \geq 0$$

This number satisfies the inequality $C(G) \leq \vartheta(G) \leq X(G)$ and provides a bound to both the maximum clique problem and minimum graph coloring problem.

Equivalent to the maximum clique problem are two other combinatorial problems. A *stable set* of *vertices* (or *vertex packing* or *independent set*) is a subset of V such that no two vertices are adjacent. A *vertex cover* is a subset of vertices that are incident to each edge in the graph. With $\overline{G}$ denoted as the graph complement of G, the following statements concerning any $S \subset V$ are known to be equivalent:

1. S is a clique of G.
2. S is a stable set of $\overline{G}$.
3. $V\backslash S$ is vertex cover of $\overline{G}$.

Accordingly, the problems of finding a maximum stable set of $\overline{G}$, a maximum clique in G, and a minimum vertex cover in $\overline{G}$ are equivalent. The *maximum stable set problem* (MSS) asks for the stable set with the maximum cardinality. Bomze *et al.* (47) provide a history of results relating to this problem.

Much like the formulation of Kleinberg and Goemans (48) the SDP relaxation of the MSS problem will assign each vertex positive or negative 1. One of the two sets will be a stable set. Given a graph G with n vertices, one formulation adds an artificial vertex v_{n+1} with no edges connecting it to other vertices. Since the artificial vertex is obviously a member of the maximal stable set of the new graph, its sign is used to identify the stable set and enforce the constraints of the problem. The MSS problem can be stated as

$$\text{maximize} \quad \frac{1}{2}\sum_{i=1}^{n}(v_i^2 + v_i v_{n+1})$$

$$(MSS)$$

$$\text{subject to} \quad |v_i + v_j + v_{n+1}| = 1 \qquad \forall (i,j) \in E,$$

$$v_i \in \{-1, 1\} \quad i = 1, \cdots, n+1$$

The semidefinite relaxation of MSS introduces a symmetric matrix $X \in \mathbb{S}^{n+1}$ and sets $X_{i,j} = v_i v_j$. Since $|v_i + v_j + v_{n+1}| = (v_i + v_j + v_{n+1})^2$, the semidefinite relaxation is

$$\text{maximize} \quad \frac{1}{2}\sum_{i=1}^{n} X_{i,i} + X_{i,n+1}$$

$$\text{subject to} \quad \sum_{i,j \in \{s,t,n+1\}} X_{i,j} = 1 \quad \forall (s,t) \in E$$

$$X_{i,i} = 1 \quad i = 1, \cdots, n+1, \quad X \geq 0$$

Clearly, there are nine variables in each equation corresponding to an edge, and one variable in the other equations. Imposing the additional constraint that the matrix X be a rank-one matrix of the form $X = vv^T$ would make it equivalent to (MSS). Relaxing this constraint to include all symmetric positive semidefinite matrices makes the feasible region convex, and the solution to this problem provides an upper bound to the integer program (MSS).

The *weighted maximal stable set* problem has a similar formulation. In order to favor the inclusion of selected vertices into the stable set. Given weights w_i on the vertices, this problem seeks to maximize

$$\frac{1}{2}\sum_{i=1}^{n}w_i\left(v_i^2 + v_i v_{n+1}\right)$$

subject to the same constraints as (MSS). The problems can also be addressed by using the semidefinite relaxation. In polyhedral relaxations of the maximal stable set problem, utilizing larger cliques is crucial for a tight approximation to the convex hull of the integer program. These cliques can also improve the semidefinite relaxation. Given cliques $C^1, \cdots, C^d$, such that C^k has n_k vertices, stable sets $v \in \{-1, 1\}^n$ must satisfy

$$\left|(n_k - 1)v_{n+1} + \sum_{v_i \in C^k} v_i\right| = 1$$

for $k = 1, \cdots, d$. This formulation has a semidefinite relaxation that more closely approximates the convex hull of the integer program.

The semidefinite relaxation of the graph coloring problem is similar to that of the maximum cut problem. Instead of assigning colors or integers to the vertices of the graph, a unit vector $\bar{v}_i \in \mathbb{R}^n$ is assigned to the each of the n vertices i in V. To capture the property of coloring, the vectors of adjacent vertices should differ in a natural way. From the definition in (15), the vector k-coloring of G is an assignment of unit vectors $\bar{v}_i \in \mathbb{R}^n$ to each vertex i in V such that for any two adjacent vertices i and j, the dot product of the vectors satisfies the inequality $\bar{v}_i^T \bar{v}_j \le -\frac{1}{k-1}$. In other words, the angle between the vectors of adjacent vertices must be sufficiently large. Define the matrix V such that column i is given by $\bar{v}_i$, and let $X = V^T V$. The matrix X is positive semidefinite and satisfies the inequalities $X_{ij} = X_{ij} \le -\frac{1}{k-1}$ for each pair of adjacent edges (i,j). Any matrix is n-colorable, so the graph coloring problem can be posed as

$$\text{Minimize} \quad \text{rank}(X)$$

$$\text{Subject to} \quad X_{ij} + X_{j,i} \le -\frac{2}{n-1} \quad \text{for} \quad (i, j) \in E \quad (COL)$$

$$X_{i,i} = 1 \quad i = 1, \cdots, n$$

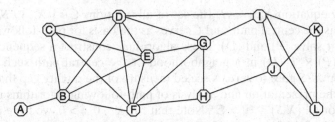

Fig. 4.1. Sample graph with 12 vertices and 23 edges.

A semidefinite relaxation of the graph k-coloring problem can be written by replacing the fraction $\dfrac{-2}{n-1}$ with $\dfrac{-2}{k-1}$. Ignoring the objective function, the problem is now a semidefinite program that seeks to find a feasible point.

Figure 4.1 shows a small graph to illustrate these combinatorial problems. In this graph, $\{A,C,F,H,I,K\}$ and $\{B,D,F,G,J,L\}$ form a maximum cut; $\{B,C,D,E,F\}$ is the maximum clique; $\{A,C,I,H,L\}$ is the maximum stable set; and $\{B,H,I\},\{C,G,J\},\{D,K\},\{E,L\},\{A,F\}$ form an optimal coloring.

4.4. AN INTERIOR-POINT ALGORITHM

The inner product in the space $\mathbb{S}^n$ of symmetric matrices is denoted by $\cdot$, which is defined as $U \cdot V = \Sigma_{i,j=1}^{n} U_{i,j} V_{i,j}$. Given input data $C, A_1, \cdots, A_m \in \mathbb{S}^n$ and scalars $b_1, \cdots b_m$, we state the pair of semidefinite programs

$$(P) \quad \inf \quad C \cdot X \quad \text{subject to} \quad A_i \cdot X = b_i, i = 1, \cdots, m \quad X \succeq 0$$

$$(D) \quad \sup \quad \sum_{i=1}^{m} b_i y_i \quad \text{subject to} \quad \sum_{i=1}^{m} A_i y_i + S = C \quad S \succeq 0$$

In this form, (P) is referred as the *primal* problem whereas (D) is referred to as the *dual* problem. Variables X and (y, S) are called feasible solutions to (P) and (D) if they satisfy the constraints in their respective problems. Interior feasible points are feasible solutions such that $X \succ 0$ and $S \succ 0$. The notation $X \succ 0$ for $X \in \mathbb{S}^n$ means that X is positive definite. The interior feasible sets of (P) and (D) will be denoted by $\mathcal{F}^0(P)$ and $\mathcal{F}^0(D)$, respectively. A well-known duality theorem states that provided there is a strictly interior point to (P) and (D), there exist primal and dual optimal solutions, (X^*, y^*, S^*) and $C \cdot X^* = b^T y^*$.

This discussion also assumes that the A_is are linearly independent, there exists $X \in \mathcal{F}^0(P)$, and $(y, S) \in \mathcal{F}^0(D)$. Optimal solutions X^* and (y^*, S^*) are also characterized by the equivalent conditions that the duality gap $X^* \cdot S^*$ is zero and the product $X^* S^*$ is zero. Moreover, for every $v > 0$, there exists a unique primal-dual feasible solution (X_v, y_v, S_v) that satisfies the perturbed optimality equation $X_v S_v = vI$. The set of all solutions $C \equiv \{(X_v, y_v, S_v): v > 0\}$ is known as the central path, and C serves as the basis for path-following algorithms that solve (P) and (D). These algorithms construct a sequence $\{(X, y, S)\} \subset \mathcal{F}^0(P) \times \mathcal{F}^0(D)$ in a neighborhood of the central path such that the duality gap $X \cdot S$ goes to zero. A scaled measure of the duality gap that proves useful in the presentation and analysis of path-following algorithms is $\mu(X,S) = X \cdot S/n$ for all $(X,S) \in \mathbb{S}^n \times \mathbb{S}^n$. Note that for $X > 0$, $S > 0$, we have $\mu(X,S) > 0$ unless $XS = 0$. Moreover, $\mu(X_v, S_v) = v$ for all points (X_v, y_v, S_v) on the central path.

Several polynomial algorithms can solve a pair of semidefinite programs. Helmberg–Rendl–Vanderbei–Wolkowicz/Kojima–Shida–Hara/Monteiro, Nesterov–Todd (see Monteiro (49) and references cited therein). All these algorithms possess $O(\sqrt{n}\log(1/\varepsilon))$ iteration complexity to yield accuracy ε. This section summarizes the dual-scaling algorithm for solving (P) and (D). For simplicity, the discussion assumes that the matrix variables are a single semidefinite variable, but the extension of the algorithm to direct products of semidefinite matrices is relatively simple.

Let the symbol $\mathcal{A}$ denote the linear map $\mathcal{A}: V \to \mathbb{R}^m$ defined by $(\mathcal{A}X)_i = \langle A_i, X \rangle$; its adjoint $\mathcal{A}: \mathbb{R}^m \to V$ is defined by $\mathcal{A}^*y = \Sigma_{i=1}^m y_i A_i$. The dual-scaling algorithm applies Newton's method to $\mathcal{A}X = b$, $\mathcal{A}^T y + S = C$, and $X = vS^{-1}$ to generate

$$\mathcal{A}(X + \Delta X) = b, \tag{4.1}$$

$$\mathcal{A}^T(\Delta y) + \Delta S = 0, \tag{4.2}$$

$$vS^{-1}\Delta SS^{-1} + \Delta X = vS^{-1} - X \tag{4.3}$$

Equations 4.1–4.3 are referred to as the Newton equations; their Schur complement is

$$v \begin{pmatrix} A_1 \cdot S^{-1}A_1 S^{-1} & \cdots & A_1 \cdot S^{-1}A_m S^{-1} \\ \vdots & \ddots & \vdots \\ A_m \cdot S^{-1}A_1 S^{-1} & \cdots & A_m \cdot S^{-1}A_m S^{-1} \end{pmatrix} \Delta y = b - v\mathcal{A}S^{-1} \tag{4.4}$$

The matrix on the left-hand side of this linear system is positive definite when $S > 0$. In this chapter, it will sometimes be referred to as M. DSDP computes $\Delta'y := M^{-1}b$ and $\Delta''y := M^{-1}\mathcal{A}S^{-1}$. For any v,

$$\Delta y := \frac{1}{v}\Delta'y - \Delta''y$$

solves Eq. 4.4.

By using Eqs. 4.2 and 4.3, and Δy, we get

$$X(v) := v(S^{-1} + S^{-1}(\mathcal{A}^T \Delta y)S^{-1})$$

which satisfies $\mathcal{A}X(v) = b$. Notice that $X(v) > 0$ if and only if

$$C - \mathcal{A}^T(y - \Delta y) > 0$$

If $X(v) > 0$, a new upper bound

$$\overline{z} := C \cdot X(v) = b^T y + X(v) \cdot S = b^T y + v(\Delta y^T \mathcal{A} S^{-1} + n)$$

can be obtained without explicitly computing $X(v)$. The dual-scaling algorithm does not require $X(v)$ to compute the step direction defined by Eq. 4.4; indeed, the solvers will not compute $X(v)$ unless specifically requested. This feature characterizes the algorithm and its performance.

For $\rho > n + \sqrt{n}$, either (y, S) or X reduces the dual potential function

$$\psi(y) := \rho \log(\overline{z} - b^T y) - \ln \det S$$

enough at each iteration to achieve linear convergence. More details about the algorithm and its implementation can be found in (17).

1. Choose an upper bound $\overline{z}$ and y such that $S \leftarrow C - \mathcal{A}^T y > 0$.
2. **for** $k \leftarrow 0, \cdots, convergence$ **do**
3.   Select v.
4.   Compute M and $\mathcal{A}S^{-1}$.
5.   Solve $M\Delta'y = b$, $M\Delta''y = \mathcal{A}S^{-1}$.
6.   **if** $C - \mathcal{A}^T(y - \Delta y) > 0$ **then**
7. $\overline{z} \leftarrow b^T y + v(\Delta y^T \mathcal{A}S^{-1} + n)$.
8. $\overline{y} \leftarrow y$, $\overline{\Delta y} \leftarrow \Delta y$, $\overline{\mu} \leftarrow v$.
9.   **end if**
10.   Find α_d to reduce ψ, and set $y \leftarrow y + \alpha_d \Delta y$, $S \leftarrow C - \mathcal{A}^T y$.
11. **end for**
12. Optional: Compute X using $\overline{y}$, $\overline{\Delta y}$, $\overline{\mu}$.

4.5. PARALLEL COMPUTING

Even relatively small graphs can lead to large SDP that are difficult to solve. The dense matrix M contains a row and column for each constraint. Although interior-point methods for semidefinite programming are computationally intensive, the high-memory requirements are usually the bottleneck that restrict the size of problems that can be solved. A graph with n vertices, for example, has a MAX-CUT relaxation such that the matrix M has n rows and columns. For the Lovász problem, the solver constructs M with dimension of $|\overline{E}| + 1$, where $|\overline{E}|$ is the number of edges in the complement of the graph, and for the MSS problem, $M \in \mathbb{S}^{|E|+n}$. Graphs with only few hundred vertices can easily contain thousands of edges. A dense matrix with 10,000 rows and columns requires about 800 MB RAM, which can easily exhaust the resources of most serial architectures. The total memory requirements of the solver may be much greater.

The most computationally expensive tasks in each iteration of the dual-scaling algorithm are usually the construction of the linear system (Eq. 4.4) and the factorization of M. As documented in (50), the worst-case computational complexity of computing M is $O(m^2n^2 + mn^3)$, and factoring it is $O(m^3)$. Sparsity in the data can reduce the cost of the former task, but its complexity remains much greater than interior-point iterations for linear or second-order cone programming.

In order to reduce the time needed to solve these applications and to satisfy the memory requirements of interior-point methods, parallel implementations distribute Eq. 4.4 over multiple processors and compute on it in parallel. Either shared-memory or distributed-memory paradigms can be used. Borchers (51) used Open MP directives and shared-memory implementations of BLAS and LAPACK to parallelize his primal-dual interior-point solver. Computational studies with 16 processors showed overall parallel efficiency on large problems between 20 and 100%. The interior-point solvers of Yamashita *et al.* (33) and PDSDP (32) assumed a distributed-memory paradigm and used MPI to pass messages between processors. Both solvers used the parallel Cholesky factorization in ScaLAPACK (29). All these solvers gave each processor local access to the data A_i and C. Furthermore, all three solvers explicitly assigned to each processor a mutually exclusive set of rows in M. As illustrated in Fig. 4.2, the solvers explicitly manage parallelism in M and have local access to the data matrices. In the distributed-memory solvers, each processor also has a local copy of the matrices X and S.

The DSDP (17) software package served as the basis for a parallel implementation of the dual-scaling algorithm. Since each element of M has the form

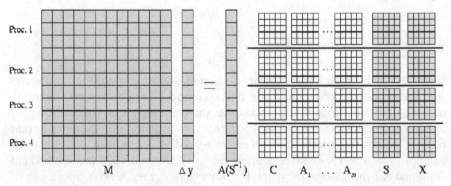

Fig. 4.2. Distribution of data structures and computations over multiple processors.

$M_{i,j} = A_i \cdot (S^{-1} A_j S^{-1})$, each element in row (or column) j requires computing the matrix $S^{-1} A_j S^{-1}$. The cost of this product usually exceeds the cost of its inner product with the data matrices A_i. In order to reduce duplication of work, it is efficient for one processor to compute all elements of Eq. 4.4 in the same row. Inserting a row of elements into a parallel matrix structure may require sending some elements to other processors. The overhead of the message, however, is small compared to the upper limit of $O(n^3 + n^2 m)$ floating-point operations (flops) to compute the elements of the row. Although an interior-point iteration for semidefinite programming is more computationally intensive that a similar iteration for linear or second-order conic programming, the additional complexity allows for better parallel scalability because the ratio of floating-point operations to interprocessor messages is relatively high.

Load balancing among processors is trivial for most combinatorial applications. Since the data constraints in (MC) all have a single nonzero, the rows of M should be divided as evenly as possible over the processors. For (MSS) and (COL), there are two types of constraint matrices; in these examples, the rows corresponding to each type constraints are divided as evenly as possible. Only in (LOV) is there one constraint, trace $(X) = 1$, whose structure is significantly different from the others. In this case, the identity matrix has more nonzeros and higher rank than do the other constraint matrices.

After factoring M and solving Eq. 4.4, PDSDP broadcasts the step direction Δy from a parallel vector structure to a serial vector structure on each processor. The serial vector structure contains all elements in Δy, and PDSDP uses it to calculate a suitable step-length, update the dual matrix S, factor it, and compute an appropriate barrier parameter v for the next iteration.

Most analysis of the scalability of interior-point algorithms for semidefinite programming has concerned three mutually exclusive parts of the algorithms: computing the elements of the Newton equations (Elements), factoring the Schur complement matrix (Factor), and other operations that consist primarily of computing X and factoring S (S). Using a Lovász problem for a graph with 100 vertices and 990 edges as an example, Figure 4.3 shows the relative amount of time spent in each part of the algorithm for five groups of processors. Normalizing times such that one processor required one unit of time to solve the problem, Figure 4.3a shows the time spent in each part of the algorithm for each group of processors. Figure 4.3b shows these times of the three parts as a percentage of the entire solution time. In this case, a single processor spent about 12% of its time computing M and 75% of the time factoring it. Using sixteen processors, about 8% of the time was spent computing the matrix and 50% of the time was spent factoring it. The remaining operations are mostly serial, so those times did not change significantly as the number of processors increased. On a single processor these operations amounted to about 10% of the time, and on sixteen processors they amounted to about 40% of the time.

A set of computational tests shown in Table 4.1 measure the overall parallel scalability and efficiency of the solver on three instances of the semidefi-

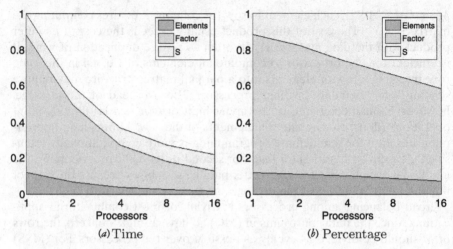

Fig. 4.3. Parallel scalability of computing M, factoring it, and other operations.

TABLE 4.1. Scalability of PDSDP on Semidefinite Relaxations

Name	$|V|$	$|E|$	n	m	Processors and Seconds				
					1	2	4	8	16
MC-1	1,000	5,909	1,000	1,000	46	30	16	11	8
MC-2	5,000	14,997	5,000	5,000	6,977	4,108	2,592	2,274	1,460
MC-3	7,000	17,148	7,000	7,000	16,030	10,590	6,392	4,721	3,928
LOV-1	100	2,970	100	1,981	43	23	13	8	4
LOV-2	150	3,352	150	7,824	3,394	1,747	995	535	271
LOV-3	150	7,822	150	3,354	196	104	49	34	17
MSS-1	100	2,970	100	2,081	261	141	75	55	31
MSS-2	150	3,352	150	7,974	22,628	11,630	6,616	3,916	1,781
MSS-3	150	7,822	150	3,504	1,671	875	494	307	159
COL-1	100	2,970	100	3,070	518	276	124	99	49
COL-2	150	3,352	150	3,502	770	407	186	157	72
COL-3	150	7,822	150	7,972	9,445	4,866	2,796	1,875	875

nite relaxations of (MC), (LOV), (MSS), and (COL). The graphs were chosen
such that the SDP's could be solved on on single a single processor with 1 GB
RAM and still scale well to additional processors. For the larger instances of
(LOV), (MSS), and (COL), the overall parallel efficiency on sixteen processors was ~80%. The time spent factoring M dominated the overall solution
time, and the scalability of ScaLAPACK heavily influenced the scalability of
the entire solver. The overall efficiency on the maximum-cut relaxation was
less because the semidefinite blocks have dimension $n = m$, and the factoriza-

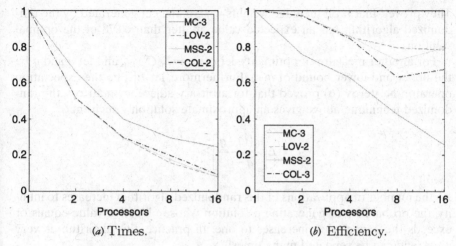

(*a*) Times.   (*b*) Efficiency.

Fig. 4.4. Overall time and parallel efficiency on four SDP.

tion of S in serial uses a significant percentage of the solution time. Figure 4.4 shows the overall scalability of PDSDP on four instances of semidefinite programs.

Distributing M across processors allows larger problems to be solved, but even this technique may not be sufficient for problems with hundreds of thousands of constraints. One idea has been to use the conjugate gradient method to solve linear Eq. 4.4. Since iterative linear solvers require only the product of the matrix with a vector, the entire matrix M does not have to be stored. Choi and Ye have used this approach on maximum cut problems (52) and Toh and Kojima (53) have explored similar ideas for primal-dual methods in conjunction with a reduced space preconditioner. Another approach for extraordinarily large problems is to use methods such as low-rank factorizations or the parallel bundle method (35).

4.6. FEASIBLE SOLUTIONS

In their randomized algorithm, Goemans and Williamson defined $V \in \mathbb{R}^{n \times n}$ such that $X = VV^T$ and selected a vector $u \in \mathbb{R}^n$ from a uniform distribution of unit vectors. Then they let

$$\hat{v} = Vu$$

and defined

$$v_i = sign(\hat{v}_i), \quad i = 1, \cdots, n$$

They proved that if all the edge weights $w_{i,j} \geq 0$, the cut generated by the randomized algorithm has an expected value greater than 0.878 of the optimal solution.

For another measure of optimality, let $q(v) := \Sigma_{i,j} C_{i,j} v_i v_j$, and let $\bar{q}$ and $\underline{q}$ be the upper and lower bound of $q(v)$. Furthermore, let $E[\cdot]$ be the expectation operator. Nesterov (6) proved that for arbitrary adjacency matrices, the randomized technique above gives an approximate solution v such that

$$E\left[\frac{q(v) - \underline{q}}{\bar{q} - \underline{q}}\right] \geq \frac{4}{7}$$

As the number of applications of this randomized algorithm increases to infinity, the probability of generating a solution whose objective value equals or exceeds the expectation increases to one. In practice, this algorithm is very quick and can be repeated many times.

For eight different graphs, we computed the semidefinite relaxation and applied the randomized approximation procedure. For each graph, Table 4.2 shows the objective value of the semidefinite relaxation and best cut, the number of processors used to solve the problem, and the times needed to solve the SDP and apply the randomized algorithm. The processors applied the randomized procedure concurrently until the procedure had been applied 1000 times. Graphs named with an "a" have edge weights of 1 and graphs named with a "b" have edge weights of ±1 in roughly equal proportion. As Table 4.2 shows, the quality of the cuts is high, especially when the edges have positive weights.

A randomized algorithm for stable sets (54) begins in a similar way: given a solution X^* to (MSS), find a $V \in \mathbb{R}^{(n+1) \times (n+1)}$ such that $X^* = V^T V$, select a unit vector $u \in \mathbb{R}^{n+1}$ from the unit sphere, and let $v = sign(V^T u)$. For each $(i,j) \in E$, if $|v_i + v_j + v_{n+1}| \neq 1$, change the sign of either v_i or v_j. The stable set will be the set of vertices with the same sign as v_n. For arbitrary graphs, the constraints

TABLE 4.2. Approximate Maximum Cuts from the Semidefinite Relaxation

Name	n	Objective Values			|P|	Seconds	
		SDP	Rand	Ratio		SDP	Rand
MC1a	1,000	29,428.5	28,158	0.957	4	66	11
MC1b	1,000	4,737.8	3,419	0.722	4	70	11
MC3a	3,000	30,226.9	28,008	0.927	4	1,590	55
MC3b	3,000	7,798.9	5,459	0.700	4	1,396	55
MC5a	5,000	43,081.4	39,390	0.914	4	6,268	152
MC5b	5,000	11,788.5	8,195	0.695	4	6,149	152
MC7a	7,000	150,646.2	141,547	0.940	4	24,089	527
MC7b	7,000	28,178.5	19,010	0.675	4	25,774	533

corresponding to the edges of the graph will be satisfied with a frequency >91% (55).

From the relaxation of the graph coloring problem, a solution X^* with rank less than or equal to k identifies a legal k-coloring. More generally, Karger *et al.* (15) propose a randomized algorithm that produces a k-semicoloring, an assignment of colors with relatively few adjacent vertices with the same color. We use a heuristic procedure for to obtain a legal coloring, albeit with more than k colors if necessary. For $k = 1, \cdots, n$, do the following: first let U^k be the uncolored vertices. If U^k is empty, terminate the algorithm. Sort the vertices of U^k in decreasing order of degree in $G[U^k]$, the graph induced by the uncolored vertices, and let i be the vertex with highest degree. Then build a vertex set W^k by examining vertices $j \in U^k$ in the decreasing order of X_{ij}. Add j to W^k if it is not adjacent to any of the vertices in W^k. Finally, assign the vertices in W^k color k. This algorithm is an extension of the popular algorithm proposed by Powell and Toint (56) to semidefinite programming.

The second set of tests computed the Lovász number and semidefinite relaxations of the minimum color relaxation for nine randomly generated unweighted graphs. The semidefinite relaxation of the maximum stable set problems on the complement of these graphs was also computed. The larger graphs created SDPs that were too large for a single processor. From the relaxations, feasible solutions were found by using the heuristic methods mentioned above. Like the randomized algorithm for the MAX-CUT relaxation, the processors applied the algorithm concurrently. Table 4.3 shows the results; recall that the clique size is the size of the stable set on the complement graph. In many of these problems, the bound provided by the semidefinite relaxation was significantly better than the bound provide the feasible solutions of the other combinatorial problem.

The use of cutting planes and lift-and-project methods can strengthen the semidefinite relaxations and generate optimal solutions. Yilderim (57) offers

TABLE 4.3. Approximate Maximum-Clique and Minimum Coloring from Semidefinite Relaxations

Name	Graphy			Objective Values			
	$|V|$	$|E|$	$|\bar{E}|$	Clique	$\vartheta(G)$	Color	$|P|$
G1	100	1,980	2,970	9	13.1	22	16
G2	100	990	3,960	17	22.1	32	16
G3	150	7,823	3,352	4	7.75	17	16
G4	150	5,588	5,587	6	12.6	26	16
G5	150	3,353	7,822	11	20.5	36	16
G6	200	5,970	13,930	5	8.8	21	32
G7	200	9,950	9,950	7	14.5	31	32
G8	200	13,930	5,970	13	23.9	46	32
G9	300	17,940	26,910	7	13.7	35	40

techniques specific to the stable set problem and and Anjos (58) applies lifting procedures for the semidefinite relaxations of the maximum-cut problem. More generally, the construction of Lasserre (59,60) and Henrion (61) uses a sequence of moment matrices and nonnegative polynomials. The work of Laurent and Rendl (16) summarizes many of these techniques.

4.7. CONCLUSIONS

Semidefinite programming provides tractable bounds and approximate solutions for several hard combinatorial optimization problems. Robust solvers have been developed that target these semidefinite programs, and some of these solvers have been implemented for parallel architectures. For interior-point methods, computing and solving the Newton equations in parallel increases the size of problems that we can solve and reduces the time needed to compute these solutions. Numerical results show that on problems of sufficient size and structure, interior-point methods exhibits good scalability on parallel architectures. The parallel version of DSDP was written to demonstrate the scalability of interior-point methods for semidefinite programming and provide computational scientists with a robust, efficient, and well-documented solver for their applications. The software is freely available from the Mathematics and Computer Science Division at Argonne National Laboratory, and we encourage its use with the terms of the license.

ACKNOWLEDGMENTS

This work was supported by the Mathematical, Information, and Computational Sciences Division subprogram of the Office of Advanced Scientific Computing Research, Office of Science, U.S. Department of Energy, under Contract W-31-109-ENG-38.

We gratefully acknowledge the use of "Jazz", a Linux cluster located at Argonne's Laboratory Computing Resource Center.

REFERENCES

1. M. Grötschel, L. Lovász, and A. Schrijver. *Geometric Algorithms and Combinatorial Opt.* Springer-Verlag, Berlin, 1988.
2. F. Alizadeh. Interior-point methods in semidefinite programming with application to combinatorial optimization. *SIAM J. Opt.*, **5**(1):13–51 (1995).
3. S. Polijak, F. Rendl, and H. Wolkowicz. A recipe for semidefinite relaxation for 0-1 quadratic programming. *J. Global Opt.*, **7**:51–73 (1995).
4. L. Lovász. On the shannon capacity of a graph. *IEEE Trans. Inf. Theory*, **25**:1–7 (1979).

5. M.X. Goemans and D.P. Williamson. Improved approximation algorithms for maximum cut and satisfiability problems using semidefinite programming. *J. ACM*, **42**:1115–1145 (1995).

6. Yu.E. Nesterov. Semidefinite relaxation and nonconvex quadratic optimization. *Opt. Methods Software*, **9**:141–160 (1998).

7. A. Frieze and M. Jerrum. Improved approximation algorithms for max *k*-cut and max bisection. *Algorithmica*, **18**:61–77 (1997).

8. E. de Klerk, D.V. Pasechnik, and J.P. Warners. Approximate graph colouring and max-k-cut algorithms based on the theta function. *J. Combinatorial Opt.*, **8**(3):267–294 (Sept. 2004).

9. M.M. Halldórsson. A still better performance guarantee for approximate graph coloring. *Inf. Proc. Lett.*, **45**:19–23 (1993).

10. Q. Zhao, S. Karisch, F. Rendl, and H. Wolkowicz. Semidefinite programming relaxations for the quadratic assignment problems. *J. Combinatorial Opt.*, **2**(1):95–27 (1998).

11. M.F. Anjos. An improved semidefinite programming relaxation for the satisfiability problem. *Math. Prog.*, **102**(3):589–608 (2005).

12. M.F. Anjos. An improved semidefinite programming relaxation for the satisfiability problem. *Math. Prog.*, **102**(3):589–608 (2005).

13. H. van Maaren and L. van Norden. Sums of squares, satisfiability and maximum satisfiability. Fahiem Bacchus and T. Walsh, eds., *Theory and Applications of Satisfiability Testing*, Vol. 3569, Springer Lecture Notes in Computer Science, 2005, pp. 293–307.

14. E. de Klerk and H. van Maaren. On semidefinite programming relaxations of (2+p)-SAT. *Ann. Math. Art. Intelligence*, **37**:285–305 (2003).

15. D. Karger, R. Motwani, and M. Sudan. Approximate graph coloring by semidefinite programming. *J. ACM*, P 246 (1998).

16. M. Laurent and F. Rendl. Semidefinite programming and integer programming. In K. Aardal, G. Nemhauser, and R. Weismante, eds., *Handbook on Discrete Optimization*, Vol. 12 of *Handbooks in Operations Research and Management Science*. Elsevier, Amsterdam, 2005.

17. S.J. Benson and Y. Ye. DSDP5: Software for semidefinite programming. Technical Report ANL/MCS-P1289-0905, Mathematics and Computer Science Division, Argonne National Laboratory, September 2005. Submitted to ACM Transactions of Mathematical Software.

18. B. Borchers. CSDP 2.3 user's guide. *Opt. Methods Software*, **11/12**(1–4):597–611 (1999).

19. J.F. Sturm. Using SeDuMi 1.02, a MATLAB toolbox for optimization over symmetric cones. *Opt. Methods Software*, **11/12**(1–4):625–653 (1999).

20. M. Yamashita, K. Fujisawa, and M. Kojima. Implementation and evaluation of SDPA 6.0 (semidefinite programming algorithm 6.0). *Opt. Methods Software*, **18**:491–505 (2003).

21. K.C. Toh, M.J. Todd, and R.H. Tutuncu. SDPT3—A Matlab software package for semidefinite programming, version 2.1. *Opt. Methods Software*, **11**:545–581 (1999).

22. M. Kočvara and M. Stingl. PENNON—a code for convex nonlinear and semidefinite programming. *Opt. Methods Software*, **18**(3):317–333 (2003).

23. S. Burer and R.D.C. Monteiro. A nonlinear programming algorithm for solving semidefinite programs via low-rank factorization. *Math. Prog. (Ser. B)*, **95**(2): 329–357 (2003).

24. C. Helmberg and F. Rendl. A spectral bundle method for semidefinite programming. *SIAM J. Opt.*, **10**(3):673–696 (2000).

25. M.J. Todd. *Semidefinite Optimization*, Vol. 10, Cambridge University Press, Cambridge, 2001, pp. 515–560.

26. H. Wolkowicz, R. Saigal, and L. Vandenberghe, eds. *Handbook of Semidefinite Programming*, Vol. 27 of *International Series in Operations Research and Management Science*. Kluwer Academic Publishers, Boston, 2000.

27. W. Gropp, E. Lusk, and A. Skjellum. *Using MPI: Portable Parallel Prog. with the Message-Passing Interface*. The MIT Press, Cambridge, MA, 1997.

28. S. Balay *et al.* PETSc 2.0 users manual. Technical Report ANL-95/11—Revision 2.3.0, Argonne National Laboratory (2005). Available at http://www.mcs.anl.gov/petsc.

29. L.S. Blackford *et al. ScaLAPACK: Users' Guide.* SIAM (1997).

30. S.J. Benson, L.C. McInnes, and J.J. Moré. A case study in the performance and sca lability of optimization algorithms. *ACM Trans. Math. Software*, **27**(3):361–376 (Sept. 2001).

31. M.A. Heroux. An overview of the Trilinos project. *ACM Trans. Math. Software*, **31**(3):397–423 (Sept. 2005).

32. S.J. Benson. Parallel computing on semidefinite programs. Technical Report ANL/MCS-P939-0302, Mathematics and Computer Science Division, Argonne National Laboratory, March 2003.

33. M. Yamashita, K. Fujisawa, and M. Kojima. SDPARA: Semidefinite programming algorithm parallel version. *Parallel Comput.*, **29**:1053–1067 (2003).

34. K. Nakata, M. Yamashita, K. Fujisawa, and M. Kojima. A parallel primal-dual interior-point method for semidefinite programs using positive definite matrix completion. Technical Report Research Report B-398, Dept. Math. & Comp. Sciences, Tokyo Institute of Technology, November 2003. *Parallel Computing*, **32**:24–43 (2006).

35. Y. Tymofyeyev. A parallel bundle method for large-scale semidefinite programming. Master's thesis, Department of Mathematics & Statistics, University of Maryland, Baltimore County, 2002.

36. S.J. Benson, Y. Ye, and X. Zhang. Mixed linear and semidefinite programming for combinatorial and quadratic optimization. *Opt. Methods Software*, **11**:515–544 (1999).

37. E. Balas and C. Sung Yu. Finding a maximum clique in an arbitrary graph. *SIAM J. Comput.*, **15**(4):1054–1068 (Nov. 1986).

38. P. Briggs, K. Cooper, K. Kennedy, and L. Torczon. Coloring heuristics for register allocation. *ACM Conference on Program Language Design and Implementation*, The Association for Computing Machinery, Portland, Oregon, 1989, pp. 275–284.

39. G.J. Chaitin. Register allocation and spilling via graph coloring. *SIGPLAN Notices (Proceedings of the SIGPLAN '82 Symposium on Compiler Construction, Boston, Mass.)*, **17**(6):98–101 (June 1982).

40. G.J. Chaitin *et al.* Register allocation via coloring. *Comput. Lang.*, **6**:47–57 (1981).

41. C. Berge. *Graphs and Hypergraphs.* North-Holland, Amsterdam, The Netherlands, 1973.

42. D. de Werra. An introduction to timetabling. *Eur. J. Operat. Res.*, **19**:151–162 (1985).

43. D.C. Wood. A technique for coloring a graph applicable to large scale time-tabling problems. *Comput. J.*, **3**:317–319 (1969).

44. A. Gamst. Some lower bounds for a class of frequency assignment problems. *IEEE Trans. Vehicular Technol.*, **35**(1):8–14 (1986).

45. M.R. Garey and D.S. Johnson. *Computers and Intractability: A Guide to the Theory of NP–Completeness.* W.H Freeman, San Francisco, CA, 1979.

46. C. Mannino and A. Sassano. An exact algorithm for the maximum cardinality stable set problem. *Comput. Opt. App.*, **3**(4):243–258 (1994).

47. I. Bomze, M. Budinich, P. Pardalos, and M. Pelillo. The maximum clique problem. In D.-Z. Du and P.M. Pardalos, eds., *Handbook of Combinatorial Optimization*, Vol. 4. Kluwer Academic Publishers, Boston, MA, 1999.

48. J. Kleinberg and M.X. Goemans. The Lováasz theta function and a semidefinite programming relaxation of vertex cover. *SIAM J. Discrete Math.*, **11**(2):196–204 (May 1998).

49. R.D.C. Monteiro. First- and second-order methods for semidefinite programming. *Math. Prog.*, **B97**:209–244 (2003).

50. S.J. Benson, Y. Ye, and X. Zhang. Solving large-scale sparse semidefinite programs for combinatorial optimization. *SIAM J. Opt.*, **10**(2):443–461 (2000).

51. B. Borchers and J. Young. Implementation of a primal-dual method for SDP on a parallel architecture, September 2005. Research Report available at http://info-host.nmt.edu/~borchers/csdp.html

52. C. Choi and Y. Ye. Solving sparse semidefinite programs using the dualscaling algorithm with an iterative solver. Working Paper, Department of Management Science, The University of Iowa, Iowa City, IA, 2000.

53. K.-C. Toh and M. Kojima. Solving some large scale semidefinite programs via the conjugate residual method. *SIAM J. Opt.*, **12**(3):669–691 (2002).

54. S.J. Benson and Y. Ye. Approximating maximum stable set and minimum graph coloring problems with the positive semidefinite relaxation. *Applications and Algorithms of Complementarity*, Vol. 50 of *Applied Optimization*, Kluwer Academic Publishers, Boston, 2000, pp. 1–18.

55. D. Bertsimas and Y. Ye. Semidefinite relaxations, multivariate normal distributions, and order statistics. In D.Z. Du and P.M. Pardalos, eds., *Handbook of Combinatorial Opt.*, Vol. 3, Kluwer Academic Publishers, Boston, MA, 1998, pp. 1–19.

56. M.J.D. Powell and P.L. Toint. On the estimation of sparse Hessian matrices. *SIAM J. Numerical Anal.*, **16**:1060–1074 (1979).

57. E.A. Yildirim and X. Fan. On extracting maximum stable sets in perfect graphs using lovasz's theta function. *Comput. Opt. Appl.*, **32**:1–30 (2005).

58. M.F. Anjos and H. Wolkowicz. Strengthened semidefinite relaxations via a second lifting for the max-cut problem. *Discrete App. Math.*, **119**(1–2):79–106 (2002).

59. J.B. Lasserre. An explicit equivalent positive semidefinite program for nonliner 0-1 programs. *SIAM J. Opt.*, **12**:756–769 (2002).

60. J.B. Lasserre. SDP versus LP relaxations for polynomial programming. *Novel Approaches to Hard Discrete Optimization*, Fields Institute Communications. American Mathematical Society, 2003. Waterloo, Canada. Fields Institute Communications, Vol. 37 pp. 143–154.

61. D. Henrion and J.B. Lasserre. GloptiPoly: Global optimization over polynomials with Matlab and SeDuMi. *ACM Trans. Math. Software*, **29**(2):165–194 (June 2003).

▪▪▪▪ CHAPTER 5

Parallel Resolution of the Satisfiability Problem: A Survey

DANIEL SINGER

LITA—EA 3097
Université Paul Verlaine de Metz, Faculté des Sciences
Île du Saulcy
57 045 Metz cedex, FRANCE

5.1. INTRODUCTION

The propositional Satisfiability problem (SAT) is one of the most studied in computer science since it was the first problem proven to be NP-complete by Cook in 1971. Nowadays, the Satisfiability problem evidences great practical importance in a wide range of disciplines, including hardware verification, artificial intelligence, computer vision and others. Indeed, one survey of Satisfiability in 1996 (1) contains >200 references of applications. SAT is especially important in the area of Electronic Design Automation (EDA) with a variety of problems, such as circuit design, FPGA routing, combinatorial equivalence checking, and automatic test and pattern generation.

In spite of its computational complexity, there is increasing demand for high-performance SAT-solving algorithms in industry Unfortunately, most modern solvers are sequential and fewer are parallel. Our intention is to review the work on parallel resolution of SAT with DPLL solvers for this last decade from the previous survey article (2).

The remainder of this chapter is organized as follows. Section 5.2 briefly introduces the SAT problem and major concepts of the field. Section 5.3 gives an overview of the main techniques used in the efficient implementation of state-of-the-art sequential DPLL solvers. Section 5.4 describes the different proposed methods to parallelize the core sequential algorithm. Section 5.5 presents some of our experimentations in parallel resolution of SAT, which is followed by a brief concluding section.

Parallel Combinatorial Optimization, edited by El-Ghazali Talbi
Copyright © 2006 by John Wiley & Sons, Inc.

5.2. PRELIMINARIES

Let $V = \{v_1, v_1, \cdots, v_n\}$ be a set of n Boolean variables. A (partial) truth assignment τ for V is a (partial) function: $V \rightarrow \{True, False\}$. Corresponding to each variable v are two literals: v and $\neg v$ called positive and negative literals. A clause C is a set of literals interpreted as a disjunction, ■ denotes the empty clause and unit clauses have a single literal. A formula F is a set of clauses interpreted as a Conjunctive Normal Form (CNF) of a formula of the propositional calculus. A truth assignment τ satisfies a formula F (τ is *a solution*) *iff* it satisfies every clause in F, and the empty formula $\varnothing$ is always satisfied. A truth assignment τ satisfies a clause C *iff* it satisfies at least one literal in C and the empty clause ■ is never satisfied.

Definition 5.2.1. The Satisfiability Problem (SAT):

Input: A set of Boolean variables V and a set of clauses C over V.

Output: Yes (gives a satisfying truth assignment τ for C if it exists) or No.

The restriction of SAT to instances where all clauses have at most k literals is denoted k-SAT. Of special interest are 2-SAT and 3-SAT; while 2-SAT is linearly solvable 3-SAT is NP-complete. The Max-SAT problem is the optimization variant problem of SAT to find a truth assignment τ that maximizes the number of satisfied clauses of C. Nevertheless, the Max-2-SAT problem is well known to be NP-hard (3).

5.2.1. Complete–Incomplete Algorithms

Current research on propositional satisfiability is focused on two classes of solving methods: complete algorithms mostly based on *Backtrack search* and incomplete ones represented by variations of *Local search* methods. Complete algorithms are guaranteed to find a satisfiable truth assignment (a solution) if the problem is satisfiable, or to terminate with the proof of the problem unsatisfiability. Incomplete algorithms, on the other hand, cannot prove the unsatisfiability of instance even though they may be able to find a solution for certain kinds of satisfiable instances very quickly.

Moreover, SAT (or Max-SAT) can be formulated as a particular Integer Linear Program such that classical Operation Research methods can be applied including Linear Programming by relaxing the integrality constraints. For example, this has been the case with linear or nonlinear cutting planes, Lagrangian or Semidefinite techniques. Incomplete methods are based on efficient heuristics that help to delay the combinatorial explosion when the size of problem increases. This category includes Simulated Annealing, Genetic Algorithms and Local Search methods. The most popular ones are GSAT (4) or WSAT (5) with a number of parallel implementations and studies (6,7). This survey will not present the work on the parallel resolution of SAT with incomplete algorithms and we refer to (2) for this approach.

Most of the more successful complete SAT solvers are instantiations of the Davis Putnam Logemann Loveland procedure (8) traditionally abbreviated as

procedure DPLL $(\mathcal{F})$
Begin
  If $\mathcal{F} = \emptyset$ then return "satisfiable"
    Else $\mathcal{F} \leftarrow$ UnitPropagation$(\mathcal{F})$;
  If $\blacksquare \in \mathcal{F}$ then return "unsatisfiable"
    Else /* Branching Rule*/
    Choose l a literal with some heuristic;
    If DPLL$(\mathcal{F} \cup \{l\})=$ satisfiable then
      return "satisfiable"
    Else DPLL$(\mathcal{F} \cup \{\neg\,l\})$
End

function UnitPropagation $(\mathcal{F})$
Begin
  While $\blacksquare \notin \mathcal{F}$ and $\exists$ unit clause $l \in \mathcal{F}$
    Satisfy(l) ; Simplify$(\mathcal{F})$;
  return$(\mathcal{F})$
End

Fig. 5.1. DPLL procedure.

DPLL (see Fig. 5.1). Other complete methods include (general) Resolution or Davis Putnam (DP) algorithms for theoretical aspects of SAT or Automatic Reasoning, Ordered Binary Decision Diagrams (OBDD) based solvers and Stälmark's methods in EDA applications. Nowadays, DPLL variants work quite well in practice and are the most widely used SAT solvers.

We may also mention a number of works on the hybridation of incomplete and complete algorithms to solve Boolean Optimization problems, Branch-and-Bound or Tabou with DPLL or DP, for example. This survey reports only these DPLL based complete methods for SAT resolution.

5.2.2. SAT-CSP

There is continuing interest in translations betwen CSP (Constraint Satisfaction Problems) and SAT (9–11). For example, (9) proposes to translate a SAT problem (F) into a binary CSP (P) as follows: to each clause C_i of F is associated a variable X_i with domain the set of literals of C_i. A constraint is defined between any pair of variables (X_i, X_j) if the clause C_i contains a literal and the clause C_j contains its complement. For each constraint (X_i, X_j) a relation R_{ij} is defined as the Cartesian product $D_i \mathrm{x} D_j$ minus the tuples (t_i, t_j) such that t_i is the complement of t_j . In this approach SAT is reduced to the Path Consistency of the CSP. Moreover it suggests to apply the *Tree Clustering Decomposition* technique for solving the particular CSP associated to 3-SAT instances, but we do not know the results. Many other translations are possible that consider the different graph structures of SAT. We mention this aspect because much more work has been done in the parallel resolution of CSP than SAT (e.g., 12, 13), but surprisingly, to our knowledge no work takes this trail.

5.2.3. Decomposition Techniques

Decomposition methods have been applied in a variety of problems, such as CSP, especially for parallel resolution in (14), but few work exist in this direction for SAT. References (15, 16) propose to solve SAT using a decomposition based on some approximation of the most constrained subproblems (those with the least number of solutions) by the c/v ratio parameter.[1] One approach decomposes a formula into a tree of partitions (i.e., subformulas) using an algorithm to find *Minimum Vertex Separators*. Then a DPLL algorithm runs with a branching heuristic based on this decompostion solving first the most constrained subformulas. At last, it performs a compilation procedure for each of the partitions and *joins* the results to answer the initial SAT problem. Another approach uses a *0–1 fractional programming optimization* algorithm to find the most constrained subformula. Then a *static* or a *dynamic* use of this algorithm may be applied by a DPLL solver. Unfortunately, we are not aware of any experimental results of these two propositions even in the sequential framework. Reference (17) studies the applicability of *Tree Decomposition* method to SAT but only in the sequential framework. Tree decomposition is a graph theoretic concept which captures the topological structure of the CNF formula represented as a hypergraph. Formulas that have bounded *Treewidth* can be checked for satisfiability in linear time by translating them into Decomposable Negation Normal Form (DNNF) (18). Reference (17) considers the integration of this decomposition method to modern DPLL solvers to achieve better performance in terms of number of decisions (branching steps). The decomposition procedure not only guides the *variable ordering* process, but also the construction of conflict clauses with guaranted bounded size (see Section 5.3.3). The reported results show consistent improvements (in terms of number of decisions) compared to traditional solver (zChaff) on benchmark problems with varying treewidth, especially with a static variable ordering approach. It is noticeable that it does not respond as well in terms of runtime because of an unoptimized implementation and overhead of the tree decomposer.

5.2.4. Experimentation: Finding Hard Problems

Empirical evaluation of SAT solvers on benchmark problems has been of particular interest for both fundamental algorithms and theoretical understanding of SAT (19). Web sites (20,21) are Satisfiability libraries that collect a number of benchmark problems, solvers and tools to provide a uniform testbed for solvers. SAT seems to have less structure than many other combinatorial problems and, in spite of impressive engineering successes on many difficult problems, there are many *easy* problems with which SAT solvers struggle. These include problems involving parity, the well known "pigeonhole problem", and problems naturally described by first-order formulas. In all of these cases, the underlying structure of the problem is lost with the poor SAT encoding (see Section 5.3.4). An anual SAT competition is held as a joint event with the SAT conference to identify new challenging benchmarks and to promote new SAT solvers. Each edition meets a great number of solvers on randomly generated or industrial benchmarks. The 2004 edition (22) pointed out the superiority of incomplete solvers on satisfiable random benchmarks

---

[1]c = number of clauses and v = number of variables.

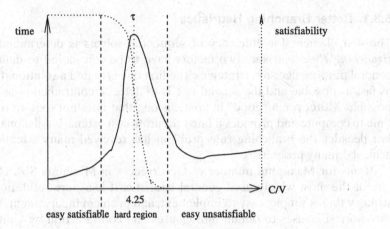

Fig. 5.2. 3-SAT phase-transition phenomenon.

contrary to industrial ones (satisfiable or not). The hardest instances for random benchmarks are generally much smaller in size than the hard structured industrial ones.

SAT has appeared to possess a property of great interest with respect to computational complexity. Random k-SAT formulas exhibit a so-called *Phase Transition Phenomenon*, that is when c clauses with exactly k literals over a set of v variables are chosen at random with a fixed ratio $r = c/v$, the probability of satisfiability falls abruptly from near 1 to near 0 as r passes some critical value τ_k called the *threshold*. Moreover, at the threshold (for $k \geq 3$) a peak of difficulty is observed and it grows exponentially as a function of v. Thus it appears that the *hard* formulas lay in this transition region near the threshold. In the case of $k = 3$, the threshold value for $\tau_k \approx 4.25$ and the best actual DPLL solver for random problems (*kcnfs* (23)) can deal such hard random unsatisfiable 3-SAT instances up to 700 variables in ~25 days, thereby approaching practical feasibility.

The SAT phase transition phenomenon (Fig. 5.2) has attracted much attention from physicists. In particular, the concept of *Backbone* of a k-SAT formula has turned out to play an important role in theoretical studies to design new hard benchmark problems and new branching heuristics (24, 25). A *backbone variable* of a formula is a variable that is assigned always the same truth value in all assignments that satisfy the maximum number of clauses or in all solutions if the problem is satisfiable.

5.3. EFFICIENCY OF SEQUENTIAL DPLL SAT SOLVERS

There has been extensive research effort to develop gradually more efficient SAT solvers (see, e.g., 20,26,27). This section presents some of the main components for efficiency of sequential state-of-the-art DPLL solvers.

5.3.1. Better Branching Heuristics

The first element for efficiency of sequential solvers is determined by the *Branching Rule* heuristic. Two factors have to be considered to define good general purpose decision strategies. The first one is to find a solution if it exists as fast as possible and the second one is to detect a contradiction as early as possible. Moreover, a "good" heuristic is one that does not require too much time to compute and provides a fairly accurate cost estimate. All along the two last decades the branching rule problem has received many attentions and achieved many progresses.

Moms for Maximum number of Occurrences in Minimum Size clauses is one of the most widely used general heuristic. It is a pure refutation based strategy that is simple, easy to implement, and problem independent. It favors the shortest clauses to obtain unit clauses and contradiction by Unit Propagation as a *First Fail Principle*. Many versions of *Moms* heuristics have been proposed. Let $m_t(l)$ = number of clauses of size t that contains the literal l, $g^+(x) = \Sigma_t m_t(x)2^{n-t}$ and $g^-(x) = \Sigma_t m_t(\neg x)2^{n-t}$ for a variable x. Let $h(x) = g^+(x) + g^-(x)$, *Moms* chooses the variable x with Maximum ($h(x)$) and the literal with Maximum($g^+(x), g^-(x)$) to be the first explored branch. The 2-sided Jeroslow-Wang heuristic (*2s-JW*), for example, combines $g^+(x)$ and $g^-(x)$ in some fashion balancing the two branches, with $h(x) = g^+(x) + g^-(x) + g^+(x)*g^-(x)$.

The Böehm and Speckenmeyer (BS) heuristic (28) chooses the literal l with maximal vector $(M_2(l), M_3(l), \cdots, M_t(l))$ under the lexicographic order where $M_i(l) = \alpha Max(m_i(l), m_i(\neg l)) + \beta Min(m_i(l), m_i(\neg l))$. Experiments have shown best results with $\alpha = 1$ and $\beta = 2$ and it calculates two elements of the vector only, $(M_s(l), M_{s+1}(l))$ where s is the size of the shortest clause of the formula (generally $s = 2$).

UP heuristic, such as the one used in Satz (29) exploits the power of Unit Propagation by choosing the literal that would produce the maximal number of unit clauses. Let $w(l)$ = number of new binary clauses obtained by running UnitPropagation ($\mathcal{F} \cup \{l\}$). Satz will branch on the variable with Maximum ($h(x)$) with $h(x) = w(x) + w(\neg x) + 1024 * w(x) * w(\neg x)$.

Recent works on dynamic learning and conflict analysis (see Section 5.3.3) define new heuristics, such as *VSIDS* for Variable State Independent Decaying Strategy in Chaff (30) that are the best actual ones for very large industrial problems. Note that heuristics may be designed to suit particular classes of instances, for example, *kcnfs* (23,25) is one of the best actual DPLL solver dedicated to solve hard random k-SAT problems. It uses a completely different heuristic based on backbone variables as branching nodes (see Section 5.2.4).

5.3.2. Careful Unit Propagation Implementation

DPLL solvers spend the bulk of their effort (>90% in most cases) searching for clauses implied in Unit Propagation, sometimes called *Boolean Constraint Propagation*. Therefore, an efficient Unit Propagation procedure implementation is the key for efficiency. GRASP (31) and Satz (29), for example, keep two counters for each clause, one for the number of value *true* literals and one for the number of value *false* literals. Each variable has two lists containing the clauses where this variable appears positively and negatively. In SATO (32), the *head–tail list* structure is introduced defining two pointers for each clause; one pointing to the first literal and the other to the last literal of the clause stored in an array. Each variable has four lists containing pointer to clauses that have their head–tail literal appearing positively and negatively respectively. The head–tail list method has been argued faster than the counters-based one because when a variable v is assigned value *true*, the clauses containing positively v will not be visited at all and vice versa. One of the best actual solver using this structure is BerkMin (33) a closed-source solver. Unfortunately, for both methods undoing a variable's assignment during backtrack has about the same complexity as assigning the variable. Chaff (30) proposed the *2-literal watching* structure that is similar to the head–tail list associating two special *watched literals* to each clause and two lists of pointers to clauses having their positive and negative watched literals corresponding to each variable. With this structure undoing an assignment takes constant time.

Reference (34) gives an interesting deep case study on cache performance of SAT solvers showing that "cache friendly data structures is one of the key elements for an efficient implementation". It gives comparative results of the three different data structures on various application domains in term of run times, data access, and cache miss rates. The counter-based solvers perform poorly due to the high cache misses. The best head–tail-based solver (BerkMin) and recent watched literals-based solver (zChaff) have similar good cache performance. It finds that there are still a lot of space for improvements because in current and future generations of microprocessors, the speed difference of main memory, L1 and L2 caches tends to be larger (see Section 5.4.3 for parallel efficiency).

Another important, but basic remark, for implementation efficiency is that a solver designed to handle a large number of variables should be quite different than a solver designed to handle fewer variables. Clearly, this explains why the best solvers for industrial benchmarks are not the best for hard random problems as mentioned in Section 5.2.4.

5.3.3. Dynamic Learning Based on Conflict Analysis and Nonchronological Backtracking

In 1996, these CSP look-back techniques were simultaneously introduced in DPLL algorithms by Marques-Silva, Sakallah (35) and by Bayardo, Schrag (36). It has now become a standard and is implemented in most of recent SAT solvers (37). At each decison step for a branching variable, choice is associated a *decision level*. All variables assigned as a consequence of implications of a certain decision will have the same decision level as the decision variable. When a conflict is encountered the DPLL algorithm analyses it for backtracking to a level so as to resolve this conflict and a 0-level backtracking means that the problem is unsatisfiable. A clause is called *conflicting clause* if it has all its literals assigned to *False*. Advanced conflict analysis relies on an *implication graph* to determine the actual reasons for the conflict. This permits us to backtrack up more than one level of the decision stack and, at the same time, to add some clauses called *conflict clauses* to a database. This last operation is the base for the *learning process* that plays a very important role in pruning the search space of SAT problems and this will be of particular interest in the parallel resolution framework. Clause learning and variable branching strategies have traditionally been studied separately, but there is great promise in developing branching strategies that explicitely take into account the order in which clauses are learned. This is the case of Chaff (30), which defines domain specific strategies using such a learning preprocessing step.

5.3.4. Specific SAT Problems Processing

DPLL solvers typically suppose CNF encoded problems, but this is seldom the natural formulation of "real-world" applications. Indeed, the CNF representation provides conceptual simplicity and implementational efficiency, it also entails considerable loss of information about the problem's structure that could be exploited in the search. There is a new interest in studying the CNF conversion for DPLL solving in different domains such as Planning, Bounded Model Checking (BMC) or Automatic Reasoning to improve search efficiency.

One approach (37) argues that this conversion is both unnecessary and undesirable. It presents a non-CNF DPLL like solver able to process any prepositional formula represented as DAGs (Directed Acyclic Graphs) such as in OBDD-based solvers. Experimental results show performance better or close to that of the highly optimized CNF solver zChaff. It seems to be promising because many other potential ways of exploiting the structure have not been experimented. One opposite approach is to "optimize" the CNF conversion with respect to the number of generated clauses, such as in (38), to the number of variables or both, such as in SATPLAN04 (39), which takes first place for optimal deterministic planning at the 2004 International Planning Competition. Another important feature to be mentioned is that for a number of real applications such as BMC, solving time may be largely dominated by encoding time thus "optimizing" may also refer to the conversion time.

Other different approaches (39–42) tackle the general problem of equivalency reasoning. Many SAT applications contain a large number of equivalences (or Xor) and this results in poor efficiency of DPLL solvers because they produce very few unit clauses. For example, the notorious *parity-32 bits* DIMACS benchmark remained unsolved by general purpose SAT solvers for a considerable time and first solved by these approaches.

5.4. PARALLEL RESOLUTION OF SAT

Sequential computer performance improvements are the most significant factor in explaining the few existing works on Parallel Algorithms for Satisfiability compared to sequential ones. Indeed, the challenge to parallel processing is substantial in this area because there are still many problems considered out of reach for the best currently available solvers. There have been several parallel computation models implemented on modern parallel or distributed computers reflecting advances in new computational devices and environments. The two computational models used in this study are *Shared Memory* and *Message Passing*. In the shared memory model, each processor has access to a single, shared address space. In practice, it is difficult to build true shared memory machines with more than a few tens of processors. A variation of the pure shared memory model is to let the processors have local memory and share only a part of the main memory such as in SMP clusters. In the message passing model, the processors have only local memory, but are able to communicate with each other by sending and receiving messages. There are different network topologies for the connections between the processors. The message passing model is highly portable since it matches the hardware of most modern supercomputers, as well as network of workstations. It is not unheard of for both models to be applied simultaneously: threads on shared memory for "node computations" and message passing among them. Such a hybrid approach could become standard and will be used in future works on Parallel Resolution of SAT for further progress.

Incomplete methods based on local search such as GSat, WalkSat or TSat are much more easily implemented on parallel machines because of their inherent parallel nature (2,43). There have been also some parallel implementations of the Davis Putnam (DP) complete algorithm (44,45). In the following, our review will be restricted to the complete, but DPLL-based parallel versions.

5.4.1. Randomized Parallel Backtrack Search

In 1992, (46) proposed a Monte Carlo-type randomized algorithm for SAT which always gives an answer but not necessarily right. A number k of instantiations are randomly generated, where k is related to the probability ε of expected failure. It concludes the input formula to be satisfiable if any instantiation makes it *true* but concludes (perhaps wrongly) unsatisfiable otherwise. The random generation step may be parallelize, but only the theoretical analysis of the polynomial average time is presented. Reference (47) introduces a generic parallel *Backtrack* search algorithm with a deterministic and a randomized method for the message passing model. Most of this work is dedicated to the *Branch-and-Bound* algorithm to prove its efficiency with a multinode-donation strategy and (48) analyses a single-node donation strategy. In 1994, (49) studies the behavior of parallel search for a complete backtrack-based algorithm for graph coloring which is a particular CSP. Independent parallel searches are easily obtained with different heuristics. It concludes by saying that such concurrent parallelization gives fairly limited improvement on hard problem instances.

More recently, *Nagging* (50) is a distributed search paradigm that exploits the speedup anomaly (see Section 5.4.2) by playing multiple reformulations of the same problem, or portions of the problem, against each other. Originally developed within the relatively narrow context of distributed automated reasoning, it has been generalized and used to parallelize DPLL algorithm. Partial results on hard random 3-SAT instances empirically show in this case the possible performance advantage of nagging over partitioning. Moreoever and aside from performance considerations, Nagging holds several additional practical advantages over partitioning; it is intrinsically fault tolerant, naturally load-balancing, requires relatively brief and infrequent interprocessor communication, and is robust in the presence of reasonably large message latencies. These properties may contribute directly to Nagging's demonstrated scalability, making it particularly well suited for use on the Grid. Unfortunately, we are not aware of any new results in this direction.

5.4.2. Search Space Partitioning

An important characteristic of the SAT search space is that it is hard to predict the time needed to complete a specific branch. Consequently, it is difficult (or impossible) to statically partition the search space at the beginning of the algorithm. To cope with this problem, most of the parallel algorithms dynamically partition the search space assigning work to the available threads during run time. The most difficult part consists of balancing the workload in such a way that on the one side idle time should be limited, and on the other side the workload balancing process should consume as few computing and communication time as possible.

In 1985, the seminal works of Speckenmeyer and co-workers (51,52) introduced the important notion of *autarky* to prove the worst case complexity of 3-SAT to be $O(1.6181^n)$, and it shows that on average the solutions of k-SAT problems are nonuniformly distributed. This was the first explanation of the experimental *superlinear speedup* obtained by a parallel backtrack search with a fixed number of processors. Nowadays, this is a well-known phenomenon sometimes called *anomaly*, corresponding to the nondeterministic treatment of the search tree by a parallel execution. Moreover, this is the reason to dissociate satisfiable from unsatisfiable problems for parallel resolution evaluation. The other one reason is that for satisfiable instances only a portion of the tree is explored, thus parallel execution highly depends on the order of the parts to be searched.

Let F be a formula as a set of clauses and $Lit(F)$ be the set of literals defined by the variables of F. An *autarky* A is a subset of $Lit(F)$ such that $F = autsat(A)$ $\oplus$ $autrem(A)$ with $autsat(A) = \{C \in F/\exists l \in A: l \in C\}$ and $autrem(A) = \{C \in$

$F/\forall l \in A: l \notin C$ and $\neg l \notin C$}. Its main property is that, after assigning *true* the literals of an autarky A if it exists, the satisfiability of F is reduced to that of *autrem*(A) for which all the variables associated to A are eliminated. There are a number of works investigating this major concept [e.g., (53)], but to our best knowledge only (45) used it for parallel resolution in a *Model Elimination* algorithm, which is not DPLL based.

In 1994, Böehm and Speckenmeyer (28) gives the first real parallel implementation of the DPLL procedure on a message based MIMD (Multiple Instructions Multiple Data) machine, and it is the reference work of the domain. Excellent efficiencies have been obtained on a Transputer system with up to 256 T800 processors and with two different connexion topologies, the linear array and the two-dimensional (2D) grid. The authors suggest the grid topology for much >256 processors! The sequential version of the solver was the fastest program at the first SAT competition in 1993. Its quality heavily depends on the branching heuristic (see Section 5.3.1) and the associated optimized dynamic data structures. Doubly chained lists with ascending order are used to assign and unassign variables. Its sophisticated dynamic workload balancing strategy was the key for parallel efficiency. Even if no reliable measure of workload for a subformula is known, a simple estimation function α^n for a partial truth assignment with n unset variables and α varying between 1.04 and 1.42 is used (remember the previous upper bound of 1.6181). If the estimated workload for some processor goes down some limit then the workload redistribution phase is activated. Each processor runs two processes, the *worker* and the *balancer*. In the initialization phase the input formula, F is sent to all processors p and a list L_p of partial assignments representing subformulas. The worker process tries to solve or split subformulas of its list by assigning *true* resp. *false* to a literal x chosen according to the branching heuristic. If its list is empty the worker process waits for either new work or a termination message of the balancer process. The balancer process of each processor p estimates its workload $\lambda(p)$ and a precomputation phase calculates the amount of workload to be sent or received by each processor. The balancing phase is performed only if at least one processor holds less than s problems (actually 3) in its list to reduce communication overhead. The sampling method to adjust the α value is presented for hard random k-SAT formulas and for hard unsatisfiable Tseitin's graph formulas. To our best knowledge, there is no recent work on modern parallel machines that report such good results with hundreds of processors.

In 1994, Zhang *et al.* (54,55) present PSATO the first DPLL solver for distributed architectures. It is based on the sequential DPLL solver SATO (32), which was at that time one of the most efficient. The constant need of more computing power and the networked workstations underused justified this approach. The other major motivation of this work was to attack open problems in the quasigroups algebraic domain. The next important concept of *guiding path* was for the first time introduced to define nonoverlapping portions of the search space to be examined. It does so by recording the list of

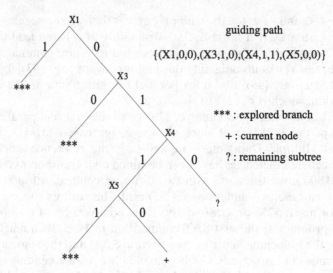

guiding path

$\{(X1,0,0),(X3,1,0),(X4,1,1),(X5,0,0)\}$

*** : explored branch

\+ : current node

? : remaining subtree

Fig. 5.3. Guiding path example.

variables to which the algorithm assigned a value up until the given point of execution (the current state of the process). Each variable of the guiding path is associated with its currently assigned truth value, as well as a Boolean flag saying whether the variable is *closed* (value 0): both truth values have been tested or *open* (value 1): one truth value remains to be tested (see Fig. 5.3, e.g.).

This notion provides a simple and effective way to define "cumulating search" allowing us to suspend and continue the run without repeating the work already done. It is also the mean to deal with the fault-tolerance problem and splitting guiding path is the workload balancing method. Surprisingly, PSATO is organized according to the centralized *master-slave model* for workload balancing, opposite to the completely distributed preceding proposition. All communications take place between the master and the slaves, but implementation was done in an obsolete language called P4. The reported experimental results show good speedup with 20 workstations, but are not significant for a number of reasons. However, PSATO made new discoveries in the quasigroup theory.

More recently, Jurkowiak *et al.* present //Satz (56), a parallel-distributed DPLL solver based on the *master-slave* communication model and *work stealing* for workload balancing. The guiding path concept is used to define the tasks associated to parts of the search tree. The sequential solver Satz on which it is based is equipped with a sophisticated experimental Unit-Propagation branching heuristic (see Section 5.3.1). The master evaluates the workload of a slave processor by the depth of the first remaining subtree to be explored in its guiding path: the smallest corresponds to the most loaded one. If two slaves have the same value, then the second remaining subtrees are compared. When a slave becomes idle it sends a work request to the master, which sends back the first remaining subtree of the most loaded slave. Every process has two threads: the working thread and the communicating one. Moreover, the communication strategy used a semaphore mechanism implemented in standard RPC (Remote Procedure Call) to be easily portable on all Unix-like networks and on the Grid. This work emphasizes the *ping–pong phenomenon* that may occur in workload balancing. A process A sends its right subtree to the idle process B, but quickly finds a contradiction in its left subtree and becomes idle. The process B then sends its right subtree to process A, but quickly becomes idle for the same reason. It is argued that experimental UP branching rule prevents //Satz from this phenomenon. Reference (57) presents experimantal results on a cluster of 216 PIII PCs interconnected by a Fast-Ethernet network. Significant speedup is obtained for hard random unsatisfiable 3-SAT instances with >500 variables up to 128 processors. For easier problems, the communication overhead and the Satz preprocessing done by all slaves penalize the overall parallel performance. For structured real-world SAT problems the results are less convincing.

5.4.3. Intelligent Backtracking and Lemma Exchange

In 2001, Blochinger *et al.* (58,59) proposed PaSAT, the first parallel DPLL solver with *intelligent backtracking* and lemma exchange for *learning*. As mentioned in Section 5.3.3, learning has now become a standard and is implemented in most of recent sequential SAT solvers. The guiding path approach for dynamic problem decomposition is used as well and the lemmas to be exchanged between the nodes of the distributed environment are the *conflict clauses*. Since at every leaf in the search tree a conflict analysis is carried out, a vast number of lemmas are generated at each node thus a selection rule has to be applied at the source. The clause size defines this criterion, which is consistent with the sequential algorithm. Experiments to determine an appropriate value for this parameter are reported. Moreover, when inserting "foreign lemmas" into a task's clauses set, these are filtered by the receiver node. Only those lemmas that are not *subsumed* by the task's initial guiding path are incorporated, to prevent insertion of superfluous lemmas for the receiver. A randomized *work stealing* strategy for workload balancing is applied in a *master-slave* communication model.

The algorithm is implemented on top of the DOTS (Distributed Object-Oriented Threads System) platform. This system is designed for the prototyping and the parallelization of highly irregular symbolic applications, such as SAT. It is natively object-oriented (C++) and it has been deployed on a number of (heterogeneous) clusters. It gives a strict multithreading programming tool in a fork-join style, located at a medium level of abstraction (compared to MPI), providing transparent synchronization and communication. A detailed experimental study discus the different parameters involved by the algorithm on a cluster of 24 SUN workstations. It used the *quasigroup* and

BMC *longmult* for unsatisfiable instances, and *DES* (3 rounds) logical crypt-analysis for satisfiable ones (see Section 5.5.4). This includes the *split-thresh-old* parameter that defines when a search space split is performed to produce an additional thread, *steal-threshold* parameter that defines when to steal a thread from a randomly chosen "victim node" and other *timing* parameters. It is not a trivial work to understand the lemma exchange effect and benefit of learning on the overall performance of the program, but it is argued in con-clusion that distributed learning can result in considerable speedup. Defini-tively in our opinion, thorough theoretical investigations and additional experimentations have to be managed in this direction.

In 2004, Feldman *et al.* (60) present a parallel multithreaded SAT solver on a single multiprocessor workstation with a *shared memory architecture*. It pro-vides experimental results for the execution of the parallel algorithm on a variety of single multiprocessor machines with a shared memory. The empha-sis has been on providing an efficient portable implementation that improves runtime by distributing the workload over several processors on the single machine. To understand low-level implementation details, the solver was designed and coded from scratch contrary to other implementations based on *zChaff* or other existing publicly available source code of solvers, such as *Satz*. The performance of the solver in a single-threaded configuration on a bench-mark suite of ~500 industrial tests is comparable to the *zChaff* one (30).

The main contribution of this paper (60) is that it shows the general dis-advantages of parallel execution of a backtrack-search algorithm on a single multiprocessor workstation, due to increased cache misses. More precisely, it observes the negative effect on otherwise highly optimized cache performance of the sequential algorithm (see Section 5.3.2). It incorporates most of the precedent ideas for parallel execution as well as state-of-the-art sequential ones presented in Section 5.3. Guiding path for search space partitioning and a fork-join style for multithreading programming are used. The search algo-rithm is parallelized by allowing threads explore the search space defined by the open variables on the guiding path of the current thread. The execution of the parallel algorithm starts with one thread that is assigned the whole problem instance, thus defining a number of open variables on its guiding path. If all threads are in suspension while waiting for an available task, this indicates that the search space has been fully explored and the formula is unsatisfiable.

A list of available tasks is maintained for dynamic workload balancing, to minimize the thread waiting times and the time to find a new task. When a thread introduces a new open variable it adds its description to the list. The number of open variables is usually much larger than the number of working threads so that they add new tasks to the list only until a ceratin threshold on the list size is reached. To reduce the overhead of task switches, the tasks are chosen as candidates for entering into the list the ones with open variable closest to the beginning of the guiding paths, such that its expected running time is higher. Moreover, the tasks list is similarly sorted according to the length of the guiding path to its open variables. As in the previous work, the parallel algorithm performs special treatment of the *conflict clause* lemmas produced by each thread for distributed learning. This is done by maintaining a list of conflict clauses that is accessible from all threads. These two lists of available tasks and conflict clauses together with the initial clauses formula are the only shared data structures. Their synchronization overhead is claimed "insignificant" compared to the overall performance, but experimental results show the contrary. This becomes worse when the number of working threads is increased. Specially severe performance degradation are reported for (physical or logical) multiprocessors systems. In the worst case, with only four threads 10% of the total running time is spent in waiting on synchronization locks for shared data structures and the authors argue that this could not explain the observed degradation. With the help of the *Intel V Tune Performance Analyser* they present a deep investigation on the reasons of this degradation, which is mainly the amount of cache misses. Their interesting conclusion is that "optimized cache performance for modern sequential SAT solvers contadicts the parallel execution efficiency on a single multiprocessor workstation"!

It is worthly to note that in 1996 Speckenmeyer *et al.* (61) already studied a multithreaded SAT solver with a dynamic load balancing strategy similar to the one described in (28) (see Section 5.4.2). It reports good performance on randomly generated 3-SAT formulas up to 32 threads but, and this perhaps makes the difference, the threads were simulated on a single processor SUN workstation with a simple round robin schedule.

5.4.4. Grid Computing

In 2003, Chrabakh *et al.* (62,63) present *GridSAT*, the first DPLL SAT solver designed to solve real "hard" and previously unsolved satisfiability problems on a large number of widely distributed and heterogeneous resources (the Grid). Its philosophy is to keep the execution as sequential as possible and to use parallelism only when it is needed. It is based on *zChaff* (30) as a sequential core solver, but it implements a distributed learning clause database system (as discribed in Section 5.4.3) that can acquire and release memory from a Grid resource pool on demand. It is developed from "first-principles" for the Grid and not a legacy parallel application with modifications for Grid execution. Two different types of resources are managed by this system: the time shared and the batch controlled ones making an important difference with all the previous parallel or distributed propositions. This initial Grid-SAT implementation uses the *Every-Ware* development toolkit in a master-slave style communication system, to prove its feasibility. The baseline Grid infrastructure is provided by the *Globus* MDS and NWS (Network Weather Service) systems. The *GridSAT* scheduler located in the master node is the focal point and is responsible for coordinating the execution and launching the clients (slaves). It uses a progressive scheme for acquiring resources and adding them to the pool because of the variability and unpredictability of resource need for a particular SAT instance. Typically, the master requests the resource list available from deployed Grid services or simply from a configuration file. The scheduler submits any batch jobs to their respective queues. When a remote client starts running, it contacts the client manager also located in the master node and registers with it. The scheduler ranks the set of available clients based on their processing power and available memory. It uses the first available client to start solving the problem. A client notifies the master that it wants to split its assigned subproblem when its memory usage exceeds a certain limit or after running for a certain period of time. The splitting process is performed by the cooperation of the splitting client, the master and the idle client and it uses a *sender-initiated strategy* for load balancing with five messages in a peer-to-peer fashion to communicate one splitting. In addition, the master can direct a client to migrate its current problem instead of splitting it. *GridSAT* implements a limited form of resilience in the presence of failures based on check pointing, except for machine crash or "out-of-memory killer" process termination.

The experimental results are obtained on different, but nondedicated, nationally distributed Grids, and all the resources were in continuous use by various other applications. A number of various challenge problems of the SAT'2002 conference is presented as test applications, including industrial, handmade, and randomly generated instances already solved by a sequential solver or open ones. One experimentation used a few dozen of machines distributed among three or four sites in California including small clusters. For the hardest problems, 100 nodes of the Blue Horizon batch system with each node having 8 CPUs and 4 GB of memory were requested moreover! Because *GridSAT* is not a traditional parallel application the results are not very good in terms of speedup for a number of reasons, but the authors conclusion is that "parallel solver is more efficient than a sequential one". Their argument is that it solved open problems, such as one *parity-32 bits* instance with 8 h of 800 CPUs of Blue Horizon plus 33 h of other resources. But this is not true, as noticed in Section 5.3.4 it was first solved in 1998, and also in 2000 with 20 min of one processor running time! In (64), improvements over the previous implementation and new experimental results are presented. In particular, it defines a new method for lemma exchange that is too complex to detail here, and new problems first solved. But as mentionned by the authors themselves, "it remains an open question to decide when using more resources increases the solver's performance", especially in this case of Grid computing.

5.4.5. Miscellaneous

In 1998, Kokotov at MIT, proposes PSolver (65) the first brick of an ambitious distributed SAT solving framework. In the spirit of Grid computing, it considers a large network of workstations that are underused or idle for significant periods of time. It allows these resources to run a client that solves portions of SAT instances in a master–slave fashion as well. A server maintains a list of subproblems to be solved (by their guiding paths), doles out these tasks to clients that connect and disconnect asynchronously, then aggregates their results. The main features of the project were the following: solver-independence, any sequential SAT solver can be used at the client end; high scalability, a network (a cluster) can run a bunch of clients and a server that in turn act as a client to a higher level network; volontary computing environment, similar to the SETI@home project, support for asynchronously connecting and disconnecting clients; fault tolerance, crashing clients do not affect the server; hardware/OS independence, PSolver is written in C++ with Solaris, Linux, and Windows distributions, and it relies on the basic TCP/IP stack for its communication. Unfortunately, this ambitious, but precursory work has not been carried on, and we are not aware of any experimental results.

To our best knowledge, Cope *et al.* (66) is the unique published work to investigate the parallel functional programming for DPLL implementation, inspite of its natural recursive expression. This proposition relies on the parallel evaluation of both left and right branches (see Fig. 5.1) when the splitting rule is applied and it is implemented in a parallel dialect of *Haskell*. It incorporates the conflict-directed backjumping (CBJ) technique, but only for nonchronological backtracking. A poor experimentation is reported and the early results obtained by simulation show "modest speedup". Unfortunately, and perhaps because of the impressive progress of the iterative implementation of DPLL, there is no new proposition in this direction.

Unlike all the presented works that may be qualified as *Macro Parallelism*, a completely different approach relies on specific hardware circuitry conception to parallelize SAT solving, and it may be qualified as *Micro Parallelism*. Among others, the *FPGA* (Field ProgrammableGates Array) technology gives another way of using the inherent parallelism inside the circuitry (pipelines, e.g.). Its first main characteristic is that it permits us to adapt (by reconfigurating) the hardware to a specific problem instance, taking into account the inherent structure of computed functions and data structures. Ultimately, this allows one to find a solution heeding the specific instance complexity rather than the general worst case one. A great deal of research effort has been done in this area from the initial works of Suyama *et al.* (67) and Platzner *et al.* (68) in 1998 [see (69) for a recent review]. FPGAs are composed of programmable gates embedded in a programmable interconnection routing network and the programmable gates are implemented using LookUp tables (LUTs). While significant speedup has been reported over software implementations for a number of applications, a few fundamental hurdles remain before it can be widely applied.

5.5. OUR EXPERIMENTATION

In this section, we present our experimentation in parallel SAT solving. It is a complementary approach of all the recent propositions for dynamic workload balancing, in the sense that it only explores an initial static decomposition for workload repartition (70). The two computational models of *Shared Memory* and *Message Passing* are compared, using OpenMP for Shared Memory and MPI for Message Passing implementations. OpenMP (71) is a complete API for directive-driven parallel programming of shared memory computers. Fortran, C and C++ compilers supporting OpenMP are available for Unix and Windows workstations. OpenMP becomes the *de facto* standard for writing portable, shared memory, parallel programs. MPI (72) is a portable standard for message passing applications and can be used on distributed-memory or shared-memory multiprocessors, as well as on homogeneous or heterogeneous workstations networks or clusters. It provides a large library of functions including point-to-point and collective communications. While message passing reigns as the practical choice for large-scale parallel computing, threads are the medium of choice for SMP multiprocessors.

5.5.1. Sequential SAT Solver Choice

Our approach is to be as possible independent of the sequential solver running on all the processors for parallel execution. We only put a parallel layer upon the sequential solver that is viewed as a blackbox. Among all the recent freeware DPLL implementations, we have experimented versions of *zChaff*, *Sato*, *kcnfs*, and *Satz*. Here, for lack of space we only present partial results obtained with *Satz* to illustrate this simple approach, however, actually the best absolute execution times have been obtained with *zChaff*. The target sequential solver *Satz* developped by Li (29,73) is written in C, which enables the use of OpenMP and MPI, as well without any extra processing. One important feature of *Satz* compared to other DPLL implementations is that it independently explores left and right subtrees making easier parallel implementation. It has no intelligent backtracking and sophisticated conflict analysis for learning, thus reducing the posible communications for lemma exchange between processors. As previously presented in Section 5.3, it uses experimental Unit Propagation as branching rule heuristic to prune the search tree as much as possible. Note that for the other solvers, intelligent backtracking and learning are restricted to one processor.

5.5.2. Initial Decomposition Strategy

The first step of our parallel proposition aims to obtain at most 2^k independent subproblems assigning both possible values *true* and *false* to some k "well-chosen" variables. The simplifications obtained by Unit Propagation are achieved at each variable choice. All the subproblems are placed in a stack that then can be dynamically allocated to processors all along the parallel execution. In OpenMP implementation, this is obtained by a simple parallel *for* loop with a dynamic allocation strategy directive. In MPI implementation, a classical master–slaves communication protocol has to be writen. The value for the k parameter may be adapted to the available processors number such that $2^k >> Nbproc$. This k parameter reflects the parallel *granularity* of our application and is studied in Section 5.5.4 giving the effective number of sub-problems to be proceed. In practice, it never goes beyond 10 giving at most 1024 potential tasks, sufficient for the maximum of 32 processors architecture we used for this reported experience. The strategy for the choice of these k variables used to initially partition the problem is of particular importance. We will consider the three following strategies:

1. *Satz*: The branching heuristic of *Satz* to give comparative results with the sequential resolution.
2. *Rand*: The random choice of variables.
3. *Moms*: The classical Maximum number of Occurrences in Minimum Size clauses heuristic (see Section 5.3.1).

5.5.3. SAT Applications

The first SAT application used for this experimentation is called the *longmult* family, and it comes from the BMC (*Bounded Model Checking*) domain. Each of the 16 instances of the family is associated with one output bit of a 16×16 shift and add multiplier. They are reputed difficult for the OBDD (Ordered Binary Decision Diagrams) approach and are classical benchmark for DPLL SAT solvers. They can be found at Armin Bieré web page,[2] and all the instances are unsatisfiable. We present only the hardest ones *longmult14* and *longmult15*. The second SAT application used is called the *DES* family, and it comes from the logical cryptanalysis domain initiated by Fabio Massacci *et al.* (74) in 1999. It is a new way to generate hard and structured SAT problems by light encoding a few numbers of tours of DES encrypton system. It can be found at SATLIB site (20), and all these instances are satisfiable. We present only the hardest ones *b1-k1.1* and *b1-k1.2* for three tours corresponding to the presentation of one block of the plaintext and one or two blocks of the cyphertext.

5.5.4. Experimental Results

We conducted the experimentation on a SGI Origin 3800 machine thanks to the CINES (*Centre Informatique National de l'Enseignement Suprieur*). The machine configuration is 768 R14000/500 MHz processors, and 384Go of memory. Its architecture is of ccNUMA type, made of a number of interconnected blocks of processors giving 1.6 GB/s data transfer rate and latency <1.4 μs. The computing environment is LSF for batch jobs submission, moreover the system guarantees the exclusive use of the requested processors number for all the job predefined duration.

Tables 5.1–5.3 present for each problem instance: its reference, the number of variables v, the number of clauses c, the sequential CPU time (in s) of *Satz*,

[2]http://www.cs.cmu.edu/modelcheck/bmc.html.

TABLE 5.1. OpenMP-MPI Comparison with *Satz* Decoposition Strategy

Pb.	Strat.	Seq	4 Pr	Ef_4	8 Pr	Ef_8	16 Pr	Ef_{16}	32 Pr	Ef_{32}
Lm14	Satz	4053	t4	e4	t8	e8	t16	e16	t32	e32
7.176v	OMP		1060	0.95	540	0.93	384	0.66	?	?
22.389c	MPI		971	1.04	503	1.00	327	0.77	284	0.44
Lm15	Satz	4865	t4	e4	t8	e8	t16	e16	t32	e32
7.807v	OMP		1251	0.97	665	0.91	?	?	?	?
24.351c	MPI		1211	1.00	622	0.97	361	0.84	274	0.55

TABLE 5.2. Decomposition Heuristics Comparison with MPI

Pb.	Strat.	Seq	4 Pr	Ef_4	8 Pr	Ef_8	16 Pr	Ef_{16}	32 Pr	Ef_{32}
Lm14	Satz	4053	971	1.04	503	1.00	327	0.77	284	0.44
7.176v	Moms		1750	0.58	891	0.57	552	0.46	291	0.43
22.389c	Rand		2050	0.49	1286	0.39	748	0.34	410	0.31
Lm15	Satz	4865	1211	1.00	622	0.97	361	0.84	274	0.55
7.807v	Moms		2027	0.60	1102	0.55	568	0.53	350	0.43
24.351c	Rand		2448	0.50	1505	0.33	1108	0.27	554	0.27
b1-k1.1	Satz	6352	1319	1.20	660	1.20	336	1.18	173	1.15
307v	Moms		1562	1.01	797	0.99	423	0.94	150	1.32
1731c	Rand		1823	0.87	702	1.13	428	1.08	187	1.06
b1-k1.2	Satz	7709	1595	1.20	839	1.14	430	1.12	220	1.10
398v	Moms		1994	0.96	921	1.04	401	1.20	154	1.56
2124c	Rand		65	29	114	8.45	105	4.58	1461	0.16

TABLE 5.3. Granularity Study

Pb.	nb.pbs	Seq	4 Pr	Ef_4	8 Pr	Ef_8	16 Pr	Ef_{16}	32 Pr	Ef_{32}
Lm14	32	4053	1308	0.77	1182	0.43	1070	0.23	1079	0.12
7.176v	60		1099	0.92	721	0.70	610	0.41	605	0.20
22.389c	112		990	1.02	513	0.99	344	0.73	292	0.43
Lm15	46	4865	1384	0.88	1009	0.60	832	0.36	786	0.19
7.807v	92		1273	0.95	728	0.83	568	0.53	456	0.33
24.351c	184		1247	0.97	628	0.97	364	0.83	277	0.55

the respective parallel time obtained with 4, 8, 16, and 32 processorrs, and their respective efficiency. Parallel efficiency is computed by:

$$Ef_{\text{nb of proc}} = \frac{\text{Satz sequential time}}{(\text{parallel time}) \times (\text{nb of proc})}$$

Table 5.1 gives comparative results of OpenMP and MPI implementations on the *longmult* family with the same *Satz* initial decomposition strategy and the same granularity giving ~120 subproblems for *longmult14* and 200 sub-problems for *longmult15*. Actually, there was a contradiction between the use of OpenMP for this application and our basic choice not to go inside the solver code. State-of-the-art DPLL solvers, such as *Satz*, make intensive use of dynamic data structures, but unfortunately OpenMP does not yet permit the dynamic private (not shared) memory allocation, thus leading to mandatory memory management overhead [see (13)]. It is especially the case for more than eight processors, and when OpenMP encounters an out-of-memory to give up the task for this reason a "?" is put in the table. In all the cases, the MPI implementation overcomes the OpenMP one, but both provide notice-able linear speedup until eight processors, then a regular decreasing efficiency for MPI and out-of-memory for OpenMP with more processors.

Table 5.2 gives the comparative results of the three decomposition strate-gies *Satz*, *Rand*, and *Moms* with MPI implementation on both *longmult* unsat-isfiable family and *DES* satisfiable one. Note that the *Satz* strategy is always near the best one in this experiment. It shows superlinear speedup for the sat-isfiable instances. A nonsurprisingly random behavior of the *Rand* strategy is observed too. It is wortwhile to note that both *Rand* and *Moms* strategies are much more easily implemented compared to the *Satz* one, which runs the solver up to a depth bound. Moreover, we have not reported the CPU time needed for the decomposition step that is not insignificant especially in the *Satz* case.

Table 5.3 presents the comparative results obtained with different granu-larity values for the *longmult* unsatisfiable family. It gives for each number of generated subproblems, its efficiency obtained with the *Satz* decomposition strategy in MPI implementation. It shows the important effect of this param-eter on the overall efficiency especially for scalability.

5.6. CONCLUSION

We have mainly reviewed the work on parallel resolution of the Satisfiability problem by a DPLL solver. After briefly introducing the different components for sequential efficiency of the state-of-the-art solvers, we give an almost chronological presentation of the essential steps toward the parallel frame-work progress of this last decade. However, significant parallel efficiencies are still obtained by a number of recent propositions, more detailed research in all the directions are needed to improve the parallel performance. Specific works on decomposition techniques, hybridation of complete–incomplete algorithms, learning ability, for example, have to be started up, as well as general study for parallel application to the Satisfiability problem. Indeed, new improvements can be made in the sequential resolution. The next step for a widespread use of Satisfiabiliy technique in real-world applications remains the parallel efficiency challenge.

REFERENCES

1. J. Gu, P.W. Purdom, J. Franco, and B.W. Wah, Algorithms for Satisfiability (SAT) problem: a survey, *DIMACS Ser Dicrete Math. TCS., AMS*, **35**, 19–152 (1996).
2. J. Gu, Parallel algorithms for Satisfiability problem, *DIMACS Series in Dicrete Maths. TCS., AMS*, **22**, 105 (1995).
3. T. Stützle, H. Hoos, and A. Roli, A review of the literature on local search algorithms for MAX-SAT, TR. AIDA.01.02, Darmstadt University of Technology, 2001.
4. D. Mitchell, B. Selman, and H. Leveque, A new method for solving hard satisfiability problems, *Proceeding of 10th National Conference on AI, AAAI 1992*, MIT Press, San Jose, CA 1992, pp. 440–446.
5. D. McAllester, B. Selman, and A. Kautz, Evidence for invariant in local search, *Proceeding of 14th. National Conference on AI, AAAI 1997*, MIT Press, Cambridge 1997, pp. 321–326.
6. A. Roli, Criticality and parallelism in GSAT, *Proc. SAT'2001*, (27) (2001).
7. K. Iwama, D. Kawai, S. Miyazaki, Y. Okabe, and J. Umemoto, Parallelizing local search for cnf satisfiability using vectorization and pvm, *ACM J. Exp. Algorithms*, **7**(2) (2002).
8. M. Davis, G. Logeman, and D. Loveland, A machine program for Theorem Proving, *CACM*, **5**(7) (1962).
9. H. Bennaceur, The Satisfiability problem regarded as a constraint satisfaction problem, *Proc. ECAI'96*, 155–159 (1996).
10. R. Génisson and P. Jégou, Davis-Putnam were already checking forward, *Proc. ECAI'96*, 180–184 (1996).
11. T. Walsh, SAT versus CSP, *Proc. of CP'2000*, LNCS **1894**, 441–456 (2000).
12. Z. Habbas, M. Krajecki, and D. Singer, Parallel resolution of CSP with OpenMP. *Proceedings of the Second European Workshop on OpenMP, EWOMP'00*, 1–8, Edinburgh, Scotland, 2000.
13. Z. Habbas, M. Krajecki, and D. Singer, Shared memory implementation of CSP resolution. *Proceedings of HLPP'2001*, Orléans, France, 2001.
14. Z. Habbas, M. Krajecki, and D. Singer, Decomposition techniques for parallel resolution of Constraint Satisfaction Problems in shared memory: a comparative study. Special issue of ICPP-HPSECA01, *Int. J. Comput. Sci. Eng. (IJCSE)*, **1**(2134):192–206 (2005).
15. E. Amir and S. McIlraith, Solving Satisfiability using decomposition and the most constrained subproblem, *Proc. SAT'2001* (27) (2001).
16. E. Amir and S. McIlraith, Partition-based logical reasoning for first Oder and propositional theories, *Art. Intel. J.* (2004).
17. P. Bjesse, J. Kukula, R. Damiano, T. Stanion, and Y. Zhu, Guiding SAT diagnosis with tree decompositions, *Proc. SAT'2003* (2003).
18. A. Darwiche, Compiling knowledge into decomposable negation normal form, *Proc. 15th.IJCAI*, 284–289 (1999).
19. S.A. Cook and D.G. Mitchell, Finding hard instance of the Satisfiability problem: a survey, *DIMACS Ser Dicrete Maths. TCS., AMS*, **35**, 1–17 (1997).

20. SATLIB—The Satisfiability Library. Available at http://www.intellektik. informatik.tu-darmstadt.de/SATLIB/.

21. Available at SATLive: http://www.satlive.org.

22. D. Leberre and L. Simon, Fifty-five solvers in Vancouver: the SAT'2004 competition, *Proceedings of SAT'2004*, LNCS **3542**, 2005.

23. G. Dequen and O. Dubois, *kcnfs*: an efficient solver for random k-SAT formulae, *Proc. SAT'2003*, LNCS **2919**, 486–501 (2003).

24. R. Monasson, R. Zecchina, S. Kirkpatrick, B. Selman, and L. Troyansky, Determining computational complexity from characteristic "phase transitions", *Nature (London)*, **400**, 133–137 (1999).

25. G. Dequen and O. Dubois, A backbone-search heuristic for efficient solving of hard random 3-SAT formulae, *Proc. 17th. IJCAI*, 248–253 (2001).

26. I. Gent, H. van Maaren, and T. Walsh, eds., *SAT 2000, Highlights of Satisfiability research in the year 2000*, Frontiers in AI and Applications, Vol. 63, Kluwer Academic Publishers Amsterdam, 2000.

27. H. Kautz and B. Selman: *Proceedings of the Workshop on Theory and Applications of Satisfiability Testing, (SAT'2001)*, Elsevier Science Publishers, Electronic Notes in Discrete Mathematics Vol.9. 2001.

28. M. Böehm and E. Speckenmeyer, A fast parallel Sat solver—efficient work load balancing, *Proceeding of the Third International Symposium on AI and Mathematics* AIMSA, Fort Lauderdale, FL, 1994.

29. C.M. Li and Anbulagan, Heuristics based on unit propagation for satisfiability problems. *Proceedings of 15th International Joint Conference on AI, IJCAI'97*, Morgan Kaufmann Pub., Nagoya Japon, 1997, pp. 366.

30. M. Moskewicz *et al*. Chaff: Engineering an efficient SAT solver, *Proceedings of the 39th DAC*, Las Vegas, 2001.

31. J.P. Marques-Silva and K.A. Sakallah, GRASP—A new search algorithm for Satisfiability, *Proc. ICCAD'96*, 220–227 (1996).

32. H. Zang, SATO: An efficient propositional prover, *Proceedings of International Conference on Automated Deduction, CADE-97*, 1997.

33. E. Goldberg and Y. Novikov, BerkMin: a fast and robust SAT-solver, *Proc. Design, Automation Test Eur. (DATE'02)*, 142–149 (2002).

34. L. Zang and S. Malik Cache performance of SAT solvers: a case study for efficient implementation of algorithms, *Proceedings of SAT'2003*, 2003.

35. J.P. Marques-Silva and K.A. Sakallah, Conflict analysis in search algorithms for propositional Satisfiability, *Proceeding of the IEEE. ICTAI*, 1996.

36. R. Bayardo, Jr. and R. Schrag, Using CSP look-back techniques to solve real-world SAT instances, *Proc. CP'96*, LNCS **1118**, 46–60 (1996).

37. C. Thiffault, F. Bacchus, and T. Walsh, Solving non-clausal formulas with DPLL search, *Proc. SAT'2004*, LNCS **3542** (2005).

38. P. Jackson and D. Sheridan, The optimality of a fast CNF conversion and its use with SAT, *Proc. SAT'2004*, LNCS **3542**, 2005.

39. H. Kautz, SATPLAN04: Planning as Satisfiability. Available at http: //www.cs. washington.edu/homes/kautz/satplan/.

40. P. Baumgartner and F. Massacci, The taming of the (X)OR, *Proc. Computational Logic—CL 2000*, LNAI **1861**, 508–522 (2000).

41. C.M. Li, Integrating equivalency reasoning into Davis-Putnam procedure. *Proceedings of AAAI-2000*, Austin, TX 2000, pp. 291–296.

42. M. Heule and H. van Maaren, Aligning CNF and equivalence reasoning, *Proc. SAT'2004*, LNCS **3542**, 145–156 (2005).

43. P.M. Pardalos, L.S. Pitsoulis, and M.G.C. Resende, A parallel GRASP for MAX-SAT problems, *Proc. PARA'96*, LNCS **1180**, 575–585 (1996).

44. D. Leberre, Exploiting the real power of unit propagation lookahed, *Proc. SAT'2001* (27) (2001).

45. F. Okushi, Parallel cooperative propositional theorem proving, *Proceedings of the 5th. International Symposium on AI and Maths.* AIMSA, Fort Lauderdale, FL, 1998.

46. L.C. Wu and C.Y. Tang, Solving the satisfiability problem by using randomized approach, *Inf. Proc. Lett.*, **41**, 187–190 (1992).

47. R.M. Karp and Y. Zhang, Randomized parallel algorithms for Backtrack search and Branch-and-Bound computation, *J. ACM.*, **40**(3):765–789 (1993).

48. Y. Zhang and A.Ortynski, Efficiency of randomized parrallel Backtrack search, *Algorithmica*, **24**, 14–28 (1999).

49. T. Hogg and C.P. Williams, Expected gains from parallelizing constraint solving for hard problems, *Proc. AAAI'94*, 331–336 (1994).

50. S. Forman and A. Segre, NAGSAT: a randomized complete, parallel solver for 3-SAT, *Proc. SAT'2002*, 236–243 (2002).

51. B. Monien and E. Speckenmeyer, Solving Satisfiability in less than $2n$ steps, *Discrete Appl. Maths.*, **10**, 287–295 (1985).

52. E. Speckenmeyer, B. Monien, and O. Vornberger, Superlinear speedup for Parallel Backtracking, *Proc. SuperComput. Conf. 87*, LNCS **297**, 985–995 (1987).

53. O. Kullmann, Investigations on autark assignments, *Disc. App. Math.*, **107**:99–137 (2000).

54. H. Zang and M.P. Bonacina, Cumulating search in a distributed computing environment: a case study in parallel satisfiability, *Proceedings of PASCO'94*, 1994.

55. H. Zang, M.P. Bonacina, and J. Hsiang, PSATO: a distributed propositional prover and its applications to Quasigroup problems, *J. Symbolic Comput.*, **21**, 543–560 (1996).

56. B. Jurkowiak, C.M. Li, and G. Utard, Parallelizing Satz using dynamic workload balancing. *Proc. SAT'2001* (27) (2001).

57. B. Jurkowiak, Programmation haute performance pour la résolution des problèmes SAT et CSP, *Thèse de l'Université de Picardie*, Amiens, 2004.

58. W. Blochinger, C. Sinz, and W. Kchlin, PaSAT-Parallel SAT-checking with lemma exchange: implementation and applications, *Proc. SAT'2001* (27) (2001).

59. W. Blochinger, C. Sinz, and W. Kchlin, Parallel propositional satisfiability checking with distributed dynamic learning. *Parallel Comput*, **29**(7):969–994 (2003).

60. Y. Feldman, N. Derschowitz, and Z. Hanna, Parallel multithreaded Satisfiability solver: design and implementation. *Proc. PDMC 2004* (2004). ENTCS, **123**(3):75–79 (2005).

61. E. Speckenmeyer, M. Böhm, and P. Heusch, On the imbalance of distributions of solutions of CNF-formulas and its impact on Satisfiability solvers, *DIMACS Ser Dicrete Maths. TCS.*, AMS, **35**, 669–676 (1996).

62. W. Chrabakh and R. Wolski, GrADSAT: a parallel SAT solver for the Grid, TR.2003–05, CS. University of California, Santa Barbara, 2003. Available at http//www.cs.ucsb.edu/research/trcs/docs/2003-05.pdf.

63. W. Chrabakh and R. Wolski, GridSAT: a Chaff-based distributed SAT Solver for the Grid, *Proceedings of SuperComputing Conference, SC'2003*, Phoenix, AR, 2003.

64. W. Chrabakh and R. Wolski, Solving "hard" satisfiability problems using GridSAT, 2004. Available at http//www.cs.ucsb.edu/~chrabakh/papers/gridsat-hp.pdf.

65. D. Kokotov and PSolver: distributed SAT solver framework. Available at http//sdg.lcs.mit.edu/satsolvers/PSolver/index.html.

66. M. Cope, I. Gent, and K. Hammond, Parallel heuristic search in Haskell, *Trends in Functional Programming*, Vol.2, S. Gilmore ed., Intellect Books, Bristol, UK, 2000, pp. 65–73.

67. T. Suyama, M. Yokoo, and H. Sawada, Solving Satifiability problems using logic synthesis and reconfigurable hardware, *Proceeding of the 31th. Hawaian International Conference on System Sciences HICSS-31*, 1998.

68. M. Platzner and G. De Micheli, Acceleration of Satifiability algorithms by reconfigurable hardware, *Proc. 8th. Int. Workshop FPL'98*, LNCS **1482**, 69–78 (1998).

69. I. Skliarova and A.B. Ferrari, Reconfigurable hardware SAT solvers: a survey of systems, *Proc. of Field-Programmable Logic and Applications (FPLA)*, P. Cheung, G. Constantinides, and J. de Sousa eds., LNCS **2778**, 468–477 (2003).

70. D. Singer and A. Vagner, Parallel resolution of the Satisfiability problem (SAT) with OpenMP and MPI, *Proc. PPAM 2005*, LNCS. **3911**, 380–388, Czeorochowa, Poland 2006.

71. OpenMP Architecture Review Board, *OpenMP C and C++ Application Program Interface*. Available at http://www.openmp.org.

72. M. Snir, S.W. Otto, S. Huss-Lederman, D.W. Walker, and J. Dongarra, MPI: the complete reference, MIT Press, Cambridge Massachusetts 1996.

73. C.M. Li and S. Gérard, On the Limit of Branching Rules for Hard Random Unsatisfiable 3-SAT. *Proceeding of 14th Eur. Conference on AI, ECAI 2000*, Berlin, 2000.

74. F. Massacci and L. Marraro, Logical cryptanalysis as a SAT-problem: Encoding and analysis of the U.S. Data Encryption Standard, *J. Automated Reasoning*, **24**(1–2), 165–203 (2000).

CHAPTER 6

Parallel Metaheuristics: Models and Frameworks

N. MELAB, E-G. TALBI, and S. CAHON

Laboratoire d'Informatique Fondamentale de Lille
UMR CNRS 8022, INRIA Futurs—DOLPHIN Project
Cité scientifique—59655, Villeneuve d'Ascq cedex—France

E. ALBA and G. LUQUE

Departamento de Lenguajes y Ciencias de la Computación,
E.T.S.I. Informática,
Campus Teatinos, 29071 Málaga (España)

6.1. INTRODUCTION

Metaheuristics are general heuristics that provide suboptimal solutions in a reasonable time for various optimization problems. They fall in two categories: local search metaheuristics (LSs) and evolutionary algorithms (EAs). A local search starts with a single initial solution. At each step of the search, the current solution is replaced by another (often the best) solution found in its neighborhood. Very often, LSs allow us to find a local optimal solution. On the other hand, EAs make use of a randomly generated population of solutions. The initial population is enhanced through a natural evolution process. At each generation of the process, the whole population or a part of the population is replaced by newly generated individuals (often the best ones).

Although the use of metaheuristics allows us to significantly reduce the temporal complexity of the search process, the exploration remains time consuming for industrial problems. Therefore, parallelism is necessary to not only reduce the resolution time, but also to improve the quality of the provided solutions. For each of the two families of metaheuristics, different parallel models have been proposed in the literature. Each of them illustrates an alternative approach to handle and deploy the parallelization. This chapter describes the different models and their characteritics.

Several parallel metaheuristics and their implementations have been proposed in the litterature. Most of them are available on the Web and can be reused and adapted to its own problems. Reusability may be defined as the ability of software components to build many different applications (1). However, one has to rewrite the problem-specific sections of the code. Such a task is tedious, error-prone, energy, and time consuming. Moreover, the newly by developed code is harder to maintain. A better way to reuse the design and code of existing metaheuristics and their associated parallel models is the use of frameworks (2). Their objective is twofold: they are reliable as they are often well tested and documented. In addition, they allow a better maintainability and efficiency.

Most existing frameworks related to metaheuristics for discrete optimization problems are object oriented (OO) (3–12). They include a set of classes that embody an abstract design of solution methods of a family of related problems (1). They are based on a strong conceptual separation of the invariant (generic) part of parallel metaheuristics and their problem-specific part. Such characteristic allows the programmer to redo very little code. The frameworks focus either only on EA (3–7) or only on LS (8,9). Only a few frameworks are dedicated on the design of both EA and LS, and their hybridization (10,12). All these frameworks are described, summarized, and compared in this chapter.

The rest of the paper is organized as follows: Section 6.2 describes the working principles and the major parallel models of evolutionary algorithms. Section 6.3 presents the principles and the major parallel models of local search metaheuristics. Section 6.4 describes the motivations and objectives of software frameworks. We also propose an overview of those dedicated to the evolutionary algorithms and local search methods. Section 6.5 concludes the chapter.

6.2. PARALLEL EVOLUTIONARY ALGORITHMS

6.2.1. Principles of Evolutionary Algorithms

Evolutionary Algorithms (13) (EAs) are population-based metaheuristics. Their principle is to improve an initial population of solutions during a given number of generations. At each generation, individuals are selected, paired, and recombined in order to generate new solutions that replace other individuals. These later are used to replace other solutions selected from the population either randomly or according to a selection strategy. Algorithm 6.2.1 illustrates the pseudocode of any Evolutionary Algorithm.

Algorithm 6.2.1. EA pseudocode.
Generate($P(0)$);
  $t := 0$;
  while not Termination_Criterion($P(t)$) **do**
    Evaluate($P(t)$);
    $P'(t)$:= Selection($P(t)$);
    $P'(t)$:= Apply_Reproduction_Ops($P'(t)$);
    $P(t + 1)$:= Replace($P(t), P'(t)$);
    $t := t + 1$;
  endwhile

The major features of EAs are the way the population is initialized, the selection strategy, the replacement approach, and the continuation–stopping criterion. The initial population is often generated at random, but is can be provided by another heuristic. The aim of the selection strategy is to foster "good" solutions. It can be either *blind* (*stochastic*), meaning individuals are selected randomly, or *intelligent* (*deterministic*), for example tournament or wheel. The replacement approach allows us to withdraw individuals selected according to a given selection strategy. The continuation–stopping criterion is evaluated at the end of each generation and the evolution process is stopped if it is satisfied.

6.2.2. Parallel Models of Evolutionary Algorithms

For nontrivial problems, executing the reproductive cycle of a simple EA on long individuals and/or large populations requires high computational resources. In general, evaluating a fitness function for every individual is frequently the most costly operation of the EA. Consequently, a variety of algorithmic issues are being studied to design efficient EAs. These issues usually consist of defining new operators, hybrid algorithms, parallel models, and so on. Parallelism arises naturally when dealing with populations, since each of the individuals belonging to it is an independent unit. Due to this, the performance of population-based algorithms is specially improved when running in parallel.

Three major parallel and distributed models for EAs stand out in the litterature: the island cooperative model, the parallel evaluation of the population model, and the parallel evaluation of a single solution model.

- *The Island Model.* The island model (Fig. 6.1) consists in running simultaneouslym several homogeneous–heterogeneous EAs that cooperate to compute better and robust solutions. They communicate by exchanging genetic stuff to improve the diversity of the search. The objective of the model is to delay the global convergence, especially when the EAs are heterogeneous regarding to the variation operators or the machines they

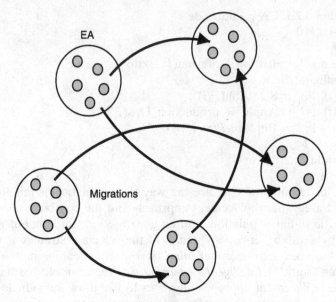

Fig. 6.1. The parallel island model.

are being executed. The migration of individuals follows a policy defined by the following parameters: the migration decision criterion, the exchange topology, the number of emigrants, the emigrants selection policy, and the replacement–integration policy. In the multiobjective context, the individuals are selected either from the population, the Pareto archive, or from the combination of the two. The design of the model is generic and could be completely provided inside a software platform for the design of parallel metaheuristics. The user will indicate how necessary the values of the different parameters of the model are.

- *The Parallel Evaluation of the Population.* The evaluation of the population is time intensive and often represents >90% of the CPU time consumed by an EA especially for real-world problems. Its parallelization is thus necessary to reduce the execution time without changing the semantics of the EA in comparison to a sequential execution. The parallel evaluation is often performed according to the farmer–worker model (see Fig. 6.2). The farmer applies the selection, transformation, and replacement operations as they require a global management of the population. At each generation, it distributes the new solutions among the workers, which evaluate them and return back their corresponding fitness values. The granularity (number of evaluators) has a great impact on the efficiency of the parallel model. This is the only parameter the user may possibly provide. The model is generic and could be provided in a software platform in a transparent way for the user.

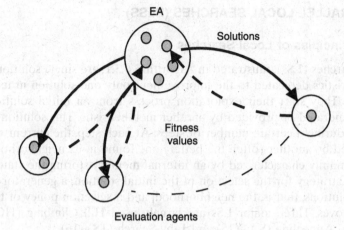

Fig. 6.2. The parallel evaluation of a population.

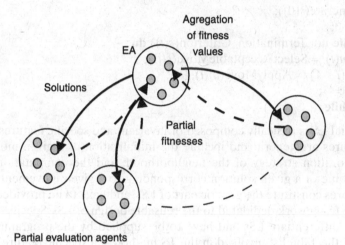

Fig. 6.3. The parallel evaluation of a single solution.

- *The Parallel Evaluation of a Single Solution.* The fitness of each solution is evaluated in a parallel centralizedway (see Fig. 6.3). This kind of parallelism could be efficient if the evaluation function is CPU time-consuming and/or IO intensive. This is often particularly true for industrial optimization problems. The function could be viewed as an aggregation of a set of partial functions. A reduction operation is performed on the results returned back by the partial functions computed by the workers. Consequently, for this model the user has to provide a set of partial functions and their associated agregation operator. The user has thus to be skilled a little bit in parallel computing. In the multiobjective context, these partial functions could be the different objectives to be optimized.

6.3. PARALLEL LOCAL SEARCHES (PLSS)

6.3.1. Principles of Local Searches

Local searches (LSs), illustrated in Algorithm 6.3.1, are single solution-based metaheuristics dedicated to the improvement only one solution in its neighborhood. They start their exploration process from an initial solution randomly generated or provided by another metaheuristic. This solution is then updated during a certain number of steps. At each step, the current solution is replaced by another (often the better) one found in its neighborhood. The LSs are mainly characterized by an internal memory storing the state of the search, a strategy for the selection of the initial solution, a generator of candidate solutions, that is, the neighborhood, and a selection policy of the candidate moves. Three major LSs are largely used Hill Climbing (HC) (14), Simulated Annealing (SA) (15) and Tabu Search (TS) (16).

Algorithm 6.3.1. Local search skeleton pseudocode.
Generate($s(0)$);
$t := 0$;
while not Termination_Criterion($s(t)$) **do**
  $m(t) :=$ SelectAcceptableMove($s(t)$);
  $s(t + 1) :=$ ApplyMove($m(t), (t)$);
  $t := 1$;
endwhile

A serial LS is basically composed of invariant and specific features. Invariant features are generic and include the initialization of a given movement, the exploration strategy of the neighborhood, and the computation of the fitness value of a given solution corresponding to a given movement. Invariant features constitute the generic part of LSs, and have to be provided by any software framework dedidated to the reusable design of LSs. Specific features allow to differentiate LSs and have to be supplied by the programmer. For instance, the Tabu list involved in the TS method is a specific feature.

There are three major parallel distributed models of LSs: the parallel exploration of the neighborhood, the multistart model, and the parallel evaluation of each solution. The two first models are illustrated in Fig. 6.4.

• *Parallel Multistart Model*. The model consists in launching in parallel several independent or cooperative homo/heterogeneous LS. Each LS is often initialized with a different solution. The independent approach is widely exploited because it is natural and easy for the user. In this case, the semantics of the model is the same as the serial execution. That is to say the results obtained with N parallel independent LSs is the same as that provided by N LSs performed in a serial way on a single machine. The parallelism allows to efficiently enhance the robustness of the execution. The model with independent LSs is generic and could be encapsulated in any framework.

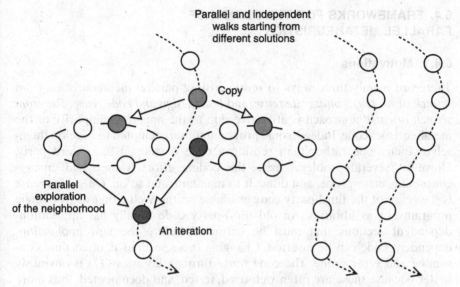

Fig. 6.4. The two first parallel models for local search.

In its cooperative mode, LSs of the parallel multistart model exchange information during execution. This information is often provided by the user and can be good visited solutions, performed move operations, and other parameters that allow to express the trajectory followed during the search. In this case, the cooperation is a specific part and must be provided by the user.

- *Parallel Moves Model.* The parallel moves model is a kind of Farmer–Worker model allowing to speed up the exploration of the possible moves without changing the semantics of the algorithm in comparison with a sequential exploration. At the beginning of each iteration of the algorithm, the farmer sends the current solution to a pool of workers. Each worker explores some neighboring candidates, and returns back the results to the farmer. The model could be efficient if the evaluation of each solution is time, consuming and/or there is a large number of candidate neighbors to be evaluated. This is particularly right for industrial applications, such as radio network design. The model is generic and easily provided by any framework for local searches. However, such model is not well suited to Simulated Annealing since only one candidate solution is evaluated at each iteration. Moreover, the efficiency of the model for Hill Climbing is not always guaranteed as the number of neighboring solutions to process before finding one that improves the current objective function may be highly variable.

- *Move Acceleration Model.* The move acceleration model corresponds to the parallel evaluation of a single solution associated to evolutionary algorithms, and decribed in Section 6.2.2.

6.4. FRAMEWORKS FOR THE DESIGN OF PARALLEL METAHEURISTICS

6.4.1. Motivations

There are mainly three ways to reuse existing parallel metaheuristics: *from scratch or no reuse*, *only code reuse*, and *both design and code reuse*. The *from scratch-oriented* approach is attractive due to the apparent simplicity of the metaheuristics code. Indeed, some programmers are tempted to develop themselves their code rather than reusing a code developed by a third party. However, several problems arise: the coding effort is time and energy-consuming, error-prone, and difficult to maintain, and so on. *Only code reuse* is the reuse of the third-party code available on the Web either as free single programs, or as libraries. An old third-party code usually has application-dependent sections that must be extracted before the new application-dependent code can be inserted. Changing these sections is often time consuming and error prone. The code reuse through libraries (17) is obviously better because these are often well tried, tested, and documented, thus more reliable. However, libraries allow us to reuse the code, but they do not make easier the reuse of the complete invariant part of algorithms, particularly their whole design.

Both code and design reuse approach is devoted to overcome this problem, that is, to redo as little code as possible each time a newoptimization problem is dealt with. The basic idea is to capture into special components the recurring (or invariant) part of solution methods to standard problems belonging to a specific domain. Frameworks provide the full control structure of the invariant part of the algorithms, and the user has only to supply the problem-specific details. In order to meet this property, the design of a framework must be based on a clear conceptual separation between the solution methods and the problems they tackle.

6.4.2. Design Requirements and Objectives

A framework is normally intended to be exploited by as many users as possible. Therefore, its exploitation could be successful only if some important user criteria are satisfied. The following criteria are the major of them:

- *Maximum Design and Code Reuse.* The framework must provide for the user a whole architecture (design) of their solution method. Moreover, the programmer may redo as little code as possible. This objective requires a clear and maximum conceptual separation between the solution methods and the problems they are dedicated to solve, and thus a deep problem domain analysis. As a consequence, the user might develop only a minimal code, that is, the problem-specific part of the code.

- *Utility and Extendibility.* The framework must allow the user to cover a broad range of metaheuristics, problems, parallel distributed models, and so on. It must be possible for the user to easily add new features–metaheuristics or change existing ones without implicating other components. Furthermore, as in practice existing problems evolve and new others arise these have to be tackled by specializing–adapting to them the framework components.
- *Transparent Use of Parallel Models.* In order to facilitate the use of the different parallel models these are implemented so that the developer can deploy their parallel algorithms in a transparent manner. Moreover, the execution of the algorithms must be robust to guarantee the reliability and the quality of the results.
- *Portability.* In order to satisfy a large number of users, the framework must support different material architectures and their associated operating systems.

6.4.3. An Overview of Existing Frameworks

It is quoted below that a framework is mainly based on the conceptual separation between the solution methods and the problems they deal with. This separation requires a deep understanding of the application domain. In (18) OO composition rather than inheritance is recommended to perform the conceptual separation. Indeed, classes are easier to reuse than individual methods. The modeling of the application domain results in a set of reusable classes with some constant and variable aspects. The implementation of the constant part is provided by the framework, and encapsulated into generic–abstract classes or skeletons (10). The variable part is problem specific, and is specified and fixed in the framework, but it is implemented by the user. This part is a set of holes or hot spots (19) that serve to fill the skeletons provided by the framework when building specific applications.

According to the extendibility requirement, two types of frameworks can be distinguished: white or glass-box frameworks and black-box frameworks. In black-box frameworks one can reuse components by plugging them together through static parameterization and composition, unaware of their internal working (2). In contrast, white-box frameworks require an understanding of the internal working of the classes so that correct subclasses (inheritance based) can be developed. Therefore, they allow more extendibility of the provided classes. Several white-box frameworks for the reusable design of parallel metaheuristics are available on the Web.

6.4.3.1. White-Box Frameworks for EAs. Table 6.1 summarizes the major of white-box frameworks dedicated to the design of parallel EAs. The different frameworks are classified according to some criteria: the parallel models they implement, the language (*lang.*) they are developed with, and the API

TABLE 6.1. White-Box Frameworks for EAs

	Model1	Model2	Model3	Lang.	Comm./Conc.
ECJ	+	−	−	Java	Java threads TCP/IP Sockets
D. Beagle	+	+	−	C++	TCP/IP Sockets
Jdeal	−	+	−	Java	TCP/IP Sockets
DREAM	+	−	−	Java	Java threads TCP/IP Sockets
MALLBA	+	+	+	C++	Netstream MPI
ParadisEO	+	+	+	C++	MPI PVM PThreads

used for communication and concurrency (*Comm./Conc*). In the table, *Model1*, *Model2* and *Model3* designate respectively the parallel island model, the parallel evaluation of the population and the parallel evaluation of a single solution. These criteria allow us to evaluate the different frameworks regarding the quality and design requirements and objectives of frameworks quoted in Section 6.4.2.

The major frameworks dedicated to the design of EAs are the following: DREAM[1] (3), ECJ[2] (4), JDEAL[3] (5), and Distributed BEAGLE[4] (7). These software are frameworks as they are based on a clear OO conceptual separation. They are portable as they are developed in the Java language except the last system, which is programmed in C++. However, they are limited regarding the parallel models. Indeed, in DREAM and ECJ only the island model is implemented using Java threads and TCP/IP sockets. DREAM is particularly deployable on peer to peer platforms. Furthermore, JDEAL provide only the Master–Slave (M/S) model using TCP/IP sockets. Distributed BEAGLE provides the island model and the parallel evaluation of the population model.

The frameworks MALLBA[5] (10) and ParadisEO[6] (12) provide all the parallel models of EAs. MALLBA and ParadisEO have numerous common char-

---

[1]Distributed Resource Evolutionary Algorithm Machine: http://www.world-wide-dream.org.
[2]Java Evolutionary Computation: http://www.cs.umd.edu/projects/plus/ec/ecj/.
[3]Java Distributed Evolutionary Algorithms Library: http://www.laseeb.isr.ist.utl.pt.sw/jdeal/.
[4]Distributed Beagle Engine Advanced Genetic Learning Environment: http://www.gel.ulaval.ca/~beagle.
[5]MAlaga+La Laguna+BArcelona: http://www.neo.lcc.uma.es/mallba/mallba.html.
[6]Parallel and distributed Evolving Objects: http://www.lifl.fr/~cahon/paradisEO.

TABLE 6.2. White-Box Frameworks for LSs

	Mod1	Mod2	Mod3	Lang.	Conc./Comm.
Easylocal ++	–	–	–	C++	–
Localizer ++	–	–	–	C++	–
MALLBA	+	+	+	C++	Netstream MPI
ParadisEO	+	+	+	C++	MPI PVM PThreads

acteristics. They are C++/MPI open source frameworks. They provide all the previously presented parallel/distributed models. However, they are quite different as ParadisEO seems to be more flexible because the granularity of its classes is finer. Moreover, ParadisEO [an extended EO(20)] provides also the PVM-based communication layer and Pthreads-based concurrency. On the other hand, MALLBA is deployable on wide area networks (10). Communications are based on *NetStream*, an *ad hoc* flexible and OOP message passing service upon MPI.

6.4.3.2. White-Box Frameworks for Local Searches.
Table 6.2 summerizes the major of white-box frameworks dedicated to the design of local search metaheuristics. The different frameworks are classified according to the same criteria presented above. The criteria *Mod1*, *Mod2*, and *Mod3* designate, respectively, the parallel multistart model, the parallel moves model, and the move acceleration model. These criteria allow us to evaluate the different frameworks regarding the quality and design requirements and objectives of frameworks quoted in Section 6.4.2.

In the local search domain, most of existing frameworks (8,9) do not allow parallel distributed implementations. Those enabling parallelism–distribution are often dedicated to only one solution method. For example (2), provides parallel skeletons for the TS method. Two skeletons are provided and implemented in C++/MPI: independent runs (multistart) model with search strategies, and a Master-Slave model with neighborhood partition. The two models can be exploited by the user in a transparent way. The software frameworks ParadisEO and MALLBA provide all the parallel models of local searches.

6.5. CONCLUSION

Although the use of metaheuristics allows us to reduce the complexity of the search process, the parallelism remains an important way to solve combinatorial optimization problems. Different models have been proposed to exploit the parallelism of metaheuristics. These models have been and are still largely experimented on a wide range of metaheuristics and applied to a large variety of problems in different areas. We believe that the best way to reuse the different models is to encapsulate them into frameworks. Frameworks provide the invariant part of the metaheuristics, therefore the user has just to supply the specific part of their problem. We have proposed an overview of existing white-box frameworks, including those dedicated either to local searchs, to evolutionary algorithms, or to both of them.

All the presented frameworks are object oriented, and are based on a clear conceptual separation between solution methods and problems. Therefore, they allow a maximum code and design reuse. Moreover, they allow a portable deployment as they are developed either in C++ or in Java. In the literature, only few frameworks provide the major parallel models. Both ECJ and DREAM implement the island model for cooperative EA, Jdeal provides the parallel evaluation of a population model, and Distributed Beable includes both of them. Finally, ParadisEO and MALLBA are particularly outstanding. They provide local searches, as well as evolutionary algorithms and all their parallel models.

In the last decade, Grid computing (22) and Peer-to-Peer (P2P) computing (23) have become a real alternative to traditional supercomputing for the development of parallel applications that harness massive computational resources. In the future, the focus in the area of parallel and distributed metaheuristics will be on the gridification of the parallel models presented in this chapter. This is a great challenge as nowadays grid and P2P-enabled frameworks for metaheuristics are just emerging (3,12).

REFERENCES

1. A. Fink, S. Vo, and D. Woodruff. Building Reusable Software Components for Heuristc Search. In P. Kall, H.-J. Luthi, eds., *Operations Research Proceedings, 1998, Springer, Berlin*, 1999, pp. 210–219.

2. R. Johnson and B. Foote. Designing Reusable Classes. *J. Object-Oriented Programming*, **1**(2):22–35 (June/July 1988).

3. M.G. Arenas *et al.* A framework for distributed evolutionary algorithms. *Proceedings of PPSN VII*, Granada, Spain September 2002.

4. S. Luke *et al.* ECJ: A Java-based Evolutionary Computation and Genetic Programming Research System. Available at http://www.cs.umd.edu/projects/plus/ec/ecj/.

5. J. Costa, N. Lopes, and P. Silva. JDEAL: The Java Distributed Evolutionary Algorithms Library. Available at http://laseeb.isr.ist.utl.pt/sw/jdeal/home.html.

6. E. Goodman. An introduction to GALOPPS—The "Genetic Algorithm Optimized for Portability and Parallelism" System. Technical report, Intelligent Systems Laboratory and Case Center for Computer-Aided Engineering and Manufacturing, Michigan State University, November 1994.

7. C. Gagné, M. Parizeau, and M. Dubreuil. Distributed BEAGLE: An Environment for Parallel and Distributed Evolutionary Computations. *Proceedings of the 17th*

Annual International Symposium on High Performance Computing Systems and Applications (HPCS) 2003, Sherbrooke, Québec, Canada May 11–14, 2003.

8. L. Di Gaspero and A. Schaerf. Easylocal++: An object-oriented framework for the design of local search algorithms and metaheuristics. *MIC'2001 4th Metaheuristics International Conference*, Porto, Portugal, July 2001, pp. 287–292.

9. L. Michel and P. Van Hentenryck. Localizer++: An open library for local search. Technical Report CS-01-02, Brown University, Computer Science, 2001.

10. E. Alba and the MALLBA Group. MALLBA: A library of skeletons for combinatorial optimization. In R.F.B. Monien, ed, *Proceedings of the Euro-Par*, Vol. 2400 of LNCS, Springer-Verlag. Paderborn, 2002, pp. 927–932.

11. N. Krasnogor and J. Smith. MAFRA: A Java memetic algorithms framework. In A.A. Freitas, W. Hart, N. Krasnogor, and J. Smith, eds., *Data Mining with Evolutionary Algorithms*, Las Vegas, NV, 2000, pp. 125–131.

12. S. Cahon, N. Melab, and E-G. Talbi. ParadisEO: A Framework for the Reusable Design of Parallel and Distributed Metaheuristics. To be published in *J. Heurs.*, Journal of Heuristics, Vol. 17(2), pp. 357–380, May 2004.

13. J.H. Holland, *Adaptation in natural and artificial systems*. Ann Arbor, MI, The University of Michigan Press, 1975.

14. C.H. Papadimitriou. The Complexity of Combinatorial Optimization Problems. Master's thesis, Princeton University, 1976.

15. S. Kirkpatrick, C.D. Gelatt, and M.P. Vecchi. Optimization by Simulated Annealing. *Science*, **220**(4598):671–680 (May 1983).

16. F. Glover. Tabu Search, Part I. *ORSA, J. Comput.*, **1**:190 (1989).

17. M. Wall. GAlib: A C++ Library of Genetic Algorithm Components. Available at http://lancet.mit.edu/ga/.

18. D. Roberts and R. Johnson. Evolving Frameworks. A Pattern Language for Developing Object-Oriented Frameworks. *Pattern Languages of Program Design* **3** (PLoPD3) pp 471–486, 1998.

19. W. Pree, G. Pomberger, A. Schappert, and P. Sommerlad. Active Guidance of Framework Development. *Software—Concepts Tools*, **16**(3):136 (1995).

20. M. Keijzer, J.J. Morelo, G. Romero, and M. Schoenauer. Evolving Objects: A General Purpose Evolutionary Computation Library, *Proceedings of the 5th International Conference on Artificial Evolution (EA'01)*, Le Creusot, France, October 2001.

21. M.J. Blesa, L.L. Hernandez, and F. Xhafa. Parallel Skeletons for Tabu Search Method. *8th International Conference on Parallel and Distributed Systems*. IEEE Computer Society Press. Kyongju City, Korea, 2001, pp. 23–28.

22. I. Foster and C. Kesselman, eds. *The Grid: Blueprint for a New Computing Infrastructure*. Morgan Kaufmann, San Fransisco, 1999.

23. N. Minar *et al. Peer-to-Peer: Harnessing the Power of Disruptive Technologies*. O'Reilly & Associates, ISBN: 0_596_00110-X 2001.

CHAPTER 7

Toward Parallel Design of Hybrids Between Metaheuristics and Exact Methods

M. BASSEUR, L. JOURDAN, and E-G. TALBI

LIFL
Bât. M3, Cité Scientifique
59655 Villeneuve d'ascq CEDEX
FRANCE

7.1. INTRODUCTION

There exist numerous exact methods, such as the family of Branch and X [Branch and Bound algorithm (1), Branch and Cut algorithm (2), Branch and Price algorithm (3)], Dynamic Programming, and so on. When instances become too large for exact methods, metaheuristics are used. There are two main categories of metaheuristics: single solution algorithms and population algorithms. The first category regroups local search (LS) (4), greedy heuristic (GH) (5), simulated annealing (SA) (6), tabu search (TS) (7), iterated local search (ILS) (8), and so on. The second category, which is more and more studied, regroups evolutionary algorithms, such as genetic algorithms (9), evolution strategies (10), genetic programming (11), and also ant colonies (AC) (12), scatter search (SS) (13), immune systems (14), and so on. However, metaheuristics may not be able to solve the problems optimality and some convergence problems can be encountered.

During the past few years, many works have been realized on cooperative (or hybrid) optimization methods. In many cases, best results are obtained with this type of method, especially on real-life problems. Initially, cooperation was mainly realized between several metaheuristics. But now, more and more cooperation schemes between metaheuristics and exact methods have been proposed. These strategies usually gave good results because they were able

Parallel Combinatorial Optimization, edited by El-Ghazali Talbi
Copyright © 2006 by John Wiley & Sons, Inc.

to exploit simultaneously the advantages of both methods while listening to the impact of their respective drawbacks. Unfortunately, only a few papers explore the interest of parallelism on such cooperation.

This chapter proposes some perspectives for parallel cooperative algorithms. The objective is to extend Talbi's taxonomy (15) to cooperation between exact methods and metaheuristics and to see the potential of parallelism for each class of cooperative method. In this chapter, cooperation and hybridization will be used in the same way. These terms will indicate algorithms that combine different optimization methods.

The remainder of the article is organized as follows. Section 7.2 recalls the taxonomy used in Ref. 15 and recalls the grammar for hybrid metaheuristics, extending it to the case of hybridization with exact methods in Section 7.3. Section 7.4 gives the potential of the parallelism, by proposing several general schemes, and schemes for cooperations between methods to optimize a biobjective flow-shop scheduling problem. Section 7.5 investigates the frameworks that could be useful to implement such cooperative methods. Conclusions are drawn in Section 7.6.

7.2. TAXONOMY

There are not many taxonomies of hybrid metaheuristics. Reference 16 only considers hybridization between metaheuristics and local search algorithms. This chapter uses the taxonomy proposed by Talbi in Ref. 15 since it is valuable for cooperative methods between metaheuristics and exact approaches.

7.2.1. Design Issues

Cooperation involves two main features: the design and the implementation. The former category concerns the cooperative algorithm itself, involving issues such as the functionality and the architecture. The implementation takes into account the hardware platform, programming paradigm, and the environment.

The design of metaheuristics can be classified in two types: a hierarchical and a flat one. The derived classes are presented for each type of classification.

7.2.1.1. Hierarchical Classification. This classification distinguishes "low-" and "high-level" cooperation. This classification also distinguishes the way to apply to cooperation "relay" or "Teamwork."

- **Low-level–high-level**

    Low-level. This cooperation is a functional composition of a single optimization method. A given function of a method is replaced by another method.

    High-level. The different algorithms are self-contained. The metaheuristic structure is never modified.

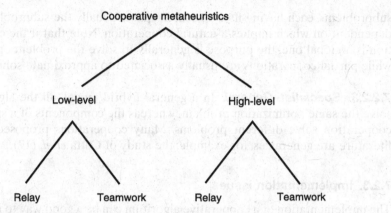

Fig. 7.1. The four classes derived from the hierarchical classification.

- **Relay–teamwork**

Relay. A set of methods is applied one after another, each using the output of the previous as its inputs, acting as in a pipeline fashion.

Teamwork represents cooperative optimization models.

Four classes are derived from this hierarchical taxonomy: Low-Level Relay (LRH), Low-Level Teamwork (LTH), High-Level Relay (HRH), High-Level Teamwork (HTH) (see Fig. 7.1).

7.2.2. Flat Classification

We decide to complete the flat classification proposed in Ref. 58 by adding the kind of resolution that is proposed by the method and to remove the nature of the cooperation as here it is always heterogeneous cooperation. Then three criteria have been selected for the flat classification of cooperation between exact and meta-heuristic methods: the complete resolution (exact or approximate), the resolution space (global or partial), and the nature of the cooperation (general or specialist).

7.2.2.1. *Exact–Approximate Resolution.* The type of whole cooperative method could be either exact or approximate. The exact cooperative approaches take useful information from heuristics to speed up the enumeration of the whole search space by upgrading bounds, finding initial solutions, defining useful cutting planes, and so on.

7.2.2.2. *Global–Partial Cooperation.* The components of the cooperative approach may work on the whole search space or only on a part. We oppose the global cooperation in which all the algorithms explore in the same search space and the partial cooperation where the problem is decomposed into

subproblems, each having its own search space. Usually the subproblems are dependent on which implies a natural cooperation. Note that if the cooperation is a global one, the purpose is generally to solve the problem optimally, while partial cooperations are usually associated to approximate solutions.

7.2.2.3. Specialist–General. In a general hybrid model, all the algorithms solve the same optimization problem, whereas the components of a specialist cooperation solve different problems. Many cooperations proposed in the literature are general, as, for example, the study of Cotta *et al.* (17).

7.2.3. Implementation Issues

The implementation of a cooperative algorithm can be a good way to improve the scalability of a method. Here, we recall the terms employed in Ref. 15 and give some remarks on meta-exact hybrid implementation.

7.2.3.1. Specific–General Purpose Computers. The specific computers differ from general purpose ones in that they usually only solve a small range of problem. Their internal structure is tailored for a particular problem, and thus can achieve much higher efficiency and hardware utilization than a processor that must handle a wide range of tasks.

7.2.3.2. Sequential–Parallel. An interesting point is to classify algorithms through the kind of implementation. In an optimization point of view, it is interesting to investigate the use of parallelism. Unfortunately, most of the hybrid algorithms between exact methods and metaheuristics are sequential.

7.2.3.3. Static–Dynamic–Adaptive. Parallel cooperation can be divided into different categories depending on the number and/or the location of work (task/data) depending on the load state of the target parallel machine:

- **Static:** The number of tasks and the location of work is fixed.
- **Dynamic:** The number of tasks is fixed, but the location of work is determined and/or changed at run-time.
- **Adaptive:** The number and location of tasks are changing dynamically.

7.3. GLOBAL OVERVIEW

We recall the grammar for cooperation schemes between metaheuristics given in Ref. 15 and extend it to exact methods (see Fig. 7.2). In our case, we consider only heterogeneous models.

In this grammar, it is interesting to know which methods use the other one. So the order in the description of a method has an importance. For example, the work of Cotta in Ref. 17 is a Low-Level teamwork Hybrid scheme. We

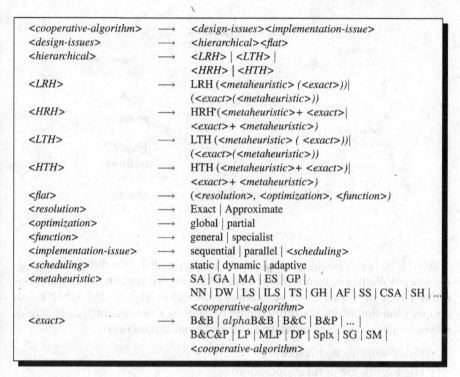

<cooperative-algorithm>	$\longrightarrow$	*<design-issues><implementation-issue>*
<design-issues>	$\longrightarrow$	*<hierarchical><flat>*
<hierarchical>	$\longrightarrow$	*<LRH>* | *<LTH>* |
		<HRH> | *<HTH>*
<LRH>	$\longrightarrow$	LRH (*<metaheuristic>* (*<exact>*))|
		(*<exact>*(*<metaheuristic>*))
<HRH>	$\longrightarrow$	HRH'(*<metaheuristic>*+ *<exact>*|
		<exact>+ *<metaheuristic>*)
<LTH>	$\longrightarrow$	LTH (*<metaheuristic>* (*<exact>*))|
		(*<exact>*(*<metaheuristic>*))
<HTH>	$\longrightarrow$	HTH (*<metaheuristic>*+ *<exact>*)|
		<exact>+ *<metaheuristic>*)
<flat>	$\longrightarrow$	(*<resolution>*, *<optimization>*, *<function>*)
<resolution>	$\longrightarrow$	Exact | Approximate
<optimization>	$\longrightarrow$	global | partial
<function>	$\longrightarrow$	general | specialist
<implementation-issue>	$\longrightarrow$	sequential | parallel | *<scheduling>*
<scheduling>	$\longrightarrow$	static | dynamic | adaptive
<metaheuristic>	$\longrightarrow$	SA | GA | MA | ES | GP |
		NN | DW | LS | ILS | TS | GH | AF | SS | CSA | SH | ...
		<cooperative-algorithm>
<exact>	$\longrightarrow$	B&B | *alpha*B&B | B&C | B&P | ... |
		B&C&P | LP | MLP | DP | Splx | SG | SM |
		<cooperative-algorithm>

Fig. 7.2. The grammar for cooperation between metaheuristics and exact methods.

write **LTH**(GA + B&B) for the Design and we means that the B&B is used as an operator by the genetic algorithm. So for the **LTH** scheme the first method uses the second in its design. For the relay model, the order indicates the order of the different methods used by the authors. For example, in Ref. 18 the authors use a **LRH**[GA (exact)] in one of their models, which means that they apply an exact method on the solution of a genetic algorithm in order to have the exact Pareto front in a multiobjective flow-shop problem. In Ref. 19, Bent and Van Hentenryck propose a **HRH**(SA (LTH(LS + B&B))) for the vehicle routing problem with time windows.

7.4. PARALLELISM ISSUE

The objective of this part is to show the potential of the parallelism in cooperation between metaheuristics and exact methods. We will use, when it is possible, elements of the literature, and when it is not possible, we will illustrate through simple examples.

In Refs. 20 and 21, the authors present interesting overviews of parallel metaheuristics. Here, we are interested in the parallelization of cooperative

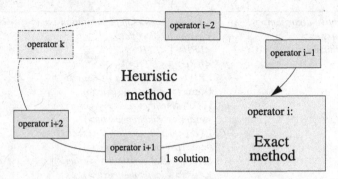

Fig. 7.3. Example of **LRH** cooperation scheme.

methods. For each possible cooperation, we distinguish two different ways to exploit parallelism in terms of type of resulting algorithms: on one hand, cooperation that proposes exact resolution approaches and on the other hand, cooperation that proposes approximate resolution. Consequently, eight classes of parallelism issues are envisaged, derived from three criteria:

- Exact–approached resolution.
- High-level–low-level cooperation.
- Relay–teamwork cooperation.

First, several general schemes of parallel cooperation are proposed. Then, parallel schemes of cooperation in a particular case to solve a biobjective flow-shop scheduling problem are proposed.

7.4.1. LRH

Figure 7.3 schematizes a general representation of **LRH** cooperation. In many cases, cooperation is realized in a unilateral way. This type of cooperation is certainly the most difficult to parallelize, because only one solution is considered, and cooperation is realized in dependent mechanisms of a single optimization method.

7.4.1.1. Parallel LRH Cooperative Metaheurisitics. For this cooperation, there is no natural way to exploit parallelism. It seems that the best idea consists in exploiting the characteristics of the problem, or the characteristics of the optimization methods. However, we propose three approaches to exploit these features:

1. The exact method usually works on a subproblem of the problem treated by the global heuristic approach. It may be interesting to simultaneously optimize, in an exact manner, several partitions of the global problem,

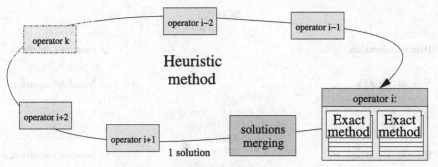

Fig. 7.4. Heuristic **LRH** cooperation scheme.

as shown in Fig. 7.4. This method will be effective only if the operator concerned by the parallelization is the most time expensive, because the other mechanism are sequential.

2. A similar idea is to iterate several executions of the global algorithm, as realized in iterated local search algorithms (8). Each processor executes one version of the global algorithm. Some information could be transmitted between the processors, as promising search areas, best solutions found, and so on.

3. A last solution could be explored if no efficient solution can be implemented: a fine grain parallelism. This parallelism is independent of the cooperation realized, and can be envisaged for all types of cooperative algorithms.

The three parallel schemes presented above can be applied to every type of cooperation.

7.4.1.2. Parallel LRH Cooperative Exact Method. Figure 7.5 represents an example of parallel cooperation for these approaches. Three sets of process are envisaged:

- **Type 1:** Several process dedicated to heuristic resolution, or only one.
- **Type 2:** Many process dedicated to exact resolution.
- A **master** process dedicated to dispatch the works to the processors dedicated to the exact resolution, and to manage information transfer between the two sets of processors.

Type 1 processor(s) are dedicated to provide bounds to the exact method. In fact, heuristics approaches are known to obtain good solutions quickly. These solutions are exploited by the exact approach to cut many nodes of the search tree. If the branch&X algorithm find new efficient solutions, it is possible to insert these solutions for one or several heuristic resolution.

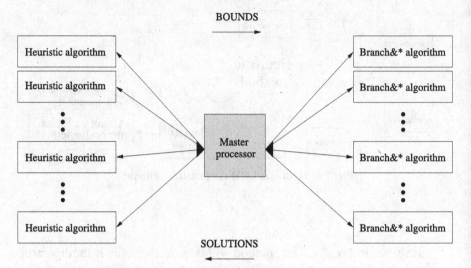

Fig. 7.5. Exact **LRH** parallel cooperation.

Type 2 processors obtain works from the master processor, which is dispatching the jobs. The jobs consist in exploring a branch of the search tree, chosen to limit the size of the search space explored by the processors.

Master processor have also two functionalities. First, it provides bounds to the type 2 processors (possibly, it could provide new solutions to the type 1 processors). Second, this processor dispatches the different nodes to explore for an exact resolution. The bounds and/or the solutions should be transmitted dynamically during the execution, each time a new information is provided by the algorithms.

7.4.2. LTH

Figure 7.6 represents a general representation of **LTH** cooperation. For this cooperation, cooperations in a unilateral way are allowed.

7.4.2.1. Parallel LTH Cooperative Metaheurisitics. Figure 7.7 shows an example of this type of cooperation. An operator of the metaheuristic is replaced by an exact approach. This exact approach is applied on the N individuals of the population of the metaheuristic.

Two major problems of this approach could be expected.

- Static approach: In this first version, N processors are exactly needed to establish this cooperation.
- The operator i is replaced by a parallel exact method, but the master processor works alone for all the others operators, if these operators can not be dispatched on the other processors.

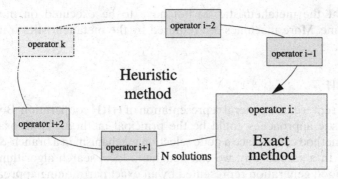

Fig. 7.6. Example **LTH** cooperation scheme.

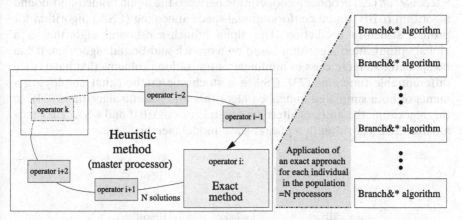

Fig. 7.7. Heuristic **LTH** parallel cooperation.

To answer these problems, we need to modify the general algorithm of the population-based heuristic approach. A dynamic approach is proposed in which a processor P selects individuals in the heuristic population each time P has no job to execute. Each time a job is terminated, the final solution is added to a list of solutions to be inserted in the population. So, despite the fact that the general algorithm is modified, the two major problems exposed are solved.

7.4.2.2. Parallel LTH Cooperative Exact Method.
For this approach, the previous parallel architecture presented could be applied. However, it does not seem interesting to exploit several metaheuristic solutions to improve an exact algorithm (a branch-&-X algorithm, e.g.). This approach can be interesting for multiobjective exact algorithms, in which each metaheuritic could optimize only one objective, the other ones being replaced by constraints.

Another scheme of parallelization is to affect, to each processor, a set of nodes to explore, as schematized in Fig. 7.7. In this parallel method, we can expect that the metaheuristic do not have to be executed on more than one machine. More machines are required by the metaheuristics if it is time expensive.

7.4.3. HRH

Figure 7.8 represents a general representation of **HRH** cooperation. Both exact and heuristic approaches could be the principal method. As an example, a heuristic method can replace a node selection mechanism in a branch-&-bound approach. In a second way, we can imagine a local search algorithm, with a neighborhood generation represented by an exact partitioning approach.

Here, we present a parallel **HRH** cooperative method of the litterature. Klepeis *et al.* (22) propose a cooperation between the alpha branch-and-bound algorithm (αBB) and a conformational space annealing (CSA) algorithm for protein structure prediction. The alpha branch-and-bound algorithm is a global optimization algorithm based on a branch-and-bound algorithm. It can be applied to a large class of nonlinear optimization problems that have twice differentiable functions (23). CSA is a stochastic method that employs elements of both simulated annealing algorithm and genetic algorithms (24). In this algorithm, the authors alternate several runs of αBB and CSA. They parallelize their algorithm in a master-slave model (see Fig. 7.9).

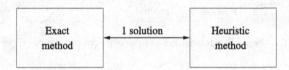

Fig. 7.8. HRH cooperation scheme.

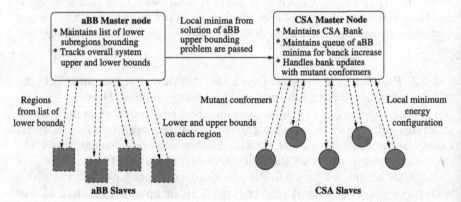

Fig. 7.9. An example of an **HLR** hybrid for the protein structure prediction.

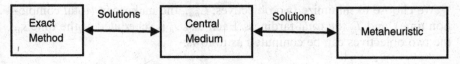

Fig. 7.10. **HTH** cooperation scheme.

7.4.4. HTH

Figure 7.10 shows a general representation of **HTH** cooperation. Both exact and heuristic approaches could be the principal method. As an example, a population-based heuristic method can replace a node selection mechanism in a branch-and-bound approach. For another kind of cooperation, we can imagine a genetic algorithm, with a mutation operator represented by a exact partitioning approach.

7.5. APPLICATION TO A BIOBJECTIVE FLOW SHOP PROBLEM RESOLUTION

This section briefly describes an exact method (25), and a population-based heuristic approach (26), in a first time. Then, we propose several parallel cooperative approaches to solve a biobjective flow shop problem.

7.5.1. Problem Description

The Flow-Shop Scheduling Problem (FSP) is one of numerous scheduling problems. The FSP has been widely studied in the literature. Proposed methods for its resolution vary between exact methods, such as the branch-&-bound algorithm (27), specific heuristics (28) and meta-heuristics (29). However, the majority of works on flow-shop problem studies the problem in its single criterion form and aims mainly to minimize makespan, which is the total completion time. Some biobjective approaches exist in the literature. Sayin and Karabati proposed a branch-and-bound strategy to solve the two-machine flow-shop scheduling problem, minimizing the makespan and the sum of completion times (27). Sivrikaya-Serifoglu and Ulusoy (30) proposed a comparison of branch-&-bound approaches for minimizing the makespan and a weighted combination of the average flowtime, applied to the two-machine flow-shop problem. Rajendran proposed a specific heuristic to minimize the makespan and the total flowtime (28). Nagar *et al.* (29) proposed a survey of the existing multicriteria approaches of scheduling problems.

FSP can be presented as a set of N jobs $J_1, J_2, \cdots, J_N$ to be scheduled on M machines. Machines are critical resources: One machine cannot be assigned to two jobs simultaneously. Each job J_i is composed of M consecutive tasks $t_{i1}, \cdots, t_{iM}$, where t_{ij} represents the jth task of the job J_i requiring the machine m_j. To each task, t_{ij} is associated a processing time p_{ij}. Each job J_i must be achieved before its due date d_i. In our study, we are interested in permutation FSP where jobs must be scheduled in the same order on all the machines.

We choose to minimize two objectives: C_{max}, the makespan (total completion time), and $\overline{T}$, the total tardiness. Each task t_{ij} is scheduled at the time s_{ij}, the two objectives can be computed as follows:

$$C_{max} = Max\{s_{iM} + p_{iM} \mid i \in [1 \cdots N]\}$$

$$\overline{T} = \sum_{i}^{N}[max(0, s_{iM} + p_{iM} - d_i)]$$

In the Graham *et al.* (31) notation, this problem is denoted: F/perm, $di/(C_{max}, \overline{T})$.

In Ref. 32, C_{max} minimization has been proved to be NP-hard for more than two machines. The total tardiness objective $\overline{T}$ has been studied only a few times for M machines (33), but total tardiness minimization for one machine has been proved to be NP-hard (34). The evaluation of the performances of our algorithm has been realized on some Taillard benchmarks for the FSP (35), extended to the biobjective case (36).[1]

7.5.2. A Biobjective Exact Method

On the Pareto front, two types of solutions may be distinguished: the supported solutions (that are on the convex hull of the set of solutions and that may be found thanks to linear combinations of criteria) and nonsupported solutions.

Based on this remark, Ulungu and Teghem have proposed the two phases method (TPM) for solving bi-criteria problems (37).

- The first phase consists in finding supported solutions with aggregations of the two objectives f_1 and f_2 in the form $\lambda_1 f_1 + \lambda_2 f_2$. It starts to find the two extreme efficient solutions that are two supported solutions. Then it looks recursively for the existence of supported solutions between two already found supported solutions r and s [we suppose $f_1(r) < f_1(s)$ and $f_2(r) > f_2(s)$] according to a direction perpendicular to the line (rs), defined as follows: $\lambda_1 = f_2(r) - f_2(s)$, $\lambda_2 = f_1(s) - f_1(r)$. Each new supported solution generates two new searches.
- The second phase consists in finding nonsupported solutions between each couple of consecutive Pareto supported solutions by reducing the search space.

This method has been adapted to solve the biobjective Flow shop problem, using a branch-&-bound approach to solve aggregations.

7.5.3. A Heuristic Approach: AGMA

This method was proposed in Ref. 26. It proposed a cooperation between a genetic algorithm (AGA), and a mimetic algorithm (AMA). Many coopera-

---

[1]Biobjective benchmarks are available on the web at http://www.lifl.fr/~basseur.

tive approaches propose pipe-lined cooperation. To improve classical hybridization methods, we propose to define dynamic transitions between AGA and AMA. The idea is to run AGA and to launch a AMA generation each time a condition is verified. Here, a progress value is assigned during the metaheuristic run. Let $P_{PO}*$ be the value of the improvement rate done on the Pareto front $PO*$. If $P_{PO}*$ goes below a threshold α, AMA is launched on the current AGA population. When AMA generation is over a threshold, the Pareto front is updated, and AGA is rerun with the previous population.

7.5.4. Parallel Cooperative Approaches

This section proposes several schemes of cooperation between AGMA and TPM. Then, several parallel implementations of these cooperations are proposed.

7.5.4.1. Exact Resolution. In this approach, we run the whole TPM. For every branch-&-bound algorithm of the TPM, we consider the best solutions given by AGMA as the initial value. Therefore we can cut many nodes of the branch-&-bound algorithm and find all optimal solutions with this method (**LRH cooperation**).

A first possible implementation is to parallelize AGMA and TPM independently. AGMA is running until a stopping criteria is reached. Then a parallel TPM can be launched with initial bounds provided by AGMA. A principal drawback can be extracted from this parallel scheme. It seems difficult to set an efficient stopping criteria. AGMA may be stopped to early to speed up the exact resolution effectively, or the running time may be lost if AGMA execution time is too long to improve the best solution during the execution.

A solution to minimize this effect is to run AGMA and TPM simultaneously. Several process are associated to each method. Each time the best solution of AGMA is improved, a new bound can be transmitted to the exact method TPM. Moreover, if a new optimal solution is founded by TPM, it can be inserted into the AGMA current population. Then, when AGMA convergence becomes too slow, process could be reaffected to TPM execution (Fig. 7.11).

7.5.4.2. Heuristic Resolution. In this approach, TPM is launched on subproblems to improve solutions founded by AGMA. We distinguish two principal schemes of cooperation that can be exposed for this type of approach. First, TPM can be embedded into a mutation operator of AGMA (**LTH cooperation**). The main problem for this cooperation is the computational time needed by the application of the exact method. We propose to assign one process to run AGMA. Then, each time a mutation has to be applied to a solution, several process are generated to this task. Then AGMAs run continue. The results obtained by TPM will be returned several generations later to the AGMA process, and inserted into the current population (see Fig. 7.12).

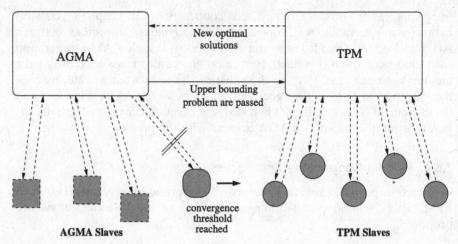

Fig. 7.11. A parallel implementation of exact **LRH** cooperation between AGMA and TPM.

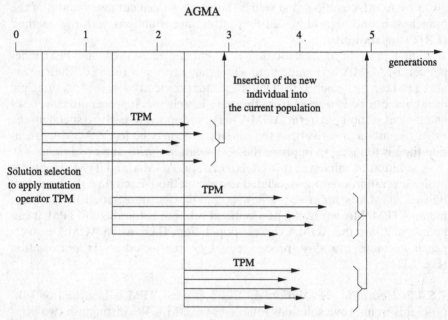

Fig. 7.12. A parallel implementation of partial **LTH** cooperation between AGMA and TPM.

Second, TPM can be applied on the final solutions provided by AGMA, in a sequential cooperation (**HTH cooperation**). In this case, the principal possible implementation is to parallelize AGMA and TPM independently.

To implement the parallel schemes, we have found the use of frameworks to be really helpful. For the basic schemes in which the methods are parallelized independantly, two different frameworks could be used. However, it is really important to get a parallel hybrid framework to establish a cooperation scheme between exact and partial approaches.

7.6. TOWARD THE USE OF FRAMEWORKS

The goal of this section, is to present a vision of the architecture, software, and frameworks, that allows us to implement the schemes present in Section 7.5.

7.6.1. Parallel Infrastructure

Here, we indicate some popular tools for implementing a parallel cooperation. We present some sophisticated environments as PVM, MPI, but also Peer-to-Peer (P2P) computing (38) and grid computing that are two powerful ways to realize high-performance applications.

7.6.1.1. PVM. Parallel Virtual Machine (PVM) is a software system that allows us to develop applications on heterogeneous networks of parallel and serial computers (39). PVM contains user-callable routines for message passing, spawning processes, coordinating tasks, and modifying the virtual machine.

7.6.1.2. MPI. The Message Passing Interface (MPI) is a library specification for message passing (40). The MPI functions support process-to-process communication, group communication, setting up and managing communication groups, and interacting with the environment.

7.6.1.3. Globus. The Globus Toolkit is an open source software toolkit used for building grids (41,42). It consists of several modules that can help to implement high-level application services.

7.6.1.4. XtremWeb. XtremWeb is a research project belonging to light weight Grid systems. It is a free open source and nonprofit software platform to explore scientific issues and applications of Desktop Grid, Global Computing, and Peer-to-Peer distributed systems (43).

There exist some frameworks that propose to develop parallel exact methods or parallel metaheuristics. First, we will present them and then show the possible way to combine them in order to propose a global framework that allows us to directly instantiate a parallel cooperative method.

7.6.2. Parallel Exact Frameworks

Here, we will present the best known exact frameworks that are "opensource". A survey of parallel branch-and-bound algorithms can be found in (44). The frameworks are presented ordered by name.

7.6.2.1. BOB++. Bob++ is a library that groups a set of C++ classes. Its goal is to easily implement sequential and parallel search algorithms (Branch and X, Dynamic programming, . . .) (45). BOB++ is a high-level framework for solving a combinatorial optimisation problem. BOB++ is available for grid computing and is fault tolerant.

7.6.2.2. COIN. The Computational Infrastructure for Operations Research (COIN-OR, or simply COIN) project is an initiative to spur the development of open-source software for the operations research community (46). This framework allows us to develop powerful exact methods and proposes a package SYMPHONY that includes a generic MILP solver for multiobjectives. It also proposes OTS for implementing Tabu Search. But for the moment there is no possible cooperation between metaheuristics and exact methods.

7.6.2.3. FATCOP. FATCOP is a parallel mixed-integer program solver written in PVM (47,48). The implementation uses the Condor resource management system to provide a virtual machine composed of otherwise idle computers. The solver differs from previous parallel branch-and-bound codes by implementing a general purpose parallel mixed-integer programming algorithm in an opportunistic multiple processor environment, as opposed to a conventional dedicated environment. It shows how to make effective use of resources as they become available while ensuring the program tolerates resource retreat. The solver performs well on test problems arising from real applications, and is particularly useful for solving long-running hard mixed-integer programming problems.

7.6.2.4. PARINO. Parino is a framework that was developed for solving large mixed-integer programs (MIPs) in parallel (49). Parino combines portability and efficiency with flexibility. It is written in C++, and is portable across any message passing platforms. The flexibility of the framework is a result of mapping the MIP computation to an entity-FSM paradigm, where it is expressed in terms of the interactions among several distributed active objects. Thus, it is possible to incrementally enhance the functionality of Parino by incorporating new dynamic objects into the framework.

7.6.2.5. PICO. PICO is a C++ framework for implementing general parallel branch-and-bound algorithms (50). The PICO framework provides a mechanism for the efficient implementation of a wide range of branch-and-bound methods on an equally wide range of parallel computing platforms.

7.6.2.6. PPBB. PPBB-Library (Portable Parallel Branch-and-Bound Library) presents an easy way to parallelize sequential branch-and-bound algorithms for several architectures. Each parallel running process of the branch-and-bound application maintains the point of view of the sequential algorithm. The library overtakes the management of the subproblems, which are created during execution of the branch-and-bound algorithm. Load balancers provided by the library take care of a balanced distribution of the subproblems. PPBB has been used for Flow Shop.

7.6.2.7. PUBB. Parallelization Utility for Branch-and-Bound algorithm (PUBB) is a generalized utility for parallel branch-and-bound algorithms (51). It has been completed in PUBB2 (52). An application on maximum clique problem is presented in Ref. 53.

7.6.3. Parallel Heuristic Framework

Many frameworks have been developed for combinatorial optimization (54). Here, we focus on opensource frameworks and present them ordered by acronym.

7.6.3.1. BEAGLE. The Distributed Beagle Engine Advanced Genetic Learning Environment is a C++ Evolutionary Computation (EC) framework that provides a high-level software environment to do any kind of EC, with support for tree-based genetic programming, bit string and real-valued genetic algorithms, and evolution strategy. The parallelism implementation is based on TCP/IP sockets (55).

7.6.3.2. DREAM. Distributed Resource Evolutionary Algorithm Machine (DREAM) is a framework that allows the automatic distribution of evolutionary algorithm (EA) processing through a virtual machine built from large numbers of individual machines linked by standard Internet protocols (56).

7.6.3.3. ECJ. An Evolutionary Computation and Genetic Programming System in Java is a framework that allows us to implement evolutionary algorithms and genetic programming. It was designed to be highly flexible, with nearly all classes (and all of their settings) dynamically determined at runtime by a user-provided parameter file. The framework uses "TCP/IP socket" and "Java threads".

7.6.3.4. J-DEAL. The Java Distributed Evolutionary Algorithms Library (J-DEAL) is an object-oriented library of Evolutionary Algorithms, with both local and distributed algorithms, for the Java language.

7.6.3.5. PARADISEO. The ParadisEO (PARAllel and DIStributed Evolving Objects) framework enables the easy and fast development of the most common parallel and distributed models of hybrid metaheuristics. The first ParadisEO implementation relies on a multiprogramming layer (Posix threads) and some communication libraries (LAM-MPI and/or PVM) for execution on dedicated resources (57,58). ParadisEO-CMWis an open source extension of the ParadisEO framework. Coupled with the Condor-MW library, it enables the execution of parallel applications on volatile and dynamic computational resources.

7.6.4. Parallel Hybrid Framework

Actually, some researchers are looking in integrative frameworks that will be able to propose developers to combine exact methods and metaheuristics and to enjoy parallelism.

7.6.4.1. A-Teams. An asynchronous team (A-Team) is a strongly cyclic computational network (59). The number of agents can be arbitrarily large and the agents may be distributed over an arbitrarily wide area. Agents cooperate by working on one another's results. Each agent is completely autonomous (it decides which results it is going to work on and when). Results that are not being worked on accumulate in shared memories to form populations.

7.6.4.2. TECHS. TECHS (TEams for Cooperative Heterogeneous Search) allow us the use of very different search agents within a search team while still achieving synergetic effects (60).

7.6.4.3. MALLBA and TRACER. In MALLBA (university of MAlaga, university of La Laguna, university of BArcelona), each optimization method is encapsulated into a skeleton (61). Different exact methods are proposed (Branch and Bound, Divide and Conquer, Dynamic Programming) and also heuristic methods. MALLBA is one of the few frameworks that proposes the possibility to directly develop parallel hybrid methods between exact and heuristic methods. The parallelism is available for LAN and WAN computer platforms. TRACER is the following project of MALLBA.

Table 7.1 proposes to present the different frameworks through some specific points: the type of available algorithms (metaheuristics and/or exact methods), the coding language, which kind of parallelism is available, the possibility to deploy the application on cluster and/or grid, and an example of application of the framework found in the literature.

7.7. CONCLUSION

This chapter presented the potential of parallelism for cooperative methods using exact methods and genetic algorithms. Also described were several frameworks that allow us to develop parallel exact methods, parallel metaheuristics, and some frameworks that allows us to develop cooperative algorithms between exact methods and metaheuristics. We have shown that there could be some interesting works in combining existing frameworks for exact methods and metaheuristics in order to obtain a more global one. The devel-

TABLE 7.1. Survey of the Presented Parallel Frameworks

Name	Methods		Language	Kind of Parallelism	Clusters	Grids	Some Applications
	MH	Exacts					
BOB++		+	C++	Thread	+	+	VRP
COIN	+	+	C++	LAM/MPI	+		Knapsack
FATCOP		+	PVM, Condor PVM		+	+	marketing delivery
PARINO		+	C++	MPI	+		VRP
PICO		+	C++	MPI	+		QAP
PPBB		+	C	PVM	+		flow-shop
PUBB		+	C++	PVM	+		Max-Clique
BEAGLE	+		C++	TCP/IP socket	+		Knapsack
DREAM	+		Java	TCP/IP socket	+	+	Job-shop
ECJ	+		Java	TCP/IP socket Java threads	+		
J-DEAL	+		Java	Java threads	+		
PARADISEO	+		C++	MPI, PVM	+	+	TSP
A-Teams	+	+	independent				TSP
			C	PVM	+		PPC
MALLBA	+	+	C++	Netstream, MPI	+		Knapsack
TECHS	+	+	independent	socket			job-shop

opment of parallel cooperative algorithms between exact methods and metaheuristics is still a challenge.

In this chapter, we saw the influence of the kind of cooperation in this kind of results: Do you want an exact result or an approximated one? Such a question will depend on the size of problem instances. The size of problem instances and the kind of cooperation will also influence the kind of parallelism. For very large instances, it will be useful to use grid compute platforms, but for small ones clusters will be easiest to find. Another question is which frameworks to use. The answers to the previous questions can help to choose the best framework. The advantage of frameworks is that some hybridizations are provided, but much work has to be done in order to take advantage of the most interesting cooperations. Only MALLBA actually provides some skeletons that makes us realize a cooperation between exact methods and metaheuristics. But some very interesting research would be to combine the most complete exact framework (COIN) with a metaheuristic framework to propose general models.

REFERENCES

1. E.L. Lawler and D.E. Wood. Branch and bound methods: A survey. *Oper. Res.*, **14**:699–719 (1966).

2. R. Gomory. Outline of an algorithm for integer solutions to linear programs. *Bull. Am. Math. Soc.*, **64**:275 (1958).

3. C. Barnhart *et al.* Branch-and-price: Column generation for solving huge integer programs. *Oper. Res.*, 316–329 (March 1998).

4. E.L. Lawler. *Combinatorial optimization: networks and matroids.* Holt, Reinhart, and Winston, New York, 1976.

5. C.H. Papadimitriou and K. Steiglitz. *Combinatorial Optimization: Algorithms and Complexity.* Prentice-Hall, 1982. Englewood Clis, NJ.

6. S. Kirkpatrick, D.C. Gelatt, and M.P. Vechhi. Optimization by simulated annealing. *Science*, **220**:671–680 (May 1983).

7. F. Glover. Future paths for integer programming and links to artificial intelligence. *Comput. Oper. Res.*, **13**:533–549 (1986).

8. H.R. Lourenço, O. Martin, and T. Stützle. *Handbook of Metaheuristics*, chapter Iterated Local Search, Kluwer Academic Publishers, Norwell, MA, 2002, pp. 321–353.

9. J. Holland. *Adaptation in Natural and Artificial Systems.* University of Michigan Press, 1975.

10. I. Rechenberg. *Evolutions Strategie: Optimierung technischer Systeme nach Prinzipien der biologischen Evolution.* Frommann-Holzboog, Stuttgart, 1973.

11. J.R. Koza. *Genetic Programming: On the Programming of Computers by Natural Selection.* MIT Press, Cambridge, MA, 1992.

12. M. Dorigo, V. Maniezzo, and A. Colorni. Positive feedback as a search strategy. Technical report, no 91016, Dipartimento di Elettronica e Informatica, Politecnico di Milano, Italy, 1991.

13. F. Glover. Heuristics for integer programming using surrogate constraints. *Decision Sci.*, **8**(1):156–166 (1977).

14. J.O. Kephart. A biologically inspired immune system for computers. In *Artificial Life IV: Proceedings of the Fourth International Workshop on the Synthesis and Simulation of Living Systems*, MIT Press, Cambridge, MA, 1994, pp. 130–139.

15. E-G. Talbi. A taxonomy of hybrid metaheuristics. *J. Heuristics*, **8**(2):541–564 (Sept. 2002).

16. I. Dumitrescu and T. Stützle. Combinations of local search and exact algorithms. In G. Raidl *et al.*, ed., *Applications of Evolutionary Computing, Proceedings of EvoWorkshops 2003*, number 2611 in Lecture Notes in Computer Science, Springer Verlag, Berlin, Germany, 2003, pp. 211–224.

17. C. Cotta, J.F. Aldana, A.J. Nebro, and J.M. Troya. Hybridizing genetic algorithms with branch and bound techniques for the resolution of the TSP. In D.W. Pearson, N.C. Steele, and R.F. Albrecht, eds., *Artificial Neural Nets and Genetic Algorithms 2*, Springer-Verlag, New York, 1995, pp. 277–280.

18. M. Basseur, J. Lemesre, C. Dhaenens, and E.-G. Talbi. Cooperation between branch and bound and evolutionary approaches to solve a biobjective flow shop problem. *Workshop on Experimental and Efficient Algorithms (WEA'04)*, Vol. 3059, Springer-Verlag, Rio de Janero, Brazil, 2004, pp. 72–86.

19. R. Bent and P. Van Hentenryck. A two-stage hybrid local search for the vehicle routing problem with time windows. Technical Report, Brown University, September 2001.

20. E. Alba, ed. *Parallel Metaheuristics: A New Class of Algorithms*. John Wiley & Sons, Live, Hobekin, NJ. 2005.

21. E. Alba and M. Tomassini. Parallelism and evolutionary algorithms. *IEEE Trans. Evol. Comput.* **6**(5):443–462 (Oct 2002).

22. J.L. Klepeis, M.J. Pieja, and C.A. Floudas. Hybrid global optimization algorithms for protein structure prediction: Alternating hybrids. *Biophys. J.*, **4**(84):869–882 (2003).

23. I. Androulakis, C. Maranas, and C. Floudas. ffbb: a global optimization method for general constrained nonconvex problems. *J. Global Op.*, **7**:337–363 (1995).

24. J. Lee, H. Scheraga, and S. Rackovsky. New optimization method for conformational energy calculations on polypeptides: conformational space annealing. *J. Comput. Chem.*, **18**:1222–1232 (1997).

25. J. Lemesre, C. Dhaenens, and E.-G. Talbi. An exact parallel method for a biobjective permutation flowshop problem. *Eur. J. Oper. Res.*, 2005. to be published. Available online at www.sciencedirect.com.

26. M. Basseur, F. Seynhaeve, and E.-G. Talbi. Adaptive mechanisms for multiobjective evolutionary algorithms. *Congress on Engineering in System Application CESA'03*, Lille, France, July 2003, pp. 72–86.

27. S. Sayin and S. Karabati. A bicriteria approach to the two-machine flow shop scheduling problem. *Eur. J. Oper. Res.*, **113**:435–449 (1999).

28. C. Rajendran. Heuristics for scheduling in flowshop with multiple objectives. *Eur. J. Oper. Res.*, **82**:540–555 (1995).

29. A. Nagar, J. Haddock, and S. Heragu. Multiple and bicriteria scheduling: A literature survey. *Eur. J. Operat. Res.*, **81**:88–104 (1995).

30. F. Sivrikaya-Serifoglu and G. Ulusoy. A bicriteria two-machine permutation flowshop problem. *Eur. J. Oper. Res.*, **107**(2):414–430 (1998).

31. R.L. Graham, E.L. Lawler, J.K. Lenstra, and A.H.G. Rinnooy Kan. Optimization and approximation in deterministic sequencing and scheduling: a survey. *Ann. Discrete Math.* **5**, 287 (1979).

32. J.K. Lenstra, B.J. Lageweg, and A.H.G. Rinnooy Kan. A general bounding scheme for the permutation flow-shop problem. *Oper. Res.*, **26**(1):53–67 (1978).

33. Y.-D. Kim. Minimizing total tardiness in permutation flowshops. *Eur. J. Oper. Res.*, **33**:511 551 (1995).

34. J. Du and J.Y.-T. Leung. Minimizing total tardiness on one machine is NP-hard. *Math. Oper. Res.*, **15**:483–495 (1990).

35. E. Taillard. Benchmarks for basic scheduling problems. *Eur. J. Oper. Res.*, **64**: 278–285 (1993).

36. E.G. Talbi, M. Rahoual, M.H. Mabed, and C. Dhaenens. A hybrid evolutionary approach for multicriteria optimization problems: Application to the flow shop. In E. Zitzler, K. Deb, and L. Thiele, eds., *Evolutionary Multi-Criterion Optimization*, volume 1993 of *Lecture Notes in Computer Science*, Springer-Verlag, Eurich, Switzerland, 2001, pp. 416–428.

37. E.L. Ulungu and J. Teghem. Multi-objectif combinatorial optimization problems: A survey. *J. Multi-criteria Dec. Anal.*, **3**:1–22 (1994).

38. A. Oram. *Peer-to-Peer: Harnessing the Power of Disruptive Technologies*. O'Reilley & Associates, Sebastopol, CA, 2001.

39. V. Sunderam. Pvm: A framework for parallel distributed computing. *Concurrency: Pract. Exper.*, **2**(4):315–319 (Dec. 1990).

40. W. Gropp, E. Lusk, N. Doss, and A. Skjellum. A high-performance, portable implementation of the MPI message passing interface standard. *Parallel Comput.*, **22**(6):789 (Sept. 1996).

41. I. Foster, C. Kesselman, and S. Tuecke. The anatomy of the grid: Enabling scalable virtual organizations. *Inter. J. Supercomput. Appl.*, **15**(3):200–222 (2001).

42. I. Foster and C. Kesselman. Globus: A metacomputing infrastructure toolkit. *Inter. J. Supercomput. Appl.*, **11**(2):115–128 (1997).

43. G. Fedak, C. Germain, V. Neri, and F. Cappello. Xtremweb: Building an experimental platform for global computing. Workshop on Global Computing on Personal Devices (CCGRID2001), May 2001. IEEE Press. Brisbane, Australia.

44. B. Gendron and T.G. Cranic. Parallel branch-and-bound algorithms: Survey and synthesis. *Oper. Res.*, **42**(5):1042–1066 (1994).

45. Bertrand Le cun and Catherine Roucairol. Bob: Branch and bound optimization library. In *INFORMS, Institute For OR and Management Science*, New Orleans, LA, October 1995.

46. R. Lougee-Heimer *et al.* The coin-or initiative: Open-source software accelerates operations research progress. *ORMS Today*, **28**(5):20 (October 2001).

47. P.K. Agarwal, J. Erickson, and L.J. Guibas. Kinetic binary space partitions for intersecting segments and disjoint triangles (extended abstract). *ACM Symposium on Discrete Algorithms*, 1998, pp. 107–116. San Francisco, CA, Acrilsian.

48. Q. Chen, M. Ferris, and J.T. Linderoth. Fatcop 2.0: Advanced features in an opportunistic mixed integer programming solver. *Ann. Oper. Res.*, **103**:17–32 (2001).

49. J.T. Linderoth. *Topics in Parallel Integer Optimization*. Ph.D. Thesis, Georgia Institute of Technology, Atlanta, 1998.

50. J. Eckstein, C.A. Phillips, and W.E. Hart. PICO: an object-oriented framework for parallel branch and bound. Technical Report RRR 40-2000, 2000.

51. Y. Shinano, M. Higaki, and R. Hirabayashi. A generalized utility for parallel branch and bound algorithms. *7nd IEEE Symposium on Parallel and Distributed Processing (SPDP '95)*, 1995, pp. 858–865.

52. Y. Shinano, T. Fujie, and Y. Kounoike. Effectiveness of parallelizing the ilogcplex mixed integer optimizer in the pubb2 framework. *Euro-Par 2003*, 2003, pp. 451–460, LNCS, Klagenfurt, Austria.

53. Y. Shinano, T. Fujie, Y. Ikebe, and R. Hirabayashi. Solving the maximum clique problem using pubb. In *12th International Parallel Processing Symposium and 9th Symposium on Parallel and Distributed Processing (IPPS '98)*, 1998, pp. 326–332.

54. E.-G. Talbi, C. Cotta, and E. Alba. *Parallel Metaheuristics*, chapter Parallel hybrid approaches. John Wiley & Sons, Live, Hobeken, NJ, 2005.

55. C. Gagné and M. Parizeau. Open beagle: A new versatile c++ framework for evolutionary computation. *GECCO Late Breaking Papers*, 2002, pp. 161–168.

56. M.G. Arenas *et al.* A framework for distributed evolutionary algorithms. *PPSN*, 2002, pp. 665–675.

57. S. Cahon, N. Melab, and E.-G. Talbi. Building with paradiseo reusible parallel and distributed evolutionary algorithms. *Parallel Comput.*, **30**(5–6):677–697 (2004).

58. S. Cahon, N. Melab, and E.-G. Talbi. Paradiseo: A framework for the reusable design of parallel and distributed metaheuristics. *J. Heuristics*, **10**(3):357–380 (2004).

59. S. Talukdar, L. Baerentzen, A. Gove, and P.S. de Souza. Asynchronous teams: Cooperation schemes for autonomous agents. *J. Heuristics*, **4**(4):295–321 (1998).

60. J. Denzinger and T. Offermann. On cooperation between evolutionary algorithms and other search paradigms. *Proceeding of CEC-99*, Washington, USA, 1999, pp. 2317–2324.

61. E. Alba *et al*. Mallba: A library of skeletons for combinatorial optimisation. *Proceedings of the Euro-Par*, volume LNCS 2004, Paderboun, Germany, 2002, pp. 927–932.

CHAPTER 8

Parallel Exact Methods for Multiobjective Combinatorial Optimization

C. DHAENENS, J. LEMESRE, N. MELAB, M-S. MEZMAZ, and E-G. TALBI

OPAC Team, LIFL, Bâatiment M3, University of Lille I, 59655 Villeneuve d'Ascq cedex FRANCE

8.1. INTRODUCTION

Optimization problems encountered in practice are seldom monoobjective. In general, there are many conflicting objectives to handle: for example, minimizing the costs and maximizing the quality. Indeed, many diverse areas (telecommunications, genomics, engineering design, finance, chemistry, and ecology among others) are concerned by multiobjective optimization problems (MOPs).

Multiobjective optimization takes its roots from the nineteenth century, with the works of Edgeworth and Pareto in economics. It has been used in economics and management science, and then gradually in engineering sciences. Nowadays, multiobjective optimization is an important area for researchers and engineers. This is due to the multiobjective nature of many real-world optimization problems, but also because many interesting questions arise in this domain.

The main difference between multiobjective optimization and single objective optimization is that the optimal solution for a MOP is not a single solution as in monoobjective optimization problems, but a set of solutions defined as Pareto optimal solutions. A solution is said to be Pareto optimal if it is not possible to improve a given objective of this solution without deteriorating another objective. This set of solutions represents the best solutions in terms of compromise between the different conflicting objectives.

Parallel Combinatorial Optimization, edited by El-Ghazali Talbi
Copyright © 2006 by John Wiley & Sons, Inc.

Difficulties in solving MOPs lie in the following general facts: the number of Pareto optimal solutions depends on several characteristics, such as the size of the problem and the number of considered objectives. The structure of the Pareto front (continuity, convexity, modality, deceptivity, etc.) depends on the studied MOP. The Pareto optimal solutions are localized on the frontier and inside the convex hull of feasible solutions. Moreover, most of the MOPs are NP-hard problems.

This chapter is interested in "*a posteriori*" multiobjective combinatorial optimization methods, where the set of Pareto solutions (solutions of best compromise) have to be generated in order to provide the decision maker with the opportunity to choose the solution according to their own criteria. This chapter uses a biobjective permutation flow-shop as an illustrative example.

This chapter is decomposed into three main parts. Section 8.2 presents the context. It introduces multiobjective concepts and gives main definitions. This section also briefly describes the biobjective permutation flowshop problem used as an illustrative example. Section 8.3 presents existing exact methods for multiobjective combinatorial optimization and analyzes their parallel design. Then, Section 8.4 gives indications about implementation of such methods on parallel systems and Grids.

8.2. GENERAL CONTEXT

This section presents multiobjective optimization concepts. Then the problem under study is exposed and finally, classical high-level parallel models are recalled.

Multiobjective combinatorial optimization is a part of combinatorial optimization. Hence, some definitions are common, but some concepts are specific to multiobjective. Below, we present the most important ones.

8.2.1. Multiobjective Combinatorial Optimization Problems

Let us describe and define Multiobjective combinatorial Problems (MOPs) in a general case. Assume that a solution to such a problem can be described by a decision vector $x(x_1, x_2, \cdots, x_n)$ in the decision space X. A fitness function $f: X \rightarrow Y$ evaluates the quality of each solution by assigning it an objective vector $y(y_1, y_2, \cdots, y_p)$ in the objective space Y, where $y_i = f_i(x)$ represents the value of the ith objective for x. In this context, multiobjective combinatorial optimization consists in finding the solutions, in the decision space, globally optimizing (minimizing or maximizing) the p objectives. In the rest of the chapter, we will consider the minimization of p objectives.

8.2.2. Optimality and Dominance Concepts

In the case of a single objective optimization, the comparison between two solutions x^1 and x^2 is immediate. If $y^1 < y^2$, then x^1 is better than x^2. For multiobjective optimization, comparing two solutions x^1 and x^2 is more complex. Only a partial-order relation exists, known as the Pareto dominance concept:

Definition 1. A solution x^i dominates a solution x^j if and only if:

$$\begin{cases} \forall k \in [1 \dots p], f_k(x^i) \leq f_k(x^j) \\ \exists k \in [1 \dots p] / f_k(x^i) < f_k(x^j) \end{cases} \tag{8.1}$$

Definition 2. A solution is Pareto optimal if it is not dominated by any other solution of the feasible set.

Figure 8.1 illustrates the notion of dominance in a minimization biobjective case. Nondominated solutions are those for which the left inferior rectangle is free of solution.

The set of optimal solutions in the decision space X is denoted as the Pareto set, and its image in the objective space is the Pareto front. In MOP, we are looking for all the Pareto optimal solutions.

8.2.3. Structure of the Pareto Front

The aim in "*a posteriori*" multiobjective optimization approaches is to give the decision maker a complete set of Pareto solutions.

A first analysis of the structure of the Pareto front shows that on the Pareto front two types of solutions may be distinguished: the supported solutions (that are on the convex hull of the set of solutions and that may be found by a linear combination of objectives), and nonsupported solutions. These solutions are important, because for some problems only few Pareto solutions are

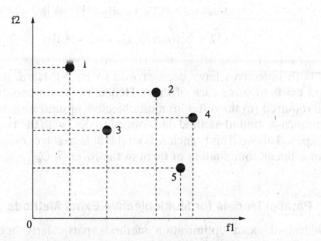

Fig. 8.1. Example of dominance. In this example, points 1, 3, and 5 are nondominated. Point 2 is dominated by point 3, and point 4 by points 3 and 5.

supported and to get a good compromise between the different objectives, it is necessary to choose one of the nonsupported solutions.

Moreover, to a given solution in the objective space (corresponding to specific values for each objective), may correspond several solutions in the decision space. Hence, it is worth it to be precise, whereas only solutions with different values for the objectives are searched (minimal complete front) or if all the Pareto solutions having different charateristics are required (maximal front). Methods may have to be designed differently in one or the other case.

8.2.4. A Biobjective Permutation Flowshop Problem

The flowshop problem is one of the numerous scheduling problems. It has been widely studied in the literature, but mostly in its monoobjective form. The flowshop problem, which we are using as an illustrative example, consists in scheduling n jobs ($i = 1 \cdots n$) on m machines ($j = 1 \cdots m$). A job consists in m operations and the jth operation of each job must be processed on machine j. So, one job can start on machine j if it is completed on machine $j - 1$, and if machine j is free. Each operation has a known processing time p_{ij}.

In the permutation flowshop, the operating sequences of the jobs are the same on every machine. If one job is at the ith position on machine one, then this job will be at the ith position on all the machines.

The two considered objectives are the makespan (C_{max}) and the total tardiness (T). The makespan is the completion time of the last job and the total tardiness (T) is the sum of tardinesses, which is the difference between the completion time of a job and its due date (d_i). In the Graham *et al.* (1) notation, this problem is denoted $F/permut, d_i/(C_{max}, T)$. The two objectives can be computed as follows, where s_{ij} represents the starting time of job i on the jth machine:

$$C_{max} = Max\{s_{iM} + p_{iM} \mid i \in [1 \cdots N]\}$$

$$T = \sum_{i=1}^{N} [max(0, s_{iM} + p_{iM} - d_i)]$$

As both objectives have been proved to be NP-Hard, no very efficient method exists to solve each of them. Hence, when a monoobjective method will be required (in the different multiobjective optimization schema), we will use a branch-&-bound method developped to deal with the two specific objectives exposed above. This branch & bound is able to solve one of the two objectives or a linear combination of them in the form ($\lambda_1 C_{max} + \lambda_2 T$) (2).

8.2.5. Parallel Models for Multiobjective Exact Methods

Parallelism of exact optimization methods, particularly branch-and-bound ones, has been largely studied in the literature (3). However, to the best of our knowledge it is rarely tackled in the multiobjective (MO) context. One of the major contributions of this chapter is to study, design, implement, and experiment the main parallel schema for MO exact methods.

There are two major approaches to deal with parallelism for exact methods: *high-* and *low-level*. The *high-level* approach consists in performing several exact methods in parallel, each of them is applied for solving one subproblem. For example, several algorithms may be performed in parallel to compute supported and/or nonsupported solutions. Each algorithm is executed as a black-box in an isolated way. The main issue to exploit such coarse-grain parallel paradigm is the management of synchronization, especially in a highly volatile Peer-to-Peer environment. In addition, only few tasks are generated, and so using large-scale environments is not required. In Section 8.3, this kind of parallelism is exploited in a small dedicated material computational platform.

The *low-level parallel* approach consists in exploring the search space in parallel, evaluating the different objectives in parallel, and so on. Parallel exploration of the search tree is the most exploited parallel model as it is problem independent. Such a model requires tackeling several issues, the major ones are knowledge sharing and synchronization, data partitioning and granularity, and work load distribution. The shared knowledge in the multiobjective context is the best Pareto solutions found so far, and can be centralized or distributed. The granularity problem consists in defining the right size of the subtrees explored by the different processors. Such grain size is the trade-off between a low-cost communication and a high degree of parallelism. Work load distribution deals with the assignment of the generated subtrees to processors in order to balance the load between processors enhancing the performance of execution.

Peer-to-Peer environments are well suited for the *low-level* parallel model, however other complex issues have to be taken into account such as fault-tolerance, heterogeneity, security, etc. In Section 8.4, a Peer-to-Peer approach is presented to deal with the *low-level* parallel model applied to multiobjective branch and bound, and the majority of these issues are discussed.

8.3. HIGH-LEVEL PARALLEL MULTIOBJECTIVE EXACT METHODS

Up to now, only few exact methods have been proposed to solve multiobjective problems. Most of the time those methods are limited to two objectives and may be applied to only very small problem instances. Hence, the parallel aspect is very important here in order to be able to cope with medium-sized problems. In this section, existing multiobjective exact methods, whose goal is to obtain the whole Pareto optimal set, are presented. For all these methods, their parallelization is discussed.

8.3.1. High-Level Model

Exposed methods use a (monoobjective) method (like a branch & bound) to search different Pareto points. In this section, the different searches are proposed to be executed in parallel and one task represents one search. In the different methods, the searches are initiated by the general method and realized with another method (like branch & bound). Therefore, the advantage to use a master–slave model is evident. With this model, each task is launched on one processor (slave–workers), and a master (dispatcher) manages a list with the different tasks that must be launched.

8.3.2. The ε-Constraint Method

The ε-constraint method is an application of the ε-constraint concept proposed by Haimes *et al.* (4,5). This concept for a problem with K objectives is to constraint $K-1$ objectives and to optimize the last one.

So the ε-constraint method, in a biobjective context, involves a constraint on one objective and optimizes the second one. The constraint problem may be expressed as follows: min $\{f_1(x): x \in X, \text{ with } f_2(x) \leq \varepsilon\}$. First, one extreme is computed, for example, the extreme with the best value for objective f_1. Then, this solution gives a bound for the objective f_2 and the best solution regarding to objective f_1 is searched below this bound (see Fig. 8.2). In general the easier objective to optimize can be used as f_1. This operation is repeated (see Fig. 8.3) until no new solution is found. Then all the efficient set is known.

8.3.2.1. Parallelization Aspect. Unfortunately, this method cannot be parallelized. Indeed, the constraint on an objective used to obtain a solution is given by the previous found solution. So, the ε-constraint method is strictly sequential.

8.3.3. Weighted Sum and Dichotomic Methods

The weighted sum concept consists in optimizing a weighted sum of objectives in the form $\lambda_1 f_1 + \lambda_2 f_2$. With well-chosen aggregations, this concept can find all

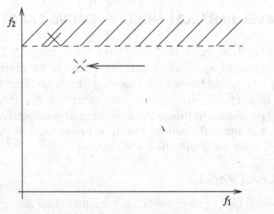

Fig. 8.2. One example of search in the ε-constraint method.

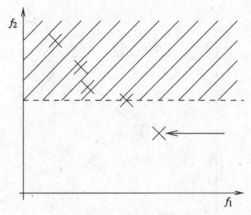

Fig. 8.3. New searches.

the supported solutions (using results from Ref. 6), but no nonsupported ones. Methods, such as the Dichotomic method or the Two-Phase method, use this concept to find the Pareto solutions. The Dichotomic method adds some constraints in order to be able to find the Pareto nonsupported solutions as well.

The principle of the Dichotomic method is a dichotomic scheme. First, the two extremes are computed. For each pair of adjacent solutions in the objective space ($f(r)$ and $f(s)$), one solution is searched between them by optimizing the following problem:

$$\left[\begin{array}{l} \min_{x \in X} f^{\sim}(x) = \lambda_1 f_1(x) + \lambda_2 f_2(x) \\ \text{with} \begin{cases} f_1(x) < f_1(s) & (C_1) \\ f_2(x) < f_2(r) & (C_2) \end{cases} \\ \qquad \text{and} \begin{cases} \lambda_1 = f_2(r) - f_2(s) \\ \lambda_2 = f_1(s) - f_1(r) \end{cases} \end{array} \right]$$

This search is presented in Fig. 8.4. At each step, this method finds a Pareto solution, if one exists between $f(r)$ and $f(s)$. If it exists, this solution belongs to the rectangle $f(r)Y f(s)Z$, where Y is the point $(f_1(s), f_2(r))$ and Z is the point $(f_1(r), f_2(s))$.* Nonsupported solutions may also be found thanks to constraints (C_1) and (C_2) that do not allow us to propose $f(r)$ or $f(s)$ as a solution of the search. Therefore, all the Pareto solutions can be found thanks to this method.

This method has been applied to assignment, knapsack, set covering, and set packing biobjective problems (the solution sets obtained with this method are available on the MCDM Numerical Instances Library, web site: *www.terry.uga.edu/mcdm/*).

*This new solution generates 2 new searches (see Fig. 8.5).

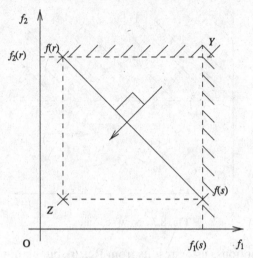

Fig. 8.4. Search direction.

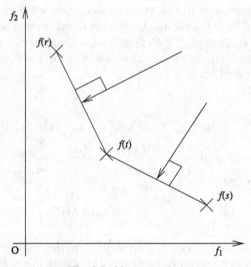

Fig. 8.5. New searches.

8.3.3.1. Parallelization Aspect. In this method, when a new solution is found, two new searches have to be launched. Hence, there is a quadratic increase of the number of searches that are independent. This allows us to establish that the parallelization will be efficient. Figure 8.6 presents the parallelization scheme obtained with this method. The two first tasks search the two extremes in parallel and a synchronous point is placed. After, when a new solution is found, two new searches are launched. The problem of the parallelization of this method is the beginning of search. To search the two extremes,

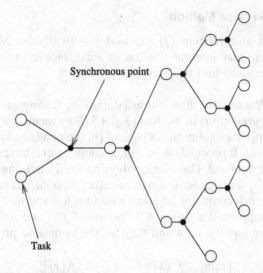

Fig. 8.6. Parallelization scheme for the Dichotomic method.

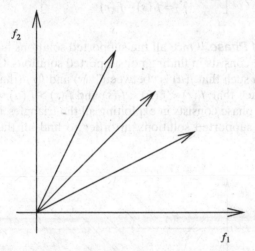

Fig. 8.7. Axis of searches uniformly scattered in search space.

only two processors are required and after that, to search between these solutions, only one processor is required.

To solve this problem, we propose to initiate random searches at the beginning of the method. Therefore, during the first step (search of the extremes) unused processors (*total number of slaves—2*) are used to look for other supported solutions in a uniform way (Fig. 8.7 illustrates an example with three unused processors). With this method, only supported solutions may be found, but if one supported solution is found, less processors will be unused in the second step.

8.3.4. The Two-Phase Method

In 1995, Ulungu and Teghem (7) exposed the Two-Phase Method (TPM), which proposes a very general scheme to solve biobjective problems. This method is decomposed into two steps.

8.3.4.1. First Phase. The first phase consists in finding all the supported solutions with aggregations in the form $\lambda_1 f_1 + \lambda_2 f_2$ by recursively exploring the existence of a supported solution "between" (in the objective space) two given supported solutions. It proceeds as in a dichotomic search but here, constraints (C_1) and (C_2) are not used. Therefore, only supported solutions are found. This first phase starts by finding the two extreme efficient solutions (supported solutions). Then, for each couple of adjacent solutions $f(r)$ and $f(s)$, the TPM looks for an existing supported solution $f(t)$ "between" $f(r)$ and $f(s)$ using an adequate aggregation (see Figs. 8.4 and 8.5). So, the optimized problem is

$$\left[\begin{array}{l} \min_{x \in X} f^\sim(x) = \lambda_1 f_1(x) + \lambda_2 f_2(x) \\ \text{with} \begin{cases} \lambda_1 = f_2(r) - f_2(s) \\ \lambda_2 = f_1(s) - f_1(r) \end{cases} \end{array} \right]$$

8.3.4.2. Second Phase. Once all the supported solutions have been found, the second phase consists in finding nonsupported solutions. Given a nonsupported solution u such that $f(u)$ is "between" $f(s)$ and $f(r)$ (that are supported solutions), u is such that: $f_1(r) < f_1(u) < f_1(s)$ and $f_2(r) > f_2(u) > f_2(s)$ (Fig. 8.8). Then the second phase consists in exploiting all the triangles, underlying each pair of adjacent supported solutions, in order to find all the nonsupported solutions.

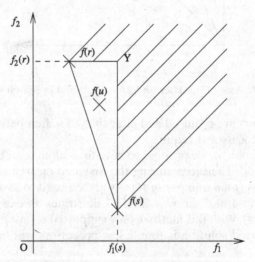

Fig. 8.8. Location of nonsupported solutions.

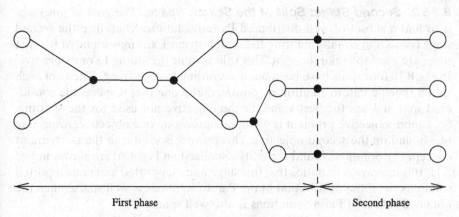

First phase   Second phase

Fig. 8.9. Parallelization scheme for the TPM.

8.3.4.3. Parallelization Aspect. The parallelization of the first phase of the method is similar to the parallelization of the dichotomic method. A similar quadratic increase of the number of first phases and the same problem of the beginning of search are noticed. So, the same optimization of the beginning of search can be made.

In the second phase, the searches are independent and may be launched simultaneously. Figure 8.9 presents the parallelization scheme of the TPM. The extremes are firstly searched. After a synchronous point, the first phase is made and then, the second phase is launched. The two phases are also indicated in this figure. The master–slave model appears also as the best model for this method.

Note that an approach may be proposed to manage in an optimal way the triggered tasks. Indeed, as soon as no more supported solution is found between two supported solutions, in the objective space, $f(r)$ and $f(s)$, the first phase is finished and a second-phase search may be launched between $f(r)$ and $f(s)$. It is not worth waiting for the end of all the first-phase searches. Hence, in the parallel version, when a processor is unused for a first-phase search, it can be used for a second-phase search (anticipation mechanism).

8.3.5. The Partitioning Parallel Method

This method provides a general scheme in order to find the whole Pareto set in three stages. It has been proposed by Lemesre et al. (8) to overcome problems related to the difficult execution of the first phase of the Two-Phase Method, when problems are already difficult to solve in the monoobjective case (problems with no structure that would allow to design polynomial monoobjective search).

8.3.5.1. First Stage: Search of the Extremes. The first stage consists in finding the two extreme efficient solutions. In order to speed up this search, we propose to use a lexicographical search on the objectives.

8.3.5.2. *Second Stage: Split of the Search Space.* The goal of this stage
is to find a subset of well-distributed Pareto solutions. Therefore the second
stage consists in equally splitting the search space. Extremes found at the first
stage are used to make the split. This split is done according to one objective.
In Fig. 8.10 four splits have been made according to objective f_2. Then, for each
split a specific Pareto solution is computed: the one that respects the considered split and has the best value for the objective not used for the splitting.
So, a monoobjective problem is obtained optimizing one objective, respecting
one bound on the second objective: This process is similar to the ε-constraint
concept (5). Solutions found for splits visualized on Fig. 8.10 are shown in Fig.
8.11. It is important to notice that this stage finds supported and nonsupported
solutions. So, if the distribution of the Pareto solutions is well sparse, then the
obtained subset of Pareto solutions is also well sparse.

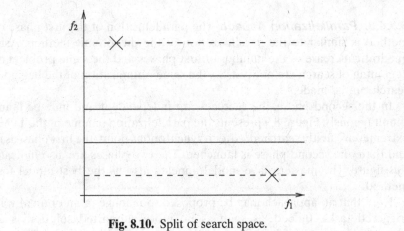

Fig. 8.10. Split of search space.

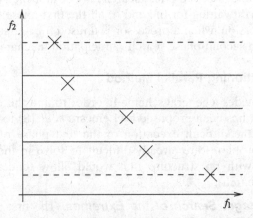

Fig. 8.11. Search of solutions well distributed on the Pareto set.

8.3.5.3. Third Stage: Search of All the Other Pareto Solutions. The third
stage consists in finding all the Pareto solutions not found during the previous
stages. For two adjacent solutions $f(s)$ and $f(r)$ the search is made in the rectangle $SY\,RO$, where Y is the point $(f_1(s), f_2(r))$, R is the point $(0, f_2(r))$, and
S is the point $(f_1(s), 0)$ (see Fig. 8.12). Note that with an adequate method, the
search can be limited to the rectangle $f(s)Y\,f(r)Z$, where Z is the point
$(f_2(s), f_1(r))$.

The whole search space explored at this stage is represented in Fig. 8.13.
No solution can dominate the extremes (gray space in the figure). Moreover
if one solution is not in this search space (if this solution is in the hatched

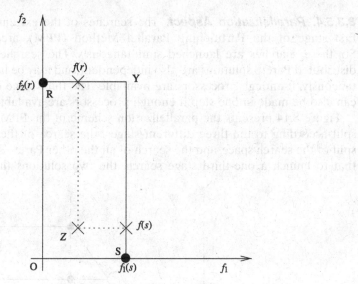

Fig. 8.12. Rectangle of search.

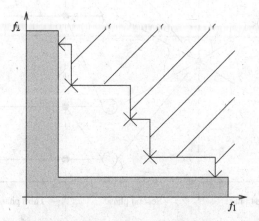

Fig. 8.13. Search space for the third stage.

space), this solution is dominated by one or more previously found solutions. To search inside the rectangles, we use the search directions obtained with λ_1 and λ_2 defined as follows (as in the Two-Phase Method).

$$\begin{cases} \lambda_1 = f_2(r) - f_2(s) \\ \lambda_2 = f_1(s) - f_1(r) \end{cases}$$

Then, the third stage consists in exploiting all the rectangles, underlying each pair of solutions found during the previous stages, in order to find all Pareto optimal solutions.

8.3.5.4. Parallelization Aspect. The searches of the extremes, during the first stage of the Partitioning Parallel Method (PPM), are independent. So, these searches are launched simultaneously. The searches of the well-distributed Pareto solutions are also independent, and may be launched simultaneously, if enough processors are available. The third stage of the method can also be made in one step if enough processors are available.

Figure 8.14 presents the parallelization scheme of the PPM. This figure is split according to the three different stages: the search of the extremes, the split of the search space, and the search of all the other Pareto solutions. Note that to launch a one-third stage search, the two solutions that delimit the

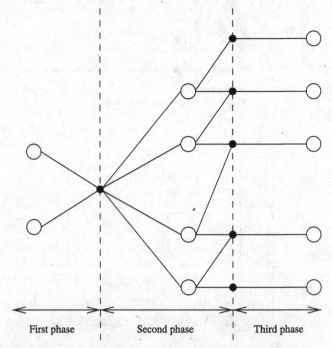

First phase   Second phase   Third phase

Fig. 8.14 Parallelization scheme for the Partitioning Parallel Method.

search space must be known. Therefore, all the Pareto solutions can be calculated into three steps with a parallel version of the PPM. In the parallel version of the Partitioning Parallel method, special attention must be made to evaluate the number of partitions. The number of partitions determines the time required to reduce the search space. In addition, during the second stage the number of searches is equal to the number of partitions minus one. Hence, the number of partitions can be adapted to the number of processors. The number of partitions may be equal to the number of processors in order to launch all the searches of the third stage in parallel. In this case, one processor is unused during the searches of the well-distributed solutions in the second stage.

8.3.6. Experiments

To evaluate the different methods on the biobjective permutation flowshop problem presented in Section 8.2.4, we use benchmarks for the problem $F/permut/C_{max}$ proposed by Taillard (9) and those proposed by Reeves (10) to which due dates for jobs have been added[1] in order to be able to compute the total tardiness criterion. For these Reeves benchmarks, we produce two types of instances; "easy" and "hard", according to the difficulty to optimize the total tardiness in the monoobjective case. Instances are described with the origin of the instance, the number of jobs, the number of machines, and the number of the instance. For example, the instance taill_20_5_1 is the first instance of Taillard with 20 jobs and 5 machines.

Experiments have been carried out on four computers with microprocessors between 2.6 and 3 GHz. The parallel communication interface used is MPI. In this section, all the results are presented for methods looking for the minimal complete Pareto set (only solutions with different values of objectives are searched). Tables 8.1 and 8.2 compare nonparallel versions with

TABLE 8.1. Results with the TPM

Instances	Time		
	TPM	Improved TPM	Parallel Improved TPM
		Taillard	
taill_20_10_1	1 day 3 h	12 h 25 mn	8 h 15 mn
taill_20_10_2	18 h 04 mn	7 h 23 mn	4 h 30 mn
		Reeves Easy	
reC_20_15_13	5 h 10 mn	2 h 10 mn	1 h 20 mn
reC_20_15_17	10 h 41 mn	6 h 01 mn	4 h 00 mn
		Reeves Hard	
reC_20_10_7	1 h 22 mn	32 mn 41 s	15 mn 50 s

[1]Details on this extension may be found at *www.lifl.fr/~lemesre*.

TABLE 8.2. Results with the PPM

Instances	Time	
	PPM	Parallel PPM
	Taillard	
taill_20_10_1	8 h 58 mn	5 h 30 mn
taill_20_10_2	5 h 01 mn	3 h 00 mn
	Reeves Easy	
reC_20_15_13	1 h 55 mn	1 h 18 mn
reC_20_15_17	3 h 42 mn	3 h 08 mn
	Reeves Hard	
reC_20_10_7	22 mn 19 s	13 mn 39 s

parallel versions of the TPM and the PPM. Table 8.1 indicates time required to solve several instances with the original TPM, an improved TPM for scheduling problems (see Ref. 12 for more details) and a parallel version of this improved TPM. This table shows an interesting decrease of time. Table 8.2 shows the same results for the PPM and its parallel version. This table shows that the search time for the parallel PPM is even smaller than for the parallel improved TPM.

It is well known that finding Pareto optimal solutions of a NP-hard problem instance, even of a reasonable size, requires a great computational power. Recently, large-scale distributed computing—peer-to-peer and grid computing—opened new prospects for solving instances of larger size. Distributed computing can encompass hundreds, even thousands, of computers interconnected through a network. It is obvious that the *high-level parallelization* methods do not fully exploit this kind of systems. Indeed, compared to the number of available machines they launch very little tasks simultaneously. A solution to have more simultaneous tasks is to parallelize these tasks themselves, it is what we call *low-level parallelization*.

8.4. LOW-LEVEL PARALLEL MULTIOBJECTIVE EXACT METHODS

Multiobjective branch-and-bound (MO-B&B) can be often efficiently used to find extremes, to execute the second phase of the TPM, the third phase of the PPM, or any other task of the *high-level parallel methods*. So, a simple way to have more tasks and thus to transform a *high-level parallel method* into a *low-level parallel* one is to replace the sequential MO-B&B by a distributed MO-B&B. However, existing distributed computing middlewares are limited regarding to applications where the generated tasks need to communicate, such as in a MO-B&B algorithm. Indeed, these environments are well suited for multiparameter applications. In this section, we will investigate these limitations in Peer-to-Peer (P2P) systems and explain the coordination model for parallel P2P multi-objective optimization proposed in (11) to enable cooperation between tasks. Then an implementation of a MO-B&B algorithm on Xtrem Web (12) will be presented.

8.4.1. Peer-to-Peer Computing Systems

Nowadays, there exist several fully distributed P2P systems meaning they do not include a central server (13). These systems are often well suited for the storage of massive data sets and their retrieval. There are also P2P systems dedicated to large-scale computing (14–16), but only few of them are fully distributed (16). Fully distributed computing P2P systems are just emerging and are not yet mature nor stable to be exploited. More mature software systems such as Xtrem Web and SETI@Home (14) are today those based on a Dispatcher-Worker architecture. In such systems, clients can submit their jobs to the Dispatcher. A set of volatile workers (peers) request the jobs from the Dispatcher according to the cycle stealing model. Then, they execute the jobs and return back the results to the Dispatcher to be collected by the clients. These middlewares, even if a central server (the Dispatcher) is required for controlling the peers (workers), are considered as P2P software environments. Indeed, an important part of these systems is executed on these peers with a high autonomy. In addition, a hierarchical design allows them to deal with a larger number of peers.

One of the major limitations of P2P computing environments is that they are well suited for embarrassingly multiparameter applications with independent tasks. In this case, no communication is required between the tasks, and thus peers. The deployment of applications needing cooperation is not straightforward. The programmer has the burden to manage and control the complex coordination between the computers. To deal with such problems existing middlewares must be extended with a software layer that implements a coordination model.

8.4.2. Coordination Models

Several interesting coordination models have been proposed in the literature (17,18). This chapter focuses only on two of the most used of them, that is, Linda (19) and Gamma (20). The model proposed in Ref. 11 for multiobjective distributed optimization is inspired from these models. In the Linda model, processes share a virtual memory space called a *tuple space* (set of tuples). The fundamental data unit, a tuple, is an ordered vector of typed values. Processes communicate by reading, writing, and consuming these tuples. A small set of four simple operations allows highly complex communication and synchronization schemes: *out(tuple)* to put a new *tuple* into *tuple-space*, *in(pattern)* to removes a (often the first) tuple matching *pattern* from *tuple-space*, *rd(pattern)* is the same as *in(pattern)*, but does not remove the tuple from *tuple-space*, and *eval(expression)* to put *expression* in *tuple-space* for evaluation. The evaluation result is a tuple left in *tuple-space*.

Gamma is a multiset rewriting model inspired by the chemical metaphor that has been proposed as a mean for a high-level description of parallel programs with minimum explicit control. The model uses a set of conditional rewriting rules defined by a pair $(R; A)$, where R is a *reaction condition* (Boolean function on multisets of data) and A is a *rewriting action* (function from multi-sets to multisets of data). When a group of molecules satisfies (subset of data) the reaction condition, it can be rewritten in the way stated by the corresponding rewriting action. Unlike in Linda, in this model a form of rewriting of tuples exists. It is defined by a consumption and production of tuples. Many extensions of this model are proposed in (21).

To take benefit from the advantages of the two models, the model proposed in Ref. 11 couples the Linda model and the Gamma model. Furthermore, the model resulting from the coupling is extended with group operations and nonblocking operations because, as explained in Section 8.4.3, they are very useful for distributed multiobjective combinatorial optimization.

8.4.3. A Coordination Model for Multiobjective Combinatorial Optimization

Designing a coordination model for distributed multiobjective combinatorial optimization requires the specification of the content of the tuple space, a set of coordination operations and a pattern matching mechanism. According to the comments of the previous subsection, the tuple space may be composed of a set of Pareto optimal solutions and their corresponding solutions in the objective space. For the distributed exact MO methods, all the solutions in the tuple space belong to the same Pareto front, that is, the actual best found one. In addition to the operations provided in Linda, distributed multiobjective optimization needs other operations. These operations can be divided in two categories: *group* operations and *nonblocking* operations. The coordination primitives are defined as follows:

- *in, rd, out and eval*: These operations are the same as those of Linda.
- *ing(pattern)*: Withdraws from *PS* all the solutions matching the specified pattern.
- *rdg(pattern)*: Reads from *PS* a copy of *all* the solutions matching the specified pattern.
- *outg(setOfSolutions)*: Inserts multiple solutions in *PS*.
- *update(pattern, expression)*: Updates *all* the solutions matching the specified pattern by the solutions resulting from the evaluation of *expression*.
- *inIfExist, rdIfExist, ingIfExist, and rdgIfExist*: These operations have the same syntax than, respectively, *in, rd, ing, and rdg*, but they are *nonblocking* probe operations.

The *update* operation allows us to locally update the Pareto space, and so to reduce the communication and synchronization cost. The pattern matching mechanism depends strongly on how the model is implemented, and in particular on how the tuple space is stored and accessed. For example, if the tuple space is stored in a database the mechanism can be the request mechanism used by the database management system.

8.4.4. Implementation on a Distributed System

The model proposed below has been implemented on top of the XtremWeb (12) middleware. XtremWeb is a P2P project developed at Paris-Sud University. It is intended to distribute applications over a set of computers, and is dedicated to multiparameter applications that have to be computed several times with different inputs. XtremWeb manages tasks following the Dispatcher–Worker paradigm. Tasks are scheduled by the Dispatcher to workers only on their specific demand since they may adaptively appear (connect to the Dispatcher) and disappear (disconnect from the Dispatcher). The tasks are submitted by either a client or a worker, and in the latter case, the tasks are dynamically generated for parallel execution. The final or intermediate results returned by the workers are stored in a MySQL database. These results can be requested later by either the clients or the workers. The database stores also different information related to the workers and the deployed application tasks.

The software layer is an implementation of the proposed model composed of two parts: a coordination API and its implementation at the worker level and a coordination request broker (CRB). The Pareto Space is a part of the MySQL database associated with the Dispatcher. Each tuple or solution of the Pareto Space is stored as a record in the database. From the worker side the coordination API is implemented in Java and in C/C++. The C/C++ version allows the deployment and execution of C/C++ applications with XtremWeb (written in Java). The coordination library must be included in these programmer applications. From the Dispatcher side, the coordination API is implemented in Java as a Pareto Space manager. The *CRB* is a software broker allowing the workers to transport their coordination operations to the Dispatcher through RMI calls.

8.4.5. P2P Multiobjective Branch-and-Bound

The MO-B&B algorithms solve MOPs by iteratively partitioning the solution space into subspaces (each subspace is associated with a sub-MOP). A distributed MO-B&B can be used as a component to get more parallelization from a *high-level parallel method*. We assume that the MOP to solve is a minimization MOP. A sequential MO-B&B algorithm consists in iteratively applying five basic operations over a list of problems: *Branching, Resolution, Bounding, Selection,* and *Elimination*.

Successive branching (decomposition) operations create a tree of MOPs rooted in the original MOP. The value of the best Pareto front found so far is used to prune the tree and eliminate the MOPs that are likely to lead to worse solutions. At each step, a MOP is selected either according to the bound values (as in *best-first* strategy) or not (as in *depth-first* and *breadth-first* strategies). The selected MOP may not be split because it has no solution or because a solution has been already found. In this case, it is solved, and if its solution can improve the best-known Pareto front this latter is updated. If the MOP can be split then it is decomposed into smaller sub-MOPs. A sub-MOP is eliminated if its bound value is not better that the best known Pareto front. Otherwise, it is added to the pool of MOPs to be solved.

There exist different parallel models in B&B algorithms (3). Here, we focus on the most general approach, in which the B&B tree is built in parallel by performing simultaneously the operations presented above on different sub-MOPs. According to such approach, the design of parallel B&B algorithms is based on three major parameters: the *execution mode*, the *work sharing strategy* and the *information sharing policy*. The execution mode defines what processes do after completion of a work unit, and may be *synchronous* or *asynchronous*. The processes (do not) wait for each other in a(n) (a)synchronous mode. The work-sharing strategy defines how work units are assigned to processes to efficiently exploit available parallelism. The information sharing policy indicates how the best-known solution is published and updated.

In Ref. 11, an asynchronous parallel cooperative Dispatcher-Worker MO-B&B algorithm was presented. Asynchrony is required by the heterogeneity nature of the P2P target execution architecture. The work-sharing strategy follows the idle cycle or work stealing paradigm. As illustrated by the Fig. 8.15, each worker maintains its local pool of MOPs to be solved and its best-known

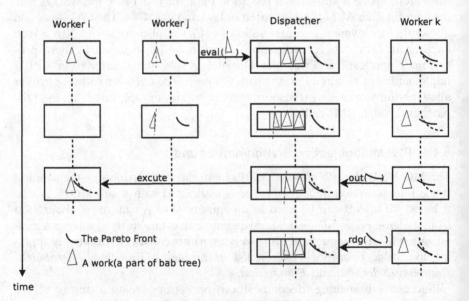

Fig. 8.15. A P2P MO-B&B.

Pareto front. The pool of works is represented by a triangle and the Pareto front by a small curve.

At each step, the worker tests if there is some MOPs to solve in its local work pool. If the pool is empty it requests work from the Dispatcher. Using *execute*, the Dispatcher replies with a pool of work units and the value of the best known Pareto front. This value is stored locally. Otherwise, if there is some work in the local pool, the worker performs a step of the sequential MO-B&B on its local pool. Thereafter, it probably requests the Dispatcher to update the best-known Pareto front by merging this latter with its local version. This is performed by using *out* coordination operation.

In the implementation of the parallel MO-B&B applied to the biobjective permutation flow-shop problem, the best-known Pareto front is updated with *rdg* if a sufficient number of iterations is already performed. The adopted selection strategy is the *depth-first* one, the node with the best bound being chosen at each step. The *update* coordination operation is executed on the Dispatcher by the Pareto Space Manager. First, it consists in performing an union between the two sets: the global best-known Pareto front (stored in the Pareto Space) and its local version. The new best-known Pareto front is then selected from this union set by considering all the nondominated solutions. The new result is returned to the calling Worker.

After a fixed number of iterations, if a Worker has remaining work in its local pool it splits it into as many pools as available workers (considering itself). The Worker saves a pool for its own need, and submits (in a client role) the other pools to the Dispatcher through the *eval* coordination operation. The Dispatcher puts these work units in its task pool to be sent to available workers at their request.

8.4.6. Experiments

The application has been deployed on the education network of the *Polytech'Lille* engineering school. The experimentation hardware platform is composed of 120 heterogeneous Linux Debian PCs. The biobjective permutation flow-shop problem benchmark is composed of 20 machines and 10 jobs (taill_20_10_1). The experimental results are summarized in Table 8.3. The total execution time is measured for the sequential and parallel versions. The execution time of the sequential version is normalized as the whole target architecture is heterogeneous. The machine where the sequential algorithm is

TABLE 8.3. Parallel MO-B&B versus Sequential MO-B&B

	Sequential B&B	Parallel B&B
Total number of tasks	1	657
Total execution time	54h51	1h53

executed is an Intel Pentium 4, 3 GHz, and is considered as a reference machine for the computation of the normalized factor. The normalized factor for each peer is obtained by using an application-specific benchmark task that is sent to all workers that join the computational pool. The speed at which the benchmark task is completed is considered as the normalized factor.

Formally, let t_{ref} and t_i be the execution time of the benchmark on, respectively, the reference machine and the machine number $i = 1 \cdots N$ of the pool of worker peers. The normalized factor α_i associated with the worker peer i is computed as follows: $a(\alpha)_i = t_i/t_{ref}$. Let α_{av} be the average normalized factor for all the worker peers. It can be formulated as: $\alpha_{av} = \Sigma_{i=1}^{N} a_i N$. The sequential time reported in Table 8.3 is the time obtained on an average peer, obtained by multiplying the sequential time obtained on the reference peer by the average factor. The results show that the execution time is divided by >29 on 120 machines. One may relativize the importance of the speedup in P2P environments, it depends strongly on the availability of the machines. It is why the experiments have been performed during a working day and on nondedicated environment. It would be interesting to get the speedup according only to the time in which peers are harnessed, unfortunately the P2P middleware used does not make it possible. The Fig. 8.16 illustrates the variation over time of the number of tasks running or waiting for a peer. One has to note that due to the nature of the application, sufficient parallelism (for the 120 peers) is generated during only 1 h over ~2 h of total execution.

8.5. CONCLUSION

Developping exact methods for multiobjective problems is an important issue as very few methods exist. The efficiency of existing methods is strongly limited

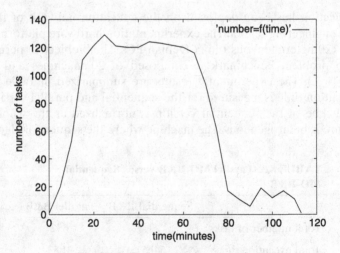

Fig. 8.16. Task generation over time.

by the size of problems that may be solved and the number of objectives to handle. Hence, parallelism may offer a good opportunity to push back the limits of these methods.

In this chapter, the high-level parallel model has been experimented and results demonstrate its efficiency. However, even for large problem instances it does not generate enough parallelism to justify its exploitation in Peer-to-Peer environments. On the other hand, the low-level parallel model allows to provide more parallelism, and the amount of parallelism is more and more important with the increase of the problem size. Therefore, it is well-suited for Peer-to-Peer computational pools. As in such environments, the amount of resources is great enough to largely meet the needs of the low-level parallel model the hybridization of this latter with the high-level model would certainly increase the amount and degree of parallelism, and better exploit the capacities provided by Peer-to-Peer systems. Indeed, the amount of work generated by the low-level model is multiplied by the number of tasks provided by the high-level model.

In the future, a perspective would be to study and experiment such hybridization in a Peer-to-Peer context.

REFERENCES

1. R.L. Graham, E.L. Lawler, J.K. Lenstra, and A.H.G. Rinnooy Kan. Optimization and approximation in deterministic sequencing and scheduling: a survey. *Ann. Discrete Math.*, **5**:287–326 (1979).

2. J. Lemesre, C. Dhaenens, and E.G. Talbi. An exact parrallel method for a bi-objective permutation flowshop problem. *Eur. J. Oper. Res.*, 2006. To be published.

3. B. Gendron and T.G. Crainic. Parallel branch-and-bound algorithms: Survey and synthesis. *Oper. Res.*, **42**(6):1042–1066 (1994).

4. Y. Haimes, L. Ladson, and D. Wismer. On a bicriterion formulation of the problems of integrated system identification and system optimization. *IEEE Trans. System, Man Cybernet.*, **1**:296–297 (1971).

5. Y. Haimes, W. Hall, and H. Freedman. Multiobjective optimization in water resources systems. *Elsevier Scientific Publishing edition*, Amsterdam 1975.

6. A. Geoffrion. Proper efficiency and theory of vector maximization. *J. Math. Anal. Appl.*, **22**:618–630 (1968).

7. E.L. Ulungu and J. Teghem. The two phases method: An efficient procedure to solve bi-objective combinatorial optimization problems. *Foundations Comput. Decision Sci.*, **20**(2):149–165 (1995).

8. J. Lemesre, C. Dhaenens, and E-G. Talbi. Parallel Partitioning Method (PPM): A new exact method to solve Bi-Objective problems. *Comput. Oper. Res.*, 2006. To be published.

9. E. Taillard. Benchmarks for basic scheduling problems. *Eur. J. Oper. Res.*, **64**:278–285 (1993).

10. C.R. Reeves. A genetic algorithm for flowshop sequencing. *Comput. Oper. Res.*, **22**:5–13 (1995).

11. M.S. Mezmaz, N. Melab, and E-G. Talbi. Towards a coordination model for parallel cooperative P2P multi-objective optimization. *Springer Verlag LNCS, Proceedings of European Grid Conf, Amsterdam, The Netherlands*, Feb. 2005.

12. G. Fedak, C. Germain, V. Neri, and F. Cappello. XtremWeb: building an experimental platform for Global Computing. *Workshop on Global Computing on Personal Devices (CCGRID2001)*, Brisbane, Australia, *IEEE Press*, May 2001.

13. M. Ripeanu. Peer-to-Peer Architecture Case Study: Gnutella Network. 1*st IEEE International Conference on Peer-to-Peer Computing (P2P2001)*, Aug. 2001.

14. D.P. Anderson, J. Cobb, E. Korpela, M. Lepofsky, and D. Werthimer. SETI@home: An Experiment in Public-Resource Computing. *Commun. ACM*, **45**(11):56–61 (Nov. 2002).

15. J. Verbeke, N. Nadgir, G. Ruetsch, and I. Sharapov. Framework for Peer-to-Peer Distributed Computing in a Heterogeneous, Decentralized Environment. *In Proceedings of the Third International. Workshop on Grid Computing (GRID'2002)*, Baltimore, MD, Jan. 2002, pp. 1–12.

16. L. Oliveira, L. Lopes, and F. Silva. P^3: Parallel Peer to Peer—An Internet Parallel Programming Environment. *International Workshop on Peer-to-Peer Computing, Pisa, Italy*, May 19–24, 2002.

17. D. Gelernter and N. Carriero. Coordination languages and their significance. *Commun. ACM*, **35**(2):97–107 (Feb. 1992).

18. G.A. Papadopoulos and F. Arbab. Coordination models and languages. *Advances in Computers: The Engineering of Large Systems, Academic Press*, Maryland, USA. 1998, Vol. 46 pp. 329–400.

19. D. Gelernter. Generative Communication in Linda. *ACM Trans. Prog. Lang. Systems*, **7**(1):80–112 (Jan. 1985).

20. C. Hankin, D. Le Métayer, and D. Sands. A Calculus of Gamma Programs. In U. Banerjee *et al.*, ed., *5th International Workshop*, on *Languages and Compilers for Parallel Computing*, Springer-Verlag, LNCS757, Berlin Aug. 1992, pp. 342–355.

21. M. Vieillot. Synthèse de programmes gamma en logique reconfigurable. *Tech. Sci. Inf.*, **14**:567–584 (1995).

CHAPTER 9

Parallel Primal-Dual Interior-Point Methods for SemiDefinite Programs

MAKOTO YAMASHITA

Kanagawa University JAPAN

KATSUKI FUJISAWA

Tokyo Denki University JAPAN

MITUHIRO FUKUDA, MASAKAZU KOJIMA, and KAZUHIDE NAKATA

Tokyo Institute of Technology JAPAN

9.1. INTRODUCTION

The Semidefinite Program (SDP) minimizes (or maximizes) a linear objective function in real variables $x_1, x_2, \cdots, x_m$ subject to a linear matrix inequality in these variables. In this chapter, we often use the term SDP to denote a pair of a primal SDP $\mathcal{P}$ and its dual $\mathcal{D}$.

$$
\text{SDP:} \begin{cases}
\mathcal{P}: & \text{minimize} & \sum_{k=1}^{m} c_k x_k \\
& \text{subject to} & X = \sum_{k=1}^{m} F_k x_k - F_0 \\
& & X \succeq O. \\
\mathcal{D}: & \text{maximize} & F_0 \bullet Y \\
& \text{subject to} & F_k \bullet Y = c_k \, (k = 1, 2, \cdots, m) \\
& & Y \succeq O.
\end{cases}
$$

The input data of the SDP are composed of real numbers $c_k \, (k = 1, \cdots, m)$ and matrices $F_k \in \mathbb{S}^n \, (k = 0, 1, \cdots, m)$, where $\mathbb{S}^n$ is the set of $n \times n$ symmetric

Parallel Combinatorial Optimization, edited by El-Ghazali Talbi

matrices. We use the notation $X \succeq O$ $(X \succ O)$ to indicate that $X \in \mathbb{S}^n$ is a positive semidefinite matrix (a positive definite matrix, respectively). The inner-product in $\mathbb{S}^n$ is defined by $U \bullet V = \sum_{i=1}^{n} \sum_{j=1}^{n} U_{ij} V_{ij}$. We call $(x, X, Y) \in \mathbb{R}^m \times \mathbb{S}^n \times \mathbb{S}^n$ a feasible solution when (x, X, Y) satisfies all constraints in $\mathcal{P}$ and $\mathcal{D}$. When X and Y are positive definite in addition to their feasibility, we call (x, X, Y) an interior feasible solution.

An SDP is a substantial extension of a linear program, and covers a wide range of applications in various fields, such as combinatorial optimization (1,2), quantum chemistry (3,4), system and control theory (5), and polynomial optimization (6,7). More applications can be found in the survey papers on SDPs (8–10). In 1994, Nesterov and Nemirovskii (11) proposed an interior-point method that solves an SDP in polynomial time. Primal-dual interior-point methods (12–16) are variants of the interior-point method, which have shown their practical efficiency by computer software packages such as SDPA (17,18), SeDuMi (19), SDPT3 (20), and CSDP (21). However, in recent applications to some SDPs arising from quantum chemistry (3,4) and polynomial optimization (6,7), we often encounter extremely large SDPs that no existing computer software package can solve on a single processor due to its limits on both computation time and memory space.

Meanwhile, the field of parallel computation has achieved a surprisingly rapid growth in the last decade. In particular, PC-cluster and grid technologies have certainly sustained the growth, and now provide enormous parallel computation resources for various fields including mathematical programming.

Solving extremely large-scale SDPs that no one could solve before is a significant work to open up a new vista of future applications of SDPs. Our two software packages, SDPARA and SDPARA-C, based on strong parallel computation and efficient algorithms have a high potential to solve large-scale SDPs and to accomplish the work. The SDPARA (SemiDefinite Programming Algorithm paRAllel version) (22) is designed for general large SDPs, while the SDPARA-C (SDPARA with the positive definite matrix Completion) (23) is appropriate for sparse large SDPs arising from combinatorial optimization.

When we consider large-scale SDPs, we need to take account of three factors: the size m of the primal vector variable x in $\mathcal{P}$ that corresponds to the number of equality constraints in $\mathcal{D}$, the size n of the primal matrix variable X (or the dual matrix variable Y), and the sparsity of the data matrices F_k $(k = 0, 1, 2, \cdots, m)$. If the matrices F_k $(k = 0, 1, 2, \cdots, m)$ are fully dense, we have at least $(m + 1)n(n + 1)/2$ real numbers as input data for the SDP; for example, if $m = n = 1000$, this number gets larger than a half-billion. Therefore, we cannot expect to store and solve fully dense SDPs with both m and n large. The most significant key to solve large-scale SDPs with sparse data matrices is how to exploit their sparsity in parallel computation.

The SDPARA, which is regarded as a parallel version of the SDPA (18), is designed to solve sparse SDPs with large m and not large n compared to m (e.g., $m = 30{,}000$ and $n = 1000$). In each iteration of the primal-dual interior-point method, the computation of a search direction (dx, dX, dY) is reduced to a system of linear equations $Bdx = r$ called the Schur complement equation. Here, B denotes an $m \times m$ positive definite matrix whose elements are computed from the data matrices $F_k (k = 1, 2, \cdots, m)$ together with the current iterate matrix variables X and Y. Fujisawa *et al.* (24) proposed an efficient method for computing B when the data matrices $F_k (k = 1, 2, \cdots, m)$ are sparse. This method is employed in the SDPA. The matrix B is fully dense in general even when all the data matrices are sparse. (There are some special cases where B becomes sparse. See, e.g., Ref. 25.) We usually employ the Cholesky factorization of B to solve the Schur complement equation. For a fixed n, most of arithmetic operations are required in the evaluation of the coefficient matrix B and its Cholesky factorization. The SDPARA executes these two parts in parallel.

One serious difficulty in applying primal-dual interior-point method to SDPs with large n lies in the fact that the $n \times n$ matrix variable Y of $\mathcal{D}$ is fully dense in general even when all the data matrices $F_k (k = 0, 1, 2, \cdots, m)$ are sparse. Note that the $n \times n$ matrix variable X of $\mathcal{P}$, which is given by $X = \Sigma_{k=1}^{m} F_k x_k\text{-}F_o$, inherits the sparsity of the data matrices. To overcome this difficulty, Fukuda and co-workers (26,27) incorporated the positive definite matrix completion technique into primal-dual interior-point methods. Their key idea can be roughly summarized as "when the aggregated sparsity pattern over the data matrices $F_k (k = 0, 1, 2, \cdots, m)$ (or the sparsity of the variable matrix X of $\mathcal{P}$) induces a sparse chordal graph structure, we can choose values for the dense matrix variable Y of $\mathcal{D}$ such that its inverse Y^{-1} enjoys the same sparsity as X"; hence we utilize Y^{-1} explicitly instead of storing and manipulating the dense matrix Y. It was reported in Ref. 27 that this technique is very effective in saving the computation time and the memory space used for SDPs with large n arising from SDP relaxations of combinatorial optimization problems on graphs. The SDPARA-C (23), the other software package presented in this chapter, is a combination of the SDPARA and a parallel positive matrix completion technique, and aims to solve sparse SDPs with large n.

Therefore, the SDPARA and the SDPARA-C have their own features and strengths, and can be used in a complementary way to solve large SDPs.

More detailed information of the SDPARA and the SDPARA-C is available at the SDPA web site.

```
http://homepage.mac.com/klabtitech/sdpa-homepage/
```

The single processor version (SDPA), and the MATLAB interface (SDPA-M) are also available there.

This chapter is composed as follows. Section 9.2 illustrates how we use the SDPARA and the SDPARA-C through their application to the maximum clique number problem. If the reader wants to use them to solve an SDP, Section 9.2 serves as a first step. The following sections deepen the understanding about the software packages. Section 9.3, an algorithmic framework of primal-dual interior-point methods and some technical details of the SDPARA and the SDPARA-C, are discussed. Their numerical results are shown on PC-clusters for large-scale SDPs in Section 9.4. Finally, future directions are given in Section 9.5.

9.2. HOW TO USE THE SDPARA AND THE SDPARA-C

First, we formulate an SDP relaxation of the maximum clique number problem (MCQ) (28). Then, we describe how we write the input data of the resulting SDP in the *SDPA sparse format*, which the SDPARA and the SDPARA-C accept as their inputs. The SDPA sparse format is a standard input format for SDPs, and many benchmark problems are written in this format (29).

Let $G(V,E)$ be a graph composed of a vertex set $V = \{1, 2, \cdots, n\}$ and an edge set $E = \{\{i, j\} : i, j \in V\}$. A subset C of V is said to be a clique when C induces a complete subgraph of G. In other words, all vertices in C are connected to each other by edges of E. Then the maximum clique number problem is to find a clique of maximum cardinality. As an illustrative example, let us consider a graph given in Fig. 9.1. In this case, $\{1, 2\}$ and $\{2, 3, 5, 6\}$ are examples of cliques, and the latter one consisting of four vertices forms a clique of maximum cardinality; hence it is a solution of the maximum clique number problem.

For a subset $C \subset V$, variables $y_i\,(i = 1, \cdots, n)$ are introduced to make a partition of V into $C = \{i : y_i \neq 0\}$ and $V \backslash C = \{i : y_i = 0\}$. Then the maximum clique number problem can be formulated as the following optimization problem.

$$(\text{MCQ}) \quad \max\left\{\sum_{i=1}^{n}\sum_{j=1}^{n} y_i y_j : \quad y_i y_j = 0\,(\{i, j\} \notin E), \sum_{i=1}^{n} y_i^2 = 1\right\}$$

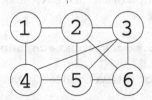

Fig. 9.1. A sample graph for the max clique number problem.

The constraint $y_i y_j = 0$ ($\{i, j\} \notin E$) ensures that $C = \{i : y_i \neq 0\}$ is a clique, while the other constraint $\sum_{i=1}^{n} y_i^2 = 1$ bounds the objective value from above. In the graph given in Fig. 9.1, a clique $\{1, 2\}$ induces a feasible solution

$$y_1 = y_2 = 1/\sqrt{2}, \, y_3 = y_4 = y_5 = y_6 = 0$$

with the objective value 2, and the maximum cardinality clique $\{2, 3, 5, 6\}$ induces an optimal solution

$$y_1 = y_4 = 0, \, y_2 = y_3 = y_5 = y_6 = 1/2$$

with the objective value 4. In general, when an optimal objective value of (MCQ) attains T, there exists a maximum clique $C^* \subset V$ of the cardinality T with

$$y_i = \begin{cases} 1/\sqrt{T} & \text{for } i \in C^* \\ 0 & \text{for } i \notin C^* \end{cases}$$

By introducing a symmetric matrix variable $Y \in \mathbb{S}^n$ and replacing each product $y_i y_j$ with Y_{ij}, we can reduce (MCQ) to an equivalent matrix formulation (MCQ$\mathcal{M}$),

$$(\text{MCQ}\mathcal{M}) \quad \max\{E \bullet Y: \quad E_{ij} \bullet Y = 0 \, (\{i, j\} \notin E)$$
$$I \bullet Y = 1, Y \geq O, \text{rank}(Y) = 1\}$$

where E denotes an $n \times n$ matrix whose all elements are one, E_{ij} an $n \times n$ matrix whose all elements are zero except the (i, j) and (j, i) elements taking one, and I the $n \times n$ identity matrix. The constraints $Y \geq O$ and rank $(Y) = 1$ are necessary to recover the vector y from the elements of Y. The (MCQ$\mathcal{M}$) [or equivalently (MCQ)] is, however, NP-complete. The difficulty is caused by the last nonconvex constraint rank $(Y) = 1$. We now relax (MCQ$\mathcal{M}$) into (MCQ$\mathcal{R}$), which is an SDP in dual form, by ignoring the difficult rank condition.

$$(\text{MCQ}\mathcal{R}) \quad \max\{E \bullet Y: \quad E_{ij} \bullet Y = 0 \, (\{i, j\} \notin E), I \bullet Y = 1, Y \geq O\}$$

The optimal objective value of (MCQ$\mathcal{R}$) is called the theta function (30). The theta function is an upper bound of the optimal value of (MCQ) as well as a lower bound of the minimum coloring number over the same graph.

In the case of the graph given in Fig. 9.1, we know that $\{1, 3\}$, $\{1, 5\}$, $\{1, 6\}$, $\{2, 4\}$, and $\{4, 6\}$ are the node pairs having no edges. Hence, (MCQ$\mathcal{R}$) turns out to be

$$\max\{F_0 \bullet Y : F_k \bullet Y = c_k (k = 1, 2, \cdots, 6), Y \geq O\}$$

where

$$c_1 = c_2 = c_3 = c_4 = c_5 = 0, c_6 = 1$$
$$F_0 = E, F_1 = E_{13}, F_2 = E_{15}$$
$$F_3 = E_{16}, F_4 = E_{24}, F_5 = E_{46}, F_6 = I$$

Thus the resulting SDP corresponds to the dual SDP $\mathcal{D}$ with $m = 6$ and $n = 6$.

The above input data is now converted into an SDPA sparse format file with the name "mcq1.dat-s", which is shown in Table 9.1. The extension "dat-s" is used to indicate that the file is written in the SDPA sparse format. The 1st line indicates the number m of input data matrices. The 2nd and the 3rd lines describe the structure of the variable matrices. The SDPA sparse format can handle a more general structure called the block diagonal structure. The lines "nBLOCK" and "bLOCKsTRUCT" are used to express this structure. We consider the entire matrix Y having only one diagonal block in this simple example, hence the bLOCKsTRUCT corresponds to the dimension n of Y. The input coefficient vector c is written in the 4th line. The other lines denote the elements of $F_k (k = 0, 1, \cdots, m)$. Each of the lines is composed of five figures, that is, the index of the input data matrix, the index of the block, the row number, the column number and the value. The index of the block in this example is always 1 because of the single diagonal block structure. For example, the 14th line indicates that the $(2, 5)$th element of F_0 is 1, and the

TABLE 9.1. mcq1.dat-s

Line 01 : 6 = m	Line 19 : 0 1 3 6 1
Line 02 : 1 = nBLOCK	Line 20 : 0 1 4 4 1
Line 03 : 6 = bLOCKsTRUCT	Line 21 : 0 1 4 5 1
Line 04 : 0 0 0 0 0 1	Line 22 : 0 1 4 6 1
Line 05 : 0 1 1 1 1	Line 23 : 0 1 5 5 1
Line 06 : 0 1 1 2 1	Line 24 : 0 1 5 6 1
Line 07 : 0 1 1 3 1	Line 25 : 0 1 6 6 1
Line 08 : 0 1 1 4 1	Line 26 : 1 1 1 3 1
Line 09 : 0 1 1 5 1	Line 27 : 2 1 1 5 1
Line 10 : 0 1 1 6 1	Line 28 : 3 1 1 6 1
Line 11 : 0 1 2 2 1	Line 29 : 4 1 2 4 1
Line 12 : 0 1 2 3 1	Line 30 : 5 1 4 6 1
Line 13 : 0 1 2 4 1	Line 31 : 6 1 1 1 1
Line 14 : 0 1 2 5 1	Line 32 : 6 1 2 2 1
Line 15 : 0 1 2 6 1	Line 33 : 6 1 3 3 1
Line 16 : 0 1 3 3 1	Line 34 : 6 1 4 4 1
Line 17 : 0 1 3 4 1	Line 35 : 6 1 5 5 1
Line 18 : 0 1 3 5 1	Line 36 : 6 1 6 6 1

33rd line indicates that the (3, 3)th element of F_6 is 1, respectively. Note that we write only the upper-right elements since all the data matrices $F_k (k = 0, 1, \cdots, m)$ are symmetric.

Now, supposing that the SDPARA and the SDPARA-C are installed, we can execute them via mpirun command. These software packages adopt the MPI (Message Passing Interface) for network communication between multiple processors.

```
$ mpirun -np 4 ./sdpara mcq1.dat-s mcq1.result.sdpara
$ mpirun -np 4 ./sdpara-c mcq1.dat-s
mcq1.result.sdpara-c
```

In the above example, we assign four processors by the argument "–np 4". The commands "./sdpara" and "./sdpara-c" are the SDPARA and the SDPARA-C executables, respectively. The last arguments "mcq1.result. sdpara" and "mcq1.result.sdpara-c" are file names in which logs and results of the computation are written.

Both the SDPARA and the SDPARA-C can solve this small example in a second. The computation logs printed out to the screen include the following information.

```
objValPrimal = 4.0000000207e+00
objValDual  = 3.9999999319e+00
```

These values are the primal and dual optimal objective values, respectively. Since we solve the relaxation problem, the dual objective value 4 is an upper bound of the maximum clique number. Recall that {2, 3, 5, 6} is a maximum cardinality clique consisting of four vertices.

We find an optimal solution (x^*, X^*, Y^*) in the assigned result file "mcq1.result.sdpara". From the optimal dual variable matrix Y^*, we construct the vector y^* via the relation $Y^*_{ij} = y^*_i y^*_j$ as follows:

$$Y^* = \begin{pmatrix} 0 & 0 & 0 & 0 & 0 & 0 \\ 0 & 1/4 & 1/4 & 0 & 1/4 & 1/4 \\ 0 & 1/4 & 1/4 & 0 & 1/4 & 1/4 \\ 0 & 0 & 0 & 0 & 0 & 0 \\ 0 & 1/4 & 1/4 & 0 & 1/4 & 1/4 \\ 0 & 1/4 & 1/4 & 0 & 1/4 & 1/4 \end{pmatrix}$$

$$y^*_1 = y^*_4 = 0, \quad y^*_2 = y^*_3 = y^*_5 = y^*_6 = 1/2$$

Hence y^* indicates that $C^* = \{2, 3, 5, 6\}$ is a maximum cardinality clique. We should mention that we can not always construct y^* from Y^* in general, because we have solved a relaxation problem obtained by ignoring the rank condition on Y.

In summary:

1. We formulate a target problem into a standard SDP and define the input data c and $F_k(k = 0, 1, \cdots, m)$.
2. We write accordingly the input file in the SDPA sparse format.
3. We obtain information regarding an optimal solution from the screen and an output file.

9.3. ALGORITHMIC FRAMEWORK AND PARALLEL IMPLEMENTATION

In Section 9.2, we described how to use the parallel software packages, the SDPARA and the SDPARA-C. This section focuses on their algorithmic framework and some details on how we receive benefits from their parallel implementation to shorten their total computation time.

9.3.1. Primal-Dual Interior-Point Method

Both of the SDPARA and the SDPARA-C are based on the Primal-Dual Interior-Point Method (PD-IPM). To explain the details of the parallel implementation, we start from the algorithmic framework of the PD-IPM. The main feature of the PD-IPM is that it deals with the primal SDP $\mathcal{P}$ and the dual SDP $\mathcal{D}$ simultaneously, keeping the positive definiteness of variable matrices X and Y along the iterations until we obtain approximate optimal solutions of $\mathcal{P}$ and $\mathcal{D}$.

The characteristics of the optimal solution are investigated first. Let (x^+, X^+, Y^+) and (x^*, X^*, Y^*) be feasible and optimal solutions of the SDP (the pair of $\mathcal{P}$ and $\mathcal{D}$), respectively. Under the assumption that the SDP has an interior feasible solution, the duality theorem ensures that there is no gap between the primal and dual optimal objective values, that is,

$$F_0 \bullet Y^+ \leq F_0 \bullet Y^* = \sum_{k=1}^{m} c_k x_k^* \leq \sum_{k=1}^{m} c_k x_k^+$$

Since the optimal solution (x^*, X^*, Y^*) satisfies the primal matrix equality and dual linear constraints, it follows that

$$X^* \bullet Y^* = \sum_{k=1}^{m} c_k x_i^* - F_0 \bullet Y^* = 0$$

Since we also know that $X^* \succeq O$ and $Y^* \succeq O$, we can further derive $X^* Y^* = O$. As a result, we obtain the Karush–Kuhn–Tucker (KKT) optimality condition:

$$\text{(KKT)} \quad \begin{cases} X^* = \sum_{k=1}^{m} F_k x_k^* - F_0, \\ F_k \bullet Y^* = c_k \, (k = 1, 2, \cdots, m) \\ X^* Y^* = O, \\ X^* \succeq O, Y^* \succeq O. \end{cases}$$

In the PD-IPM, the central path plays a crucial role in computing an optimal solution. The central path is composed of points defined by a perturbed KKT optimality condition:

The central path $\equiv \{(x(\mu), X(\mu), Y(\mu)) \in \mathbb{R}^m \times \mathbb{S}^n \times \mathbb{S}^n : \mu > 0\}$,

where $(x(\mu), X(\mu), Y(\mu))$ satisfies

$$\text{(perturbed KKT)} \quad \begin{cases} X(\mu) = \sum_{k=1}^{m} F_k x(\mu)_k - F_0 \\ F_k \bullet Y(\mu) = c_k \, (k = 1, 2, \ldots, m) \\ X(\mu) Y(\mu) = \mu I \\ X(\mu) \succ O, Y(\mu) \succ O \end{cases}$$

For any $\mu > 0$, there exists a unique $(x(\mu), X(\mu), Y(\mu)) \in \mathbb{R}^m \times \mathbb{S}^n \times \mathbb{S}^n$ satisfying (perturbed KKT), and the central path forms a smooth curve. We also see from $X(\mu)Y(\mu) = \mu I$ that $X(\mu) \bullet Y(\mu) = n\mu$. It should be emphasized that the central path converges to an optimal solution of the SDP; $(x(\mu), X(\mu), Y(\mu))$ converges to an optimal solution of the SDP as $\mu \to 0$. Thus the PD-IPM traces the central path numerically as decreasing μ toward 0.

Algorithmic Framework of the PD-IPM

Step 0: (Initialization). We choose an initial point (x^0, X^0, Y^0) with $X^0 \succ O, Y^0 \succ O$. Let $\mu^0 = X^0 \bullet Y^0/n$ and $h = 0$. We set the parameters $0 < \beta < 1$ and $0 < \gamma < 1$.

Step 1: (Checking Convergence) If μ^h is sufficiently small and (x^h, X^h, Y^h) approximately satisfies the feasibility, we print out (x^h, X^h, Y^h) as an approximate optimal solution and stop.

Step 2: (Search Direction). We compute a search direction (dx, dX, dY) toward a target point $(x(\beta\mu^h), X(\beta\mu^h), Y(\beta\mu^h))$ on the central path with $\mu = \beta\mu^h$.

Step 3: (Step Length). We compute step lengths α_p and α_d such that $X^h + \alpha_p dX$ and $Y^h + \alpha_d dY$ remain positive definite. In the course of this computation, γ is used to keep positive definiteness.

Step 4: (Update). We update the current point by $(x^{h+1}, X^{h+1}, Y^{h+1}) = (x^h + \alpha_p dx, X^h + \alpha_p dX, Y^h + \alpha_d dY)$. Let $\mu^{h+1} = X^{h+1} \bullet Y^{h+1}/n$ and $h \leftarrow h + 1$. Go to Step 1.

In general, it is not required that the initial point (x^0, X^0, Y^0) is a feasible solution. When (x^h, X^h, Y^h) is infeasible, the step lengths α_p and α_d in Step 3 need to be chosen so that some feasibility measure improves as well as $X^h + \alpha_p dX$ and $Y^h + \alpha_d dY$ remain positive definite.

The computation of the search direction (dx, dX, dY) in Step 2 usually consumes most of the computation time. A fundamental strategy to shorten the total computation time in parallel processing is to use a distributed computation in Step 2. This will be described in the next subsection. Ideally, we want to take a search direction (dx, dX, dY) so that $(x^h + dx, X^h + dX, Y^h + dY)$ coincides with the targeting point $(x(\beta\mu^h), X(\beta\mu^h), Y(\beta\mu^h))$ on the central trajectory with $\mu = \beta\mu^h$, which leads to

$$\begin{cases} X^h + dX = \sum_{k=1}^{m} F_k(x_k^h + dx_k) - F_0 \\ F_k \bullet (Y^h + dY) = c_k (k = 1, 2, \cdots, m) \\ (X^h + dX)(Y^h + dY) = \beta\mu^h I \end{cases}$$

Here, we ignore the positive definite conditions $X^h + dX \succeq O$ and $Y^h + dY \succeq O$ because we recover the conditions by adjusting the step lengths α_p and α_d in Step 3. The above system is almost a linear system except the term $dXdY$ in the last equality. Neglecting the nonlinear term and introducing an auxiliary matrix $\widetilde{dY}$, the system of nonlinear equations above can be reduced into the following system of linear equations:

$$\begin{cases} Bdx = r, \\ dX = P + \sum_{k=1}^{m} F_k dx_k, \\ \widetilde{dY} = (X^h)^{-1}(R - dXY^h), \quad dY = (\widetilde{dY} + \widetilde{dY}^T)/2 \end{cases}$$

where

$$\begin{cases} B_{ij} = \left((X^h)^{-1} F_i Y^h\right) \bullet F_j (i = 1, 2, \cdots, m, j = 1, 2, \cdots, m) \\ r_i = -d_i + F_i \bullet \left((X^h)^{-1}(R - PY^h)\right)(i = 1, 2, \cdots, m) \\ P = \sum_{k=1}^{m} F_k x_k^h - F_0 - X^h \\ d_i = c_i - F_i \bullet Y^h (i = 1, 2, \cdots, m) \\ R = \beta\mu^h I - X^h Y^h \end{cases} \tag{9.1}$$

We call the system of linear equations $Bdx = r$ the *Schur complement equation* (SCE) and its coefficient matrix B the *Schur complement matrix* (SCM). First, solve the SCE, then compute dX and dY. Note that the size of the SCM B corresponds to the number m of equality constraints in $\mathcal{D}$. Since the SCM

B is positive definite through all iterations of the PD-IPM, we apply the Cholesky factorization to B for computing the solution dx of the SCE. The computation cost to evaluate the SCM B is $O(m^2 n^2 + m n^3)$ arithmetic operations when the data matrices F_k ($k = 1, 2, \cdots, m$) are fully dense, while its Cholesky factorization requires $O(m^3)$ arithmetic operations since B becomes fully dense in general even when some of the data matrices are sparse. The auxiliary matrix $\widetilde{dY}$ is introduced to make dY symmetric. The search direction used here is called the HRVW/KSH/M direction (13–15).

The name "interior-point method" comes from Step 3. We adjust the step lengths α_p and α_d to retain X^{h+1} and Y^{h+1} in the interior of the cone of positive definite matrices, that is, $X^{h+1} \succ O$ and $Y^{h+1} \succ O$ for all h. Using the Cholesky factorization of X^h, we first compute the maximum $\bar{\alpha}_p$ of possible step lengths α such that $X^h + \alpha dX \succeq O$. Then the step length α_p in Step 3 is chosen such that $\alpha_p = \gamma \min\{1, \bar{\alpha}_p\}$ by the given parameter $\gamma \in (0, 1)$, for example, $\gamma = 0.9$. Let L be the lower triangular matrix from the Cholesky factorization of $X^h = LL^T$ and let $P\Lambda P^T$ be the eigenvalue decomposition of $L^{-1} dX L^{-T}$. Then, we have

$$X^h + \alpha dX \succeq O \Leftrightarrow LL^T + \alpha dX \succeq O \Leftrightarrow I + \alpha L^{-1} dX L^{-T} \succeq O$$
$$\Leftrightarrow I + \alpha P\Lambda P^T \succeq O \Leftrightarrow P^T I P + \alpha P^T P\Lambda P^T P \succeq O \Leftrightarrow I + \alpha\Lambda \succeq O$$

Hence, $\bar{\alpha}_p$ is given by

$$\bar{\alpha}_p = \begin{cases} -1/\lambda_{\min} & \text{if} \quad \lambda_{\min} < 0 \\ +\infty & \text{otherwise} \end{cases}$$

where $\lambda_{\min}$ is the minimum diagonal value of Λ. In the computation of $\bar{\alpha}_p$ above, we need only $\lambda_{\min}$, but not the full eigenvalue decomposition $P\Lambda P^T$. In the software packages SDPA, SDPARA and SDPARA-C, we adopt the Lanczos method (31) to compute the minimum eigenvalue of $L^{-1} dX L^{-T}$. The step length α_d is computed in the same way.

9.3.2. Parallel Computation in the SDPARA

To apply parallel processing to the PD-IPM, we need to investigate which components of the PD-IPM are bottlenecks when we solve SDPs on a single processor. In general, the following four components occupy >90% of the computation time.

1. [ELEMENTS] The evaluation of the SCM B ($O(m n^3 + m^2 n^2)$ arithmetic operations in dense computation).
2. [CHOLESKY] The Cholesky factorization of the SCM B ($O(m^3)$ arithmetic operations).
3. [DMATRIX] The computation of dY ($O(n^3)$ arithmetic operations).
4. [DENSE] The other matrix manipulations ($O(n^3)$ arithmetic operations).

TABLE 9.2. Time Consumption of Each Component for control11, theta6, and maxG51 on a Single Processor[a]

	control11		theta6		maxG51	
	Time	Ratio, %	Time	Ratio, %	Time	Ratio, %
ELEMENTS	463.2	91.6	78.3	26.1	1.5	1.0
CHOLESKY	31.7	6.2	209.8	70.1	3.0	2.1
DMATRIX	1.8	0.3	1.8	0.6	47.3	33.7
DENSE	1.0	0.2	4.1	1.3	86.5	61.7
Others	7.2	1.4	5.13	1.7	1.8	1.3
Total	505.2	100.0	292.3	100.0	140.2	100.0

[a]Time unit is second.

Table 9.2 shows how much computation time is spent in each component when we solve three SDPs with the SDPA 6.00 (18) on a single processor Pentium 4 (2.2 GHz) and 1 GB memory space. The SDPs, control11, theta6 and maxG51, are from the benchmark collection SDPLIB (31). The SDP control11 is formulated from a stability condition in control theory, while theta6 and maxG51 are SDP relaxations of combinatorial optimization problems; the maximum clique number problem and the maximum cut problem, respectively.

Although the SDPA effectively utilizes the sparsity of input data matrices $F_k (k = 1, \cdots, m)$ (24), the ELEMENTS component still occupies 90% of the computation time in the case of control11. On the other hand, 70% is consumed by the CHOLESKY component in the case of theta6. In either case, the components regarding the SCM B spend >95% of the computation time. Therefore they are obviously bottlenecks on a single processor. The main strategy in the SDPARA (22) is to replace these two components by their parallel implementation. The other two components, DMATRIX and DENSE, are left as a subject of the SDPARA-C.

Let us examine the formula for the elements of the SCM B,

$$B_{ij} = \left(\left(X^h \right)^{-1} F_i Y^h \right) \bullet F_j \quad (i = 1, \cdots, m, j = 1, \cdots, m)$$

When multiple processors are available, we want each processor to work independently from the other processors, because a network communication among the processors prevents them from devoting their full performance to computation. We remark that each element can be evaluated on each processor independently, when each processor stores input data matrices $F_k (k = 1, \cdots, m)$ and the variable matrices $(X^h)^{-1}$ and Y^h. Furthermore, all elements in the ith row of B share the computation $(X^h)^{-1} F_i Y^h$. Therefore, it is reasonable that only one processor computes all elements in each row of B to avoid duplicate computation in the evaluation of the entire B.

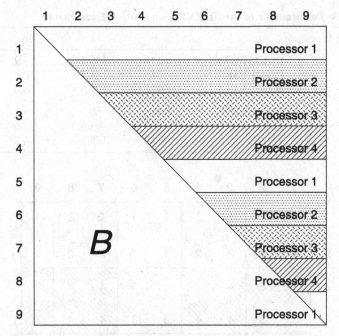

Fig. 9.2. Parallel evaluation of the Schur complement matrix.

In the SDPARA, we implement the row-wise distribution for the ELE-MENTS component. Figure 9.2 shows the row-wise distribution where the size of the SCM B is 9 and 4 processors are available. Since B is symmetric, we compute only the upper triangular part. In the row-wise distribution, we assign each processor to each row in a cyclic manner. To be precise, in the general case, let m be the size of the SCM B and U be the number of available processors. Then the uth processor computes the elements $B_{ij} ((i, j) \in \mathcal{P}_u)$, where

$$\mathcal{P}_u = \{(i, j): 1 \leq i \leq m, \ (i-1)\%U = (u-1), i \leq j \leq m\}$$

and $a\%b$ denotes the remainder of the division a by b. We can verify easily that any row of B is covered by exactly one processor.

Before starting the PD-IPM, we duplicate the input data matrices F_k ($k = 1, \cdots, m$) and the initial point X^0 and Y^0 on each processor. Hence, we can evaluate the SCM B at the initial iteration without any communication between multiple processors. Updating X^h and Y^h on each processor ensures that the independence can be held until the algorithm terminates. Although the basic concept of the row-wise distribution seems very simple, it provides us with the following three advantages. The first is that the row-wise distribution attains a high scalability owing to no communication, which is shown by the numerical results in Table 9.3. The second is that we can combine the row-wise distribution with the technique developed for exploiting the sparsity

TABLE 9.3. Performance of the SDPARA on control11 and theta6

Number of Processors		1	4	16	64
control11	ELEMENTS	603.4	146.8	35.9	9.0
	CHOLESKY	54.5	18.7	10.1	5.3
	Total	685.3	195.0	66.6	31.8
theta6	ELEMENTS	166.0	60.3	18.6	5.5
	CHOLESKY	417.3	93.3	35.6	17.3
	Total	600.6	166.9	66.7	35.5

[a]time in second

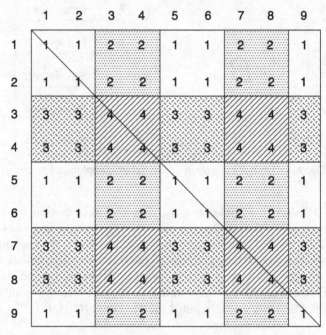

Fig. 9.3. Two-dimensional blockcyclic distribution of the Schur complement matrix for parallel Cholesky factorization.

in (24). The last advantage is that the memory space attached to each processor is also independent from the other processors. In addition, the memory space is almost equally divided into all processors, because the size m of B is usually much greater than the number of available processors.

After the evaluation of the SCM B, we proceed to its Cholesky factorization for computing the solution of the SCE $Bdx = r$. We adopt the parallel Cholesky factorization equipped by the ScaLAPACK (32). Here, we briefly explain how to distribute the elements of B to the processors for the Cholesky factorization. For the ELEMENTS component, not only the computation but also the memory space are divided by the row-wise distribution. However, the ScaLAPACK assumes that the matrix is distributed in a specific memory distribution called the Two-Dimensional Block-Cyclic Distribution (TD-BCD) to accelerate its parallel processing performance. Figure 9.3 illustrates the TD-BCD when B is a 9×9 matrix and 4 processors are used. For example, the (2, 4)th and the (7, 5)th elements are stored on the memory space attached to the 2nd processor and the 3rd processor, respectively.

To bridge the two different memory distributions, we redistribute the SCM B from the row-wise distribution to the TD-BCD in each PD-IPM iteration. The network communication cost for the redistribution is justified by a significant difference in the computation times between the Cholesky factorization on the TD-BCD and that on the row-wise distribution.

Except the ELEMENTS and CHOLESKY components, the SDPARA works in the same way as the SDPA on a single processor. Therefore, saving computation time in the SDPARA is entirely done in these two parallel components. Table 9.3 shows numerical results on the SDPARA applied to control11 and theta6. More numerical results on extremely large SDPs from quantum chemistry will be reported in Section 9.4. All numerical experiments on the SDPARA and the SDPARA-C in this chapter, except Section 9.4.1, were executed on the PC-cluster Presto III at Tokyo Institute of Technology. Each node of the cluster has an Athlon 1900+ processor and 768 MB memory, and all nodes are connected by Myrinet 2000. The high-speed network via Myrinet 2000 is necessary to get enough performance of the parallel Cholesky factorization.

From Table 9.3, we observe that the SDPARA can solve control11 and theta6 faster as more processors participate. Scalability is a criterion to evaluate the effectiveness of parallel computation, which measures how much faster a parallel software package can solve problems on multiple processors compared to a single processor case. Here, we emphasize that the ELEMENTS component attains a very high scalability; in particular, it is almost an ideal scalability (linear scalability) in the case of control11. In both cases, the CHOLESKY component also attains a high scalability. We obtain 3.5 times total speed up on 4 processors and 21.5 times total speed up on 64 processors, respectively, in the case of control11, while we obtain 3.6 times total speed up on 4 processors and 16.9 times total speed up on 64 processors, respectively, in the case of theta6. The difference can be explained by the fact that the ELEMENTS component occupies 88% of the computation time on a single processor in the former case while the CHOLESKY component occupies 69% in the latter case.

9.3.3. The Positive Definite Matrix Completion Method and the SDPARA-C

The SDPARA works effectively on general SDPs whose computation time is occupied mostly by the ELEMENTS and CHOLESKY components. However, some SDPs arising from combinatorial optimization consume most of their computation time on the other components, the DMATRIX and DENSE. Particularly, this feature becomes clearer when the input data matrices are extremely sparse, for instance, when each input data matrix involves only one or two nonzero elements. The SDPARA-C (SDPARA with the positive definite matrix Completion) (23) is designed to solve such sparse SDPs. First we present the basic idea behind the positive definite matrix completion method using a simple example, and then mention how we combine the method with parallel computation in the SDPARA.

As an illustrative example, we consider the SDP with the following input data

$$m = 2 \quad n = 4 \quad c_1 = 3 \quad c_2 = 5$$

$$F_0 = \begin{pmatrix} -7 & 0 & 0 & -1 \\ 0 & -5 & 0 & 0 \\ 0 & 0 & -8 & 3 \\ -1 & 0 & 3 & -4 \end{pmatrix} \quad F_1 = \begin{pmatrix} 2 & 0 & 0 & -1 \\ 0 & 0 & 0 & 2 \\ 0 & 0 & -3 & 0 \\ -1 & 2 & 0 & 1 \end{pmatrix}$$

$$F_2 = \begin{pmatrix} -1 & 0 & 0 & 0 \\ 0 & -2 & 0 & -1 \\ 0 & 0 & 3 & 1 \\ 0 & -1 & 1 & -2 \end{pmatrix}$$

Define *the aggregate sparsity pattern* over the input data matrices by

$$\mathcal{A} = \{(i, j) \; : \; \text{the } (i, j)\text{th element of } F_k \text{ is nonzero}$$
$$\text{for some } k(k = 0, 1, \cdots, m)\}$$

We can represent the aggregate sparsity pattern $\mathcal{A}$ as a matrix A and a graph in Fig. 9.4 that we call the *aggregated sparsity pattern matrix* and *graph*, respectively.

When we deal with the primal SDP $\mathcal{P}$ with the input data given above, we only need the elements $X_{ij} ((i, j) \in \mathcal{A})$ to verify the feasibility of a given (x, X), and we can perform all computation in the PD-IPM without using the other elements $X_{ij} ((i, j) \notin \mathcal{A})$. For example, dX as well as the Cholesky factor L of X have the same sparsity pattern as A, and we can use them to compute the step length α_p.

Now we focus our attention on the dual SDP $\mathcal{D}$. First, we observe that only elements $Y_{ij} ((i, j) \in \mathcal{A})$ are also used to evaluate the objective function $F_0 \bullet$

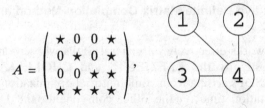

$$A = \begin{pmatrix} \star & 0 & 0 & \star \\ 0 & \star & 0 & \star \\ 0 & 0 & \star & \star \\ \star & \star & \star & \star \end{pmatrix},$$

Fig. 9.4. Aggregate sparsity pattern graph.

Y and the equality constraints $F_k \bullet Y = c_k (k = 1, 2, \cdots, m)$. But the other elements $Y_{ij} ((i, j) \notin \mathcal{A})$ are necessary to evaluate the positive definiteness and/or semidefiniteness of Y. Therefore, the following problem is a key to an effective use of the sparsity in the dual side: when $Y_{ij} = \overline{Y}_{ij} ((i, j) \in \mathcal{A})$ are given, choose $Y_{ij} = \overline{Y}_{ij} ((i, j) \notin \mathcal{A})$, so that the resulting entire matrix $Y = \overline{Y}$ is positive definite. This problem is known as the positive definite matrix completion problem. In the example under consideration, the matrix Y with known $Y_{ij} = \overline{Y}_{ij} ((i, j) \in \mathcal{A})$, but unknown values for all other elements has *a positive definite matrix completion* (a positive definite matrix $\hat{Y}$ with $\hat{Y}_{ij} = \overline{Y}_{ij} ((i, j) \in \mathcal{A})$), if and only if

$$\begin{pmatrix} \overline{Y}_{11} & \overline{Y}_{14} \\ \overline{Y}_{41} & \overline{Y}_{44} \end{pmatrix} \succ O, \begin{pmatrix} \overline{Y}_{22} & \overline{Y}_{24} \\ \overline{Y}_{42} & \overline{Y}_{44} \end{pmatrix} \succ O, \begin{pmatrix} \overline{Y}_{33} & \overline{Y}_{34} \\ \overline{Y}_{43} & \overline{Y}_{44} \end{pmatrix} \succ O$$

Furthermore, we can choose $\hat{Y}$ such that its inverse $\hat{Y}^{-1}$ is a sparse matrix with the same sparsity pattern as A although $\hat{Y}$ itself becomes fully dense. We can also compute the Cholesky factor M of $\hat{Y}^{-1}$, which has the same sparsity pattern as A, without knowing the elements $\hat{Y}_{ij} ((i, j) \notin \mathcal{A})$.

Using the same example as above, we now briefly mention how we incorporate the positive definite matrix completion in each iteration of the PD-IPM. Suppose that the hth iterate (x^h, X^h, Y^h) is given. Here, we assume that X^h is a positive definite matrix with the sparsity pattern A, and that Y^h is a partial matrix with known elements $Y_{ij}^h = \overline{Y}_{ij}^h ((i, j) \in \mathcal{A})$ satisfying the condition:

$$\begin{pmatrix} Y_{11}^h & Y_{14}^h \\ Y_{41}^h & Y_{44}^h \end{pmatrix} \succ O, \begin{pmatrix} Y_{22}^h & Y_{24}^h \\ Y_{42}^h & Y_{44}^h \end{pmatrix} \succ O, \begin{pmatrix} Y_{33}^h & Y_{34}^h \\ Y_{43}^h & Y_{44}^h \end{pmatrix} \succ O$$

this condition ensures that the partial matrix Y^h has a positive definite matrix completion. To compute the search direction (dx, dX, dY), we first apply the Cholesky factorization to X^h and $(Y^h)^{-1}$; $PX^hP^T = LL^T$ and $Q(Y^h)^{-1}Q^T = MM^T$. Here P and Q denote some permutation matrices. For simplicity of notation, we assume that we adequately permutate the rows and columns of X^h and $(Y^h)^{-1}$ by a preprocessing so that P and Q are the identify matrix in the remainder of this section. Note that both L and M have the same sparsity pattern as A, and that we can compute M directly from the known elements $Y_{ij}^h ((i, j) \in \mathcal{A})$ of Y^h without generating the dense positive definite completion of Y^h. We then replace X^h by LL^T and Y^h by $(MM^T)^{-1}$ in the formula we have given in Section 9.3.1 for the search direction (dx, dX, dY). This replacement makes it possible for us to compute (dx, dX, dY) by using only matrices with the same sparsity pattern as A. In particular, dX has the same sparsity pattern as A and dY is a partial matrix with known elements $dY_{ij} = d\overline{Y}_{ij} ((i, j) \in \mathcal{A})$. Then we compute the primal step length α_p and the next primal iterate (x^{h+1}, X^{h+1}) as in Section 9.3.1, and the dual step length α_d and the next dual iterate Y^{h+1} (a partial matrix with elements $Y_{ij}^{h+1} ((i, j) \in \mathcal{A})$ such that

$$\begin{pmatrix} Y_{11}^{h+1} & Y_{14}^{h+1} \\ Y_{41}^{h+1} & Y_{44}^{h+1} \end{pmatrix} = \begin{pmatrix} Y_{11}^{h} & Y_{14}^{h} \\ Y_{41}^{h} & Y_{44}^{h} \end{pmatrix} + \alpha_d \begin{pmatrix} dY_{11} & dY_{14} \\ dY_{41} & dY_{44} \end{pmatrix} \succ O$$

$$\begin{pmatrix} Y_{22}^{h+1} & Y_{24}^{h+1} \\ Y_{42}^{h+1} & Y_{44}^{h+1} \end{pmatrix} = \begin{pmatrix} Y_{22}^{h} & Y_{24}^{h} \\ Y_{42}^{h} & Y_{44}^{h} \end{pmatrix} + \alpha_d \begin{pmatrix} dY_{22} & dY_{24} \\ dY_{42} & dY_{44} \end{pmatrix} \succ O$$

$$\begin{pmatrix} Y_{33}^{h+1} & Y_{34}^{h+1} \\ Y_{43}^{h+1} & Y_{44}^{h+1} \end{pmatrix} = \begin{pmatrix} Y_{33}^{h} & Y_{34}^{h} \\ Y_{43}^{h} & Y_{44}^{h} \end{pmatrix} + \alpha_d \begin{pmatrix} dY_{33} & dY_{34} \\ dY_{43} & dY_{44} \end{pmatrix} \succ O$$

The positive definite matrix completion method described above for this simple example can be extended to general cases where the aggregated sparsity pattern graph $G(V, E)$ of the input data matrices $F_0, F_1, \cdots, F_m$ has a sparse chordal extension. Here, a graph is said to be chordal if any minimal cycle contains at most three edges. We recall that the aggregated sparsity pattern graph of the example itself (Fig. 9.4) is a chordal graph since there is no cycle, and that the principal submatrices, whose positive definiteness have been checked to see whether the partial matrix Y has a positive definite matrix completion, are corresponding to the maximal cliques of the graph. As another example, consider an SDP with data matrices whose aggregated sparsity pattern graph $G(V, E)$ is given by Fig. 9.5. This graph is not chordal because $C = \{2, 5, 3, 6\}$ is a minimal cycle having four edges. Adding an edge $\{2, 3\}$, we make a *chordal extension* $\bar{G}(V, \bar{E})$ of $G(V, E)$, which is illustrated in Fig. 9.6. The extended graph $\bar{G}(V, \bar{E})$ is corresponding to an extended aggregated sparsity pattern

$$\bar{\mathcal{A}} = \{(i, j) : i = j \text{ or } \{i, j\} \in \bar{E}\}$$

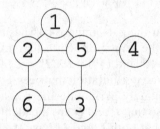

Fig. 9.5. Aggregate sparsity pattern.

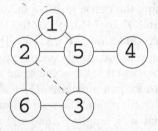

Fig. 9.6. Extended sparsity pattern.

The set of maximal cliques of the extended graph is given by

$$C = \{\{1, 2, 5\}, \{2, 3, 5\}, \{2, 3, 6\}, \{4, 5\}\}$$

For each $C \in C$ and each $Y \in S^n$, let Y_C denote the principal submatrix consisting of the elements Y_{ij} with $(i, j) \in C \times C$. Then, we can state the basic property on the positive definite matrix completion as follows. A partial matrix Y with known elements $Y_{ij} = \bar{Y}_{ij} ((i, j) \in \mathcal{A})$ has a positive definite matrix completion if and only if $\bar{Y}_C \succ O$ for every $C \in C$. If Y has a positive definite matrix completion, we can compute the Cholesky factor M of $\hat{Y}^{-1}$ with the property that both M and $\hat{Y}^{-1}$ have the same sparsity pattern as $\mathcal{A}$. Using these facts, we can extend the positive definite matrix completion method to general cases where the aggregated sparsity pattern graph $G(V, E)$ of the input data matrices has a sparse chordal extension. Usually a chordal extension of a sparse graph is not unique, and we employ heuristic methods implemented in SPOOLES (33) and/or METIS (34) to choose an effective chordal extension. See the Refs. 26 and 27 for more details.

Now we proceed to how we incorporate the positive definite completion method into parallel computation. Specifically, we present how we compute the elements of the SCM B in the SDPARA-C. Let $G(V, E)$ be the aggregated sparsity pattern graph of data matrices $F_0, F_1, \cdots, F_m$ of an SDP to be solved, and $\bar{A}$ be an extended aggregated sparsity pattern matrix induced from a chordal extension $\bar{G}(V, \bar{E})$ of $G(V, E)$. Suppose that $(x^h, X^h, Y^h) \in \mathbb{R}^m \times S^n \times S^n$ is an iterate of the PD-IPM where we assume that X^h and $(Y^h)^{-1}$ are matrices with the sparsity pattern $\bar{A}$. Let L and M be the Cholesky factors of X^h and $(Y^h)^{-1}$, respectively; $X^h = LL^T$ and $(Y^h)^{-1} = MM^T$. Note that both L and M have the same sparsity pattern as $\bar{A}$. Substituting $X^h = LL^T$ and $Y^h = (MM^T)^{-1}$ in the formula to compute the elements of the SCM B, we have

$$B_{ij} = B_{ji} = F_i \bullet \left(L^{-T} L^{-1} F_j M^{-T} M^{-1} \right)$$

$$= \sum_{\ell=1}^{n} e_\ell^T F_i L^{-T} L^{-1} F_j M^{-T} M^{-1} e_\ell$$

$$= \sum_{\ell=1}^{n} \left(L^{-T} L^{-1} [F_i]_{*\ell} \right)^T F_j \left(M^{-T} M^{-1} e_\ell \right)$$

where e_ℓ denotes the ℓth coordinate unit vector and $[F_i]_{*\ell}$ is the ℓth column of F_i. Since L and M are sparse lower triangular matrices, the formula does not require any dense matrix computation; for example, $w = L^{-1}[F_i]_{*\ell}$ is computed by solving the sparse triangular system of linear equations $Lw = [F_i]_{*\ell}$.

From the viewpoint of parallel processing, we emphasize that the modified formula above preserves row-wise independence. That is, assuming that each processor maintains the sparse matrices L, M and $F_j (j = 1, 2, \cdots, m)$, it can compute the ith row of the SCM B independently without communicating to the other processors. Therefore we could distribute the computation of the elements of the SCM B to each processor row-wisely as done in the SDPARA. We need, however, to take account of two more facts for efficient parallel computation of the elements of the SCM B. The one is that the computation cost of the ith row of B according to the above formula using L and M is more expensive than the cost according the original formula using $(X^h)^{-1}$ and Y^h mentioned in Section 9.3.2. The other fact, which is more crucial, is that the computation cost of the ith row of B is proportional to the number of nonzero columns of F_i; if $[F_i]_{*\ell} = 0$ in the formula above, the term $(L^{-T}L^{-1}[F_i]_{*\ell})^T$ $F_j(M^{-T}M^{-1}e_\ell)$ vanishes in the summation. Due to these two facts, the direct use of the simple row-wise distribution of B over the processors would cause considerable unbalance between the computation costs of some ith and i'th rows in SDPs when F_i has many nonzero columns and $F_{i'}$ has a few nonzero columns. In (MCQ$\mathcal{R}$) mentioned in Section 9.2, only one data matrix I has n nonzero columns and all other data matrices of the form E_{pq} has two nonzero columns, so the computation cost of the row of B corresponding to the identity matrix I is about $n/2$ times expensive than that corresponding to the data matrix E_{pq}.

In order to resolve the unbalance in the row-wise parallel computation of the SCM B, we separate the row indices $\{i : 1 \leq i \leq m\}$ of B into two disjoint subsets $\mathcal{Q}$ and $\mathcal{R}$ according to the number of nonzero columns of F_i ($i = 1, 2, \cdots, m$):

$$\mathcal{Q} = \left\{ i: \begin{array}{l} 1 \leq i \leq m, \text{ the number of nonzero columns of } F_i \\ \text{exceeds some threshold} \end{array} \right\}$$

$$\mathcal{R} = \{i: \ 1 \leq i \leq m\} \setminus \mathcal{Q}$$

In applications to combinatorial optimization, such as the maximum clique number problem and the maximum cut problem, the cardinality of $\mathcal{Q}$ is expected small and the cardinality of $\mathcal{R}$ is much larger than the number of processors. We apply the row-wise parallel computation to all rows with indices $i \in \mathcal{R}$, while for each row with index $i \in \mathcal{Q}$ and each ℓ with $[F_i]_{*\ell} \neq 0$, we assign the computation of terms $(L^{-T}L^{-1}[F_i]_{*\ell})^T F_j(M^{-T}M^{-1}e_\ell)$ ($i \leq j \leq m$) to a single processor, and then all such terms are gathered and accumulated with respect to ℓ to compute the entire ith row of B. We call this way of distribution of the elements of the SCM as a *hashed row-wise distribution*.

A similar modification is performed to compute $d\widetilde{Y}$ (the DMATRIX component). We use the following formula:

$$[d\widetilde{Y}]_{*\ell} = \beta\mu L^{-T}L^{-1}e_\ell - M^{-T}M^{-1}e_\ell - L^{-T}L^{-1}dXM^{-T}M^{-1}e_\ell$$

$$(\ell = 1, 2, \cdots, n)$$

instead of the original one

$$d\widetilde{Y} = X^{-1}(R - dXY) = \beta\mu X^{-1} - Y - X^{-1}dXY$$

TABLE 9.4. Computation Time and Memory Space for SDPA, SDPARA, and SDPARA-C

	SDPA	SDPARA	SDPARA-C
ELEMENTS	82.0 s	7.7 s	10.5 s
CHOLESKY	25.3 s	2.9 s	4.0 s
DMATRIX	69.4 s	69.0 s	2.4 s
DENSE	125.7 s	126.1 s	2.3 s
Total computation time	308 s	221 s	26 s
Memory space for B	27 MB	1 MB	1 MB
Memory space for $n \times n$ matrices	237 MB	237 MB	8 MB
Total memory space	279 MB	265 MB	41 MB

The computation of each $[d\widetilde{Y}]_{*\ell}$ is distributed to a single processor, and thus the entire $d\widetilde{Y}$ is computed in parallel. See Ref. 23 for more technical details.

As we have discussed so far, we have three parallelized components in the SDPARA-C. The first is the ELEMENTS in which the hashed row-wise distribution is adopted. The second is the CHOLESKY, which is identical to the CHOLESKY components of the SDPARA. The last one is the DMATRIX. Table 9.4 shows the computation time and the required memory space on each processor when we apply the SDPA, the SDPARA and the SDPARA-C to (MCQ$\mathcal{R}$) with $m = 1891, n = 1000$ on Presto III. We use 64 processors for the latter two parallel software packages.

The ELEMENTS and CHOLESKY components are successfully shortened by the SDPARA as in the previous test problems control11 and theta6 in Table 9.3. However, the total scalability in Table 9.4 is not so good because the computation time for the DMATRIX and DENSE components remains large without any reduction. On the other hand, the SDPARA-C works effectively on the latter two components owing to the positive definite matrix completion method. Storing the sparse Cholesky factor M of $(Y^h)^{-1}$ instead of the full dense matrix Y^h considerably saves the memory space. The time reduction in the DMATRIX component is owing to the combination of the positive definite matrix completion method and parallel computation. We also notice that the computation time for the ELEMENTS component in the SDPARA-C is slightly larger than that in the SDPARA. The reason is that the modified formula for computing the elements of B using the Cholesky factors L of (X^h) and M of $(Y^h)^{-1}$ is a little more expensive than the original formula used for the SDPA and SDPARA.

9.4. NUMERICAL RESULTS

This section presents numerical results on the SDPARA and the SDPARA-C applied to large-scale SDPs from quantum chemistry and combinatorial optimization. We also report numerical results on some benchmark problems from DIMACS challenge and SDPLIB (31), which exhibit a clear difference between the two software packages.

9.4.1. Numerical Results on the SDPARA

Applications of SDPs to quantum chemistry are found in Refs. 3 and 4. Computing the ground-state energies of atomic–molecular systems with high accuracy is essential to investigate chemical reactions involving these systems, and it is one of the most challenging problems in computational quantum chemistry, too. It is known that the statuses of the electrons involved in these systems can be expressed by positive semidefinite matrices called *reduced density matrices*. Since Coleman (35), we know that a lower bound of the ground-state energy of a system, under a certain discretization, can be formulated as an SDP, if we only consider a subset of the conditions that define the original reduced density matrices. An interesting fact is that if we restrict ourselves to just characterize the diagonal elements of the reduced density matrices for any system, this problem becomes equivalent to the description of all facets of the cut polytope, and therefore, an NP-hard problem (36).

The resulting SDP, which approximates the ground-state energy via a subset of the above conditions is extremely large even for small atoms–molecules. This SDP involves a large number m of equality constraints that a single processor requires a huge amount of time to solve or even can not store it in the physical memory space.

We apply the SDPARA to the six SDPs formulated from the ground-state energy computation of atoms/molecules: CH_3^+, Na, O, HNO, HF and CH_3N (3). The number m of equality constraints, the size n of data matrices, the number of diagonal blocks of data matrices "#blocks", and the sizes of the four largest diagonal blocks "largest" are given in Table 9.5. As briefly mentioned in Section 9.2, if the SDP can be written in block diagonal structure, all the routines of the PD-IPM can be executed separately for each block diagonal matrix, and then combined later. Suppose that the data–variable matrices consist of s diagonal blocks whose sizes are $n_1, n_2, \cdots, n_s$. Then the total size of the data/variable matrices are $n = \Sigma_{r=1}^{s} n_r$. The computation cost for the

TABLE 9.5. SDPs from Quantum Chemistry

Atoms–Molecules	m	n	#blocks	Largest
CH_3^+	2,964	3,162	22	[736, 736, 224, 224]
Na	4,743	4,426	22	[1053, 1053, 324, 324]
O	7,230	5,990	22	[1450, 1450, 450, 450]
HNO	10,593	7,886	22	[1936, 1936, 605, 605]
HF	15,018	10,146	22	[2520, 2520, 792, 792]
CH_3N	20,709	12,802	22	[3211, 3211, 1014, 1014]

TABLE 9.6. Performance of the SDPARA on SDPs from Quantum Chemistry

Number of Processors		8	16	32	64	128	256
CH_3^+	ELEMENTS	1202.8	620.0	368.3	155.0	67.9	42.5
	CHOLESKY	22.6	15.8	14.7	7.7	11.5	18.7
	Total	1551.7	917.3	699.5	461.2	431.3	573.6
Na	ELEMENTS	5647.8	2876.8	1534.6	768.8	408.7	212.9
	CHOLESKY	95.0	64.3	54.8	38.9	30.9	63.4
	Total	7515.6	4132.7	2468.2	1706.1	1375.7	1334.7
O	ELEMENTS	*	10100.3	5941.5	2720.4	1205.9	694.2
	CHOLESKY	*	218.2	159.9	87.3	68.2	106.2
	Total	*	14250.6	7908.2	4453.7	3281.1	2951.6
HNO	ELEMENTS	*	*	*	8696.4	4004.0	2083.3
	CHOLESKY	*	*	*	285.4	218.2	267.9
	Total	*	*	*	14054.7	9040.6	7451.2
HF	ELEMENTS	*	*	*	*	13076.1	6833.0
	CHOLESKY	*	*	*	*	520.2	671.0
	Total	*	*	*	*	26797.1	20780.7
CH_3N	ELEMENTS	*	*	*	*	34188.9	18003.3
	CHOLESKY	*	*	*	*	1008.9	1309.9
	Total	*	*	*	*	57034.8	45488.9

ELEMENT component, for example, becomes $O(m^2\Sigma_{r=1}^{s} n_r^2 + m\Sigma_{r=1}^{s} n_r^3)$ arithmetic operations instead of $O(mn^3 + m^2n^2)$.

Table 9.6 shows how much computation time the SDPARA spends to solve the SDPs changing the number of available processors. The numerical results in Table 9.6 were executed on AIST (National Institute of Advanced Industrial Science and Technology) super cluster P32. Each node of P32 has two Opteron 2-GHz processors and 6-GB Memory space. The marks "*" in Table 9.6 mean that we avoid solving the SDPs by smaller number of processors due to enormous computation time.

First, we observe that the ideal scalability is attained in the ELEMENTS component on all SDPs. This is owing to the row-wise distribution of the elements of the SCM **B**, which requires no communication among multiple processors. The SDPARA also speeds up the CHOLESKY component. Although the scalability of the CHOLESKY component is not so good when more than 128 processors participate, it enables the SDPARA to obtain sufficient computation time reduction compared to a single processor. As a result, the SDPARA attains a high total scalability; for example, the SDPARA on 256 processors solves the oxygen atom O 4.8 times faster than the SDPARA on 16 processors.

We also emphasize that the computation time owing to the SDPARA enable us to solve the largest SDP CH_3N. Since the ELEMENTS components attains almost the ideal scalability, we would require >1000 h if we used only a single processor. The SDPARA shrinks 40 days computation into a half-day.

9.4.2. Numerical Results on the SDPARA-C

In Table 9.7, we apply the SDPARA-C to three SDPs, which arise from combinatorial optimization. They are SDP relaxations of the maximum cut problems and the max clique number problems on lattice graphs, respectively. A lattice graph $G(V, E)$ is defined by the following vertex set V and edge set E,

$$V = \{(i, j): 1 \leq i \leq P, 1 \leq j \leq Q\}$$
$$E = \{((i, j), (i+1, j)): 1 \leq i \leq P-1, 1 \leq j \leq Q\}$$
$$\cup \{((i, j), (i, j+1)): 1 \leq i \leq P, 1 \leq j \leq Q-1\}$$

Here P and Q denote positive integers. The aggregate sparsity patterns of cut-10-500 and clique-10-200 are covered by the corresponding lattice graphs.

The numerical results on the SDPARA-C applied to the three SDPs are shown in Table 9.8. In the table, we exclude components that can be computed in <10s even on a single processor. In the case of cut-10-200, all three parallel components, ELEMENTS, CHOLESKY, and DMATRIX in the

TABLE 9.7. Sparse SDPs from Combinatorial Optimization

Name	m	n		
cut-10–500	5000	5000	max cut problem	with $P = 10$, $Q = 500$
clique-10–200	3791	2000	max clique problem	with $P = 10$, $Q = 200$
maxG51	1000	1000	from SDPLIB (31)	

TABLE 9.8. Performance of the SDPARA-C on SDPs from Combinatorial Optimization

Number of Processors		1	4	16	64
cut-10–500	ELEMENTS	937.0	270.4	74.6	23.0
	CHOLESKY	825.1	142.0	49.7	19.9
	DMATRIX	459.5	120.4	30.9	9.2
	Total	2239.7	544.4	166.8	70.7
clique-10–200	ELEMENTS	2921.9	802.8	203.6	55.6
	CHOLESKY	538.9	100.1	38.2	17.1
	DMATRIX	197.4	51.9	14.6	5.5
	Total	3670.1	966.2	266.5	95.6
maxG51	ELEMENTS	228.1	65.2	17.9	6.3
	DMATRIX	220.1	60.1	20.3	18.4
	DENSE	26.8	26.4	26.7	26.9
	Total	485.7	157.2	70.1	61.1

SDPARA-C clearly contribute to shortening the total computation time. We obtain 31.6 times speed up on 64 processors in comparison to the computation time on a single processor. In the case of clique-10-200, the ELEMENTS component attains a very high scalability, 52.6 times speed up on 64 processors over the computation time on a single processor. We should remind the discussion in Section 9.3.3 on unbalance among the computation costs of rows of the SCM **B** and the hashed row-wise distribution of elements of the SCM **B** to resolve it. Without the hashed row-wise distribution, we could not attain the high scalability. On the other hand, parallel processing does not yield any benefit on the DENSE component of maxG51 although the other two components are considerably shortened. However, it should be mentioned that the computation time of the DENSE component has already been shortened by positive matrix completion method before applying parallel processing.

9.4.3. Comparison between the SDPARA and the SDPARA-C

The test problems in this subsection are from SDPLIB (31) and the 7th DIMACS implementation challenge: semidefinite and related optimization problems. Table 9.9 shows numerical results on the SDPARA and the SDPARA-C using the 64 processors of Presto III. The unit of computation time and memory space used are second and Megabytes, respectively.

The column ρ denotes the average density of the aggregated sparsity pattern matrix, that is, the number of nonzeros in the aggregated sparsity pattern matrix divided by $n \times n$. When ρ is small, we regard that the SDP is sparse. The SDPs whose names start with "torus" are the benchmark test problems from DIMACS, and all other problems are from SDPLIB.

In Table 9.9, "M" means that the SDPARA cannot solve the problem due to lack of memory space. This fact shows us that the positive definite matrix

TABLE 9.9. Performance on SDPLIB and DIMACS Challenge Problems

	m	n	ρ	SDPARA		SDPARA-C	
				time	memory	time	memory
maxG32	2000	2000	1.6e-2		M	31.8	51
thetaG11	2401	801	2.9e-2	130.3	182	22.7	15
equalG11	801	801	4.4e-2	141.3	177	17.2	40
qpG51	2000	1000	6.7e-2	416.4	287	654.8	139
thetaG51	6910	1001	1.4e-1		M	107.9	107
control11	1596	165	4.5e-1	29.9	67	2017.6	84
equalG51	1001	1001	5.3e-1	230.1	263	528.5	482
torusg3–8	512	512	1.5e-1	45.4	88	14.7	51
toruspm3–8–50	512	512	1.5e-1	34.7	88	14.8	51
torusg3–15	3375	3375	6.3e-2		M	575.0	463
toruspm3–15–50	3375	3375	6.3e-2		M	563.3	463

completion method incorporated in the SDPARA-C saves memory space effectively. From the view point of computation time, we notice their performance significantly depends on ρ. When the input data matrices of an SDP are considerably sparse or ρ is <5.0e-2, the SDPARA-C works more efficiently than the SDPARA. On the other hand, when the input data matrices of an SDP are dense as in the cases of control11 with $\rho = 4.5e-1$ and equalG51 with $\rho = 5.3e-1$, the SDPARA works better. Some characteristics such as the number m of equality constraints and the extended aggregated sparsity other than the average density ρ of the aggregated sparsity pattern matrix also affect the performance of the SDPARA and the SDPARA-C. In particular, it is not clear which of them works better for the moderately dense cases with $5.0e-2 \leq \rho \leq 2.0e-1$ in Table 9.9. We conclude that the SDPARA and the SDPARA-C complement each other.

9.5. FUTURE DIRECTIONS

In Section 9.4.3, we have shown that the SDPARA and the SDPARA-C can successfully solve large-scale sparse SDPs in short time. Each software performs more efficiently than the other on some of the test problems, and their roles are complementary. Also there are some small-scale (even dense or small) SDPs, which the SDPA on a single processor solves faster than the SDPARA and the SDPARA-C because they are not large enough (and/or not sparse enough) to apply parallel computation effectively. It is our future work to develop a method of judging which software package is suitable for a given SDP to be solved. With such method, we could provide an interface that automatically assigns a given SDP to a suitable software package.

Under current circumstances, many readers do not have any hardware for parallel computation. We will provide an online solver for SDPs; if the users send an SDP written in the SDPA sparse format to the online solver via the Internet, then the SDP is solved with a suitable software package among the SDPA, the SDPARA and the SDPARA-C selected by the method mentioned above, an the computational results are sent back to the user through the Internet. We will attach a link of the online solver to the SDPA web site below as soon as it is available.

`http://homepage.mac.com/klabtitech/sdpa-homepage/`

The source codes and manuals of the SDPA, the SDPARA and the SDPARA-C are already available at this web site.

REFERENCES

1. M. X. Goemans and D. P. Williamson, "Improved approximation algorithms for maximum cut and satisfiability problems using semidefinite programming", *J. Ass. Comput. Mach.*, **42**, 1115 (1995).

2. L. Lovász and A. Schrijver, "Cones of matrices and set-valued functions and 0-1 optimization", *SIAM J. Opt.*, **1**, 166 (1991).

3. M. Fukuda *et al.*, "Large-scale semidefinite programs in electronic structure calculation", To be published in *Math. Prog.*

4. M. Nakata *et al.*, "Variational calculations of fermion second-order reduced density matrices by semidefinite programming algorithm", *J. Chem. Phys.*, **114**, 8282 (2001).

5. S. Boyd, L. E. Ghaoui, E. Feron, and V. Balakrishnan, *Linear matrix inequalities in system and control theory*, Society for Industrial and Applied Mathematics, Philadelphia, 1994.

6. S. Kim, M. Kojima, and H. Waki, "Generalized Lagrangian duals and sums of squares relaxations of sparse polynomial optimization problems", *SIAM J. Opt.*, **15**, 697 (2005).

7. J. B. Lasserre, "Global optimization with polynomials and the problems of moments", *SIAM J. Opt.*, **11**, 798 (2001).

8. M. J. Todd, "Semidefinite optimization," *Acta Num.*, **10**, 515 (2001).

9. L. Vandenberghe and S. Boyd, "Positive-Definite Programming", In J. R. Birge and K. G. Murty, eds., *Mathematical Programming: State of the Art 1994*, University of Michigan, MI, Ann Arbor, 1994.

10. H. Wolkowicz, R. Saigal, and L. Vandenberghe, *Handbook of Semidefinite Programming, Theory, Algorithms, and Applications*, Kluwer Academic Publishers, Boston, 2000.

11. Yu. E. Nesterov and A. S. Nemirovskii, *Interior Point Polynomial Methods in Convex Programming: Theory and Applications*, Society for Industrial and Applied Mathematics, Philadelphia, 1994.

12. F. Alizadeh, J. P. A. Haeberly, and M. L. Overton, "Primal-dual interior-point methods for semidefinite programming: Convergence rate, stability and numerical results", *SIAM J. Optim.*, **8**, 746 (1998).

13. C. Helmberg, F. Rendl, R. J. Vanderbei, and H. Wolkowicz, "An interior-point method for semidefinite programming," *SIAM J. Opt.*, **6**, 342 (1996).

14. M. Kojima, S. Shindoh, and S. Hara, "Interior-point methods for the monotone semidefinite linear complementarity problems", *SIAM J. Opt.*, **7**, 86 (1997).

15. R. D. C. Monteiro, "Primal-dual path following algorithms for semidefinite programming", *SIAM J. Opt.*, **7**, 663 (1997).

16. Yu. E. Nesterov and M. J. Todd, "Primal-dual interior-point methods for self-scaled cones," *SIAM J. Opt.*, **8**, 324 (1998).

17. K. Fujisawa, M. Kojima, K. Nakata, and M. Yamashita, "SDPA (SemiDefinite Programming Algorithm) User's Manual—Version 6.00," Research Report B-308, Dept. of Mathematical and Computing Sciences, Tokyo Institute of Technology (2002).

18. M. Yamashita, K. Fujisawa, and M. Kojima, "Implementation and Evaluation of SDPA6.0 (SemiDefinite Programming Algorithm 6.0)", *Opt. Methods Software*, **18**, 491 (2003).

19. J. F. Strum, "SeDuMi 1.02, a MATLAB toolbox for optimization over symmetric cones", *Opt. Methods Software*, **11, 12**, 625 (1999).

20. M. J. Todd, K. C. Toh, and R. H. Tütüncü, "SDPT3—a MATLAB software package for semidefinite programming, version 1.3", *Opt. Methods Software*, **11, 12**, 545 (1999).

21. B. Borchers, "CSDP, a C library for semidefinite programming", *Opt. Methods Software*, **11, 12**, 613 (1999).

22. M. Yamashita, K. Fujisawa, and M. Kojima, "SDPARA: SemiDefinite Programming Algorithm paRAllel version", *Paral. Comput.*, **29**, 1053 (2003).

23. K. Nakata, M. Yamashita, K. Fujisawa, and M. Kojima, "A parallel primaldual interior-point method for semidefinite programs using positive definite matrix completion", *Paral. Comput.*, **32**, 24 (2006).

24. K. Fujisawa, M. Kojima, and K. Nakata, "Exploiting sparsity in primal dual interior-point methods for semidefinite programming", *Math. Prog.*, **79**, 235 (1997).

25. H. Waki, S. Kim, M. Kojima, and M. Muramatsu, "Sums of squares and semidefinite programming relaxations for polynomial optimization problems with structured sparsity", Research Report B-411, Dept. of Mathematical and Computing Sciences, Tokyo Institute of Technology, 2004.

26. M. Fukuda, M. Kojima, K. Murota, and K. Nakata, "Exploiting sparsity in semidefinite programming via matrix completion I: General framework", *SIAM J. Opt.*, **11**, 647 (2000).

27. K. Nakata, K. Fujisawa, M. Fukuda, M. Kojima, and K. Murota, "Exploiting sparsity in semidefinite programming via matrix completion II: Implementation and numerical results", *Math. Progr.*, *Se. B*, **95**, 303 (2003).

28. M. Grötschel, L. Lovász, and A. Schrijver, *Geometric Algorithms and Combinatorial Optimization*, 2nd ed., Springer-Verlag, New York, 1993.

29. B. Borchers, "SDPLIB 1.2, a library of semidefinite programming test problems", *Opt. Methods Software*, **11, 12**, 683 (1999).

30. L. Lovász, "On the Shannon Capacity of a Graph", *IEEE Trans. Inf. Theory*, **IT-25**, 1 (1979).

31. K. C. Toh, "A note on the calculation of step-lengths in interior-point methods for semidefinite programming", *Comput. Opt. Appl.*, **21**, 301 (2002).

32. L. S. Blackford *et al.*, *ScaLAPACK Users' Guide*, Society for Industrial and Applied Mathematics, Philadelphia, 1997.

33. C. Ashcraft, D. Pierce, D. K. Wah, and J. Wu, "The reference manual for SPOOLES, release 2.2: An object oriented software library for solving sparse linear systems of equations", Boeing Shared Services Group, Seattle, WA 98124 (1999). Available at http://netlib.bell-labs.com/netlib/linalg/spooles/spooles.

34. G. Karypis and V. Kumar, "METIS—A software package for partitioning unstructured graphs, partitioning meshes, and computing fill-reducing orderings of sparse matrices, version 4.0—", Department of Computer Science/Army HPC Research Center, University of Minnesota, Minneapolis, (1998). Available at http://www-users.cs.umn.edu/~karypis/metis/metis.

35. A. J. Coleman, "Structure of fermion density matrices", *Rev. Mod. Phys.*, **35**, 668 (1963).

36. M. Deza and M. Laurent, *Geometry of Cuts and Metrics*, Springer-Verlag, Berlin, 1997.

■■■■ **CHAPTER 10**

MW: A Software Framework For Combinatorial Optimization On Computational Grids

WASU GLANKWAMDEE and JEFF LINDEROTH

Department of Industrial and Systems Engineering Lehigh University, Bethlehem PA USA

10.1. INTRODUCTION

Branch and bound is the backbone of many algorithms for solving combinatorial optimization problems, dating at least as far back as the work of Little et al. (1) in solving the traveling salesman problem. Branch and bound and similar tree-search techniques have been implemented on a variety of parallel computing platforms dating back to the advent of multiprocessor machines. See Gendron and Crainic (2) for a survey of parallel branch-and-bound algorithms, including references to early works.

The goal of this chapter is to demonstrate that branch-and-bound algorithms for combinatorial optimization can be effectively implemented on a relatively new type of multiprocessor platform known as a *computational grid* (3). A computational grid consists of collections of loosely coupled, nondedicated, heterogeneous computing resources. Computational grids can be quite powerful, consisting of a large number of processors, but they can be difficult to use effectively. We will argue that to easily and effectively harness the power of computational grids for branch-and-bound algorithms, the master–worker paradigm should be used to control the algorithm. While recognizing that the master–worker paradigm is inherently not scalable, we will also show that the manner in which the tree search is performed can have a significant impact on the resulting parallel branch-and-bound algorithm's scalability and efficiency. Many of these ideas were (implicitly) present in the branch-and-bound implementation of Anstreicher et al. (4), used to solve a number of quadratic

Parallel Combinatorial Optimization, edited by El-Ghazali Talbi
Copyright © 2006 by John Wiley & Sons, Inc.

assignment problems to optimality. In this work, we show that these ideas equally well apply to more general branch-and-bound implementations. We will also briefly describe a software framework MW that can ease an application developer's burden when implementing master–worker based parallel algorithms on computational grids. The focus will specifically be on features of MW that are of the most utility to users wishing to implement branch-and-bound algorithms. To illustrate the impact of the issues we discuss, the Chapter ends with a case study implementation of a branch-and-bound solver to solve the 0–1 knapsack problem running on a wide-area computational grid of hundreds of processors.

10.2. COMPUTATIONAL GRIDS

Networks of computers, such as the Internet, that have been highly successful as communication and information-sharing devices, are beginning to realize their enormous potential as computational grids: collections of loosely coupled, geographically distributed, heterogeneous computing resources that can provide significant computing power over long time periods. As an example of the vast computing power available on a computational grid, consider the SETI@home project (5), which since its inception in the 1990s has delivered >18,000 *centuries* of CPU time to a signal processing effort. Computational grids are generally used in this manner: as *high-throughput computing devices*. In high-throughput computing, the focus is on using resources over long time periods to solve larger problems than would otherwise be possible. This is in contrast to *high-performance computing* in which the performance is usually delivered and measured on a shorter time scale. Another important distinction in our work is that high-performance resources are typically scheduled: a user must request a fixed number of processors for a fixed computing time. It is extremely difficult to accurately predict the CPU time required for branch-and-bound algorithms, which makes using resources in such a rigid manner nearly impossible for purveyors of branch and bound. Our grid computing approach must be more flexible.

This work will focus on computational grids built using the Condor software system (6), which manages distributively owned collections of workstations known as *Condor pools*. A unique and powerful feature of Condor is that each machine's owner specifies the conditions under which jobs are allowed to run. In particular, the default policy is to stop a Condor job when a workstation's owner begins using the machine. In this way, Condor jobs only use cycles that would have otherwise been wasted. Because of the minimal intrusion of the Condor system, workstation owners are often quite willing to donate their machines, and large computational grids from Condor pools can be built.

In recent years, Condor has been equipped with a variety of features that allow collections of Condor pools to be linked together. One mechanism, called *flocking* (7), allows for jobs submit to one Condor pool to be run in a different (perhaps geographically distant) pool. A second mechanism, called *glide-in*, allows for scheduled (usually high performance) resources to temporarily join existing Condor pools (8). With mechanisms such as flocking and glide-in, large-scale computing configurations can be built, but this increase in available CPU power comes at a price. Additional CPU decentralization leads to further loss of authority and control of the resources, which implies that the fault tolerance aspects of algorithms running on such computational grids will be extremely important. The use of flocking and glide-in to solve a large-scale knapsack problem in will be demonstrated Section 10.6.4

10.2.1. Related Work

Aida et al. (9) describe a *hierarchical* master–worker paradigm aimed at reducing application performance degradation that may occur as a result of a single master. Their framework is applied on a branch-and-bound algorithm to minimize the maximum eigenvalue of a matrix function and run on a distributed computational grid testbed of up to 50 processors. Aida and Osumi extend this work in Ref. 10, scaling the algorithm up to 384 processors. In Ref. 9, the authors conclude that "the conventional master–worker paradigm is not suitable to efficiently solve the optimization problem with fine-grain tasks on the WAN setting, because communication overhead is too high compared to the costs of the tasks". While this conclusion is certainly true, it is our contention that a significant majority of branch-and-bound algorithms can be made to consist of coarse-grained tasks, and the loss of coordinated control induced by such an algorithmic decision does not result in significant redundant work being done. Fault tolerance is not addressed in the works reported in Refs. 9 and 10. Our grids will draw CPU power from the Condor system of nondedicated processors, so fault tolerance is of extreme importance to our work.

Tanaka et al. (11) describe a master–worker based, grid-enabled algorithm for the 0–1 knapsack problem. Section 10.6 gives such an algorithm. In Ref. 11, the focus is to enable communication links between processors on opposite sides of a firewall, and for this, they use software components from the Globus toolkit (12). The focus is less on the performance or load balancing aspects of the branch-and-bound algorithm itself.

Other notable works for implementing parallel branch-and-bound algorithms include ALPS (13), BOB (14), PICO (15), and PPBB-Lib (16). However, these works do not explicitly address the significant fault tolerance issues necessary to run on computational grids composed of harnessed idle CPU cycles.

Iamnitchi and Foster (17) propose a fully decentralized branch-and-bound algorithm that addresses the fault recovery issue by propagating messages about the completed subtrees to all processors through a gossip mechanism (18). This mechanism may result in significant overhead, both in terms of redundant work and in bandwidth usage. However, simulated results on reasonably sized configurations show that in many cases the overhead is acceptable.

The works of Drummond et al. (19) and Filho et al. (20) describe a decentralized branch-and-bound algorithmic framework that is used to solve instances of the Steiner Problem using a branch-and-bound algorithm. Fault tolerance is achieved via sharing checkpoint information among processors in a round-robin fashion. Simultaneous failures of worker processes are difficult from which to recover, so the approach may be suited for "moderate" levels of fault recovery. Good computational results are presented on configurations of up to 48 processors.

10.3. BRANCH AND BOUND

Branch-and-bound algorithms are generally applied to $\mathcal{NP}$-Hard problems, so harvesting the enormous computing power of computational grids for branch-and-bound algorithms is a natural idea to consider. However, a fundamental drawback of using nondedicated resources in the case of branch and bound is that if a processor leaves the computation, then the nodes on that processor must be reevaluated. Thus, on a computational grid, we may wish to favor parallelization strategies in which nodes are centralized on a master processor that is under our direct control. Failure of the master processor can be dealt with through a checkpointing mechanism—by periodically writing the nodes to the disk. Having a single master processor responsible for managing the list of nodes that must be evaluated is also appealing from the standpoint that it provides a simple mechanism for dealing with the dynamic, error-prone nature of computational grids. If a new resource becomes available during the course of the computation, it can simply be assigned active nodes from the master processor. Likewise, should a resource be reclaimed (or fail) while evaluating a node, the master processor can simply assign that node to a different processor. Thus, for reasons of simplicity, the master–worker paradigm is very appealing for a grid computing environment.

However, the master–worker paradigm is inherently not scalable. That is, for configurations consisting of a large number of workers, the master processor may be overwhelmed in dealing with requests from the workers and *contention* may occur. Many parallel branch-and-bound methods have a more loosely coupled form of coordinated control that allows for more scalability. It is our goal in this work to show the limits to which branch-and-bound algorithms can be scaled using the master–worker paradigm, with a well-engineered version of the algorithm running on a computational grid.

Contention. The lack of scalability of the master–worker paradigm comes from the bottleneck of a single master process serving many worker requests. The contention problem can be quite serious in a grid computing environment, as our goal is to have hundreds or thousands of workers served by a single master. To ease the contention problem, it is useful to think of the master–worker paradigm as a simple G/G/1 queueing model. There are two ways to increase the efficiency of the model:

1. *Decrease the arrival rate.* This can be accomplished by increasing the *grain size* of the computation. In the context of branch and bound, the grain size can be increased by making the base unit of work in the parallel branch-and-bound algorithm a *subtree*, not a single node. The grain size can be limited by giving an upper bound on the CPU time (or number of nodes) spent evaluating the subtree.
2. *Increase the service rate.* This can be accomplished by searching the subtrees in a depth-first manner. Searching the subtrees depth-first minimizes the number of nodes that will be left unexplored if the evaluation limit on the subtree is reached. This has two positive effects for increasing the service rate of the master processor. First, the size of the messages passed to the master is reduced, and second, the size of the list of unexplored nodes on the master is kept small. We will demonstrate the effect of node selection on contention and parallel efficiency of a master–worker branch-and-bound algorithm in Section 10.6.3.1.

Clean-Up. The unit of work in our parallel branch-and-bound algorithm will be a time or node limited subtree in order to ease contention effects at the master. However, a subtle point as regards to this strategy is that even though we may wish a worker to evaluate a subtree for γ seconds, it may take significantly less than γ seconds to *completely* evaluate and fathom the subtree. Somehow, we would like to ensure that if a node enters the master's task queue, then it is *likely* that it will require the full time γ (or close to the full-time γ) to evaluate. This is accomplished with a second (or clean-up) phase in every task. The goal of the clean-up phase is to fathom nodes that are unlikely to lead to full-length tasks. Nodes deeper in the branch-and-bound tree are likely to lead to short tasks, so in the clean-up phase, the focus is on evaluating these nodes. One strategy for implementing clean-up is the following. When the time limit γ is reached on the worker, the worker computes the average depth $\bar{d}$ of its unevaluated nodes. Then, the worker is given an additional $t_1\gamma$ seconds to attempt to evaluate every node whose depth is larger than $\psi_1\bar{d}$. Note that if the worker is evaluating nodes in a depth-first fashion, this simply amounts to "popping up" the stack of nodes to depth $\psi_1\bar{d}$. This simple idea can be extended to a multi-phase clean up, wherein if the first phase of clean-up is not successful in removing all nodes of depth larger than $\psi_1\bar{d}$, the worker is given an additional $\tau_2\gamma$ seconds to remove all nodes whose depth is larger than $\psi_2\bar{d}$. Typically, $\psi_2 > \psi_1$, the goal is to make it more likely for subsequent clean-up phases to complete. We will demonstrate the effectiveness of clean-up in removing short tasks in the case study in Section 10.6.

Ramp-Up and Ramp-Down. Contention is not the only issue that may cause a lack of efficiency of a parallel branch-and-bound algorithm. *Ramp-up* and *ramp-down*, referring to the times at the beginning and the end of the computation when there are more processors available than active nodes of the search tree, can also reduce efficiency. A simple and effective way to deal with these issues is to exploit the fact that the grain size of the branch-and-bound algorithm can be dynamically altered. If the number of tasks in the master's list is less than α, the maximum task time is set to a small number of seconds β. Note that this strategy works to improve the efficiency in both the ramp-up and ramp-down phases.

10.4. MW API

MW consists of an Application Programming Interface (API) designed to be *easy* for application programmers to use, but one that also allows users to exploit specific properties of the algorithm in order to build an efficient implementation. The main characteristic of the parallel branch-and-bound algorithm that we exploit in order to increase parallel efficiency will be *dynamic grain size*.

In order to parallelize an application with MW, the application programmer must re-implement three abstract base classes: MWDriver, MWTask, and MWWorker.

10.4.1. MWDriver. To create the MWDriver, the user need reimplement four pure virtual methods:

- `get_userinfo(int argc, char *argv[])`: Processes arguments and does basic setup.
- `setup_initial_tasks(int *n, MWTask ***tasks)`: Returns the address of an array of pointers to tasks on which the computation is to begin. For branch-and-bound algorithms, $n = 1$, and the task is a description of the root node.
- `pack_worker_init_data()`: Packs the initial data to be sent to the worker upon startup. Typically this consists of at least a description of the problem instance to be solved.
- `act_on_completed_task(MWTask *task)`: Is called every time a task finishes. For branch-and-bound algorithms, typically this method involved calling the `MWDriver::addTasks(int n, MWTask **tasks)` method if the recently completed task has resulted in new nodes (tasks) that must be completed.

The MWDriver manages a set of MWTasks and a set of MWWorkers to execute those tasks. The MWDriver base class handles workers joining and leaving the computation, assigns tasks to appropriate workers, and rematches running tasks when workers are lost. All this complexity is hidden from the application programmer.

10.4.2. MWTask. The MWTask is the abstraction of one unit of work. The class holds both the data describing the work to be done by a task and the results computed by the worker. For branch-and-bound algorithms implemented in the manner suggested in Section 10.3, the input portion of the task consists of a description of one node. For the input node, the goal is to evaluate the entire subtree rooted at this node. The result portion of the task is a list of nodes that were unevaluated when the task CPU limit was reached. The derived task class must implement functions for sending and receiving its data between the master and worker. The names of these functions are self-explanatory: `pack_work()`, `unpack_work()`, `pack_results()`, and `unpack_results()`. These functions will call associated `pack()` and `unpack()` functions in the MWRMComm class (described in Section 10.5.4) to perform the communication.

10.4.3. MWWorker. The MWWorker class is the core of the worker executable. Two pure virtual functions must be implemented:

- `unpack_init_data()`: Unpacks the initialization information passed in the MWDriver's `pack_worker_init_data()`. This method can also perform any computations necessary to initialize a worker before receiving tasks.
- `execute_task(MWTask *task)`: Given a task, computes the results.

The MWWorker asks the master for a task and sits in a simple loop. Given a task, it computes the results, reports the results back, and waits for another task. The loop finishes when the master asks the worker to end.

10.5. ADDITIONAL MW FEATURES

10.5.1. Task List Management

In MW, the master class manages a list of uncompleted tasks and a list of workers. The default scheduling mechanism in MW is to simply assign the task at the head of the task list to the first idle worker in the worker list. However, MW gives flexibility to the user in the manner in which each of the lists are ordered.

For example, MW allows the user to easily implement both a Last-In-First-Out policy (LIFO) and a First-In-First-Out policy (FIFO) by simply specifying the location at which new tasks are added to the task list (the MWTaskAdditionMode) to be one of ADD_AT_END or ADD_AT_BEGIN in the method

```
MWDriver::set_task_add_mode(MWTaskAdditionMode t).
```

A more dynamic way in which to manage the task list is through *task keys*. Each (derived) MWTask may be assigned a key value through the method

```
MWDriver::set_task_key_function(MWKey(*)(MWTask *)
key_func),
```

where **key_func** is the address of a function that takes a pointer to a **MWTask** and returns the MWKey of the task, which is typed to be a double. The task_key may be changed dynamically during the course of the computation by using this method. The task list can be sorted through the method

```
MWDriver::sort_task_list(),
```

and once sorted, tasks can be added and retrieved from the sorted list by task key value. In MW, the task list is sorted from smallest key value to largest key value.

The ability to dynamically alter the task key during the course of the search is important for some branch-and-bound computations. For example, many branch-and-bound algorithms search the tree in a best-first manner. For large branch-and-bound trees, this can lead to the number of active nodes becoming very large, exhausting the available memory on the master processor. Instead, by dynamically altering the task list ordering, the user can adopt an approach where the nodes are searched best-first until the number of tasks at the master exceeds a "high-water" level h, and then the task list is reordered so that the tasks with the worst bound are searched. The task list can be kept in this order until its size of becomes smaller than a "low-water" level ℓ, at which time the list can be reordered in a best-first fashion.

One final method that can be of particular importance to branch-and-bound applications is a call that can delete all tasks in the task list whose key values are larger than a specified value:

```
MWDriver::delete_tasks_worse than(MWKey).
```

10.5.2. User-Level Checkpointing

Long running computations will invariably at some point fail. A program bug, a power loss, an operating system upgrade, or a network failure will cause the program to stop execution. Being able to easily deal with failures of the worker executables is precisely the purpose of MW, so these failures cause little problem: MW can detect each failure and resend the task the failed worker was executing to another worker. A crash on the master is more serious. To mitigate this risk, MW provides a mechanism for user-level checkpointing of the master state. To implement checkpointing in MW the users need implement the following four methods that read and write the state of the master and a task to a file:

- MWDriver::write_master_state(FILE *fp),
- MWDriver::read_master_state(FILE *fp),

- `MWTask::write_ckpt_info(FILE *fp)`,
- `MWTask::read_ckpt_info(FILE *fp)`

10.5.3. Statistics and Benchmarking

At the end of a computation, MW reports various performance statistics. MW relies on a (dynamically changing) set of workers W, and for each worker $j \in W$, a variety of statistics are collected, including

- u_j, the wall clock time that worker j was available,
- c_j, the CPU time that worker j used to execute tasks, and
- s_j, the wall clock time that worker j was suspended by the resource manager.

MW will report to the user the overall parallel performance η:

$$\eta = \frac{\sum_{j \in W} c_j}{\sum_{j \in W} (u_j - s_j)}.$$

Benchmarking computations that run on dynamically available, heterogeneous processors is a very difficult issue. In order to compute an algorithmic performance statistic that is comparable between runs, users can register a *benchmark task* with MW. When a worker is available to begin computation, the `MWDriver` will send the worker the benchmark task to compute, record the CPU time required to perform this task, and use this number to compute a normalized total CPU time. If $b_j = 1/t_j$, $\forall j \in W$ is the the reciprocal of the CPU time worker j required to complete the benchmark task, and $b_M = 1/t_M$ is the reciprocal of the time time for the master processor to complete the task, then MW will report a normalized CPU time of

$$\mathcal{T} = \frac{\sum_{j \in W} c_j b_j}{b_M}.$$

Branch-and-bound algorithm developers find the normalized benchmark feature quite useful for tuning the myriad of parameters in the algorithm.

10.5.4. The RMComm Layer

MW contains an abstract interface to different resource management and communication mechanisms. Thus, by simply linking with the appropriate libraries, users can rely on different software to find appropriate worker processors and communicate between master and worker processors. Currently, there are four RMComm implementations in the standard MW distribution: Condor-Sockets, Condor-PVM, Condor-Files, and an Independent layer, useful for debugging, in which both master and worker exist in a single process. In our case study of Section 10.6, we use both the Condor-PVM and Condor-Sockets RMComm layers.

10.6. CASE STUDY: THE KNAPSACK PROBLEM

10.6.1. Background

This section describes a branch-and-bound implementation of MW to solve the 0–1 knapsack problem. In the 0–1 knapsack problem, there is a set $N = \{1, \cdots, n\}$ of items each with profit c_i and weight a_i, a knapsack of capacity b, and the objective is to fill the knapsack as profitably as possible, that is, solve

$$z^* = \max\{c^T x \mid a^T x \le b, x \in \mathbb{B}^n\}. \tag{10.1}$$

Our MW implementation MWKnap has three goals. First, we would like to demonstrate that building a parallel branch-and-bound solver is easily accomplished with MW. Second, we would like the solver to be flexible enough to show the improvement in efficiency that can be obtained by tuning the search appropriately, as discussed in Section 10.3. Finally, we wish to demonstrate that very large problem instances can be solved with branch-and-bound by harnessing the CPU cycles of a computational grid.

Without loss of generality, we assume that the items are sorted in decreasing order of profit to weight ratio c_i/a_i. The lower bound in the branch-and-bound algorithm is computed by greedily inserting items while the knapsack capacity is not exceeded. The upper bound in the algorithm is obtained by additionally inserting the fractional part of the last item that exceeds the knapsack capacity in order to fill the knapsack exactly. This can be seen as solving the linear programming relaxation of Eq. 10.1 (21). Note that in the solution there is at most one fractional item, which we denote as f. Therefore, the solution to the LP relaxation is $x_i = 1$ for $i = 1, \ldots, f-1$, $X_f = \{b - \Sigma_{i=1}^{f-1} a_i\}/a_f$, and $x_i = 0$ for $i = f+1, \ldots, n$. The lower bound on the optimal solution value z_L is given by the formula

$$z_L = \sum_{i=1}^{f-1} c_i,$$

and the upper bound on the optimal solution value z_U is given by

$$z_U = \sum_{i=1}^{f-1} c_i + \left(b - \sum_{i=1}^{f-1} a_i\right)\frac{c_f}{a_f}.$$

If all items fit into the knapsack ($f = n$), then the lower and upper bounds are

$$z_L = z_U = \sum_{i=1}^{f} c_i.$$

Let us make a few definition to precisely define the algorithm. We use the term *node* ($\mathcal{N}$) to denote the problem associated with a certain portion of the feasible region of the problem. A node is characterized by the sets of variables fixed to 0 and 1.

1. Namely, $\mathcal{N} = (N_0, N_1, N_F)$, where

$$N_0 \stackrel{\text{def}}{=} \{i \mid x_i = 0\}$$

$$N_1 \stackrel{\text{def}}{=} \{i \mid x_i = 1\} \quad \text{and}$$

$$N_F \stackrel{\text{def}}{=} \{i \mid i \notin N_0 \cup N_1\} = N \setminus N_0 \setminus N_1$$

Again, we assume WLOG that N_F is ordered in decreasing order of c_i/a_i. The lower and upper bounds of a node $\mathcal{N}$ are denoted by $z_L^{\mathcal{N}}$ and $z_U^{\mathcal{N}}$, respectively. $\mathcal{L}$ is a set of nodes that must still be evaluated, and z^* holds the current best solution value. With these definitions, the general branch-and-bound algorithm for 0–1 knapsack problem is summarized in Algorithm 1.

ALGORITHM 1. The Branch and Bound Algorithm for 0–1 Knapsack Problem

Require: $c_i > 0$, $a_i > 0$. c_i/a_i are sorted in decreasing order.
  $z^* = 0$. Put the root node in $\mathcal{L}$.
  while $\mathcal{L} \neq \varnothing$ **do**
    Choose and delete node $\mathcal{N} = (N_0, N_1, N_F)$ from $\mathcal{L}$.
    Let f be the smallest index such that $\Sigma_{i \in N_F, i=1}^{f} a_i > b - \Sigma_{i \in N_1} a_i$.
    if $\Sigma_{i \in N_F, i=1}^{f} a_i \leq b - \Sigma_{i \in N_1} a_i$ **then**
      $z_L^{\mathcal{N}} = z_U^{\mathcal{N}} = \Sigma_{i \in N_1} c_i + \Sigma_{i \in N_F, i=1}^{f} c_i$
    else
      $z_L^{\mathcal{N}} = \Sigma_{i \in N_1} c_i + \Sigma_{i \in N_F, i=1}^{f-1} c_i$
      $z_U^{\mathcal{N}} = z_L^{\mathcal{N}} = (b - \Sigma_{i \in N_F, i=1}^{f-1} c_i) \frac{c_f}{a_f}$
    end if
    if $z_L^{\mathcal{N}} > z^*$ **then**
      $z^* = z_L^{\mathcal{N}}$.
      Remove nodes $\mathcal{N}' \in \mathcal{L}$ such that $z_U^{\eta} < z^*$.
    end if
    if $z_L^{\mathcal{N}} = z_U^{\mathcal{N}}$ or $z_U^{\mathcal{N}} < z^*$ **then**
      Fathom node $\mathcal{N}$.
    else
      Add a new node $\hat{\mathcal{N}} = (N_0 \cup \{f\}, N_1, N_F \setminus \{f\})$ to $\mathcal{L}$, with $z_U^{\hat{\mathcal{N}}} = z_U^{\mathcal{N}}$.
      if $\Sigma_{i \in N_1} a_i + a_f < b$ **then**
        Add a new node $\hat{\mathcal{N}} = (N_0, N_1 \cup \{f\}, N_F \setminus \{f\})$ to $\mathcal{L}$, with $z_U^{\hat{\mathcal{N}}} = z_U^{\mathcal{N}}$.
      end if
    end if
  end while

At each node, a branching operation may be performed on the sole fractional variable x_f. The node is fathomed if the lower bound is equal to the upper bound, if the upper bound is lower than the current best solution value, or if all items are able to be placed into the knapsack. The next node in the list $\mathcal{L}$ to be evaluated might be chosen in a depth-first fashion, as suggested by Greenberg and Hegerich (22), or in a best-first fashion, in which the node $\mathcal{N}$ with the largest value of $z_U^{\mathcal{N}}$ is chosen. For more sophisticated, improved variants of Algorithm 1, see the work of Horowitz and Sahni (23) and a survey by Pisinger and Toth (24).

10.6.2. MW Implementation

To create a parallel solver for the knapsack problem with MW, we must reimplement MWTask, the MWWorker that executes these tasks, and the MWDriver that guides the computation by acting on completed tasks.

MWTask. Algorithm 1 will solve the 0–1 knapsack instance to optimality. As discussed in Section 10.3, we wish to parallelize Algorithm 1 within the master–worker framework by making the base unit of work a limited subtree. Thus, in our parallel implementation Algorithm 1 becomes a *task*, with the exception that the grain size is controlled by specifying the maximum CPU time or maximum number of nodes that a worker is allowed to evaluate before reporting back to the master. In MW, there are two portions of a task, the work portion and the result portion. For our solver MWKnap, a KnapTask class is derived from the base MWTask, and the work portion of the KnapTask consists of a single input node. The result portion consists of an improved solution (if one is found), and a list containing the nodes of the input subtree that are not able to be evaluated before reaching the task's node or time limit. Figure 10.1 shows a portion of the KnapTask C++ header file.

```
 1   class KnapTask : public MWTask
 2   {
 3     // Work portion
 4     KnapNode inputNode_;
 5
 6     // Result portion
 7     bool foundImprovedSolution_;
 8     double solutionValue_;
 9     std::vector<KnapNode *> outputNode_;
10   };
```

Fig. 10.1. The work and result portions of KnapTask.

MWWorker. In MW, the (pure virtual) `MWWorker::execute_task` (`MWTask *task`) method is entirely in the user's control. Therefore, when implementing branch-and-bound algorithms for which the task is to evaluate a subtree, the user is responsible for writing code to manage the heap of unevaluated subtree nodes. For MWKnap, we implement a heap structure using C++ Standard Template Library to maintain the set of active nodes. The heap can be ordered by either node depth or node upper bound, so we can quantify the effect of different worker node selection techniques on overall parallel efficiency. Figure 10.2 shows portions of the derived worker's execute_task method.

Note on line 3 of Fig. 10.2, we need to downcast the abstract `MWTask` to an instance of the `KnapTask` that can be executed. On line 4, the node heap is created and instantiated to be either a best-first or depth-first heap by setting the variable `currentNodeOrder_`. The while-loop from lines 6 to 46 contains the implementation of Algorithm 1. The procedure `finished(heap)` on line 6 is implemented separately and ensures that the worker will evaluate the given subtree as long as there are active nodes left in that subtree or the node or time limit of the task is not violated. The purpose of the for-loop from lines 12–20 is to identify the fractional item f. The if-statement beginning at line 23 is used to check the feasibility of the solution and compute lower and upper bounds of the node. The if-statement from lines 34–37 is exercised when a better lower bound is found and infeasible nodes are fathomed. The child nodes are generated from the result of the if-statement from lines 39–43. On line 47, when the grain size limit is reached, the nodes left on the heap are copied to the result portion of the task and returned back to the master task pool.

MWDriver. In MWKnap, a `KnapMaster` class is derived from the base `MWDriver` class. The `MWDriver::act_on_completed_task`(`MWTask *t`) method is implemented to handle the results passing back from the workers. Figure 10.3 shows a portion of this method. The if-statement from lines 6–12 is used to update the improved solution value, and remove nodes in the master pool that have their upper bounds less than the current best solution value. New tasks, which are unevaluated nodes left from the completed task, are added to the master task list by the for-loop beginning at line 15. Here we assume that the master is in best-first mode.

10.6.3. Computational Experience

This section contains experiments showing the impact of varying algorithmic parameters on the effectiveness of MWKnap. The goals of this section are to answer the following questions:

1. In what order should the master send nodes to the workers?
2. How should the workers search the subtrees given to them by the master? Namely,

```
1   void KnapWorker::execute_task(MWTask *t)
2   {
3     KnapTask *kt = dynamic_cast<KnapTask *> (t);
4     NodeHeap *heap = new NodeHeap(currentNodeOrder_);
5     heap->push(new KnapNode(kt->getInputNode()));
6     while (!finished(heap)) {
7       KnapNode *node = heap->top(); heap->pop();
8       double remainingSize = instance_.getCap() - node->getUsedCap();
9       double usedValue = node->getUsedValue();
10      int f = 0;
11
12      for (KnapInstance::itemIterator it = instance_.itemsBegin();
13           it != instance_.itemsEnd(); ++it) {
14        if (node->varStatus(f) == Free) {
15          fSize = it->getSize(); fProfit = it->getProfit();
16          remainingSize -= fSize; usedValue += fprofit;
17        }
18        if (remainingSize < 0.0) break;
19        f++;
20      }
21
22      bool branch = false;
23      if (remainingSize >= 0) {
24        nodeLb = usedValue; nodeUb = usedValue;
25      }
26      else {
27        usedValue -= fProfit; remainingSize += fSize;
28        nodeLb = usedValue;
29        nodeUb = usedValue + fProfit/fSize * remainingSize;
30        node->setUpperBound(nodeUb);
31        if (nodeUb > kt->getSolutionValue()) branch = true;
32      }
33
34      if (nodeLb > kt->getSolutionValue()) {
35        kt->setBetterSolution(nodeLb);
36        heap->fathom(nodeLb);
37      }
38
39      if (branch) {
40        heap->push(new KnapNode(*node, f, FixedZero, fSize, fProfit));
41        if (node->getUsedCap() + fSize < instance_.getCap())
42          heap->push(new KnapNode(*node, f, FixedOne, fSize, fProfit));
43      }
44
45      delete node;
46    }
47    kt->addNodesInHeap(*heap);
48    return;
49  }
```

Fig. 10.2. Algorithm 1 in MWWorker.

```
1   MWReturn KnapMaster::act_on_completed_task(MWTask *t)
2   {
3     KnapTask *kt = dynamic_cast<KnapTask *> (t);
4
5     // Remove infeasible nodes portion
6     if (kt->foundImprovedSolution()) {
7       double blb = kt->getSolutionValue();
8       if (blb > bestLB_) {
9         bestLB_ = blb;
10        delete_tasks_worse_than(-bestLB_);
11      }
12    }
13
14    // Add new tasks portion
15    for (vector<KnapNode *>::const_iterator it = kt->newNodeBegin();
16        it != kt->newNodeEnd(); ++it) {
17      if ((*it)->getUpperBound() > bestLB_) addTask(new KnapTask(**it));
18      delete *it;
19    }
20  }
```

Fig. 10.3. The portions of act_on_completed_task(MWTask *t) in KnapMaster.

- In what order should the subtree nodes be evaluated?
- For how long should the subtree be evaluated before reporting back to the master?

We test MWKnap on a family of instances known as *circle(2/3)* (25). In these instances, the weights are randomly generated from a uniform distribution, $a_i \sim U[1, 1000]$, and the profit of item i is a circular function of its weight: $c_i = (2/3)\sqrt{4000^2 - (a_i - 2000)^2}$. These instances are contrived to be challenging for branch-and-bound algorithms, and various algorithms in the literature can solve the instances with up to 200 items in less than one hour on a single machine (26, 27).

In the first phase of our computational experiments, we use solely a Condor pool at Lehigh University consisting of 246 heterogeneous processors. In the pool, there are 146 Intel Pentium III 1.3-GHz processors and 100 AMD Opteron 1.9-GHz processors. All machines run the Linux operating system.

10.6.3.1. Contention. The first experiment is aimed at demonstrating the effect of task grain size and node selection strategy on contention effects at the master processor. For this experiment, the grain size is controlled by limiting the maximum number of nodes the worker evaluates before reporting back to the master (MNW). Different combinations of master node order, worker node order, and grain sizes varying between MNW = 1 and MNW = 100,000 nodes are tested on cir200, a circle(2/3) instance with 200 items. The

TABLE 10.1. Performance of MWKnap with Best-First Master Task Pool on `cir200`

MNW	Worker Node Order							
	Best-First				Depth-First			
	W (s)	$\mathcal{N}$	η	T (s)	W (s)	$\mathcal{N}$	η	T (s)
1	304.0	1.0E6	0.59	84.95	758.9	1.3E6	0.19	204.63
10	155.4	1.6E6	2.44	103.3	1111	4.5E6	0.34	574.15
100	119.0	5.4E6	8.66	302.5	2214	2.5E7	1.41	2,736.0
1,000	151.3	2.7E7	22.5	1340	362.6	1.5E8	28.9	14,839
10,000	140.0	5.1E7	50.0	2436	111.6	3.5E7	46.5	3,327.4
100,000	122.4	5.1E7	58.2	2417	186.1	1.3E8	60.1	12,121

TABLE 10.2. Performance of MWKnap with Depth-First Master Task Pool on `cir200`

MNW	Worker Node Order							
	Best-First				Depth-First			
	W (s)	$\mathcal{N}$	η	T (s)	W (s)	$\mathcal{N}$	η	T (s)
1	56,122	3.1E6	0.01	292.45	492.3	1.3E6	0.63	205.77
10	13,257	6.0E6	0.04	379.28	1171	4.6E6	0.32	569.97
100	5,004.8	1.8E7	0.25	999.60	2521	2.9E7	0.80	3,159.5
1,000	4,859.7	1.1E8	1.52	5,832.6	520.4	1.5E8	21.5	14,659
10,000	4,718.4	5.5E8	7.27	25,464	484.1	4.2E7	12.7	4,004.4
100,000	4,216.5	8.6E8	12.8	40,153	187.9	1.1E8	57.4	10,297

maximum number of workers is limited to 64. Tables 10.1 and 10.2, show the wall clock time (W), the total number of nodes evaluated ($\mathcal{N}$), the parallel performance (η), and the normalized CPU time (T) for each trial in the experiment.

Even though each combination of master node-order, worker node-order, and grain size is attempted only once, we can still draw some meaningful conclusions from the trends observed in Tables 10.1 and 10.2.

- The parallel performance increases with the grain size, but at the price of a larger total number of nodes evaluated.
- Small grain sizes have very low parallel efficiency.
- A master search order of best-first is to be preferred.

The best-first search strategy in the worker performs well on the relatively small instance `cir200`, but when this strategy is employed on larger instances, it leads to extremely high memory usage on the master. For example, Fig. 10.4 shows the memory usage of the master processor when the workers employ

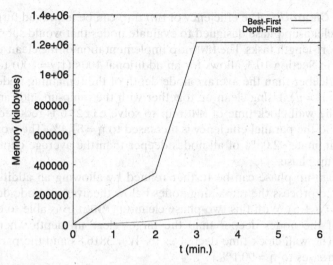

Fig. 10.4. Memory usage of different worker node orders on `cir250`.

a best-first search strategy on `cir250`, a circle(2/3) instance with 250 items. After only 3 min, the master processor memory usage goes to over one GB. At this point, the master process crashes, as it is unable to allocate any more memory to add the active nodes to its task list. Therefore, in subsequent experiments, we will employ a best-first node ordering strategy on the master and a depth-first node selection strategy on the workers. Further, we will use a relatively large CPU limited grain size for the tasks. For example, with a grain size of $\gamma = 100$ s and a maximum number of workers of 128, `MWKnap` can solve `cir250` in $W = 4674.9$ s of wall clock time with an average parallel efficiency of $\eta = 65.5\%$.

10.6.3.2. Ramp-Up and Ramp-Down.
Even with careful tuning of the grain size and the master and worker search strategies, the parallel efficiency (65.5%) of `MWKnap` on the test instance `cir250` is relatively low. Some loss of efficiency is caused because there is a dependence between tasks in the branch-and-bound algorithm. This task dependence leads to situations where workers are sitting idle waiting for other workers to report back their results to the master. In the case of `MWKnap`, this occurs at the beginning and at the end of the computation when the master pool has less tasks than participating workers.

As mentioned in Section 10.3, the master pool can be kept populated by dynamically changing the grain size. The efficiency improvement during ramp-up and ramp-down is achieved by reducing γ to 10s when there are less than 1000 nodes in the master pool. Using this worker idle time reduction strategy, the efficiency of `MWKnap` on `cir250` is increased to $\eta = 77.7\%$ with a wall clock time of $W = 4230.3$ s.

10.6.3.3. Clean-Up.

The efficiency of MWKnap can be improved further with a worker clean-up phase designed to evaluate nodes that would subsequently lead to short-length tasks. The MWKnap implementation of the clean-up phase, discussed in Section 10.3, allows for an additional 100 s ($\tau_1 \gamma = 100$) to process all nodes deeper than the average node depth of the remaining nodes on the worker ($\psi_1 d = d$). Using clean-up together with the ramp-up and ramp-down strategy, the wall clock time of MWKnap to solve cir250 is reduced to $W = 4001.4$ s, and the parallel efficiency is increased to $\eta = 81.4\%$. The workers are able to eliminate 92.06% of all nodes deeper than the average depth during the clean-up phase.

The clean-up phase can be further refined by allowing an additional 50 s ($\tau_2 \gamma = 50$) to process the remaining nodes below the average node depth plus five ($\psi_2 d = d + 5$). With this two-phase clean-up, MWKnap is able to eliminate 99.87% of the nodes deeper than the target clean-up depth when solving cir250. The wall clock time decreases to $W = 3816.8$ s and the parallel efficiency increases to $\eta = 90.1\%$.

Figure 10.5 shows the distribution of task execution times before the optimal solution is found for the initial MWKnap implementation, MWKnap with a single-phase clean-up, and MWKnap with two-phase clean-up. Figure 10.6 compares the distribution of task execution times for the same three implementations after the optimal solution is found. Since $\gamma = 100$, task times greater than 100 s correspond to tasks in which clean-up was necessary. Even though the distributions of task times look nearly the same for all three implementations, the parallel efficiency increases by over 12%. Thus, an interesting conclusion that can be drawn from our work is that a small improvement in the distribution of

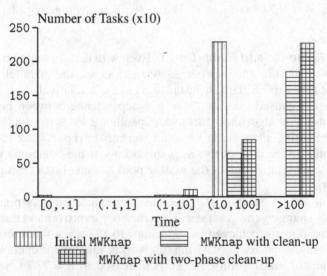

Fig. 10.5. Distribution of task time on cir250 before optimal solution is found.

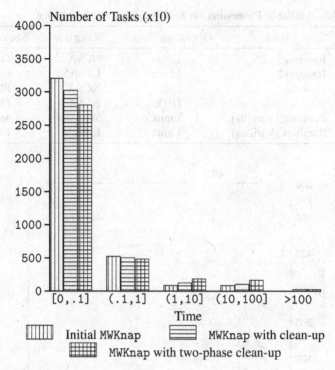

Fig. 10.6. Distribution of task time on `cir250` after optimal solution is found.

task times can lead to a significant increase in parallel efficiency for master–worker applications.

10.6.4. Large-Scale Computation

In this section, we demonstrate the true power of a computational grid—the ability to harness diverse, geographically distributed resources in an effective manner to solve larger problem instances than can be solved using traditional computing paradigms. Our demonstration is made on an instance `cir300`, a circle(2/3) knapsack instance of size 300. To solve this instance, we will use a subset of over 4000 available processors whose characteristics are given in Table 10.3. There are three different processor types, running two different operating systems, and located at four different locations in the United States. The processors at the University of Wisconsin compose of the main Condor pool to which our worker jobs are submit. Processors at NCSA and the University of Chicago are part of the Teragrid (http://www.teragrid.org). These processors are scheduled using the Portable Batch Scheduler (PBS), and join our knapsack computation through the Condor glide-in mechanism. Other processors join the computational via Condor flocking.

TABLE 10.3. Available Processors for Solution of `cir300` Instance

Number	Type	Operating System	Location	Access Method
1756	Itanium-2	Linux	NCSA	Glide-in
302	Itanium-2	Linux	UC-ANL	Glide-in
252	Pentium	Linux	NCSA	Flock
508	SGI	IRIX	NCSA	Flock
1182	Pentium (Various)	Linux	Wisconsin	Main
52	Pentium (Various)	Linux	Lehigh	Flock

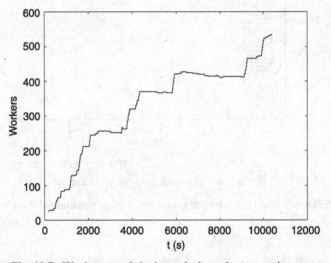

Fig. 10.7. Workers used during solution of `cir300` instance.

For this instance, we used a grain size of $\gamma = 250$ CPU s. Initial testing on the `cir300` instance showed that we could not continually send nodes with the best upper bounds to the worker processors and keep the size of the master task list within the memory bounds on the master processor. Thus, the master node list is kept in best-bound order while there are less than $h = 50,000$ tasks, then it is switched to worst-bound order until the number of tasks is reduced to $\ell = 25,000$ tasks, at which point the order is again reversed.

The instance is solved in a wall clock time of less than 3 h, using on average 321.2 workers, and at a parallel efficiency of $\eta = 84.8\%$. The total CPU time used on all workers is 2,795,897 s, or over 1 CPU month. Figure 10.7 shows the number of workers available to use while the run is proceeding. We see that the maximum number of workers is achieved at the end of the run, showing that the grid could likely have delivered computing power to solve a larger instance. In Fig. 10.8, the number of tasks in the master task list is plotted during the course of the run. The effect of switching the master node ordering from best-first to worst-first at 50,000 tasks is clearly seen.

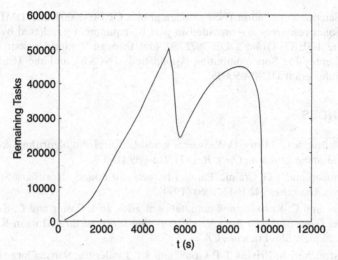

Fig. 10.8. Number of tasks in master list during solution of `cir300` instance.

10.7. CONCLUSIONS

We have introduced MW, a framework for implementing master–worker style computations in a dynamic computational grid computing environment. While the master–worker paradigm is not scalable, we have shown that by carefully tuning search parameters, the algorithm can be made to scale reasonably efficiently, even when there are hundreds of worker processors being served by a single master. Future work will focus on making it even easier for users to build branch-and-bound algorithms with MW. First, MW will be augmented with a general branch-and-bound interface. In our envisioned implementation, the users will need only provide mechanisms for computing bounds and for branching. The efficiency improvement features detailed in this work will be implemented in the base class, relieving the users from this burden. We also have begun working on a "black-box" implementation of MW in which the `MWWorker::execute_task(MWTask *)` method is implemented with a user-supplied executable. MW source code, including the `MWKnap` solver described here, is available from the MW homepage:

`http://www.cs.wisc.edu/condor/mw`.

ACKNOWLEDGMENTS

The authors would like to sincerely thank the whole Condor team for their tireless efforts in providing a robust and useful software tool. In particular, Greg Thain is instrumental in helping us run the computational experiments and for providing comments that helped to improve the exposition. This work is supported in part by the US

National Science Foundation (NSF) under grants OCI-0330607 and DMI-0522796. Computational resources are provided in part by equipment purchased by the NSF through the IGERT Grant DGE-9972780, and through Teragrid resources at the National Center for Supercomputing Applications (NCSA) and the University of Chicago under grant DDM-050005.

REFERENCES

1. J.D.C. Little, K.G. Murty, D.W. Sweeney, and C. Karel. An algorithm for the traveling salesman problem. *Oper. Res.*, **21**:972–989 (1963).

2. B. Gendron and T.G. Crainic. Parallel branch and bound algorithms: Survey and synthesis. *Oper. Res.*, **42**:1042–1066 (1994).

3. I. Foster and C. Kesselman. Computational grids. In I. Foster and C. Kesselman, ed., *The Grid: Blueprint for a New Computing Infrastructure*. Morgan Kaufmann, 1999, Chapt. 2. San Franciso, CA.

4. K. Anstreicher, N. Brixius, J.-P. Goux, and J.T. Linderoth. Solving large quadratic assignment problems on computational grids. *Math. Prog. Ser B*, **91**:563–588 (2002).

5. Seti@home: Search for extraterrestrial intelligence at home. Available at http://setiathome.ssl.berkeley.edu.

6. M. Livny, J. Basney, R. Raman, and T. Tannenbaum. Mechanisms for high throughput computing. *SPEEDUP*, 11 (1997).

7. D.H.J. Epema, M. Livny, R. van Dantzig, X. Evers, and J. Pruyne. A worldwide flock of condors: Load sharing among workstation clusters. *J. Fut. Gener. Comput. Systems*, 12 (1996).

8. J. Frey, T. Tannenbaum, I. Foster, M. Livny, and S. Tuecke. Condor-G: A computation management agent for multi-institutional grids. *Cluster Comput*, **5**:237–246 (2002).

9. K. Aida, W. Natsume, and Y. Futakata. Distributed computing with hierarchical master-worker paradigm for parallel branch and bound algorithm. *Proceedings of the 3rd IEEE/ACM International Symposium on Cluster Computing and the Grid (CCGrid 2003)*, 2003, pp 156–163.

10. K. Aida and T. Osumi. A case study in running a parallel branch and bound application on the grid. *Proceedings of the IEEE/IPSJ: The 2005 Symposium on Applications & the Internet (SAINT2005)*, 2005, pp. 164–173.

11. Y. Tanaka, M. Hirano, M. Sato, H. Nakada, and S. Sekiguchi. Performance evaluation of a firewall-compliant globus-based wide-area cluster system. *9th IEEE International Symposium on High Performance Distributed Computing (HPDC 2000)*, 2000, pp. 121–128.

12. I. Foster and C. Kesselman. Globus: A metacomputing infrastructure toolkit. *Intl. J. Supercomput. App.*, **11**:115–128 (1997).

13. Y. Xu, T.K. Ralphs, L. Ladányi, and M.J. Saltzman. ALPS: A framework for implementing parallel search algorithms. *The Proceedings of the Ninth Conference of the INFORMS Computing Society*, 2005. To appear, Available from http://www.lehigh.edu/~tkr2/research/pubs.html.

14. M. Benechouche et al. Building a parallel branch and bound library. *Solving Combinatorial Optimization Problems in Parallel*, Springer, Berlin, 1996.

15. J. Eckstein, C.A. Phillips, and W.E. Hart. PICO: An object-oriented framework for parallel branch-and-bound. *Proceeding of the Inherently Parallel Algorithms in Feasibility and Optimization and Their Applications*, 2001, pp. 219–265.

16. S. Tschöke and T. Polzer. Portable parallel branch and bound library user manual, library version 2.0. Technical report, Department of Computer Science, University of Paderborn, Paderborn, Germany, 1998.

17. A. Iamnitchi and I. Foster. A problem specific fault tolerance mechanism for asynchronous, distributed systems. In *Proceedings of 2000 International Conference on Parallel Processing (29th ICPP'00)*. IEEE, 2000.

18. N. Alon, A. Barak, and U. Mander. On disseminating information reliably and without broadcasting. *7th Internaltional Conference on Distributed Computing Systems ICDCS97*. IEEE Press, 1997. Baltimore, USA

19. L.M.A. Drummond et al. A grid-enabled branch-and-bound algorithm with application on the steiner problem in graphs. Unpublished Manuscript.

20. J.V. Filho, L.M.A. Drummond, E. Uchoa, and M.C.S. de Castro. Towards a grid enabled branch-and-bound algorithm. Available at http://www.optimization-online.org/DB_HTML/2003/10/756.html.

21. G.B. Dantzig. Discrete variable extremum problems. *Oper. Res.*, **5**:266–277 (1957).

22. H. Greenberg and R.L. Hegerich. A branch search algorithm for the knapsack problem. *Manag. Sci.*, 16 (1970).

23. E. Horowitz and S. Sahni. Computing partitions with applications to the knapsack problem. *J. ACM*, **21**:277–292 (1974).

24. D. Pisinger and P. Toth. Knapsack problems. In D.Z. Du and P. Pardalos, eds., *Handbook of Combinatorial Optimization*, Kluwer, 1998, pp. 1–89. Boston, MA.

25. D. Pisinger. Where are the hard knapsack problems? *Comput. Oper. Res.*, **32**:2271–2284 (2005).

26. S. Martello and P. Toth. A new algorithm for the 0–1 knapsack problem. *Manag. Sci.*, **34**:633–644 (1988).

27. D. Pisinger. An expanding-core algorithm for the exact 0–1 knapsack problem. *Eur. J. Oper. Res.*, **87**:175–187 (1995).

CHAPTER 11

Constraint Logic Programming on Multiple Processors

I. SAKELLARIOU and I. VLAHAVAS

Department of Informatics, Aristotle University Thessaloniki, Greece

11.1. INTRODUCTION

Logic programming (LP) is identified as one of the major programming paradigms, based on sound theoretical foundations. It has been an active area of research for the past three decades, especially from the mid-1970s until the late 1990s. This research effort has lead not only to a large number of theoretical results and proposed models, but also to industrial strength implementations of logic programming languages, as, for example, Prolog that is undoubtedly the main representative of this class of languages.

The interest in logic programming, and especially in its main representative Prolog, stems from its significant advantages in developing applications involving symbolic computation and reasoning. This comes as no surprise, since one of the funding works on logic programming was the effort of Colmeraurer and Russel in Marseille, to develop a language for natural language applications. Close interaction between the Marseille group and the research group of Edinburgh gave rise to the idea of using first-order predicate logic as a programming language, an idea first described in the seminal paper of Kowalski (1).

A major criticism of Prolog and its approach to programming is inefficiency. This criticism seems to carry on even today where the maturity of the field both in implementation technology, as well as optimization techniques, has resulted in very efficient LP platforms.

However, rather early two orthogonal approaches to the solution of the above problem where identified: parallelization and constraint solving. The former exploits parallelism that is naturally embedded in the declarative semantics of logic programs, in order to decrease the execution time of logic

Parallel Combinatorial Optimization, edited by El-Ghazali Talbi
Copyright © 2006 by John Wiley & Sons, Inc.

programs by utilizing multiple processing units. The latter replaces the standard unification mechanism of Prolog with constraint solving over some computational domain, resulting to an extended paradigm named constraint logic programming (CLP). This programming focuses on an increase to the efficiency of the paradigm in the area of combinatorial problems, by drastically reducing the search space that has to be explored through constraint reasoning. Thus, CLP aims to reduce the effects of combinatorial explosion that manifests itself on most AI and "real-world" industrial applications.

The above two approaches are orthogonal, in the sense that they can be employed simultaneously. Indeed, a number of (constraint) logic programming models and languages aim to exploit the power and elegance of combining parallel execution and constraint solving.

This chapter aims to present models and languages for multiprocessor execution of constraint logic programs. The chapter starts with a presentation of the close relation of logic and constraint logic programming semantics. The same section (Section 11.2) also outlines available platforms for constraint logic programming and various applications areas of the CLP technology. Section 11.3 introduces the basic ideas and models proposed for executing LP programs in parallel. How the parallel LP models have been extended to support constraint solving is described in Section 11.4. Section 11.5 presents three concrete implementations of languages that support the development of parallel CLP applications. Finally, Section 11.6 concludes the chapter.

11.2. CONSTRAINT LOGIC PROGRAMMING

The general idea behind programming with constraints is to facilitate the representation of complex relations, or constraints, between user defined entities in the problem to be solved. Although other paradigms, such as object oriented programming, do provide the necessary means for defining entities and operations reflecting entities' behavior, the maintenance of relations between these entities is entirely left to the programmer. Constraint programming eliminates the need for explicitly encoding such maintenance tasks by providing all necessary underlying machinery (2,3).

Thus, in constraint programming a problem is usually represented as a set of variables, each belonging to a domain and a set of constraints (relations) imposed on them. In such a setting a solution is a valid assignment of values to variables, that is, an assignment that satisfies all the stated constraints. The importance here is that constraints offer a way to declaratively state "what" has to hold among problem variables and not "how" can such a task can be achieved (3), that is, constitute a declarative approach to problem solving.

The declarative nature of constraint programming adheres well to the declarative semantics of logic programming (4), since the later allows us to easily state relations and implement search algorithms that are crucial to the solution of any constraint problem. In other words, LP offers the means to create a single and powerful framework for various cooperating constraint solving algorithms. In this sense, one can say that CLP merges two declarative paradigms: logic programming and constraint solving.

The integration of CP and LP was further motivated by the observation that the algorithm of unification used in logic programming is in fact a constraint solving algorithm, and as such it could be combined with, or replaced by, various other constraint solving algorithms.

The generalization of LP into CLP offers important application areas to the former. Solutions based on CLP have been used in a variety of applications like, for example, scheduling, resource allocation, timetabling, financial planning, and frequency assignment for cellular phones.

11.2.1. Extending the Classical Logic Programming

Classic or conventional logic programming allows easily encoding combinatorial problems because problem constraints are stated as relations and the implementation of search algorithms is rather straightforward due to nondeterminism. However, the conventional approach is rather inefficient, since the "passive" use of constraints inside the standard "backtracking" or "generate-and-test" search procedures of logic programming suffers from *thrashing*, that is repeatedly failing search for the same reason (5). Even heuristics or more sophisticated search algorithms cannot deal efficiently with this class of problems.

On the other hand, constraint solving can help toward a more efficient use of stated constraints. Instead of passive checks whenever a variable is bound to a value, an "active" use of constraints is used to infer information on restricting possible values to variables. The newly inferred information is reused to further restrict the variables, a process that is referred to as *constraint propagation*. Constraint propagation reduces the search space that has to be explored to find a solution, thus leads to more efficient logic programming systems. This concept of *a priori* pruning of domain variables has permitted the application of the LP paradigm to a much broader class of real-world applications.

This active use of constraints can be easily integrated into both the declarative and procedural semantics of logic programs. Integration into the declarative semantics is rather straightforward: constraints are simply a "new" kind of relations that have to hold in order to prove a goal. The operational semantics of the two paradigms although closely related require more careful consideration. The rest of this section will briefly present the operational semantics of logic and constraint logic programs, to demonstrate their close relation. Our description is based on the work described in Refs. 6–8.

11.2.1.1. LP Operational Semantics. Logic programming is based on the resolution proof procedure introduced by Robinson (9). A logic program P consists of a finite set of program clauses, or *Horn* clauses, of the form $H \leftarrow B$,

where H is an atom of the form $p(a_1, a_2 \cdots a_n)$ and B and conjunction of literals. The *unit* clause is represented by H and the empty clause by the symbol ■. The notion of unification is central in logic programming; *unification* makes two terms syntactically identical through appropriate variable substitutions. Thus a *unifier* θ of two terms s_1 and s_2 is a substitution of the form v_1/t_1, v_2/t_2 $\cdots v_n/t_n$, where v_i are variables and t_i are terms, such that when θ is applied to s_1 and s_2, the equality $s_1\theta = s_2\theta$ holds. Each v_1/t_1 is called a *binding* and if t_1 is a variable, free term is called a *ground binding*. A composition of substitutions presented as $\theta = \theta'\sigma$ on a term s is an application of $s\theta = (s\theta')\sigma$, that is, the two substitutions are applied in order.

The most general unifier (*mgu*) θ of a set of expressions S is a unifier such that for every other unifier σ of the set, there exists a substitution γ such that $\sigma = \theta\gamma$. We assume that there exist a function $\text{unif}(s_1 = s_2)$ returns the most general unifier of a term equation if one exists, or fail otherwise.

Given an atom a of the form $p(s_1, \cdots, s_n)$ and a program P, the set of program clauses $H \leftarrow B$, such that H is in the form $p(t_1, \cdots, t_n)$ is called the *definition* of a and is represented by the symbol $\text{defn}_P(a)$. The set contains variants of the clauses such that the new variables introduced in the body of the rules are distinct new variables (renaming).

The operational semantics are given in terms of reductions between *states*. The latter are tuples of the form $\langle G|\theta \rangle$, where G is a set of goals or equations over terms and θ a substitution. Given a state $\langle g_1, \cdots, g_n|\theta \rangle$ there can be the following reductions:

- $\langle g_1, \cdots, g_n|\theta \rangle \rightarrow \langle g_1, \cdots, g_{i-1}, s_1 = t_1, \cdots, s_n = t_n, B, g_{i+1} \cdots g_n|\theta \rangle$ if g_i is a goal selected from G and $(H \leftarrow B) \in \text{defn}_P(gi)$.
- $\langle g_1, \cdots, g_n|\theta \rangle \rightarrow \langle ■|false \rangle$ if g_i is a goal selected from G and the definition of g_i is the empty set, that is, $\text{defn}_P(g_i) = \phi$.
- $\langle g_1, \cdots, g_n|\theta \rangle \rightarrow \langle g_1, \cdots, g_{i-1}, g_{i+1}, \cdots, g_n|\theta\theta' \rangle$ if g_i is an equation over terms of the form $s_i = t_i$ selected from G and $\text{unif}(s_i\theta = t_i\theta) = \theta'$.
- $\langle g_1, \cdots, g_n|\theta \rangle \rightarrow \langle ■|false \rangle$ if g_i is an equation over terms of the form $s_i = t_i$ selected from G and $\text{unif}(s_i\theta = t_i\theta)$ fails.

In the above semantics, we assume that there is a *selection* or *computation rule* that selects a goal or a equation from G and a *search rule* that selects a clause from the definition of g_i in the first reduction. For example, Prolog language uses a left-to-right selection rule and depth first search.

Given a goal G and a program P, a *successful* derivation is a *finite* sequence of states $\langle G|true \rangle \rightarrow \langle G_1|\theta_1 \rangle \rightarrow \cdots \rightarrow \langle ■|\theta_n \rangle$, where a reduction from the ones mentioned above holds between two states $\langle G_i|\theta_i \rangle$ and $\langle G_{i+1}|\theta_{i+1} \rangle$. A derivation is *failed* is it is a *finite* derivation of the form $\langle G|true \rangle \rightarrow \langle G_1|\theta_1 \rangle \rightarrow \cdots \rightarrow \langle ■|false \rangle$. The substitution θ of a successful derivation is the *answer* to G given P. Note that there also exists the case of infinite derivations.

Search for a successful derivation(s) occurs in a search tree, called *derivation tree*, where each node is a state and arcs are derivations. The root of the tree is the original goal and a branch of the tree from the root to some leaf node are derivations. In such a tree, there are *success* branches, *failure* branches, or *infinite* branches corresponding to successful, failed or infinite derivations.

11.2.1.2. CLP Operational Semantics.

The operational semantics of conventional logic programs can be generalized to constraint logic programs. However, before introducing CLP semantics the notion of a constraint domain has to be introduced. Informally, a *constraint domain* contains *constraints*, that is, first-order logic formulas build from a set of allowed symbols, predicates and functions, their interpretation and a *solver*: a function (solv) that maps a constraint to *true, false*, or *unknown*, if the formula is satisfiable, unsatisfiable or not able to tell with respect to interpretation of the domain (solver incompleteness). The domain is assumed to contain the equality "=" constraint.

For example, the constraint domain *Real* has the $\leq, \geq, <, >, =$ relation symbols, the $+, -, *, /$ function symbols, and sequences of digits with a (optional) decimal point as constants. The interpretation of the above is the usual interpretation of the same symbols in the domain of real numbers. An implementation of a *solver* that can be used in this domain could use the simplex algorithm and Gauss–Jordan elimination, as, for example, in the CLP(R) language (10).

The *finite domain* (FD), contains the relation symbols $\leq, \geq, <, >, =, in[a, b]$, the $+$ function symbol and has as constant symbols the set of integers $\mathbf{Z}$. The semantics of $\leq, \geq, <, >, =, +$ are interpreted in the usual way and the relation symbol *in* is the interval constraint $(Xin[a, b]))$, which holds between two integer values a, b and a domain variable X, which denotes that $a \leq X \leq b$. The finite domain has been enhanced with a number of ad hoc primitive constraints, such as the *element* and *cumulative* constraints, apart from the ones stated above. This additional constraints significantly increased the applicability of the FD domain in large combinatorial optimization problems, such as scheduling and resource allocation.

To justify the view that constraint logic programming is in fact a generalization of conventional logic programming, consider that the latter is a CLP system over finite trees, with the identity relation "=", and the unification algorithm as the constraint solver.

The operational semantics of constraint logic programs, can be given simply by generalizing the operational semantics given before for any constraint domain. A computational state is now a tuple of the form $\langle G|c \rangle$, where G is a set of goals or primitive constraints and c the *constraint store*. Given a computational state $\langle g_1, \cdots, g_n|c \rangle$ there can be the following reductions:

- $\langle g_1, \cdots, g_n|c \rangle \rightarrow \langle g_1, \cdots, g_{i-1}, s_1 = t_1, \cdots, s_n = t_n, B, g_{i+1} \cdots g_n|\theta \rangle$ if g_i is a goal selected from G and $(H \leftarrow B) \in defn_P(g_i)$
- $\langle g_1, \cdots, g_n|c \rangle \rightarrow \langle \blacksquare|false \rangle$ if g_i is a goal selected from G and the definition of g_i is the empty set, i.e. $defn_P(g_i) = \phi$

- $\langle g_1, \cdots, g_n | c \rangle \rightarrow \langle g_1, \cdots, g_{i-1}, g_{i+1}, \cdots, g_n | c \wedge g_i \rangle$ if the g_i selected from G is a primitive constraint and $solv(c \wedge g_i) = true$ or $solv(c \wedge g_i) = unknown$.
- $\langle g_1, \cdots, g_n | c \rangle \rightarrow \langle \blacksquare | false \rangle$ if g_i is a primitive constraint selected from G and $solv(c \wedge g_i) = false$.

The notion of a successful derivation introduced in the context of conventional logic programming is still applicable, however, the answer to such a derivation is now the constraint c.

The resulting scheme defines the class of languages $CLP(\mathbb{X})$ obtained by instantiating the parameter $\mathbb{X}$, that stands for the constraint domain. The most common domains are the domain of real numbers, of rational numbers, the Boolean domain, and the well known and probably the most studied and widely applied finite domain.

Finally, we should mention that a number of solving algorithms have been incorporated in the CLP framework. Algorithms that have already been used include linear equality and inequality solvers (10,11), nonlinear constraint solvers (12), finite domain constraint solvers (11,13,14), linear Diophantine constraint solvers (15), finite set constraint solvers (16) to name a few. These algorithms must have certain characteristics, such as incrementality (17) and efficient test for satisfiability. An in depth study of both the operational semantics and properties of constraint solvers is provided in (7).

11.2.2. CLP Platforms

A number of constraint logic programming systems have been developed; for example $CLP(\mathbb{R})$ (10) over the domain of reals, clp(L) over the lattice domain (18), CHIP (19) one of the earlier clp systems supporting constraint solving over the finite domain, Prolog-III (20), clp(FD) (21), which was the base for GNU-Prolog (22), cc(FD) (23), and industrial strength tools like CHIP v.5 from COSYTEC.[1]

Most modern industrial strength CLP systems, like ECLiPSe Prolog (24,25), SICStus (26), offer constraint solving over multiple domains such as finite domains, rationals, or reals.

ECLiPSe (24) is currently developed by the IC-Parc of the Imperial College in London and is the result of integration of various logic programming extensions in the area of constraint programming, logic programming, parallel systems, and databases that were developed in ECRC. The system has a number of interesting features that allow the development of logic programming applications for solving large combinatorial problems. ECLiPSe offers constraint handling over integer finite domains and the related constraints, as well as global constraints, that is, constraints employing special propagation algorithms dedicated to specific problems, such as the *cumulative* constraint for disjunctive scheduling problems. Moreover, ECLiPSe offers constraint handling facilities for finite symbolic domains, as well as support for user-

---

[1]http://www.cosytec.com.

defined constraints through Constraint Handling Rules (27) and the Propia library. Additionally, the platform offers constraint solving over finite sets of integers and support for the usual relations, that is, membership and inclusion, as well as support using external libraries for mathematical programming.

To further support the implementation of real world applications, ECLiPSe libraries include advanced search methods, such as heuristic search, as well as a branch-and-bound library that contains variations of the standard algorithm and greatly facilitates the implementation of optimization problems. ECLiPSe has been used in a number of applications, for example, a Multiprotocol label switching bandwidth protection application developed by CISCO, scheduling applications, resource allocation, AI planning, and many more.

SICStus Prolog (26) is a product of the Swedish Institute of Computer Science (SICS) and has been developed for >15 years. It is a successful and very robust Prolog implementation that follows the ISO standard and has a number of extensions and libraries. SICStus offers constraint handling over finite domains (14), rationals and reals (28), as well as support for Boolean domains. SICStus also supports user-defined constraints in the form of Constraint Handling Rules (22). As in the case of ECLiPSe, SICStus also provides a set of necessary primitives that allow easily implementing search algorithms. The platform has been used in a number of industrial applications like a network resource manager for the ERICSSON telecommunication company, optimization engine for logistics, biotechnology (29).

Both platforms (ECLiPSe and SICStus) were commercially supporting efficient and robust parallel execution schemes in their earlier versions, as well as support for parallel execution of constraint logic programs. However, this support has dropped due to a rather high cost of maintaining the parallel execution mechanisms.

Finally, we should mention that the ideas of constraint solving have been used through other programming languages as well. For example, ILOG provides constraint handling in the form of C++ libraries,[2] COSYTEC that also offers constraint libraries in C and C++, apart from the CHIP LP system. In fact, a great number of industrial applications have been implemented in these platforms and CP in the context of object oriented programming has been quite successful, so much that although originally derived as an extension to logic programming, it is considered now to be an "autonomous" programming paradigm. Still the belief of the authors of this Chapter, is that the match between the declarative semantics of LP and CP paradigms is unparallel.

11.2.3. CLP Applications

Applications of the constraint programming paradigm in general and CLP in particular are numerous, since the introduction of constraint solving in logic programming has significantly increased the applicability of the resulting languages. Thus, CLP has been successfully employed in the development of

[2]http://www.ilog.com.

industrial applications, such as scheduling and digital circuit verification. This section briefly outlines some research areas where CLP has been successfully employed.

One class of applications of great interest are *modeling* applications, where CLP is used as a specification language to derive "executable specifications". CLP seems to fit well to this class since its declarative nature allows us to describe easily the problem's relationships in the form of constraints. Examples of applications of this class are analysis and synthesis of analog circuits, VLSI circuit verification, real-time control systems, options trading, and so on.

However, the main application area of constraint technology seems to be that of *combinatorial search* and *optimization* problems. We outline a few possible application areas below; an exhaustive overview of the applications in this area would be impossible, both due to the plethora of applications developed so far and to their constantly increasing number.

Scheduling seems to be the ideal area of applications for finite domain constraints. There is an important number of scheduling applications for productions processes of chemical factories, glass factories, aircraft manufacturing, television production, and so on (30, 31). As mentioned earlier, most of the current CLP implementations, such as CHIP, ECLiPSe, and SICStus support specialized primitive constraints, such as the cumulative constraint for efficient solution of large disjunctive scheduling problems. Such specialized primitive constraints have been used, for example, in the PLANE system, employed by the Dassault Aviation company for scheduling the production of aircrafts (CHIP platform).

Another area of application of CLP platforms are *cutting* problems, that is, problems were the task is to cut two-dimensional large pieces, or a continuous roll, to pieces of given smaller size, and have been used as an example of application of constraint technology rather early (32). Over time, CLP technology has been applied on different settings of the cutting stock problem and reports on successful cutting stock applications continue to appear in the literature. Moreover, in Ref. 33 the authors claim that the use of CLP in this kind of problem will increase because CLP is more cost effective than conventional languages and optimization libraries.

A typical example of *allocation* problems tackled by CLP is aircraft stand allocation, where airport parking locations have to be assigned to aircrafts. This specific application has a dynamic character with reallocation taking place frequently due to delays and changes to air traffic. Allocation problems are mainly expressed by disequality constraints or more complex aggregate constraints. Normally, reallocation can be done very quickly, as in the case of the APACHE system used by Roissy airport of Paris, which allocates stands when changes to the flights' departures–arrivals occur.

Crew rotation is the task of assigning personnel to, for example, flights or other transport services or activities and presents another major area of application for CLP. A number of systems have been developed, like the GYMNASTE system, which produces schedules of nurses in a hospital,

OPTI-SERVICE, which creates weekly plans of activities of technicians and journalists in the French TV and a radio station, workforce management problems in BT, to name a few real-world applications available.

CLP has also been applied to transport problems, where the problem is to schedule the transport of goods between known locations by a set of lorries with fixed capacity. The task has been successfully solved by using global constraints. The system described in Ref. 31 has completely replaced the manual scheduling process. While a manual solution to the problem required up to 8 h of work, the developed system needs 15 min. Different scenarios can be compared and sudden changes can be better handled.

The above list is not exhaustive. CLP applications include, AI planning systems, routing and management in Telecommunication networks, bioinformatics, for example, DNA sequencing and protein folding and resource allocation. A more detailed description of the CLP applications can be found in Refs. 3, 17, 30.

11.3. PARALLELISM IN LOGIC PROGRAMMING

The idea of executing logic programs in parallel has long been investigated by researchers, especially during the 1980s and 1990s. The research reported in the field is enormous and various approaches to parallelism in logic programs have been developed. Although automatic parallelization of logic programs was one of the main aims of these research efforts, other approaches also attracted a significant amount of research, such as explicit parallelism through message passing mechanisms, like in CSP-II Prolog that is presented in the final section, or blackboard primitives and extensions to the standard Prolog language, such as Guarded Horn clauses and concurrency.

Research in parallel logic programming was motivated by two reasons. The first reason is that parallelism and the expected gains in execution efficiency, presented an excellent answer to one of the points that received most criticism, that of inefficiency related to the execution of logic programs. Indeed, even today, when far more efficient sequential implementations of LP languages exist, this myth still holds, among researchers and students in computer science.

The second and probably most important reason, is that exploitation of the parallelism that is naturally embedded in logic programs, offers the significant advantage of programming in parallel without explicit user annotations, thus overcoming one of the major difficulties of imperative parallel languages. This stems from two important properties of logic programming:

1. *Control* is separated from the *logic* of the problem. This is best presented by the equation:

$$algorithm = logic + control$$

originally introduced by Kowalski (34). This (almost) clear separation allows the employment of different control strategies, possibly parallel, without altering the problem's description in logic.

2. Logic programming languages are *single assignment languages*, thus the order of execution of the different operations in a logic program, has no effect to their soundness (35).

We can distinguish four main types of parallelism in logic programming: *unification parallelism, search parallelism, OR-parallelism, and AND-parallelism.* The first two types of parallelism do not change the order of execution of sequential Prolog, whereas AND- and OR-parallelism involve the application of alternative control strategies than the standard Left-to-Right-Depth-First used in sequential implementations. Although some research was reported in the first two types of parallelism (e.g., Ref. 36), the LP community was mainly focused on OR- and AND-parallelism.

As mentioned, the execution of a logic program consists of finding a successful derivation of the given query in a derivation tree. For example, assume that the query q(X,Y,Z) and the following logic program are given. Figure 11.1 presents the derivation tree of the program and depicts the two main types of parallelism (AND- and OR-) that are explained in more details in the following sections.

$$q(X,Y,3):-a(X,Y)$$
$$a(X,Y):-b(X),c(Y)$$
$$a(X,Y):-d(X,Y),c(Y)$$
$$b(3)$$
$$c(1)$$
$$d(1,1)$$

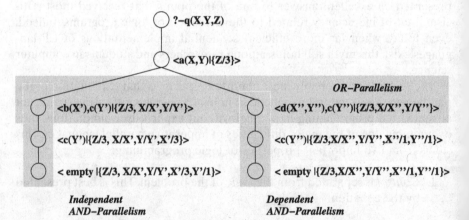

Fig. 11.1. The derivation tree of a Simple Prolog Program.

The potential efficiency gain from applying OR- and AND-parallelism, depends on the structure of the executed program. OR-parallelism offers speed up in the execution time, when the program is nondeterministic, that is, contains multiple resolvents for a given goal. AND-parallelism, on the other hand, can speed up even determinate programs since it involves the parallel construction of a single branch. Note here that the above types of parallelism are orthogonal to each other, that is, they can be exploited simultaneously (35) and a number of systems aims at exploiting both types of parallelism simultaneously.

11.3.1. OR-Parallelism

OR-parallelism arises from the fact that a goal can be matched with multiple heads of program clauses, a property referred to as nondeterminism in logic programming. For example, in the above example the goal $a(X,Y)$ unifies with the heads of two program clauses, namely the $a(X,Y):-b(X),c(Y)$ and $a(X,Y): -d(X,Y),c(Y)$ and forms a choice point as shown in the figure.

Each such match leads to a search path that can be explored independently from the other branches of the Prolog search tree. The name OR-parallelism derives from the fact that each branch represents an alternative answer to the original query and is searched in parallel; the multiple matching to the goal clauses, form a disjunction.

In an ideal OR-parallel system, the execution proceeds in a sequential manner until the resolution of a nondeterministic goal is encountered in the search procedure. At that point each of the alternative paths that is formed by each of the alternative resolutions can be explored in parallel, that is, assigned to a different processing element, often call a worker. Each such path can lead to either an alternative solution or a failure.

In the example, although computation proceeds independently in each path, the binding of the variable Z must be shared in both paths, whereas the variables X and Y are bound to different values in each path. In general, two nodes that belong in two different paths in the OR-tree must share all the variable bindings generated during all the inference steps that were performed before their least common ancestor node and at the same time be able to independently assign values to the variables that were unbound at their last ancestor node. This is the main problem of implementing OR-Parallelism; there must be an efficient way of representing and accessing the multiple bindings to variables that are created in each independent path.

Thus, variables at each choice point can be classified as either conditional or unconditional. *Unconditional* variables are variables that were created and bound at or before the least common ancestor node and are shared between the alternative paths. For example, variable Z in the example is an unconditional variable. *Conditional* variables are variables that were created, but remain unbound at the least common ancestor node. These might be bound to different values in each of the alternative OR-paths. In the example above, variables X and Y are conditional variables.

The implementation of an OR-Parallel system requires the existence of an efficient mechanism that allows each branch to have its own "private" store, to record the bindings of the conditional variables and at the same time provides access to the bindings of the unconditional variables. This problem is referred to as the *multiple bindings environment* problem and several methods and execution models have been proposed in the literature that aim to its efficient solution. These methods can be classified in three main approaches (37): the shared bindings environment, the closed bindings environment, and the nonshared bindings environment approach.

Methods that follow the *shared binding environment* approach use a shared space to record the bindings of all variables, regardless of whether the latter are conditional or unconditional. In these approaches, auxiliary data structures are used, to provide a form of bookkeeping, that records in which OR-branch the bindings to the conditional variables occurred. Examples of such methods are the *Directory Tree Method* (38), the *Hashing Windows Method* (39), the *Bindings Array Method* (40), the *Time Stamping Method* (41), the *Version Vectors Method* (42) and the *Favored Bindings Method* (43).

In the *closed-binding environment* approach, independent processes, each corresponding to an alternative matching clause, perform the computation of *one* goal statement, forming a process tree with explicit parent–child relationships. Each process has an isolated self-contained environment that restricts the variable access to a local level. Communication occurs only between processes related by a child–parent relationship. Such methods are the *Variable Importation Method* (44) and the *Closed Bindings Environment* (45).

Finally, the *nonshared bindings approach* consists of execution models in which each processing element maintains its own independent environment in which all variable bindings are recorded. When a search path is assigned to a processor, the environment is either copied or reconstructed and the computation proceeds independently. This class avoids the need of managing complex binding schemes and aim to reduce the amount of communication in the system. The *Muse Model* (46), the *Kabu-Wake Model* (47) and *The Delphi Model* (48, 49) belong to the class of OR-parallel models that follow this approach. Recently, the *Stack Splitting* (50) method that belongs to this approach was proposed for the efficient implementation of AND/OR parallel systems. Note that the techniques and models that belong to this approach seem to best-fit distributed memory architectures, as, for example, networks of machines operating in parallel.

11.3.2. Types of AND-Parallelism

AND-parallelism refers to the simultaneous execution of the goals in the body of a program clause (36). In other words, AND-parallelism refers to the parallel construction of the nodes in the same branch of the Prolog search tree (Fig. 11.1). The name AND derives from the fact the (sub)goals in the same branch of the search tree form a conjunction, that is, must all be resolved for the branch to be successful.

The main issue when evaluating a conjunction of subgoals in parallel is that of *data dependencies*, that is, the existence of shared variables between the subgoals. During parallel execution, such dependencies can lead to *binding conflicts*. For example, the subgoals d(X″,Y″) and c(Y″) share variable Y″ (Fig. 11.1) and thus potentially can lead to a binding conflict. Data dependency is not restrictive for AND-parallelism, in the sense that it makes parallel execution impossible, but should be approached with care in order to obtain any efficiency gains. The presence or absence of shared variables gives rise to the two types of AND-parallelism, that present different problems and issues in their implementation:

- *Independent AND-parallelism* that involves the parallel execution of multiple subgoals that do not share any variables. For example, goals b(X′) and c(Y′) in Fig. 11.1 are candidates for independent AND-parallel execution.
- *Dependent AND-parallelism*, which is the parallel execution of subgoals that contain shared variables, as, for example, the goals d(X″,Y″) and c(Y″), and has to be done under certain conditions, in order to provide some efficiency gains.

The sections that follow briefly present the principles and models proposed in the literature for AND parallel execution of logic programs.

11.3.3. Independent AND-parallelism

Exploiting independent AND-parallelism involves finding efficient and correct methods to three main issues: *detection of data dependencies, forward execution*, and *backtracking mechanisms*. Actually, these issues correspond to the three main execution phases of an independent AND-parallel system.

The *detection of data dependencies* involves discovering the data dependencies of the subgoals and based on these imposing an order in which the subgoals are to be executed. It is often referred to as *ordering phase*, as, for example, in Refs. 35, 51 and 52. Although, this might seem a simple issue that could be handled at compile time, this is not possible in all cases, since two variables might become related, that is, point to each other, during execution. Thus, not all dependencies can be detected at compile time and in order to exploit as much parallelism as possible some data dependency checking should be performed at run time.

During the *forward execution*, the subgoals that have to be executed in parallel are selected. This phase depends on the outcome of the data-dependency determination phase, in order to decide which goals are ready for execution and in some models a forward execution phase is followed by a reinitialization of the ordering phase. The outcome of this phase can be either a solution, a failure, or an initialization of the backward execution phase.

Finally, the *backward execution phase* is in fact the analog of the backtracking procedure of Prolog and thus involves selecting an appropriate backtracking point and restoring the state of the computation, before reentering the forward execution phase. Two issues that have to be dealt with in this phase is intelligent backtracking and termination of sibling AND subgoals, when a failure in a conjunct of a conjunction that is executed in parallel occurs.

The independent AND-parallelism models proposed in the literature fall into three major classes according to when they perform data-dependency checks. The *static approach* models, such as the static data dependency analysis model (SDDA) (53), perform all checks at compile time. In models that follow the *dynamic approach*, data dependency checks are performed at run time, as, for example, in the Connery's model (51). Although this approach can potentially exploit the maximum amount of AND-parallelism in a program, the cost of performing checks at run time is relatively high. The last class of models combines the two previous approaches, by performing the most expensive tests at compile time and less demanding ones at runtime. Examples of models that follow the *hybrid approach* are the RAP model (54) and its extension the RAP-WAM model (55). The two models mentioned before are based on *conditional graph expressions* (CGE) that are created at compile time for each clause in the program. CGEs specify the set of conditions that must hold for a set of goals, so that the latter can be executed in parallel at runtime. Obviously, the test defined in the conditions are checked at runtime. These ideas were used to build some very efficient Prolog systems as the &ACE (56) and &-Prolog/Ciao (57) system.

11.3.4. Dependent AND-parallelism

The exploitation of *dependent AND-parallelism* presents more problems than the previous types of parallelism. Not only the different bindings to shared variables between subgoals that are executed in parallel have to be checked for consistency, but also the order of solutions produced by the system, compared to the sequential version should be maintained. Additionally, the issue of identifying promising candidate subgoals for dependent AND execution is not an easy task.

A number of models have been proposed in the literature that address the problems mentioned above. Some of them aim at preserving the standard Prolog semantics, while others sacrifice normal Prolog semantics in exchange for simple and efficient implementations, like the committed choice family of languages. An excellent classification of the models and their advantages–disadvantages is given in Ref. 52.

Enforcing the standard Prolog semantics requires that a *consumer–producer relationship* is established for each shared variable. The producer of the binding for the shared variable is the "leftmost" subgoal, while consumers are all other subgoals in which the variables appears. In this sense, the shared variable can be viewed as a communication channel, or *stream*, between the two subgoals. The shared variable can act as a two-way communication channel: if the producer binds the variable to a complex term that contains uninstatiated variables, then the consumer subgoal might bind these variables to ground terms; these bindings might later be consumed by the original producer. This communication gives rise to a *coroutining effect*.

Although there exist approaches that allow both producer and consumer subgoals to produce bindings on shared variables and later perform a consistency check, as, for example, Epilog and ROPM (58), this approach proved to have a rather high parallel overhead. Most successful approaches are following the preventing model (52), that is, not allow bindings to occur if Prolog semantics are not preserved.

The principle that governs the computation in dependent AND-systems is the suspension of subgoals, if they try to bind their "input" variables, that is, the variables that the clause is a consumer of. Suspended subgoals are resumed when these variables are instantiated by producer subgoals. This computation presents two problems apart from the problems mentioned in independent AND-parallelism: that of determining which subgoal is the producer of a shared variable and the implementation of an efficient mechanism to resume the execution of suspended consumer goals, when the variables that caused their suspension are instantiated.

A number of models have been proposed in the literature, with or without coroutining. Without the presence of coroutining, devising an efficient model is simpler. A classic example is the *Dynamic Dependent And-Parallel Scheme* (DDAS), that was proposed by Shen (59), aims to exploit as much AND-parallelism as possible. The model is based on the use of *Extended Conditional Graph Expressions* (ECGE), that extend DeGroot's *Conditional Graph Expressions* with one more "test" that detects whether a variable is dependent or not. In the DDAS model, the execution of subgoals that have data dependencies between them, proceeds in parallel until one of the subgoals tries to bind the shared variable. In the case where such an event occurs, then two cases are possible: either the subgoal is the *producer* of the variable and the binding takes place, or the subgoal is the *consumer* and its execution suspends. The producer of a shared variable is determined by a priority system that is generated based on the left-to-right ordering of goals of the sequential Prolog. The leftmost goal (highest priority), which is active, is considered to be the producer of the shared variable. The model also includes a *backward execution scheme* used to control backtracking; when an unbinding of a dependent variable occurs, the consumers of the variable to the right in the ECGE, which have consumed at least one dependent variable, are forced to backtrack (redo).

The presence of coroutining results to added complexity, since for an efficient implementation communication of the bindings on the shared variables has to be done when nondeterminism of both producer and consumer goals are eliminated. If not, then a lot of speculative work of the workers operating on the parallel goals might occur. Eliminating nondeterminism is the approach followed by the committed choice Languages presented in Section 11.3.4.1. Although the Andorra family of languages follows a similar approach to dependent AND parallelism, it will be presented in the following section, since it aims at systems exploiting OR- and AND-Parallelism simultaneously.

11.3.4.1. Committed Choice Languages. A well-known family of languages that exploit dependent AND-parallelism with coroutining are the Committed Choice Non-Deterministic languages (CCND). There languages significantly alter standard Prolog semantics, since they eliminate *don't know nondeterminism* altogether. The four major representatives of this class of languages are *Parlog* (60), *Concurrent Prolog* (61) and *Guarded Horn Clauses* (*GCH*) (62) and its extension KL1 (63).

In these languages, the basic notion introduced is that of *guards*. A guarded horn clause has the form:

$$H :- G_1, G_2 \cdots G_n \mid B_1, B_2 \cdots B_n$$

where the conjunction $G_1, G_2, \cdots, G_n$ is the *guard* of clause H, B_i are the body goals, and the symbol "|" is the *commit (or commitment)* operator. While the declarative semantics of the above expression remains the same as in Prolog, if the commitment operator is read like a conjunction, the operational semantics is different. Upon the resolution of a goal, the clauses of the matching relation (procedure) try to prove their guards in parallel. Once one or more succeed in proving their guards, the execution proceeds with *one* of them while the execution of all other clauses is aborted. The clause selected is called the *committed clause*. Note that the selection is arbitrary (*don't care nondeterminism*). If the body of the committed clause fails, no other alternative paths are investigated, resulting in the absence of *don't know nondeterminism*. In such a case, the goal simply fails. There are many instances of committed-choice languages and the notion of guards has been extended successfully in constraint logic programming as well, as described in a later section.

For example, in *Parlog* (60), annotations are used to determine the direction of unification in relations (predicates). Each relation has at least one such declaration that specifies whether its arguments are input or output variables. If during head unification, an attempt is made to bind an input variable to a nonvariable term then the clause is suspended. In *Concurrent Prolog* (61), read only variables are denoted by the symbol "?" (e.g., X?). Any attempt to bind a read-only variable, leads to suspension of the process that attempted the binding, until some other process with appropriate permission binds the variable.

Guarded Horn Clauses (GHC) (62), does not use variables annotations at all, but instead, it restricts the unifications performed in the guard of the clause. Note here that the head of the clause is considered to be part of the guard too. The rule of suspension in GCH states that any unification of a variable to nonvariable term that is attempted in the guard of the clause leads to suspension of the clause. This forces that all the bindings to variables are to be performed in the body of the clause and executed *after* the clause has been selected for commitment. KL1 (63) is an extension of the GCH that allowed processes to control (meta-control) other processes so as to solve problems such as load balancing, allocation to processing elements, and so on.

Note that allowing arbitrary user-defined predicates to act as guards (deep guards) gives rise to complex implementation problems and thus *flat* versions of CCND languages were introduced, in which only a set of predefined predicates were allowed to act as guards.

11.3.5. Exploiting More Than One Types of Parallelism

A number of other models aim at exploiting different forms of parallelism simultaneously. The PEPSys model (Parallel ECRC Prolog System) (64,65) was developed to exploit independent AND- and OR-Parallelism. The model uses a combination of the *hashing windows* and the *time stamping* method to record variable bindings. The *Reduce-Or Parallel Model* (*ROPM*), was introduced by Kalé (66), in which the basic idea was to divide the problem into independent subproblems that can be executed on their own. In this sense, a node in the ROPM representation of the search tree (Reduced-Or) has enough information and can be solved without references to the nodes above it.

The AO-WAM model (67,68) combines independent AND-parallelism, exploited though the *Conditional Graph Expressions* and OR-parallelism, using an extension of the bindings array technique, to represent multiple environments. IDIOM (35,69), is a model that integrates Independent AND, determinate Dependent AND- and OR-parallelism, by combining the basic Andorra model with the Extended AND-OR tree of the AO-WAM. The model can be viewed as an extension of the AO-WAM, in order to support determinate Dependent AND-parallelism.

The ACE model (56,70) aims to exploit Independent AND- and OR-parallelism simultaneously. The model can be considered as a combination of the MUSE model and &-Prolog; it uses the stack-copying approach of MUSE to maintain multiple environments for the OR-parallel Prolog execution and the CGE of &-Prolog (57) for the exploitation of Independent AND-parallelism.

11.3.5.1. The Basic Andorra Model. Another class of models, and a corresponding set of languages implemented that exploits parallelism in LP, is based on the well-known *Andorra principle*. This approach can be considered as an effort to integrate the features of CCND languages and the standard Prolog paradigm (71). The Andorra family of languages aims at exploiting all three kinds of parallelism in LP.

The *Basic Andorra Model* was proposed by D.H.D. Warren (72) as an execution model for logic programs that will permit the exploitation of both

AND- and OR-parallelism. Execution in Andorra in based on the notion of *determinacy*, that is, having only one clause to reduce a subgoal. Thus all determinate goals are reduced in an AND-parallel manner regardless of the order that they would have in a sequential Prolog system (*determinate phase*). If no determinate goals exist, then one of the nondeterminate goals, usually the leftmost, is selected and explored in an OR-parallel manner(*nondeterminate phase*). A determinate phase is then invoked for each alternative OR-branch, giving rise to OR-parallelism.

Eagerly executing determinate goals provides a mechanism for search space reduction, due to pruning of the search space of nondeterminate goals caused by the bindings produced in the determinate phase. It also imposes a form of synchronization, since determinate goals act as producers of bindings for nondeterminate ones (consumers) that are not allowed to execute until the determinate phase ends.

A number of implementations of the basic Andorra model have been realized. In Andorra-I (73,74), processing elements, called *workers*, are organized in groups called *teams*. Each team is assigned a separate OR-branch, and during the *determinate phase* the workers of a team operate in parallel to reduce all determinate goals in the branch. When no more determinate goals are left to be reduced, choice point is created for the leftmost goal (nondeterminate phase) and one of the OR-branches is initialized for the team.

Pandora (75) integrates features from CCND languages and Andorra. Pandora is an extension of Parlog to support nondeterminism. The latter is achieved by the introduction of the *don't know* relation. Having the usual committed choice relations of Parlog, as well as the don't know relations, Pandora is able to achieve operational semantics similar to that described by the Basic Andorra Model. More specifically, the computation of a conjunction of clauses begins with the reduction of committed choice clauses (Parlog clauses) and all don't know clauses that are determinate (and-parallel phase). If the computation deadlocks, that is, all goals suspend, and among the suspended goals exist calls that match "don't know" relations, then the execution proceeds with the reduction of one of these clauses, creating OR-branches for the alternative path (*deadlock phase*). Then, the computation proceeds by initiating an AND-parallel phase for each of the branches.

11.3.5.2. The Extended Andorra Model.
The Extended Andorra Model (*EAM*) extends the idea of executing *determinate* goals ahead of their "turn", originally introduced in the Basic Andorra Model. In EAM, nondeterminate goals are allowed to execute, but up to the point that they do not try to try to instantiate any "outside" variables. If it tries to do so it must suspend. Note that if the goal produces a single binding for the variable, then it does not need to suspend, but instead it "publishes" the binding to the "outside" environment, becoming the *producer* of the variable, thus being in accordance with the Basic Andorra Model in which the determinate goals become the producers of the shared variables. When the system reaches the state that all the

goals are suspended, each goal that is the producer of a variable publishes its bindings to the "outside environment". The producer goal typically defined as the leftmost goal that contains the shared variable. For each binding published, a copy of the consumer goal is created and its execution is resumed. This operation is known as the *nondeterminate promotion step*. A recent implementation of the EAM model was attempted with promising results in the BEAM system (76,77).

The Andorra Kernel Language (AKL) (78), is a sequential implementation of an instance of the Extended Andorra model. The difference in AKL is that the language provides full control over parallelism to the programmer through the *wait* guard. An initial parallel implementation of the AKL is described in Ref. 79. Note that AKL has different syntax and semantics than Prolog, and therefore a Prolog to AKL translator was developed, which is described in Ref. 80.

The AKL was further developed and resulted to the Agents Kernel Language, a concurrent constraint LP platform with deep guards. A parallel implementation of the Agents Kernel Language was implemented in the Penny targeting shared memory multiprocessors (81), however, it supported only constraints over rational trees, that is, an extension of the finite trees used in conventional LP programs.

EAM is a very powerful and general model that exploits all types of parallelism in logic programs. In the EAM, there is no distinction between dependent and independent AND-parallelism; the model tries to exploit as much parallelism whenever it is possible. The disadvantage of the proposed model is that it presents difficulties in its efficient implementation due to its complexity, even until today.

11.4. PARALLELISM IN CONSTRAINT LOGIC PROGRAMMING

Parallel execution and constraint reasoning seem to be complementary techniques for the solution of large combinatorial problems. The former aims in exploring alternative solution paths in parallel, thus reducing the time required in order to traverse the search space, while the latter aims to reduce the size of the search space, thus increasing the efficiency of search procedures. Consequently, approaches that exploit some sort of parallelism together with constraint satisfaction have been proposed in the literature.

Although it might seem natural that all the Parallel LP research would be easily extended to the constraint logic programming paradigm, this was not a trivial task in some cases. As it will be discussed in the corresponding section, although the application of OR-parallelism in CLP is relatively straightforward, AND-parallelism is difficult to be applied directly, mainly because the notions of goal independence that are central to AND-parallelism, are not directly applicable. This is due to the fact that the constraint store allows one goal to "affect" another in more ways than in standard logic programming.

However, most models of executing CLP programs in parallel are extensions of ideas and principles originally introduced in the context of parallel logic programming.

11.4.1. OR-Parallelism in CLP

The benefits of exploiting OR-parallelism in a CLP language were first reported by Van Hentenryck in (82), where the finite constraint solver of the CHIP system was combined with the PEPsys (63) parallel system. Parallel execution involved exploring choice points created during the assignment of values to variables (labeling phase) in an OR-parallel manner and the results reported were quite promising.

Probably the first complete logic programming system that efficiently combines OR-parallelism and constraint satisfaction is the Elipsys system (ECRC Logic Inference Parallel System). Elipsys (83,84) is a logic programming system developed in ECRC, and combined all major research trends in logic programming at the time. The system adopted the shared-binding approach to the multiple bindings representation problem. More specifically, the system used the binding arrays method originally proposed by Warren (40), according to which an additional data structure is used to record bindings of conditional variables locally on each processor exploring an alternative path. Scheduling on the other hand, that is, assignment of work to processors is done via a message passing mechanism. Elipsys executed on a variety of platforms, including both shared memory and distributed memory architectures.

Parallelism in Elipsys is not automatic in the sense that the user has to annotate appropriate goals that are to be executed in parallel (85). However, the platform hides away all other details involved in parallel execution, such as load balancing and synchronization. The suitability of the Elipsys system to industrial applications was demonstrated during a 3-year EU funded research project named APPLAUSE (86).

During the APPLAUSE project, another parallel CLP logic programming platform was developed in ECRC, namely, the well-known ECLiPSe platform (87). After the termination of the ECRC research activities, the development of the ECLiPSe platform was continued in the IC-PARC of the Imperial College in London, as described in Section 11.2.2.

OR-parallelism in ECLiPSe adopted a hybrid approach to the multiple bindings problem, in order to fit multiprocessor environments consisting of networks of computers. In such a network, it is common that multiprocessor and single processor machines coexist. Thus, when work has to be shared between processing units (workers) on shared memory multiprocessor machines, OR-parallelism relies on a stack-copying method, whereas when work is shared between processing units of distributed memory machines, a recomputation approach is employed.

This approach was originally proposed by Mudambi and Schimpf in Ref. 88. In the same paper, authors describe in detail the recomputation model of exploiting OR-parallelism in CLP programs and investigate the benefits of adopting this approach to OR-parallel CLP systems. The implementation is based on the notion of oracles (48,49), initially proposed in the Delphi model. Oracles record nondeterministic choice points during execution that are used by a new processor to which a path is assigned to guide the recomputation phase. The motivation behind adopting the recomputation approach was that it fits well in a heterogeneous machine network, since the communication of oracles can be implementation independent and that the size of stacks in a CLP program are typically larger than those in a LP, thus the stack copying approach would yield much higher overheads. Authors extended the ECLiPSe language for supporting the use of oracles and tested the prototype implementation on a number of machines connected via a TCP/IP network. The results were rather promising, showing that good speedups can be obtained by the recomputation approach to parallel CLP, in a heterogeneous environment.

Firebird (89) is a concurrent constraint programming system that supports finite domains, concurrency and OR data-parallelism. The model was targeted toward a massively parallel SIMD computer architecture with distributed local memory. The language follows the syntax of flat GHC, that is, clauses have the form:

$$H :- C_{ask} \mid B, C_{tell}$$

where C_{ask}, B and C_{tell} are conjunctions of *ask* constraints, and *tell* constraints, respectively.

Ask and tell constraints have been introduced originally to concurrent constraint programming (23,90) and extend the synchronization and control mechanisms of concurrent logic languages to constraint programming. Processes interact through a global constraint store by either *telling* a constraint, that is, posting a new constraint to the store or by *asking* whether a constraint is entailed or disentailed by the constraint store. The later is used for synchronization, that is, if neither entailment or disentailment can be determined by the execution of the process blocks.

Although Firebird resembles the Andorra model, the semantics of the language are different. In Firebird, execution consists of committed choice indeterministic and nondeterministic derivation steps. Although the former closely follows the model of committed choice languages, that is, consists of guard tests, commitment, and spawning, the nondeterministic step differs more radically than that of Andorra. A nondeterministic step sets up choice points by selecting one of the domain variables and trying all possible values (labeling) in an OR-parallel manner. Thus, each branch that is tried in parallel contains the domain variable labeled, that is, instantiated to one of the values of its domain.

Execution proceeds by indeterministic and nondeterministic derivations steps. In the case that both are applicable, execution proceeds by one of them.

However, the model does specify which is to be selected in each case, leaving room for eager nondeterminism when nondeterministic steps always take precedence over indeterministic and lazy nondeterminism in the opposite case.

Firebird follows a strategy for allocating work to processor elements that avoid interprocessor communication. Alternative computations produced by a nondeterministic step are allocated to groups of processors. For example, if a choice point contains K alternatives and there are N processing elements at the time, each alternative is assigned to N/K elements. Each processor has a unique ID, it "knows" which alternative to execute without communicating with other processors. However, since not all alternatives might have the same size or the execution of some might end, processors elements might remain idle. To overcome the problem, the model performs an *equalization*, that is, reallocation of idle processors to groups that are still executing. A variation of equalization called *apportion* performs the reallocation using some heuristics.

The model has been implemented on a DECmpp machine of 8192 processors with distributed local memory and was tested on various benchmark problems, including the N-queens problem and demonstrated significant speedups in the computation.

11.4.2. AND-Parallelism in CLP

Applying AND-parallelism on CLP programs is somewhat more difficult, mainly due to the fact that the classical notions of independence of logic programs do not hold. This is due to the fact that even if two goals do not share any variables, changes in the domains of the variables appearing in the first might affect through constraint variables appearing in the second, thus the two goals are dependent. Therefore, a more careful definition of independence is necessary, which takes into account the relationships imposed by the constraints.

The work described in Refs. 8 and 91 defines new notions of independence that are applicable to constraint logic programs. Authors formally define notions of *weak*, *strong*, and *search* independence based on derivations, answers, and partial answers of these programs. A partial answer is defined as the constraint store to some state that is not a final state, that is, an answer of a derivation $\langle G|c\rangle$ to a state $\langle G'|c'\rangle$, where G' is not the empty clause ■.

Thus, informally given a constraint c and two goals g_1 and g_2 that are executed in parallel:

- *Weak* independence holds between g_1 and g_2 if the answers obtained by the execution of the two goals are consistent.
- *Strong* independence, holds if every partial answer of g_2 is consistent with the answers of g_1.
- Finally, *search* independence holds if all partial answers of g_1 are consistent with all partial answers of g_2.

However, although the above notions, are of major theoretical importance, they cannot be used in the implementation of practical systems, since they rely on the notion of solution answers. Thus, authors introduce the notion of *projection* independence, which can be detected using runtime tests during the execution of a program. Two goals $g_1(\bar{X})$ and $g_2(\bar{Y})$, where $\bar{X}, \bar{Y}$ are variables $x_1 \cdots x_n$ and $y_1 \cdots y_k$, are projection independent if their common variables are *fixed* by the constraint store c; that is, they have a unique value that satisfies c, and the conjunction of the projection of c to the variables $\bar{X}$ with the projection of c to the variables of $\bar{Y}$ imply the projection of c to the union of variables $\bar{X}$ and $\bar{Y}$. The above is more formally described as

$$(\bar{X} \cap \bar{Y} \subseteq \text{fixed}(c)) \wedge (\exists_{-\bar{X}}c \wedge \exists_{-\bar{Y}}c \rightarrow \exists_{-\bar{Y} \cup \bar{X}}c)$$

where $\exists_{-\bar{x}}$ is the projection of c to the variables of g_1 and *fixed*(c) the set of all fixed variables of c. Since in some cases computing the projection of the store to a set of variables might be a costly operation, authors also introduce the notion of link independence as a test for practical CLP systems. *Link independence* relaxes the second conjunct of the above condition to a simpler test of checking where any of the $\bar{X}$ variables is directly or indirectly "linked" by primitive constraints of c to any of the variables $\bar{Y}$, thus ensuring that the two goals will not affect each other. In the same work, authors generalize the notion of independence for constraint logic programming with delayed goals.

Garcia de la Banda *et al.* (92) preliminary provides results of an AND-parallel system based on CIAO Prolog, which demonstrates very promising results. The CIAO Prolog system is described in Section 11.5.2.

Guarded Definite Clauses with Constraints (GDCC) (93) is a parallel implementation of a concurrent constraint logic language based on the KL1. GDCC was an effort to exploit parallelism in two ways: parallel execution of the language in which the program is expressed and parallel execution of constraint solving algorithms at each execution step. The former is provided by the KL1 language on which GDCC is implemented in. The latter is implemented through a set of parallel constraint solvers with which execution is synchronized. The main components of the GDCC system are a compiler that compiles the source code to KL1, an interface for dispatching ask and tell constraints to the solvers, and the solvers themselves. Thus, constraint solvers are executing in parallel with the GDCC program and synchronize only when required by the concurrent semantics of the language. In the same work, authors describe available parallel constraint solvers for the algebraic domain (nonlinear polynomial equations), Boolean domain and integer linear domain.

Finally, an approach to exploiting both OR- and Dependent AND- parallelism through an extension of the Andorra-I language is reported by Gregory and Yang in Ref. 94. The determinate phase in this case includes executing constraint goals as early as possible in order to reduce the variable domains, exploiting dependent AND-parallelism. The nondeterminate phase might include assigning a new OR-branch to each of the values in the variable domains and proceeds the execution with a new determinate phase. The system provided constraint solving facilities similar to those of the ECRC CHIP system, that is, finite domain constraint solving. One of the advantages of the proposed language was that regardless of the order in which the constraints and search were stated in the original user program, domain reduction through constraints was always executed as early as possible.

11.5. EXECUTING CLP PROGRAMS ON MULTIPLE PROCESSORS

While research for exploitation of implicit parallelism in CLP has experienced a slowdown in the last few years, the same cannot be said for languages that implement the research results described in the previous sections. This section briefly presents some of the currently available platforms for implementing parallel CLP applications. We have chosen to present three concrete implementations of CLP languages that can be used for the development of parallel applications: *Mozart/OZ*, a concurrent multiparadigm constraint language that is influenced by AKL among other things; *CIAO Prolog*, a multiparadigm system based on LP that is an implementation of many of the major results described in the corresponding sections; and *CSPCONS*, a CLP system that offers explicit communication primitives between Prolog processes that run in parallel.

11.5.1. The Mozart/OZ System

A platform that supports constraints, logic programming, and distributed execution is the Mozart/OZ platform (95–97), that is being developed by the Universitat des Saarlandes (Germany), the Swedish Institute for Computer Science, and the Universite' Catholique de Louvain (Belgium). Mozart is in fact a multiparadigm language that supports logic, functional, constraint, object-oriented, concurrent, distributed programming that is the successor of DFKI[3] OZ (98).

Concurrent programs in Mozart/OZ are implemented through the use of explicit thread creation and synchronization over logic variables (single assignment variables). The latter are stored in an area called *constraint store* that in the simple case contains equalities over the domain of rational trees, that is, logic variables bound to some term. Thread execution proceeds following a concurrent execution model, that is, it is allowed to proceed as long as some conditions are satisfied (*ask* constraint over the store that contains the bindings) and a binding is allowed to take place as long as it is consistent with the store (*tell* constraint), or an exception is raised. Thread communication is achieved through shared references in the constraint store. This concurrent model of Mozart allows encoding deterministic logic programs easily. Non-

---

[3]German Research Center for Artificial Intelligence.

deterministic logic programs are supported through the special primitives, such as the *choice* primitive.

Thus, computation in OZ takes place in the so-called *computation space*. Informally, a *computational space* consists of the constraint store, the thread store, that is, the set of program threads, the mutable store, and the trigger store. The mutable store contains cells, that is, mutable references to the constraint store that are used for the implementation of concurrent object system of OZ and the trigger store contains triggers employed for lazy execution (Byneed computations). We are not going to present these concepts in more detail. However, for more information the reader is referred to Refs. 98–100. As described in the next paragraph, a few extensions in the concept of computation spaces allow the implementation of constraint handling over any constraint domain and any search algorithm.

11.5.1.1. *Constraints in Mozart/OZ.*

Mozart supports constraint handling over finite domains, finite sets, and real intervals. To support constraint programming, Mozart extends the constraint store by allowing other constraint systems, such as, finite domains. In these cases, the store contains *basic* constraints of the computational domain, as well as algorithms to decide whether the constraints in the store are satisfiable or whether a basic constraint is entailed by the store, that is, every value assignment that satisfies the store also satisfies the basic constraint. Examples of basic constraints for the finite domain are $X = 8 \land Y \in 3\#10$, that is, the variable X has the unique value 8 and Y belongs to the integer interval (29,49).

More complex constraints, as, for example, $X + 34 * Y < Z + W$, are implemented as *propagators*. The latter are computational entities executing on their own thread that change the store by posting new basic constraints on those variables given the constraints on those variables that exist in the store. However, these newly posted by the propagator basic constraint must be consistent with the store and, obviously, it further constrains the domain of the variable. These propagators modify the constraint store in a concurrent manner: They resume execution if any of their variables (parameters) are modified, after which they suspend. If during its execution a propagator detects an inconsistency or entailment, it returns a corresponding value and is terminated.

The status of the attached propagators determines the status of their computation space. A space is *failed* if one of its propagators has failed, or it is *stable* if its propagators have either failed or are suspended. A space is *solved* if it has not failed and has no more propagators, that is, all its propagators have been entailed.

To implement search algorithms that are necessary for complete solutions of constraint problems, nesting of computation spaces is supported, together with seven primitive operations, like space creation, cloning, merging, exploring alternative computations and asking the status of a space. Nesting allows the creation of a hierarchy of spaces on which a set of visibility rules on variable access apply between different spaces. This hierarchy allows the creation of child computation spaces that explore alternative computations through which the search tree is explored. Mozart/OZ already has a number of search algorithms implemented, which are based on these concepts, for example, depth-first search, iterative deepening and branch and bound.

One of the most interesting features of Mozart/OZ is that it provides a transparent distribution of search to a set of networked machines. The search tree is explored in a parallel manner by delegating entire subtrees of the search to multiple workers, thus yielding a kind of OR-parallelism. This operation is transparent to the user in the sense that all that has to be done is to state the available machines for the parallel execution and apply little modifications to the sequential code. Benchmarks on a set of problems reported linear speedup on a network of six machines (100).

However, that the syntax of the OZ language differs significantly from standard logic programming syntax (i.e., Prolog), presents some problems to the novice programmer. Mozart/OZ is currently used in a number of projects, such as scheduling and analysis of biochemical networks.[4]

11.5.2. Ciao Prolog

CIAO is a logic programming system based on Prolog, extended with constraints, parallelism, and concurrency (101,102). The platform supports all major programming paradigms of logic programming, constraint logic programming, and CC languages, including object oriented and functional programming. The programming environment is a collective effort of the CLIP group in the Technical University of Madrid and several other groups around the world and includes results from various areas of research, such as parallelization and program analysis.

The CIAO design allows for extensions by using a minimal kernel to which all extended features are implemented as libraries. The kernel language supports sentential, parallel, concurrent, and distributed execution primitives, which are exploited by a source-to-source transformation of the user program. This architecture relies on the view that most parallel–concurrent models and implementations are essentially applications of variations of a few basic principles, as, for example, determinacy, which allows the parallel execution of dependent threads. This independence allows parallel execution as long as threads do not "affect" each other, nonfailure for avoiding speculative work, and task granularity for minimizing computational overheads associated with parallel execution (103).

11.5.2.1. The CIAO Kernel. The CIAO kernel language supports a set of explicit control operators, such as the "," operator for sequential execution, "&/2" for parallel execution, "&/1" for concurrency. The kernel language also

---

[4]For more details please see http://www.mozart-oz.org

supports an AND fairness operator "&&/1", which ensures that the ask anno-tated will be assigned to either a worker, or a new worker will be created for it, as well as an operator for controlling task placement in a distributed envi-ronment. Among the features of the kernel language is explicit synchroniza-tion by appropriate operators, that is, blocking execution until a variable is bound (wait/1 operator) or until a constraint is entailed (ask/1 operator).

This kernel language is supported by a simple abstract machine based on &-Prolog (57) and its improvements are described in Ref. 104. The abstract machine also includes support for *attributed variables* on which depends the implementation of constraint solvers and communication among concurrent tasks. The former, that is, implementing constraints on top of existing logic pro-gramming systems by using attributed variables has been often used, as, for example, in ECLiPSe and SICStus Prolog. The latter, that is, communication of concurrent processes using attributed variables, was first introduced in Ref. 105. In CIAO, implementing communication between concurrent tasks is performed by shared (attributed) variables posted to a Linda-like blackboard system. This communication scheme allows synchronization to be imple-mented at the source level, that is, as a Prolog program. Details of this imple-mentation are described by Hermenegildo *et al.* in Ref. 105.

Distributed execution in CIAO involves a number of *workers* (processing units), organized in *teams* (106). Teams share the same code and cooperate toward its execution. Appropriate primitives (*add worker/1, add worker/2, delete_worker/1*) are used to change the configuration of teams. All commu-nication of workers is based on a Linda-like blackboard structure on which all workers have access. Idle workers obtain goals to execute from the blackboard and post results in the same area. The distributed execution model of CIAO also includes *active modules*, that is, Prolog modules with a team attached to them. Active modules allow remote execution of predicate calls by applica-tions. Once an active module receives queries via its private blackboard struc-ture it executes them and posts results on the same area from, where the calling application can obtain them.

As mentioned earlier, CIAO supports multiple paradigms via source-to-source transformations to the kernel language. In the current CIAO system, a preprocessor is responsible for all code analysis and transformations. The CIAO preprocessor (107) relies on an abstract interpretation technique in order to perform global and local analysis of logic programs both for debug-ging and code optimization. The latter also includes automatically annotating programs for parallel execution and automatic granularity control, that is, automatically including run-time test to ensure that tasks are of sufficient size to be executed in parallel. A more detailed description of the above as well as pointers to the relevant literature can be found in Ref. 101.

Finally, note that CIAO allows not only the development of applications, but also makes an excellent testbed for experimenting with language design.

11.5.3. The CSPCONS Prolog

CSPCONS adopts a different approach to the parallel–distributed execution of logic programs, by allowing the creation of independent sequential Prolog processes that synchronize though message and event passing. Although this approach does not follow the main stream of automatic parallelization of the execution of logic programs, it offers a set of rich programming constructs that allow the implementation of parallel–distributed constraint logic programming applications. The CSPCONS (108,109) platform is based on the Communicating Sequential Prolog II (CSP-II), which has been developed since 1995 (110,111) and offers advanced communication facilities, all under the logic programming framework.

CSPCONS is an extension of CSP-II, which inherits all its advanced features and at the same time supports constraint programming. Both platforms have extended features like modularity, multitasking, real-time programming, and of course, network communication. The main feature of the two systems is that they support the communicating sequential process (112) programming methodology in a Prolog environment. Processes run in parallel and communication between them is achieved through message passing over channels or events. This process-based model allows an elegant implementation of any parallel and distributed algorithms. The channel-based communication has been extended with networking capabilities over the TCP–IP protocol, thus providing the ability to establish connections between applications residing in different hosts. Furthermore, under this schema a plethora of features are provided, such as communication with foreign applications, an interface to relational database systems, real-time programming methods like cyclic behavior, reaction to predefined events, and timed interrupts.

11.5.3.1. CSPCONS Processes. CSPCONS processes are defined as the execution flow of a Prolog goal and every process has its own Prolog execution environment and dynamic database. Thus the progress of a process is independent of the execution of other processes. This separation of dynamic databases ensures that CSPCONS processes may have influence on each other only by the specified communication techniques, that is, channels, events and inter rupts, or through external objects like files. In general, each CSPCONS process can have active instances of several different solvers, as, for example, a Finite Domain and a Linear solver. However, the set of constraints and domain variables maintained by instances of a solver that belong to different processes are independent of each other, resulting to a communicating sequential CLP system. On a single processor machine, a time-sharing scheduler controls the concurrent processes.

Processes are identified by a unique system-wide symbolic name. Two kinds of processes are provided: *self-driven or normal* and *event-driven or real-time* processes.

A *self-driven* process is characterized by its (Prolog) goal; after its creation, it will begin the execution of this goal. The nonfatal termination of a self-driven process is determined by the termination of its goal. A *real-time* process is characterized by one goal for the initialization, one goal for the event handling, and by the description of the events that trigger its execution. The initialization goal is executed once and provides the means for performing any necessary setup actions. After the successful termination of the initializing goal, the process switches to acyclic behavior. From that moment on it is controlled by the incoming events. For every real-time process, the incoming events are gathered in a separate first-in-first-out input queue, from which the process consumes them by initiating its event-handling goal. The number of events that real-time processes can be triggered for is unlimited. The successful termination of a process is signaled by the failure of its event-handling goal. Such termination is considered as regular; it does not affect the overall success or failure of the application.

Interprocess communication is achieved by synchronous messages or by event passing. Messages are passed through *communication channels* that implement a one-way communication between two processes. Communication channels act as system-wide available resources, identified by unique names and may appear and disappear dynamically during the program's lifetime. As stated, *events* serve for triggering real-time processes and can be generated explicitly by built-in predicates or implicitly by the internal clock in order to invoke execution of the real-time process in specific time intervals. Every occurrence of an event may carry an optional arbitrary Prolog term except the case of a single unbound variable.

Finally, note that processes can backtrack, however, communication is not backtrackable.

As a natural extension of the original interprocess channel concept, the external communication over TCP–IP networks conceptually consists of message streams. In order to facilitate speed-up of external communication, asynchronous message passing is introduced as an option. For the Prolog programmer, the communication environment appears as a homogeneous address space (community) in which all fellow applications (partners) are accessed via channel messages. Partner configuration requires detailed knowledge of its network information, that is, its name, port, IP address or hostname, and the IP port it listens to. Although this might seem a somewhat difficult and tedious task, it provides a more versatile connection schema. Various versions of simple and more sophisticated naming service applications have been implemented as CSPCONS processes that can be included in applications as simple Prolog libraries and help significantly to reduce programming efforts toward establishing remote connections.

One important characteristic of the platform is that at any given time the network status of each agent in the community is known to all fellow agents via an alert mechanism: changes in the status of an agent trigger network related events to the fellow agents participating in the community, thus informing them of the change that took place, as, for example, the nonavailability of an agent.

11.5.3.2. Constraints in CSPCONS. The CSPCONS system consists of two main subsystems: the *solver* and the *core*. The solver is responsible for maintaining the constraint store and performing any constraint related tasks, that is, it is responsible for storing domain variables and the set of constraints, as well as for constraint propagation. The core is the extended CSP-II system that keeps track of the active instances of the different solvers, dispatches requests originated by the Prolog program to the appropriate solver instance, and performs other system-related tasks, includingll normal Prolog predicate calls. The design aim behind such a model was to allow the introduction of new constraint handling facilities easily. The solver is in fact a C linkable library that implements a set of function calls defined by the CLP-Interface of CSPCONS. The model offers independence of the code concerning constraint handling and provides the means to easily extend the system to support any constraint domain and any algorithm. Currently, CSPCONS support a finite domain solver and a linear equations–disequations solver. CSPCONS runs on a variety of platforms and has been tested and performed well on a number of applications.

11.6. CONCLUSIONS

Undoubtedly, an enormous research effort in the past two decades was devoted to increasing the efficiency of the standard logic programming paradigm. The two directions, parallelizing the execution of LP and extending the standard unification to constraint solving in order to efficiently deal with large combinatorial problems, have led to a large number of research results, as well as concrete implementation languages.

Future directions in the area include application of research results to other logic-based paradigms, such as inductive logic programming and nonmonotonic-reasoning, new implementations targeting in distributed network-based computer environments, and, of course, new constraint reasoning techniques.

The parallel constraint logic programming approach seems to have significant advantages for the development of practical applications, especially in the area of combinatorial search problems. Its declarative semantics drastically reduce the development time required to build complex applications, since only the logic of the problem has to be stated. Building parallel applications is either a transparent operation through the employment of automatic parallelization tools, such as the CIAO Prolog, or significantly facilitated by language constructs, such as those provided by Mozart/OZ or CSPCONS. Large combinatorial problems are handled efficiently by the integrated constraint solving algorithms.

The technology in language implementation issues has reached a maturity level that allows the development of real-world applications, exploiting parallelism and constraints simultaneously. The latter might also help to change the general view regarding the unsuitability of the LP/CLP paradigm for large scale applications.

REFERENCES

1. R.A. Kowalski. Predicate logic as programming language. In *Proceedings of the IFIP Congues 1974*, North-Holland Pub Co, Amsterdam, The Netherlands, 1974, pp. 569–574.

2. K. Marriott and P.J. Stuckey. *Introduction to Constraint Logic Programming*. MIT Press, 1998. Cambridge, MA, USA.

3. F. Rossi. Constraint (Logic) Programming: A Survey on Research and Applications. In K.R. Apt, A.C. Kakas, E. Monfroy, and F. Rossi, eds., *Proceedings of the ERCIM/Compulog Net Workshop on Constraints (Oct. 1999)*, No. 1865 in LNAI. Springer, 2000.

4. P.V. Henteryck. Constraint logic programming. *Knowledge Eng. Rev.*, 6(3):151–194 (1991).

5. A.K. Mackworth. Consistency in Networks of Relations. *Art. Intel.*, 8(1):99 (1977).

6. J.W. Lloyd. *Foundations of Logic Programming*. Springer-Verlag, 1987. Heidelberg, RG.

7. J. Jaffar, M.J. Maher, K. Marriott, and P.J. Stuckey. The semantics of constraint logic programs. *J. Logic Prog.*, 37(1–3):1 (1998).

8. M. Garcia de la Banda, M. Hermenegildo, and K. Marriott. Independence in CLP languages. *ACM Trans. Prog. Lang. Syst.*, 22(2):296–339 (2000).

9. J.A. Robinson. A Machine-Oriented Logic Based on the Resolution. *J. ACM*, 12(1):23–41 (1965).

10. J. Jaffar, S. Michaylov, P.J. Stuckey, and R. Yap. The CLP($\mathcal{R}$) Language and System. *ACM Trans. Prog. Lang. Systems*, 14(3):339–395 (July 1992).

11. A. Aggoun and N. Deldiceanu. Overview of the CHIP Compiler System. *Logic Programming: Proceedings of the 1991 International Symposium*, 1991, pp. 775–789.

12. H. Hong. Non-Linear Constraint Solving over Real Numbers in Constraint Logic Programming (Introducing RISC-CLP). Technical Report 92-08, Research Institute for Symbolic Computation, Johannes Kepler University, Linz, Austria, 1992.

13. D. Diaz and P. Codognet. A Minimal Extension of the WAM for clp(FD). In D.S. Warren, ed., *Proceedings of the Tenth International Conference on Logic Programming*, The MIT Press, 1993, pp. 774–790. Budapest, Hungary.

14. M. Carlsson, G. Ottosson, and B. Carlson. An Open-ended Finite Domain Constraint Solver. *Ninth International Symposium on Programming Languages, Implementations, Logics, and Programs (PLILP'97)*, Vol. 1292, Springer-Verlag, Berlin, 1997, pp. 191–206.

15. E. Contejean. Solving Linear Diophantine Constraints Incrementally. In D.S. Warren, ed., *Proceedings of the Tenth International Conference on Logic Programming,* The MIT Press, 1993, pp. 532–549. Budepest, Hungary.

16. C. Gervet. Conjunto: Constraint Logic Programming with Finite Set Domains. In M. Bruynooghe, ed., *Proceedings of the 1994 International Symposium on Logic Programming, ILPS'94,* The MIT Press. Ithaca, New York, November 1994, pp. 339–358.

17. J. Jaffar and M. Maher. Constraint Logic Programming: A Survey. *J. Logic Prog.,* **19**:20 (1994).

18. A.J. Fernández and P.M. Hill. An interval constraint system for lattice domains. *ACM Trans. Prog. Lang. Syst.,* **26**(1):1–46 (2004).

19. M. Dincbas *et al.* The constraint logic programming language chip. *Proceedings of the International Conference on Fifth Generation Computer Systems.* Tokyo, Japan, 1988.

20. A. Colmerauer. An introduction to Prolog III. *Commun. ACM,* **33**(7):69–90 (1990).

21. P. Codognet and D. Diaz. Compiling Constraints in clp(FD). *J. Logic Prog.,* **27**(3):185–226 (June 1996).

22. D. Diaz and P. Codognet. The GNU Prolog system and its implementation. *SAC '00: Proceedings of the 2000 ACM symposium on Applied computing,* ACM Press, 2000, pp. 728–732. Como, Italy.

23. P. Van Hentenryck, V.A. Saraswat, and Y. Deville. Design, implementation, and evaluation of the constraint language cc(fd). *Selected Papers from Constraint Programming,* Springer-Verlag, 1995, pp. 293–316.

24. A.M. Cheadle *et al.* ECLiPSe: A tutorial introduction (ver5.8). vTechnical Report IC-Parc-05–1, IC-Parc, Imperial College London, 2005.

25. H. Simonis. Developing applications with ECLiPSe. Technical Report IC-Parc-03–2, IC-Parc, Imperial College London, 2003.

26. Intelligent Systems Laboratory. *SICStus Prolog User's Manual.* Swedish Institute of Computer Science, PO BOX 1263, S-164 28 Kista, Sweden, November 2004. Release 3.12.0.

27. T.W. Frühwirth. Theory and Practice of Constraint Handling Rules. *J. Logic Prog.,* **37**(1–3):95–138 (1998).

28. C. Holzbaur. Ofai clp(q,r) manual, edition 1.3.3. Technical Report TR-95-09, Austrian Research Institute for Artificial Intelligence, Vienna, 1995.

29. M. Carlsson. Dispensation order generation for pyrosequencing. ERCIM News, **60** (2005).

30. M. Wallace. Practical applications of constraint programming. *Constraints,* **1**(1):139–168 (Sept. 1996).

31. H. Simonis, P. Charlier, and P. Kay. TACT: An integrated transportation problem solved with CHIP. *Practical Applications of Constraint Technology,* 1998.

32. M. Dincbas, H. Simonis, and P van Hentenryck. Solving a Cutting-Stock Problem in CLP. In R.A. Kowalski, K.A. Bowen, eds., *Proceedings of the Fifth International Conference and Symposium on Logic Programming.* The MIT Press, 1988. Japan, Tokyo.

33. C. Pearson, M. Birtwistle, and A.R. Verden. Reducing material wastage in the carpet industry. *Proceeding of the fourth Practical Applications of Constraint Technology*, 1998, London, UK.

34. R.A. Kowalski. *Logic for Problem Solving*. North-Holland, Publishing Co, Amsterdam, The Netherlands, 1979.

35. G. Gupta. *Multiprocessor Execution of Logic Programs*, Kluwer Academic Publishers, 1994, Dordrecht, Northerland.

36. J.S. Conery and D.F. Kibler. Parallel Interpretation of Prolog Programs. *Conference on Functional Programming Languages and Computer Architecture*, ACM, Oct. 1981, pp. 163–170.

37. S.A. Delgado-Rannauro. OR-Parallel Logic Computational Models. In P. Kacsuk and M.J. Wise, eds., *Implementations of Distributed Prolog*, John Wiley & Sons, New York, 1992, Chapt. 1.

38. A. Ciepielewski and S. Haridi. A formal model for or-parallel execution of logic programs. In R.E.A. Mason, ed., *Information Processing 83. Proceedings of The IFIP 9th World Computer Congress*, North-Holland, Amsterdam, The Netherlands, 1983, pp. 299–305.

39. P. Borgwardt. Parallel Prolog using Stack Segments on Shared Memoty Multiprocessors. *1984 International Symposium on Logic Programming*, IEEE-CS, February 1984, pp. 2–11.

40. D.S. Warren. Efficient Prolog Memory Management for flexible control strategies. *New Genera. Comput.*, **2**:361–369 (1984).

41. P. Tinker and G. Lindstrom. A Performance Oriented Design for OR-Parallel Logic Programming. *Fourth International Conference on Logic Programming*, MIT Press, May 1987, pp. 601–615. Nelbourne, Australia.

42. B. Hausman, A. Ciepielewski, and S. Haridi. OR-Parallel Prolog Made Efficient on Shared Memory Multiprocessor. *1987 Symposium on Logic Programming*, IEEE Computer Society Press, September 1987, pp. 69–79.

43. T. Disz, E. Lusk, and R. Overbeek. Experiments with OR-parallel logic programs. In J.-L. Lassez, ed., *Proceedings of the Fourth International Conference on Logic Programming (ICLP '87)*, MIT Press, Melbourne, Australia, May 1987, pp. 576–600.

44. G. Lindstrom. Or-parallelism on applicative architectures. In S.-Å. Tärnlund, ed., *Proceedings of the Second International Conference on Logic Programming*, Uppsala, 1984, pp. 159–170.

45. J.S. Conery. Binding Environments for Parallel Logic Programs in Non-Shared Memory Multiprocessors. *1987 Symposium on Logic Programming*, IEEE Computer Society Press, September 1987, pp. 457–467.

46. K.A.M. Ali and R. Karlsson. The MUSE Approach to OR-parallel Prolog. *Int. J. Parallel Prog.*, 19(2):129–162 (1990).

47. K. Kumon, H. Masuzawa, and A. Itashiki. Kabu-wake: A new parallel inference method and its evaluation. *Proceedings of the IEEE COMPCON 86*, San Francisco, March 1986, pp. 168–172. IEEE CS Press, NY.

48. W.R. Clocksin and H. Alshawi. A method for efficiently executing horn clause programs using multiple processors. Technical report, Department of Computer Science Cambridge University, Cambridge, 1986.

49. H. Alshawi and D.B. Moran. The delphi model and some preliminary experiments. In R.A. Kowalski and K.A. Bowen, eds., *Proceedings of the Fifth International Conference and Symposium on Logic Programming*, Seatle, ALP, IEEE, The MIT Press, 1988, pp. 1578–1589.

50. G. Gupta and E. Pontelli. Stack-splitting: OR-/AND-parallelism on distributed memory machines. *Proceedings of the 1999 International Conference on Logic Programming*, Massachusetts Institute of Technology, Cambridge, MA, 1999, pp. 290–304.

51. J.S. Conery and D.F. Kibler. AND Parallelism in Logic Programs. *8th International Joint Conference on Artificial Intelligence*, August 1983.

52. G. Gupta, E. Pontelli, K.A.M. Ali, M. Carlsson, and M.V. Hermenegildo. Parallel execution of prolog programs: a survey. *ACM Trans. Program. Lang. Syst.*, **23**(4):472–602 (2001).

53. J.-H. Chang. High performance execution of prolog programs based on a static data dependence analysis. Technical Report CSD 86/263, University of California, Berkeley, 1985.

54. D. DeGroot. Restricted and-parallelism. *Proceedings of Int. Conference on Fifth Generation Computer Systems 1984*, North-Holland and OHMSHA, November 1984, pp. 471–478. Tokyo, Japan.

55. M.V. Hermenegildo. An abstract machine for restricted AND-parallel execution of logic programs. In E. Shapiro, ed., *Proceedings of the Third International Conference on Logic Programming*, Lecture Notes in Computer Science, Springer-Verlag, London, 1996, pp. 25–39.

56. E. Pontelli, G. Gupta, and M. Hermenegildo. &ACE: A highperformance parallel prolog system. *Proceedings of the 9th International Symposium on Parallel Processing (IPPS'95*, IEEE Computer Society Press, Los Alamitos, CA, April 1995, pp. 564–571.

57. M.V. Hermenegildo and K.J. Greene. &-Prolog and its performance: Exploiting independent And-Parallelism. In D.H.D. Warren and P. Szeredi, eds., *Proceedings of the Seventh International Conference on Logic Programming*, The MIT Press, Jerusalem, 1990, pp. 253–268.

58. L.V. Kalé and B. Ramkumar. The Reduce-OR Process Model for Parallel Logic Programming on Non-shared Memory Machines. In P. Kacsuk and M.J. Wise, eds., *Implementations of Distributed Prolog*, John Wiley & Sons, New York, 1992. Chapt. 9.

59. K. Shen. Exploiting Dependent And-Parallelism in Prolog. The Dynamic Dependent And-Parallel scheme (DDAS). In K. Apt, ed., *Proceedings of the Joint International Conference and Symposium on Logic Programming*, The MIT Press, Washington, 1992, pp. 717–731.

60. K. Clark and S. Gregory. PARLOG: Parallel programming in logic. *TOPLAS*, **8**(1):1 (Jan. 1986).

61. E.Y. Shapiro. A subset of concurrent prolog and its interpreter. TR 003, ICOT, Institute for New Generation Computer Technology, Tokyo, Japan, January 1983.

62. K. Ueda. Guarded horn clauses. In E. Wada, ed., *Logic Programming conference*, number 221 in LNCS, Springer-Verlag, 1986, pp. 168–179. Tokyo, Japan.

63. K. Hirata *et al.* Parallel and Distributed Implementation of Concurrent Logic Programming Language KL1. *FGCS*, 1992, pp. 436–459.

64. J. Chassin, H. Westphal, P. Robert and J. Syre. The PEPSys model: Combining backtracking, AND- and OR- parallelism. *Proceedings of the Fifth International Conference and Symposium on Logic Programming*, IEEE, Computer Society Press, San Francisco, August–September 1987, pp. 436–448.

65. U. Baron *et al.* The parallel ECRC prolog system PEPSys: An overview and evaluation results. Institute for New Generation Computer Technology (ICOT), editor, *Proceedings of the International Conference on Fifth Generation Computer Systems.* Vol. 3, Springer-Verlag, Berlin, FRG, November 28–December 2 1988, pp. 841–850.

66. L.V. Kalé. The REDUCE-OR process model for parallel evaluation of logic programs. In J.-L. Lassez, ed., *Proceedings of the Fourth International Conference on Logic Programming (ICLP '87)*, MIT Press, Melbourne, Australia, May 1987, pp. 616–632.

67. G. Gupta. *Parallel Execution of Logic Programs on Shared memory Multiprocessors.* Ph.D. thesis, University of North Carolina at Chapel Hill, 1991.

68. G. Gupta and B. Jayaraman. And-or parallelism on sharedmemory multiprocessors. *J. Logic Prog.*, **17**(1):59–8 (Oct. 1993).

69. G. Gupta, Vítor Santos Costa, Rong Yang, and Manuel V. Hermenegildo. IDIOM: Integrating dependent And-, independent And-, and Or-parallelism. In V. Saraswat and K. Ueda, eds., *Logic Programming, Proceedings of the 1991 International Symposium,* The MIT Press, San Diego, 1991, pp. 152–166.

70. G. Gupta, Manuel Hermenegildo, Enrico Pontelli, and Vítor Santos Costa. ACE: And/Or-parallel Copying-based Execution of logic programs. In P. Van Hentenryck, ed., *Logic Programming—Proceedings of the Eleventh International Conference on Logic Programming,* Massachusetts Institute of Technology, The MIT Press, 1994, pp. 93–109. Samta Nargherita Ligure, Italy.

71. J. Chassin de Kergommeaux and P. Codognet. Parallel logic programming systems. *ACM Comput. Surv.*, **26**(3):295–336 (1994).

72. D.H.D. Warren. The Andorra Principle. *GigaLips Workshop*, 1987.

73. V.S. Costa, D.H.D. Warren, and R. Yang. The andorra-I engine: A parallel implementation of the basic andorra model. In K. Furukawa, ed., *Proceedings of the 8th International Conference on Logic Programming*, MIT, June 1991, pp. 825–839.

74. R. Yang, T. Beaumont, I. Dutra, V. Santos Costa, and D.H.D. Warren. Performance of the compiler-based Andorra-I System. D.S. Warren, ed., *Proceedings of the Tenth International Conference on Logic Programming,* The MIT Press, Budapest, Hungary, 1993, pp. 150–166.

75. R. Bahgat and S. Gregory. Pandora: Non-deterministic Parallel Logic Programming. In G. Levi and M. Martelli, eds., *Proceedings of the Sixth International Conference on Logic Programming,* The MIT Press, pp. 471–486 1989. Lisbon, Porlügal.

76. R. Lopes, V.S. Costa, and F.M.A. Silva. A novel implementation of the extended andorra model. *PADL '01: Proceedings of the Third International Symposium on Practical Aspects of Declarative Languages,* Springer-Verlag, London, 2001, pp. 199–213.

77. R. Lopes, V.S. Costa, and F.M.A. Silva. On the beam implementation. In F. Moura-Pires and S. Abreu, eds., *Progress in Artificial Intelligence, 11th Protuguese Conference on Artificial Intelligence, EPIA 2003, Beja, Portugal, December 4–7, 2003, Proceedings*, Vol. 2902 of *Lecture Notes in Computer Science*, Springer, 2003, pp. 131–135.

78. S. Haridi and S. Janson. Kernel andorra Prolog and its computation model. In D.H.D. Warren and P. Szeredi, eds., *Proceedings of the Seventh International Conference on Logic Programming*, The MIT Press, Jerusalem, 1990, pp. 31–46.

79. R. Moolenaar and B. Demoen. A Parallel Implementation for AKL. In M. Bruynooghe and J. Penjam, eds., *Proceedings of Programming Language Implementation and Logic Programming, 5th International Symposium*, number 714 in LNCS, Springer, 1993, pp. 246–261. Tallin, Estonia.

80. F. Bueno and M.V. Hermenegildo. An Automatic Translation Scheme from Prolog to the Andorra Kernel Language. ICOT Staff, editor, *Proceedings of International Conference on Fifth Generation Computer Systems 92*, IOS Press, June 1992, pp. 759–769, Tokyo, Japan.

81. J. Montelius and S. Haridi. An evaluation of penny: a system for fine grain implicit parallelism. *PASCO '97: Proceedings of the second international symposium on Parallel symbolic computation*, ACM Press, New York, 1997, pp. 46–57.

82. P. Van Hentenryck. Parallel constraint satisfaction in logic programming: Preliminary results of chip within pepsys. *ICLP*, 1989, pp. 165–180.

83. M. Dorochevsky, Liang-Liang Li, M. Reeve, K. Schuerman, and A. Veron. ElipSys: a parallel programming system based on logic. In A. Voronkov, ed., *Logic programming and automated reasoning: international conference, LPAR '92, St. Petersburg, Russia, July 15–20, 1992: proceedings*, volume 624 of *Lecture Notes in Artificial Intelligence and Lecture Notes in Computer Science*, Springer Verlag, Berlin, Germany / Heidelberg, Germany / London, UK / etc., 1992, pp. 469–471.

84. S.A. Delgado-Rannauro, M. Dorochevsky, K. Schuerman, A. Veron, and J. Xu. ElipSys: An integrated platform for building large decision support systems. Technical Report ECRC-DPS-104, ECRC, January 1991.

85. S. Prestwich. Elipsys programming tutorial. Technical Report ECRC-93-2, ECRC, 1993.

86. L.-L. Li *et al.* Applause: applications using the elipsys parallel clp system. In *ICLP'93: Proceedings of the tenth international conference on logic programming on Logic programming*, MIT Press, 1993, pp. 847–848. Budapest, Hungary.

87. A. Herold. The handbook of parallel constraint logic programming applications. Technical Report, ECRC, 1995.

88. S. Mudambi and J. Schimpf. Parallel CLP on Heterogeneous Networks. In P. Van Hentenryck, ed., *Logic Programming—Proceedings of the Eleventh International Conference on Logic Programming*, MIT, The MIT Press, 1994, pp. 124–141. Santa Nargheuta Ligure, Italy.

89. B.-M. Tong and H.-F. Leung. Data-parallel concurrent constraint programming. *J. Logic Prog.*, **35**:103–150 (1998).

90. V.A. Saraswat and M. Rinard. Concurrent constraint programming. *POPL '90: Proceedings of the 17th ACM SIGPLAN-SIGACT symposium on Principles of programming languages*, ACM Press, New York, 1990, pp. 232–245.

91. M. Garcia de la Banda, M. Hermenegildo, and K. Marriott. Independence in Constraint Logic Programs. *ILPS '93: Proceedings of the 1993 International Symposium on Logic Programming*, MIT Press, 1993, pp. 130–146. Vancouver, Canada.

92. M. Garcia de la Banda, F. Bueno, and M.V. Hermenegildo. Towards Independent And-Parallelism in CLP. *PLILP '96: Proceedings of the 8th International Symposium on Programming Languages: Implementations, Logics, and Programs*, Springer-Verlag, 1996, pp. 77–91.

93. S. Terasaki *et al.* Parallel Constraint Logic Programming Language GDCC and its Parallel Constraint Solvers. In *FGCS*, 1992, pp. 330–346.

94. S. Gregory and R. Yang. Parallel constraint solving in andorra-i. In *FGCS*, 1992, pp. 843–850. Tokyo, Japan.

95. P. Van Roy *et al.* Logic programming in the context of multiparadigm programming: the Oz experience. *Theo. Pract. Logic Prog.*, **3**(6):715–763 (2003).

96. P. Van Roy and S. Haridi. Mozart: A programming system for agent applications. *International Workshop on Distributed and Internet Programming with Logic and Constraint Languages*, November 1999. Part of International Conference on Logic Programming (ICLP 99).

97. S. Haridi, P. Van Roy, and G. Smolka. An overview of the design of Distributed Oz. *Proceedings of the Second International Symposium on Parallel Symbolic Computation (PASCO '97)*, ACM Press, Maui, Hawaii, July 1997, pp. 176–187.

98. G. Smolka. The Oz programming model. In J. van Leeuwen, ed., *Computer Science Today*, Lecture Notes in Computer Science, Vol. 1000, Springer-Verlag, Berlin, 1995, pp. 324–343.

99. P. Van Roy and S. Haridi. *Concepts, Techniques, and Models of Computer Programming*. MIT Press, March 2004.

100. C. Schulte. *Programming Constraint Services*, volume 2302 of *Lecture Notes in Artificial Intelligence*. Springer-Verlag, Berlin, Germany, 2002.

101. M. Hermenegildo *et al.* The CIAO Multi-Dialect Compiler and System: An Experimentation Workbench for Future (C)LP Systems. In I. de Castro Dutra *et al.* eds., *Parallelism and Implementation of Logic and Constraint Logic Programming*, Nova Science, April 1999, pp. 65–85. Las Cruces, USA.

102. D. Cabeza and M. Hermenegildo. Distributed Concurrent Constraint Execution in the CIAO System. *Proceedings of the 1995 COMPULOGNET Workshop on Parallelism and Implementation Technologies, U. Utrecht / T.U. Madrid*, September 1995.

103. M.V. Hermenegildo. Some Methodological Issues in the Design of CIAO, a Generic, Parallel Concurrent Constraint Logic Programming System. In A. Borning, ed., *Proceedings of Principles and Practice of Constraint Programming, Second International Workshop, PPCP'94*, volume 874 of *Lecture Notes in Computer Science*, Springer, 1994, pp. 123–133. Sealtle, USA.

104. E. Pontelli, G. Gupta, D. Tang, M. Carro, and M.V. Hermenegildo. Improving the Efficiency of Nondeterministic Independent AND-Parallel Systems. *Comput. Lang.*, **22**(2–3):115–142 (1996).

105. M. Hermenegildo, D. Cabeza, and M. Carro. Using Attributed Variables in the Implementation of Concurrent and Parallel Logic Programming Systems. In

L. Sterling, ed., *Proceedings of the 12th International Conference on Logic Programming*, MIT Press, Cambridge, June 13–18, 1995, pp. 631–646.

106. D. Cabeza and M.V. Hermenegildo. Implementing Distributed Concurrent Constraint Execution in the CIAO System. In P. Lucio, M. Martelli, and M. Navarro, eds., *1996 Joint Conference on Declarative Programming, APPIA-GULP-PRODE'96*, 1996, pp. 67–78.

107. M. Hermenegildo, G. Puebla, F. Bueno, and P. López-Garcia. Program Development Using Abstract Interpretation (and The Ciao System Preprocessor). *10th International Static Analysis Symposium (SAS'03)*, number 2694 in LNCS, Springer-Verlag, June 2003, pp. 127–152.

108. I.P. Vlahavas, I. Sakellariou, I. Futo, Z. Pasztor, and J. Szeredi. CSPCONS: A Communicating Sequential Prolog with constraints. *Methods and Applications of Artificial Intelligence, Procs of the 2nd Hellenic Conference on AI, SETN 2002*, volume 2308 of *Lecture Notes in Computer Science*, Springer, 2002, pp. 72–84.

109. I. Sakellariou, I. Vlahavas, I. Futo, Z. Pasztor, and J. Szeredi. Communicating Sequential Processes for Distributed Constraint Satisfaction. *Infor. Sci.*, 2006, **76**(5):490–521.

110. I. Futo. Prolog with Communicating Processes: From T-Prolog to CSR-Prolog. In D.S. Warren, ed., *Proceedings of the 10th International Conference on Logic Programming*, The MIT Press, 1993, pp. 3–17. Budapest, Hungary.

111. I. Futo. A Distributed Network Prolog System. *Proceedings of the 20th International Conference on Information Technology Interfaces, ITI 99*, 1998, pp. 613–618.

112. C.A.R. Hoare. Communicating Sequential Processes. *Commun. ACM*, **21**(8):666–677 (Aug. 1978).

CHAPTER 12

Applications of Parallel Metaheuristics to Optimization Problems in Telecommunications and Bioinformatics

S. L. MARTINS, C. C. RIBEIRO, and I. ROSSETI

Universidade Federal Fluminense
Departamento de Ciência da Computação
Niteró, RJ 22410-240, Brazil

12.1. INTRODUCTION

Recent years have witnessed huge advances in areas, such as computer technology, communication networks, biology, and genetics. Many hard optimization problems in network design and routing are related with new applications and technologies, such as cellular mobile radio systems and optical fibers. The research in genomics pushed the need for solving optimization and graph problems in biology.

Combinatorial optimization problems in telecommunications and other areas involve finding optimal solutions from a discrete set of feasible solutions. However, even with the advent of new computer technologies and parallel processing, many of these problems could not be solved to optimality in reasonable computation times, due to their inner nature or to their size. Moreover, reaching optimal solutions is meaningless in many practical situations, since often we are dealing with rough simplifications of reality and the available data is not precise. The goal of approximate algorithms (or heuristics) is to quickly produce good approximate solutions, without necessarily providing any guarantee of solution quality.

Metaheuristics are general high-level procedures that coordinate simple heuristics and rules to find good (often optimal) approximate solutions to

Parallel Combinatorial Optimization, edited by El-Ghazali Talbi

computationally difficult combinatorial optimization problems. Among them, are simulated annealing, tabu search, Greedy Randomized Adaptive Search Procedure (GRASP), genetic algorithms, scatter search, Vanialde Neighborhood Search (VNS), ant colonies, and others. They are based on distinct paradigms and offer different mechanisms to escape from locally optimal solutions, contrarily to greedy algorithms or local search methods. Metaheuristics are among the most effective solution strategies for solving combinatorial optimization problems in practice and they have been applied to a very large variety of areas and situations. The customization (or instantiation) of a metaheuristic to a given problem yields a heuristic to the latter.

Metaheuristics offer a wide range of possibilities for effective parallel algorithms running in much smaller computation times, but requiring efficient implementations. Cung *et al.* (1) showed that parallel implementations of metaheuristics appear quite naturally as an effective approach to speedup the search for good solutions to optimization problems. They allow solving larger problems and finding better solutions with respect to their sequential counterparts. They also lead to more robust algorithms and this is often reported as the main advantage obtained with parallel implementations of metaheuristics: they are less-dependent on parameter tuning and their success is not limited to few or small classes of problems.

Parallel implementations of metaheuristics and their applications to problems in telecommunications, network design and routing, and bioinformatics are studied in this chapter. Section 12.2 summarizes the main issues on parallelization strategies of metaheuristics. Section 12.3 reviews the main principles and ideas involved in parallelizing algorithms derived from four widely and successfully used metaheuristics: GRASP, simulated annealing, genetic algorithms, and tabu search. Case studies regarding applications of parallel metaheuristics to some problems in telecommunications and bioinformatics are presented in detail in Section 12.4. Applications of metaheuristics to problems in telecommunications and bioinformatics are listed and reviewed in Section 12.5.

12.2. PARALLELIZATION STRATEGIES

Even though parallelism is not yet systematically used to speed up or to improve the effectiveness of metaheuristics, parallel implementations abound in the literature. Parallelization strategies considerably differ from one technique to another. An architecture-independent classification of parallelization strategies considering the underlying parallel local search strategy, inspired from that proposed in (2) was proposed by Cung *et al.* (1).

Metaheuristics based on local search may be seen as the exploration of the *neighborhood graph* (or state space graph) associated with a problem instance, in which nodes correspond to solutions and edges connect neighbor solutions. Each iteration consists basically in the evaluation of the solutions in the neighborhood of the current solution, followed by a move toward one of them, avoiding as much as possible to prematurely stop in a local optimum and until no further improvement of the best known solution can be achieved. The solutions visited along the search define a *walk* (or a *trajectory*) in the neighborhood graph. Parallel implementations of metaheuristics use several processors to concurrently generate or explore the neighborhood graph. Since this graph is not known beforehand, parallelizations of metaheuristics are *irregular applications*, whose efficiency strongly depends on the appropriate choice of the granularity of the algorithm and on the use of load balancing techniques.

We distinguish between two approaches for the parallelization of the local search, according with the number of trajectories investigated in the neighborhood graph:

1. Single walk: fine-to-medium grained tasks.
2. Multiple walks: medium-to-coarse grained tasks.
   a. Independent search threads.
   b. Cooperative search threads.

In the case of a *single-walk parallelization*, one unique trajectory is traversed in the neighborhood graph. The search for the best neighbor at each iteration is performed in parallel, either by the parallelization of the cost function evaluation or by domain decomposition (the neighborhood evaluation or the problem instance itself are decomposed and distributed over different processors). The goal of this strategy is basically to speed up the sequential traversal of the neighborhood graph. The task whose execution is distributed among the processors may be the evaluation of the cost function at each neighbor of the current solution or the construction of the neighborhood itself. In the first case, speedups may be obtained without any modification in the trajectory followed by the sequential implementation. In the second case, the neighborhood decomposition and its distribution over several processors often allow more deeply examining a larger portion of the neighborhood than that examined by a sequential implementation, which often uses neighborhood reduction techniques. Thus, the trajectory followed in the neighborhood graph may be better guided in parallel than in sequential mode, possibly leading to improved solutions. Single-walk parallelizations have small or medium granularity and need frequent synchronizations.

A *multiple-walk parallelization* is characterized by the investigation in parallel of multiple trajectories, each of which by a different processor. We call by a *search thread* the process running in each processor traversing a walk in the neighborhood graph. These threads can be either *independent* (the search threads do not exchange any information they collect) or *cooperative* (the information collected along each trajectory is disseminated and used by the other threads).

When using independent search threads, we distinguish between two basic approaches:

- Exploration in parallel of multiple trajectories originating from different nodes of the neighborhood graph: Each walk starts from a different solution. The search threads may use the same local search algorithm or different ones, with the same parameter values or not. The trajectories may intersect at one or more nodes of the neighborhood graph. If p processors are used, this strategy corresponds to the successive execution of p sequential independent searches.
- Exploration in parallel of subgraphs of the neighborhood graph, obtained by problem decomposition (e.g., by variable fixation): Several subgraphs of the neighborhood graph are explored in parallel, without intersection of the corresponding trajectories. We have a total and permanent decomposition of the neighborhood graph formed by complete solutions.

Cooperative strategies are the most general and promising, demanding more programming efforts and implementation skills. The search threads exchange and share information collected along the trajectories they investigate. This shared information is implemented either as global variables stored in a shared memory, or as a pool in the local memory of a dedicated central processor that can be accessed by all other processors. In this model, in which the search threads cooperate and the information collected along each trajectory is used to improve the other trajectories, one expects not only to speed up the convergence to the best solution but, also, to find better solutions than independent-thread strategies within the same computation time. The most difficult aspect to be set up is the determination of the nature of the information to be shared or exchanged to improve the search, without taking too much additional memory or time to be collected. We may cite elite solutions and their costs, best solutions found, move frequencies, and tabu lists, among others.

Toulouse *et al.* (3) attempted to show how this cooperation behaves by modeling cooperative procedures as discrete-time dynamical systems. They performed simulations describing different cooperative procedures with the same sequential programs, initial conditions, and parameter values, which exhibit completely different search patterns under the influence of systemic cooperations.

12.3. PARALLELIZATION OF METAHEURISTICS

This section reviews the main principles and ideas involved in parallelizing algorithms derived from four widely and successfully used metaheuristics: GRASP, simulated annealing, genetic algorithms and tabu search. The reader is referred, for example, to Ref. 1, for a more comprehensive overview of parallel algorithms based on metaheuristics.

12.3.1. GRASP

A greedy randomized adaptive search procedure (GRASP) (4,5) is a multi-start algorithm, in which each iteration consists of two phases. In a construction phase, a feasible solution is iteratively constructed, one element at a time, by a greedy randomized procedure. Next, in a local search phase, a local optimum in the neighborhood of the constructed solution is sought. The best solution over all iterations is kept as the result.

Most parallel implementations of GRASP are independent-thread multiple-walk strategies (6–11), based on the distribution of the iterations over the processors. In general, each search thread has to perform Max_Iterations/p iterations, where p and Max_Iterations are, respectively, the number of processors and the total number of iterations. Each processor has a copy of the sequential algorithm and a copy of the problem data. One of the processors acts as the master, reading and distributing problem data, generating the seeds that will be used by the pseudorandom number generators at each processor, distributing the iterations, and collecting the best solution found by each processor.

Path-relinking is often used in the implementation of cooperative strategies (13). Computational results illustrate the effectiveness of path-relinking procedures used in conjunction with GRASP to improve the quality of the solutions found by the latter.

12.3.2. Simulated Annealing

Simulated annealing in the context of optimization methods was introduced by Kirkpatrick *et al.* (14). As the first metaheuristic to be parallelized, several papers describing parallelization efforts appeared subsequently (15–21).

Most of the first parallelizations (22,23) followed the single-walk strategy and were based on the ideas of *move acceleration* and *parallel moves*. In the first case, each move is evaluated by breaking it up into several subtasks executed in parallel: selection of a feasible move, evaluation of the associated cost change, acceptance or rejection of the move, and global information update.

In the case of parallel moves (16,21–26), each processor generates, evaluates, and accepts a different move. Synchronization can be done after only one or after several steps. Other coarse-grained parallelizations (18,27) of simulated annealing are based on the use of multiple Markov chains, which is equivalent to the multiple-walk strategy. The readers are also referred to Refs. 28–30 for other surveys about parallel simulated annealing and its hybrids.

12.3.3. Genetic Algorithms

A genetic algorithm is a basic search procedure, proposed and developed by Holland (31,32). It is based on the process of natural evolution, following the principles of natural selection and survival of the fittest (33,34). First, a population of individuals (solutions) is created. Each individual is evaluated according to a fitness function. Individuals with higher evaluations (i.e., more fitted) are selected to generate a new generation of this population. Crossover is a genetic operation that combines parts from pairs of individuals to generate new ones. Mutation is a unary genetic transformation that creates a new individual by small changes applied to an existing one. New individuals created by crossover or mutation replace all or part of the initial population. The process of evaluating fitness and creating a new population generation is repeated until a termination criterion is achieved.

Many different approaches to the parallelization of genetic algorithms can be found in the literature and they differ in many aspects. Basically, there are three types of parallelization strategies (35–38): global (single-walk parallelization), diffusion model, and island model. Fine- (diffusion model) and coarse-grained (island model) parallelizations characterize cooperative multiple-walk strategies.

Global (single-walk) parallelization strategies (39–41) manipulate a single population, but the individuals are distributed among several processors for fitness evaluation. The trajectory followed by the parallel implementation is the same followed by the sequential algorithm. Almost-linear speedups may be obtained whenever the evaluation of the objective function is significantly more computationally expensive than the other steps (i.e., the genetic operators) of the algorithm.

Fine-grained parallelizations (38,42,43) using the *diffusion model* are developed to take advantage of massively parallel computers. The population is divided into many small subpopulations, usually formed by a single individual. Each subpopulation is mapped onto the processing elements. Selection and mating are only possible within a small, restricted neighborhood defined by the topology of the massively parallel computer. The use of local selection and reproduction rules leads to a continuous diffusion of individuals over the population (38).

Coarse-grained or *island model* algorithms (35,44–49) are currently the most used strategies. They are based on dividing the population into few subpopulations. Each subpopulation is assigned to a different processor, which performs a sequential genetic algorithm starting from this subpopulation. Mating involves only individuals within the same subpopulation. Occasionally, the processors exchange individuals through a migration operator. Some important technical issues influence the implementation of this strategy, such as the size of the subpopulations, the topology of the interprocessor connection network that defines the exchange of individuals, and the migration rate (i.e., the number of individuals to be exchanged during a migration phase and the frequency in which migration takes place).

12.3.4. Tabu Search

Tabu search is an adaptive procedure for solving combinatorial optimization problems, which guides an improvement heuristic to continue exploration without being confounded by an absence of improving moves (see, e.g., Refs. 50–52). Tabu search goes beyond local search by employing a memory-based strategy for modifying the neighborhood of the current solution as the search progresses. Depending on the search stage, this modified neighborhood may be an extension or a restriction of the regular one. As a consequence, and contrary to the basic local search scheme, moves toward solutions that deteriorate the cost function are permitted under certain conditions.

Single-walk parallelization has been the first strategy applied to tabu search methods (29), aiming to accelerate the search in the neighborhood. Most of these implementations use a master–worker paradigm. The master process executes a sequential tabu procedure and, at each iteration, asks the workers to evaluate the possible moves in the neighborhood of the current solution. Usually, workers may perform this evaluation by two variants: slaves evaluate candidate moves only or they also perform a few local search iterations. The master receives and process the information obtained from workers and then selects and implements the next move.

Some implementations of tabu search based on neighborhood decomposition are reported in Refs. 53–62 and show very good results, specially when neighborhoods are very large and the time to evaluate and perform a move is relatively small. Almost all the time near linear speed-ups are achieved. This type of parallelization depends heavily upon the problem characteristics. The results are not so good, when the time required for one sequential iteration is relatively large compared to the total solution time (63).

Other implementations (64,65) combine single- and multiple-walk strategies. First, a master processor distributes the problem data to slaves running initialization processes. Each of these slave processors builds a different initial solution and returns it to the master. The master combines the solutions it received, to generate a unique initial solution which is decomposed into several subproblems that are sent to the slaves. Each subproblem is solved by variants of the same sequential tabu search algorithm by the slaves and the solutions generated by them are sent to the master. These solutions are combined by the master to obtain an improved solution. A new iteration of this procedure resumes, until some stopping criterion is attained.

Multiple-walk implementations using independent search threads can be found in Refs. 66–69. Each thread starts from possibly different initial solutions and use diverse tabu search strategies. The experimental results show that this kind of implementation leads to very efficient and robust heuristics.

Cooperative multiple-walk implementations (70–73) are among the most promising tabu search parallelization strategies, due to their effectiveness and robustness. In most implementations, the processors start from different initial solutions and their searches follow paths generated by different sequential tabu search algorithms. Communication is performed through a central pool of elite solutions.

12.4. CASE STUDIES IN NETWORK DESIGN AND BIOINFORMATICS PROBLEMS

This section describes in detail some parallel implementations of the metaheuristics described in the previous section to optimization problems in network design and bioinformatics.

12.4.1. Parallel GRASP for 2-Path Network Design

12.4.1.1. Problem Formulation. Let $G = (V,E)$ be a connected graph, where V is the set of nodes and E is the set of edges. A k-path between nodes $s, t \in V$ is a sequence of at most k edges connecting them. Given a non-negative weight function $w : E \to R_+$ associated with the edges of G and a set D of pairs of origin-destination nodes, the 2-path network design problem (2PNDP) consists of finding a minimum weighted subset of edges $E' \subseteq E$ containing a 2-path between every origin–destination pair.

Applications of 2PNDP can be found in the design of communications networks, in which paths with few edges are sought to enforce high reliability and small delays. 2PNDP was shown to be NP-hard by Dahl and Johannessen (74).

12.4.1.2. GRASP Construction. The construction of a new solution begins by the initialization of modified edge weights with the original edge weights. Each iteration of the construction phase starts by the random selection of an origin–destination pair still in D. A shortest 2-path between the extremities of this pair is computed, using the modified edge weights. The weights of the edges in this 2-path are set to zero until the end of the construction procedure, the origin–destination pair is removed from D, and a new iteration resumes. The construction phase stops when 2-paths have been computed for all origin–destination pairs.

12.4.1.3. Local Search. The local search phase seeks to improve each solution built in the construction phase. Each solution may be viewed as a set of 2-paths, one for each origin–destination pair in D. To introduce some diversity by driving different applications of the local search to different local optima, the origin–destination pairs are investigated at each GRASP iteration in a circular order defined by a different random permutation of their original indices.

Each 2-path in the current solution is tentatively eliminated. The weights of the edges used by other 2-paths are temporarily set to zero, while those which are not used by other 2-paths in the current solution are restored to their original values. A new shortest 2-path between the extremities of the origin–destination pair under investigation is computed, using the modified weights. If the new 2-path improves the current solution, then the latter is modified; otherwise the previous 2-path is restored. The search stops if the current solution was not improved after a sequence of $|D|$ iterations along which all

2-paths have been investigated. Otherwise, the next 2-path in the current solution is investigated for substitution and a new iteration resumes.

12.4.1.4. Path-Relinking.

A solution to 2PNDP is represented as a set of 2-paths connecting each origin–destination pair. Path-relinking starts by determining all origin–destination pairs whose associated 2-paths are different in the starting and guiding solutions. These computations amount to determining a set of moves that should be applied to the initial solution to reach the guiding one. Each move is characterized by a pair of 2-paths, one to be inserted and the other to be eliminated from the current solution.

In the case of the independent-thread parallel implementation of GRASP with path-relinking for 2PNDP, each processor has a copy of the sequential algorithm, a copy of the data, and its own pool of elite solutions. One processor acts as the master, reading and distributing the problem data, generating the seeds that will be used by the pseudo-random number generators at each processor, distributing the iterations, and collecting the best solution found by each processor. All the p available processors perform GRASP iterations.

However, in the case of the cooperative-thread parallel implementation of GRASP with path-relinking for 2PNDP, the master handles a centralized pool of elite solutions, collecting and distributing them upon request. The $p - 1$ slaves exchange the elite solutions found along their search trajectories. In the proposed implementation for 2PNDP, each slave may send up to three different solutions to the master at each iteration: the solution obtained by local search, and the solutions w^1 and w^2 obtained by forward and backward path-relinking (13) between the same pair of starting and guiding solutions, respectively.

12.4.1.5. Computational Results.

The results illustrated in this section concern an instance with 100 nodes, 4950 edges, and 1000 origin–destination pairs. The methodology proposed in Ref. 75 is used to assess experimentally the behavior of randomized algorithms. This approach is based on plots showing empirical distributions of the random variable *time-to-target solution value*. To plot the empirical distribution, a solution target value is fixed and each algorithm executes 200 times, recording the running time when a solution with cost at least as good as the target value is found. For each algorithm, the i th sorted running time t_i is associated with a probability $p_i = (i - \frac{1}{2})/200$ and the points $z_i = (t_i, p_i)$, for $i = 1, \cdots, 200$ are plotted.

Results obtained for both the independent-thread and the cooperative-thread parallel implementations of GRASP with path-relinking on the above instance with the target value set at 683 are reported in Fig. 12.1. The cooperative implementation is already faster than the independent one for eight processors. For fewer processors, the independent implementation is naturally faster, since it employs all p processors in the search (while only $p - 1$ slave processors take part effectively in the computations performed by the cooperative implementation).

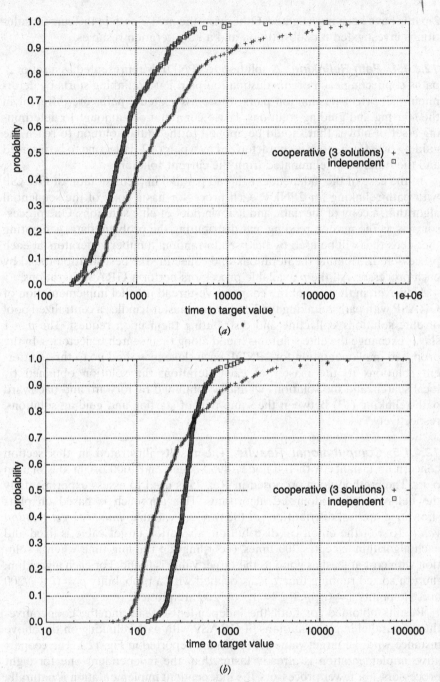

Fig. 12.1. Running times for 200 runs of the multiple-walk independent-thread and the multiple-walk cooperative-thread implementations of GRASP with path-relinking using (*a*) two processors and (*b*) eight processors, with the target solution value set at 683.

Three different strategies were investigated to further improve the performance of the cooperative-thread implementation, by reducing the cost of the communication between the master and the slaves when the number of processors increases:

1. Each send operation is broken in two parts. First, the slave sends only the cost of the solution to the master. If this solution is better than the worst solution in the pool, then the full solution is sent. The number of messages increases, but most of them will be very small ones with light memory requirements.
2. Only one solution is sent to the pool at each GRASP iteration.
3. A distributed implementation, in which each slave handles its own pool of elite solutions. Every time a processor finds a new elite solution, the latter is broadcast to the others.

Comparative results for these three strategies on the same problem instance are plotted in Fig. 12.2. The first strategy outperformed all others.

Table 12.1 shows the average computation times and the best solutions found over 10 runs of each strategy when the total number of GRASP iterations is set at 3200. There is a clear degradation in solution quality for the independent-thread strategy when the number of processors increases. As fewer iterations are performed by each processor, the pool of elite solutions

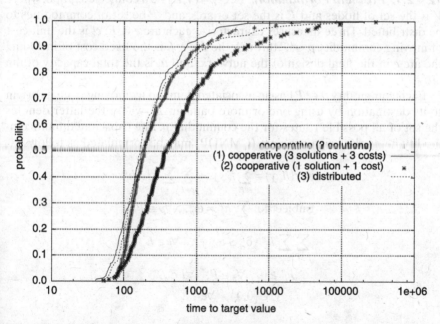

Fig. 12.2. Strategies for improving the performance of the centralized multiple-walk cooperative-thread implementation on eight processors.

TABLE 12.1. Average Times and Best Solutions Over 10 Runs for 2PNDP

Processors	Independent		Cooperative	
	Best Value	Avg. Time, s	Best Value	Avg. Time, s
1	673	1310.1		
2	676	686.8	676	1380.9
4	680	332.7	673	464.1
8	687	164.1	676	200.9
16	692	81.7	674	97.5
32	702	41.3	678	74.6

gets poorer with the increase in the number of processors. Since the processors do not communicate, the overall solution quality is worse. In the case of the cooperative strategy, the information shared by the processors guarantees the high quality of the solutions in the pool. The cooperative implementation is more robust. Very good solutions are obtained with no degradation in quality and significant speedups.

12.4.2. Parallel Tabu Search for Capacitated Network Design

12.4.2.1. Problem Formulation. Let $G = (V, E)$ be a connected graph, where V is the set of nodes and E is the set of arcs, and $\mathcal{P}$ be set of commodities to be distributed. Three measures characterize each arc $e \in E$: c_e^p is the unit cost of moving commodity $p \in \mathcal{P}$ through the arc e; f_e is the fixed cost of including the arc e in the final design of the network; and u_e is the total capacity of the arc e.

Each commodity $p \in \mathcal{P}$ has an associated demand w_p moving from its origin to its destination by using one or more paths in $\mathcal{L}^p$, where the latter denotes the set of all possible routes for the commodity p. The capacitated multicommodity network design problem (CMNDP) may be formulated as follows:

$$\min z(h, y) = \sum_{e \in E} f_e \cdot y_e + \sum_{p \in \mathcal{P}} \sum_{l \in \mathcal{L}^p} k_l^p \cdot h_l^p$$

$$\text{subject to: } \sum_{l \in \mathcal{L}^p} h_l^p = \omega_p, \quad \forall p \in \mathcal{P}$$

$$\sum_{p \in \mathcal{P}} \sum_{l \in \mathcal{L}^p} h_l^p \cdot \delta_{el}^p \le u_e \cdot y_e, \quad \forall e \in E$$

$$h_l^p \ge 0, \quad \forall_p \in \mathcal{P}, \quad \forall l \in \mathcal{L}^p$$

$$y_e \in \{0, 1\}, \quad \forall e \in E$$

where $\delta_{el}^p = 1$ if the arc e belongs to lth path for commodity p, $\delta_{el}^p = 0$ otherwise. The unit transportation cost of path $l \in \mathcal{L}^p$ is $k_l^p = \Sigma_{e \in E} c_e^p \cdot \delta_{el}^p$. $y_e = 1$ if the arc e

is included in the final design of the network, and $y_e = 0$ otherwise. h_l^p represents the flow of commodity $p \in \mathcal{P}$ on path $l \in \mathcal{L}^p$, and H is the set of all selected h_l^p of a solution.

Applications of CMNDP can be found in transportations, logistics, telecommunications, power system design, and production planning.

12.4.2.2. Sequential Tabu Search.
The sequential implementation is based on the exploration of the space of the extreme points of the polyhedron of the linear relaxation. To determine the neighbors solutions of any given solution, Crainic and Gendreau (71) used the revised pivoting rules of the simplex method (76).

An initial solution can be generated performing simplex pivots without the use of tabu mechanisms until a first feasible solution is obtained. The neighborhood of the current solution is defined as the subset of all extreme points that can be reached from this solution by one simplex pivot. The best element (e.g., the move with the largest decrease in the objective function) of this subset is selected. Nonimproving moves are accepted. Moves conducting to nonfeasible solutions are also accepted if they represent the best local option. The corresponding overflows are assigned to artificial arcs with arbitrarily high costs.

Since not all variables are available to the local search procedure at each iteration, column generation is used to expand the neighborhood and to enrich the set of candidates whenever a local optimum solution appears to have been reached. This condition is detected when the best solution identified during the current series of pivot moves, Z_{local}, did not improve for *max_move* consecutive moves. A modified shortest path algorithm is used to generate new paths. In this method, all saturated arcs are eliminated. To capture the interplay between the fixed costs and the capacities of the arcs, a relaxation of the formulation is used. A fixed number, *k_gen*, of paths is generated for all commodities each time the column generation procedure is executed.

Local search terminates when no improvement to the current local best solution is obtained after *max_col_gen* consecutive column generation cycles. The method stops or proceeds to diversify the search. A small number of arcs is selected for diversification. Paths containing these arcs are not allowed to enter the basis during their tabu tenure. These arcs are not available to be used during the column generation phase. The tabu tenure is defined in terms of a number of column generation cycles.

12.4.2.3. Parallel Implementations.
In the independent-thread parallel implementation of tabu search for CMNDP, each processor has a copy of the sequential tabu search algorithm and a copy of the data. One processor acts as the master, reading and distributing the problem data, and collecting the best solution found by each processor. All the p available processors perform the tabu search method.

In the case of the cooperative-thread parallel implementation of tabu search for CMNDP, the master handles a centralized pool of solutions, collecting and distributing them upon request. The $p - 1$ slaves exchange the solutions found along their search trajectories. Each slave executes the sequential tabu search procedure and sends its solution to the pool whenever it improves the local best solution (Z_{local}). Solutions are sent during regular local search phases, as well as immediately after a diversification move.

A solution is requested from the pool by a slave before a diversification operation. If the imported solution is better than the current best, then the latter is replaced by the former, and the diversification proceeds from the new solution. Otherwise, the imported solution is simply discarded, and the diversification proceeds as usual.

12.4.2.4. Computational Results. The implementation of the sequential tabu search heuristic was done in FORTRAN 77. The cooperation mechanisms are programmed in C. The parallel experiments have been performed on a cluster of SUN Ultra SPARC 1/140 workstations with a 143-MHz clock, 512 KB of cache memory, and 64 MB of RAM memory (3 out of the 16 processors had 128 MB of RAM memory). No other applications were running during the parallel experimentation.

A set of 10 instances was used in the experiments. These problems are identified with the letter C and a quintuple containing the number of nodes, the number of arcs, the number of commodities, an indicator showing whether the fixed costs are relatively high (F) or low (V), and another indicator showing if the problem is tightly (T) or somewhat loosely (L) capacitated.

The objective of the runs was to analyze the influence of the information exchanged among the processors in solution quality. Tables 12.2–12.4 display results obtained with 4, 8, and 16 processors, respectively. For each instance,

TABLE 12.2. Percentage Improvement in Solution Quality for Parallel Executions on 4 Processors

C	IND	SBest	SProb	SMobil	SHigh	SLow
(25,100,10,F,T)	0.46	0.46	1.87	1.87	0.61	0.46
(25,100,30,F,T)	0.00	−0.04	0.14	0.14	0.19	−0.17
(100,400,10,F,T)	1.50	0.52	1.77	1.77	1.50	1.50
(20,230,40,F,T)	0.13	0.02	0.00	0.00	0.00	0.02
(20,300,40,F,T)	0.16	0.00	0.16	0.16	0.16	0.00
(20,300,200,F,T)	5.08	8.01	7.74	7.38	5.50	5.31
(30,520,100,F,T)	4.03	2.41	3.13	3.13	3.13	3.13
(30,520,400,F,T)	1.37	1.44	1.08	2.12	1.03	1.36
(30,700,100,F,T)	1.17	1.65	1.31	1.17	1.17	1.31
(30,700,400,F,T)	2.77	2.00	1.70	1.70	0.55	0.54
Avg. Improvement	1.67	1.64	1.89	1.95	1.38	1.38

TABLE 12.3. Percentage Improvement in Solution Quality for Parallel Executions on 8 Processors

C	IND	SBest	SProb	SMobil	SHigh	SLow
(25,100,10,F,T)	0.46	0.46	1.19	0.81	0.61	0.46
(25,100,30,F,T)	0.00	-0.04	0.19	0.19	0.19	-0.17
(100,400,10,F,T)	1.50	0.52	-0.84	-0.46	1.52	3.16
(20,230,40,F,T)	0.13	0.02	0.02	0.02	0.00	0.13
(20,300,40,F,T)	0.16	0.00	0.16	0.16	0.16	0.16
(20,300,200,F,T)	5.08	9.26	8.84	5.93	7.98	8.94
(30,520,100,F,T)	4.03	3.27	4.03	3.51	4.03	3.64
(30,520,400,F,T)	1.37	3.68	5.16	4.20	3.60	3.25
(30,700,100,F,T)	1.17	1.72	1.71	1.71	1.53	1.31
(30,700,400,F,T)	2.77	3.70	4.06	2.77	2.77	3.53
Avg. Improvement	1.67	2.26	2.45	1.88	2.24	2.24

TABLE 12.4. Percentage Improvement in Solution Quality for Parallel Executions on 16 Processors

C	IND	SBest	SProb	SMobil	SHigh	SLow
(25,100,10,F,T)	0.56	0.61	0.79	0.46	0.50	0.79
(25,100,30,F,T)	0.00	0.09	0.11	0.14	0.23	0.23
(100,400,10,F,T)	1.50	1.89	1.50	1.50	1.77	1.77
(20,230,40,F,T)	0.13	0.00	0.02	0.02	0.02	0.02
(20,300,40,F,T)	0.16	0.16	0.16	0.16	0.16	0.16
(20,300,200,F,T)	5.08	7.98	7.72	7.98	7.54	8.05
(30,520,100,F,T)	4.03	3.51	4.03	4.03	3.51	3.51
(30,520,400,F,T)	1.37	1.93	1.37	2.08	3.90	1.42
(30,700,100,F,T)	1.17	1.50	1.17	1.17	1.33	1.68
(30,700,400,F,T)	2.77	3.47	2.97	2.84	2.84	2.77
Avg. Improvement	1.67	2.12	1.98	2.04	2.18	2.18

these tables indicate results for the independent parallel search (column *IND*), and five selection strategies to extract a solution from the pool in cooperative strategies:

- *SBest*: extracts the minimum cost solution from the pool of solutions.
- *SProb*: randomly selects a solution among the best in the pool.
- *SMobil*: randomly selects a solution of the pool according to weighted probabilities.
- *SHigh*: similar to *SMobil*, except that it randomly selects a solution among those with high weighted probability values.
- *SLow*: similar to *SMobil*, except that it randomly selects a solution among those with low weighted probability values.

The performance of each strategy is measured for each problem as the percentage improvement in solution quality, with respect to the corresponding result obtained by the sequential procedure. A negative value indicates that a worse solution was found.

According with Tables 12.2–12.4, the parallel strategies found better solutions. Only 6 out of the 180 parallel runs found a solution worse than that obtained by the sequential algorithm, while in 11 runs the same solution was obtained. The results also indicate that cooperative search performs better than independent search. This observation is true for two selection strategies when 4 processors were used. When 8 or 16 processors were used, all cooperative strategies significantly outperformed the independentsearch approach.

12.5. APPLICATIONS IN TELECOMMUNICATIONS AND BIOINFORMATICS

Presented here are some applications of parallel implementations of metaheuristics to optimization problems in telecommunications and bioinformatics. As many problems in these areas are NP-hard and exact methods can only solve small problems, approximate algorithms based on metaheuristics play a very important role in their solution in practice.

The parallel algorithms presented here are developed aiming the achievement of lower execution times and/or finding better quality solutions. Parallelizations of metaheuristics designed to accelerate sequential procedures are usually simple to implement and quite often lead to linear speedups. The cooperative work, performed by parallel execution threads exchanging information during their execution, shows that better results can be achieved in less computational times for different types of metaheuristics.

12.5.1. Applications in Telecommunications and Network Design

The outbreak of new technologies in telecommunications networks, together with the demand for more computer intensive applications, leads to huge developments and needs in network design and routing.

Communication networks consist of nodes that can be computers, database repositories, instruments like tomography equipments or radio transmitters, connected by data transmission links, such as copper cables, optical fibers, satellite, and radio links. Their design involves making decisions on many issues, such as the number of nodes and their locations, routing paths, capacity installation, wavelength allocation, and frequency assignment. The main objective is often to obtain a least cost network configuration, subject to constraints involving issues, such as delay, throughput, reliability, link capacity, and cross-talk level.

Applications of metaheuristics to problems in telecommunications are plentiful in the literature (77,78). Some parallel applications are surveyed below, according to the main metaheuristic used by each of them.

As shown in Section 12.4.1, GRASP with path-relinking for the 2-path network design problem has been shown to be efficiently implemented in parallel with linear speedups. As noticed before, applications can be found in the design of communications networks, in which paths with few edges are sought to enforce high reliability and small delays.

Canuto et al. (79) developed a parallel GRASP heuristic for the prize-collecting Steiner tree problem. Given an undirected graph with prizes associated with its nodes and weights associated with its edges, this problem consists of finding a subtree of this graph minimizing the sum of the weights of its edges plus the prizes of the nodes not spanned. It has important applications in the design of local access networks. The authors proposed a multi-start local search algorithm. Path-relinking is used to improve the solutions found by local search. Their results show that the local search with perturbations approach found optimal solutions on nearly all of the instances tested, in much smaller computation times than an exact branch-and-cut algorithm that is able to handle only small problems. An independent parallelization obtained important speedups.

The parallelization of the reactive GRASP heuristic developed by Prais and Ribeiro (12) for the problem of traffic assignment in TDMA communication satellites led to linear speedups in Ref. 80.

Bastos and Ribeiro (66) implemented an independent-thread multiple-walk parallel reactive tabu search strategy, which is among the most effective and robust heuristics for the Steiner problem in graphs. Although the threads are independent, they cooperate either periodically or at a postoptimization phase using a pool of good solutions.

The multicommodity location–allocation problem with balancing requirements (73) was one of the first applications addressed by cooperative-thread implementations of tabu search. The algorithm is centralized, as in most parallelizations of this type. The trajectories start from different initial solutions and communicate through a central pool of elite solutions. In a similar domain, another application to the design of capacitated multiresource networks is described in Ref. 71. Improved solutions and smaller computation times are obtained for both applications, with respect to the sequential algorithms.

Buriol et al. (81) presented a hybrid genetic algorithm for solving the OSPF weight setting problem, combining a genetic algorithm with a local search procedure applied to improve the solutions obtained by crossover. Experimental results showed that the hybrid heuristic found better solutions and led to a more robust implementation than the best known heuristic in the literature. Preliminary parallelization results have shown almost linear speedups.

Watanabe et al. (82) proposed a new type of parallel genetic algorithm model for multiobjective optimization problems. It was applied to solve an antenna arrangement problem in mobile communications. Their algorithm showed a very good performance when compared to other methods.

Guo et al. (83) presented a parallel genetic algorithm for finding solutions to the third-generation radio network planning problem. They presented a genetic encoding of the problem and proposed an implementation of a coarse grained genetic program, but they did not implement the parallel algorithm.

Alba *et al.* (84) developed some parallel evolutionary algorithms for designing error correcting codes, and finding optimal placements for antennas in radio networks. They reported several results obtained using steady-state, generational, and cellular evolutionary algorithms. From a global point of view, the results have been very satisfactory for the two problems.

Alba and Chicano (85) presented a new local search algorithm (repulsion algorithm) for the problem of finding an error coding code. They used a hybrid between a parallel genetic algorithm and this new algorithm, and compared it against a pure parallel genetic algorithm. The results showed that improvements were achieved with the repulsion algorithm and parallelism.

Melab *et al.* (86) developed a white-box object-oriented framework dedicated to the reusable design of parallel and distributed metaheuristics. It provides features for evolutionary algorithms, local search procedures, most common parallel and distributed models and hybridization mechanisms. They show results obtained for solving a radio network design problem. The problem consists in finding a set of sites for antennas from a set of predefined candidate locations, determining the type and the number of antennas, and their configuration parameters. They investigated a parallel distributed multiobjective genetic algorithm developed to solve this problem using this framework. Three parallel–distributed models are available from this framework. They implemented the three models and compared their performance.

12.5.2. Applications in Bioinformatics

Bioinformatics is a multidisciplinary area, where computational and mathematical techniques are used to solve problems in biology. The cost of biological experiments is quite high and many of them are also time consuming. Therefore, many computational methods for analyzing and interpreting results of genetic experiments have been developed. Usually, solving biological problems involves an enormous amount of collected data, and the interpretation of the results of biochemical experiments requires complicated combinatorial models.

This area is quite new, with relatively few applications of metaheuristics reported in the literature to date. Parallel evolutionary algorithms are most often used in these applications.

Bhandarkar *et al.* (87) developed a parallel genetic algorithm for physical mapping of chromosomes in the presence of errors. The main goal was to obtain a minimal set of clones and probes that covers the entire chromosome. They implemented a two-tier parallel strategy. The upper level comprised a parallel discrete optimization using a genetic algorithm, while the lower level was performed by a parallel conjugate gradient descent procedure for continuous optimization. They obtained some results showing that for some instances this implementation was able to achieve linear and superlinear speed-ups.

Jourdan et al. (88) presented a parallel genetic algorithm to treat the linkage disequilibrium, used to discover haplotypes, which are candidates to explain multifactorial diseases, such as diabetes or obesity. Since the evaluation of the fitness of the individuals is time consuming, they developed a synchronous parallel implementation of the evaluation phase. The implementation was based on a master–slave model. During the fitness evaluation phase, the master gives to each slave an individual to be evaluated. The slave computes the fitness of this individual and sends it back to the master.

A well-known model used for the protein-folding problem is the 2D-HP model (89). Santos et al. (90) performed a theoretical analysis of some parallel genetic algorithms to solve this problem. They analyzed some configurations for the parallel implementation, including master–slave, fine-grained, coarse-grained, and their variants. They used the LogP model (91) of a distributed memory multiprocessor, in which processors communicate by point-to-point messages. They also implemented the algorithms analyzed theoretically, and showed that their performance prediction was correct.

A genetic algorithm-based method was proposed by Nguyen et al. (92) for solving the sum-of-pairs multiple protein sequence alignment. First, a chromosome representation and the genetic operators were proposed. Next, two kinds of local search heuristics were combined with this algorithm: one used to generate individuals in the initial population and the other used as the mutation operator for improving individuals during the search. Then, a parallel implementation of this method was presented. Experimental results of benchmarks from the BAliBASE benchmark showed that the proposed method is superior to other well-known methods in terms of solution quality and running time.

Gras et al. (93) presented a new classification of metaheuristics considering the property of cooperation between entities exploring the search space. This classification scheme involves three subclasses: centralized, individual, and concerted cooperation, depending on how the cooperation is accomplished. They gave new definitions and described new developments of these approaches, and tried to show their individual benefits. They show that a hierarchical division of the problem into independent tasks can lead to spread and simplify optimization steps. The results of these optimizations are then associated to produce a global solution benefiting from the structures appearing in the different levels considered. They applied these techniques to two central problems of proteomics: automatic protein identification and multiple sequence alignment based on motif inference. For the first problem, they developed a parallel cooperative ant algorithm (94), where the ants find some solutions and exchange information about these solutions among them. For the second problem, a cooperative multiagent strategy was developed, which takes advantage of concerted cooperation to achieve a fully automated clustering of biological sequences. The global algorithm follows an asynchronous course where each agent performs a succession of actions independently of the progress of other agents. Once the agents are initialized, they run an evolutionary algorithm to compute a preliminary solution. The agents exchange information about their solutions, so that some individuals from one agent can be sent to another agent to improve the quality of population.

Brauer et al. (95) presented a parallel genetic algorithm for phylogenetic inference under the maximum-likelihood optimality criterion. Parallelization was accomplished by assigning each individual of the population to a separate processor, so that the number of processors used was equal to the size of the evolving population. The genetic algorithm incorporated branch-length and topological mutation, recombination, selection on the maximum-likelihood score, and migration and recombination among subpopulations. They tested this parallel genetic algorithm with empirically observed and simulated DNA sequence data. For both observed and simulated data, the improvement in search time was nearly linear with respect to the number of processors. They also explored various ways of optimizing and tuning the parameters of the genetic algorithm.

REFERENCES

1. V.-D. Cung, S.L. Martins, C.C. Ribeiro, and C. Roucairol. Strategies for the parallel implementation of metaheuristics. In C.C. Ribeiro and C.C. Ribeiro, eds., *Essays and Surveys in Metaheuristics*, Kluwer, 2002, pp. 263–308. Dordrecht.

2. M.G.A. Verhoeven and E.H.L. Aarts. Parallel local search. *J. Heuristics*, **1**:43–65 (1995).

3. M. Toulouse, T.G. Crainic, and B. Sansó. Systemic behavior of cooperative search algorithms. *Parallel Comput.*, **30**(1):57–79 (2004).

4. T.A. Feo and M.G.C. Resende. Greedy randomized adaptive search procedures. *J. Global Opt.*, **6**:109–133 (1995).

5. M.G.C. Resende and C.C. Ribeiro. Greedy randomized adaptive search procedures. In F. Glover and G. Kochenberger, eds., *Handbook of Metaheuristics*, Kluwer, 2003, pp. 219–249. Dordrecht.

6. A.C. Alvim. Parallelization strategies for the metaheuristic GRASP. Master's thesis, Department of Computer Science, Catholic University of Rio de Janeiro, Brazil, 1998. (In Portuguese).

7. Y. Li, P.M. Pardalos, and M.G.C. Resende. A greedy randomized adaptive search procedure for the quadratic assignment problem. In P.M. Pardalos and H. Wolkowicz, eds., *Quadratic Assignment and Related Problems*, Vol 16 of *DIMACS Series on Discrete Mathematics and Theoretical Computer Science*, American Mathematical Society, 1994, pp. 237–261. Rutgers University Piscataway, WS, USA.

8. S.L. Martins, M.G.C. Resende, C.C. Ribeiro, and P.M. Pardalos. A parallel GRASP for the Steiner tree problem in graphs using a hybrid local search strategy. *J. Global Opt.*, **17**:267–283 (2000).

9. R.A. Murphey, P.M. Pardalos, and L.S. Pitsoulis. A greedy randomized adaptive search procedure for the multitarget multisensor tracking problem. In P.M.

Pardalos and D.-Z. Du, eds., *Network design: Connectivity and Facilities Location*, Vol. 40 of *DIMACS Series on Discrete Mathematics and Theoretical Computer Science*, American Mathematical Society, 1998, pp. 277–301. Piscataway, USA.

10. P.M. Pardalos, L.S. Pitsoulis, and M.G.C. Resende. A parallel GRASP implementation for the quadratic assignment problem. In A. Ferreira and J. Rolim, eds., *Parallel Algorithms for Irregularly Structured Problems—Irregular'94*, Kluwer, 1995, pp. 115–130. Dordrecht.

11. P.M. Pardalos, L.S. Pitsoulis, and M.G.C. Resende. A parallel GRASP for MAX-SAT problems. *Lect. Notes Comput. Sci.*, **1184**:575–585 (1996).

12. M. Prais and C.C. Ribeiro. Reactive GRASP: An application to a matrix decomposition problem in TDMA traffic assignment. *INFORMS J. Comput.*, **12**:164–176 (2000).

13. M.G.C. Resende and C.C. Ribeiro. GRASP with path-relinking: Recent advances and applications. In T. Ibaraki, K. Nonobe, and M. Yagiura, eds., *Metaheuristics: Progress as Real Problem Solvers*, Springer, 2005, pp. 29–63. Berlin.

14. S. Kirkpatrick, C.D. Gelatt, Jr., and M.P. Vecchi. Optimization by simulated annealing. *Science*, **220**:671–680 (1983).

15. A. Casotto, F. Romeo, and A. Sangiovanni-Vincentelli. A parallel simulated annealing algorithm for the placement of macro-cells. *IEEE Trans. Comput.-Aided Design Integ. Circ. Syst.*, **CAD-6**:727–751 (1987).

16. P. Banerjee and M. Jones. A parallel simulated annealing algorithm for standard cell placement on a hypercube computer. *Proceedings of the 1986 International Conference on Computer—Aided Design*, 1986, pp. 34–37.

17. A. Casotto and A. Sangiovanni-Vincentelli. Placement of standard cells using simulated annealing on the connection machine. *Proceedings of the 1987 International Conference on Computer-Aided Design*, 1987, pp. 350–353.

18. E.H.L. Aarts, F.M.J. de Bont, J.H.A. Habers, and P.J.M. van Laarhoven. Parallel implementations of the statistical cooling algorithm. *Integration*, **4**:209–238 (1986).

19. F. Darema, S. Kirkpatrick, and V. Norton. Parallel algorithms for chip placement by simulated annealing. *IBM J. Res. Dev.*, **31**:391–402 (1987).

20. S. Kim, J.A. Chandy, S. Parkes, B. Ramkumar, and P. Banerjee. Proper-PLACE: A portable, parallel algorithm for cell placement. *Proceedings of the 8th International Parallel Processing Symposium*, 1994, pp. 932–941.

21. P. Banerjee, M. Jones, and J. Sargent. Parallel simulated annealing algorithms for standard cell placement on hypercube multi-processors. *IEEE Trans. Parallel Dist. Syst.*, **1**:91–106 (1990).

22. S.A. Kravitz and R.A. Rutenbar. Placement by simulated annealing on a multiprocessor. *IEEE Trans. Comput. Aided Des.*, **6**:534–549 (1987).

23. R.A. Rutenbar and S.A. Kravitz. Layout by annealing in a parallel environment. *Proceedings of the IEEE International Conference on Computer Design*, 1986, pp. 434–437.

24. J.R. Allwright and D.B. Carpenter. A distributed implementation of simulated annealing for the travelling salesman problem. *Parallel Comput.*, **10**:335–338 (1989).

25. E.E. Witte, R.D. Chamberlain, and M.A. Franklin. Parallel simulated annealing using speculative computation. *IEEE Trans. Parallel Dist. Syst.*, **2**:483–494 (1991).

26. P. Roussel-Ragot and G. Dreyfus. A problem-independent parallel implementation of simulated annealing: Models and experiments. *IEEE Trans. Comput.-Aided Des.*, **9**:827–835 (1990).

27. S.-Y. Lee and K.G. Lee. Synchronous and asynchronous parallel simulated annealing with multiple markov chains. *IEEE Trans. Parallel Dist. Syst.*, **7**:993–1008 (1996).

28. R. Azencott. *Simulated annealing: Parallelization techniques*. John Wiley & Sons, Inc., New York, 1992.

29. T. Crainic and M. Toulouse. Parallel strategies for metaheuristics. In G. Kochenberger and F. Glover, eds., *State-of-the-Art Handbook in Metaheuristics*. Kluwer Academic Publishers, 2002. Norwell, MA.

30. D.R. Greening. Parallel simulated annealing techniques. *Physica D*, **42** (1990).

31. J.H. Holland. *Adaptation in natural and artificial systems*. University of Michigan Press, 1975. Ann Anbor.

32. J.H. Holland. Genetic algorithms. *Sci. Am.*, **267**:44–50 (1992).

33. Z. Michalewicz. *Genetic algorithms + Data structures = Evolution Programs*. Springer-Verlag, 1996. London, UK.

34. C.R. Reeves. Genetic algorithms. In C.R. Reeves, ed., *Modern Heuristic Techniques for Combinatorial Problems*, John Wiley & Sons, Inc., 1993, pp. 151–196. New York.

35. E. Cantú-Paz. A survey of parallel genetic algorithms. *Cal. Parallèles, Rés. Sys. Rép.*, **10**:141–171 (1998).

36. E. Cantú-Paz. *Efficient and Accurate Parallel Genetic Algorithms*. Kluwer, 2000. Boston, NA.

37. E. Cantú-Paz and D.E. Goldberg. Parallel genetic algorithms: Theory and practice. *Comput. Methods Appl. Mech. Eng.*, **186**:221–238 (2000).

38. A. Chipperfield and P. Fleming. Parallel genetic algorithms. In A.Y. Zomaya, ed., *Parallel and Distributed Cmputing Handbook*, pp. 1118–1143. McGraw-Hill, 1996. New York.

39. D. Abramson and J. Abela. A parallel genetic algorithm for solving the school timetabling problem. *Proceedings of the 15th Australian Computer Science Conference*, 1992, pp. 1–11.

40. H. Muhlenbein. Parallel genetic algorithms in combinatorial optimization. In O. Balci, R. Sharda, and S. Zenios, eds., *Computer Science and Operations Research: New Developments in their Interfaces*, Pergamon Press, 1992, pp. 441–456.

41. P. Chalermwat, El.-G. Talbi, and J. LeMoigne. 2-phase GA-based image registration on parallel clusters. *Future Gener. Comput. Syst.*, **17**:467–476 (2001).

42. U. Kohlmorgen, H. Schmeck, and K. Haase. Experiences with fine-grained parallel genetic algorithms. *Ann. Oper. Res.*, **90**:203–220 (1999).

43. E.-G. Talbi and T. Muntean. Hill-climbing, simulated annealing and genetic algorithms: A comparative study. In H. El-Rewini and T. Lewis, eds., *Proceedings of the International Conference on Systems Sciences: Task Scheduling in Parallel and Distributed Systems*, IEEE Computer Society Press, 1993, pp. 565–573. Los Alamites, CA, USA.

44. D. Andre and J.R. Koza. Parallel genetic programming: A scalable implementation using the transputer network architecture. In P.J. Angeline and K.E. Kinnear, Jr., eds., *Advances in Genetic Programming 2*, MIT Press, 1996, pp. 317–338. Cambridge, MA, USA.

45. T.C. Belding. The distributed genetic algorithm revisited. In L. Eschelman, ed., *Proceedings of the Sixth International Conference on Genetic Algorithms*, Morgan Kaufmann, 1995, pp. 114–121. Pittsburgh, PA.

46. M. Bubak and K. Sowa. Object-oriented implementation of parallel genetic algorithms. In R. Buyya, ed., *High Performance Cluster Computing: Programming and Applications*, Vol. 2, Prentice Hall, 1999, pp. 331–349. NJ, USA.

47. E. Cantú-Paz. Implementing fast and flexible parallel genetic algorithms. In L.D. Chambers, ed., *Practical Handbook of Genetic Algorithms*, Vol. III, CRC Press, 1999, pp. 65–84. Boca Raton, FL.

48. E. Cantú-Paz and D.E. Goldberg. Predicting speedups of idealized bounding cases of parallel genetic algorithms. In T. Bäck, ed., *Proceedings of the Seventh International Conference on Genetic Algorithms*, Morgan Kaufmann, 1997, pp. 113–121. East Lansing, Michigan.

49. I. De Falco, R. Del Balio, A. Della Cioppa, and E. Tarantino. A parallel genetic algorithm for transonic airfoil. *Proceedings of the IEEE International Conference on Evolutionary Computing*, 1995, IEEC Perth, Australia, pp. 429–434.

50. F. Glover. Tabu search—Part I. *ORSA J. Comput.*, **1**:190–206 (1989).

51. F. Glover. Tabu search—Part II. *ORSA J. Comput.*, **2**:4–32 (1990).

52. F. Glover and M. Laguna. *Tabu Search*. Kluwer Academic Publishers, 1997. Nowell, MA, USA.

53. B.-L. Garcia, J.-Y. Potvin, and J.-M. Rousseau. A parallel implementation of the tabu search heuristic for vehicle routing problems with time windows constraints. *Comput. Oper. Res.*, **21**:1025–1033 (1994).

54. J. Chakrapani and J. Skorin-Kapov. Connection machine implementation of a tabu search algorihm for the traveling salesman problem. *J. Comput. Inf. Technol.*, **1**:29–63 (1993).

55. J. Chakrapani and J. Skorin-Kapov. Massively parallel tabu search for the quadratic assignment problem. *Ann. Oper. Res.*, **41**:327–341 (1993).

56. C.N. Fiechter. A parallel tabu search algorithm for large traveling salesman problems. *Discrete Appl. Mathe.*, **51**:243–267 (1994).

57. S.C. Porto and C.C. Ribeiro. Parallel tabu search message-passing synchronous strategies for task scheduling under precedence constraints. *J. Heuristics*, **1**:207–223 (1995).

58. S.C. Porto and C.C. Ribeiro. A tabu search approach to task scheduling on heterogeneous processors under precedence constraints. *Int. J. High Speed Comput.*, **7**:45–71 (1995).

59. S.C. Porto and C.C. Ribeiro. A case study on parallel synchronous implementations of tabu search based on neighborhood decomposition. *Invest. Oper.*, **5**:233–259 (1996).

60. S.C. Porto, J.P. Kitajima, and C.C. Ribeiro. Performance evaluation of a parallel tabu search task scheduling algorithm. *Parallel Comput.*, **26**:73–90 (2000).

61. E. Taillard. Robust taboo search for the quadratic assignment problem. *Parallel Comput.*, **7**:443–455 (1991).

62. T.G. Crainic, M. Toulouse, and M. Gendreau. Synchronous tabu search parallelization strategies for multicommodity location-allocation with balancing requirements. *OR Spektrum*, **17**:113–123 (1995).

63. T.G. Crainic and M. Toulouse. Parallel metaheuristics. In T.G. Crainic and G. Laporte, eds., *Fleet Management and Logistics*, Kluwer, 1998, pp. 205–251. Norwell, NA.

64. P. Badeau, F. Guertin, M. Gendreau, J.-Y. Potvin, and E. Taillard. A parallel tabu search heuristic for the vehicle routing problem with time windows. *Trans. Res.-C*, **5**:109–122 (1997).

65. M. Gendreau, F. Guertin, J.-Y. Potvin, and E. Taillard. Parallel tabu search for real-time vehicle routing and dispatching. *Trans. Sci.*, **33**:381–390 (1999).

66. M.P. Bastos and C.C. Ribeiro. Reactive tabu search with path relinking for the steiner problem in graphs. In C.C. Ribeiro and P. Hansen, eds., *Essays and Surveys in Metaheuristics*. Kluwer, 2001. Dordrecht.

67. C. Rego and C. Roucairol. A parallel tabu search algorithm using ejection chains for the vrp. In I.H. Osman and J.P. Kelly, eds., *Metaheuristics: Theory and Applications*, Kluwer, 1996, pp. 253–295. Dordrecht.

68. J. Schulze and T. Fahle. A parallel algorithm for the vehicle routing problem with time window constraints. *Ann. Oper. Res.*, **86**:585–607 (1999).

69. E. Taillard. Parallel taboo search techniques for the job shop scheduling problem. *ORSA J. Comput.*, **6**:108–117 (1994).

70. C.B. Cavalcante, V.C. Cavalcante, C.C. Ribeiro, and C.C. de Souza. Parallel cooperative approaches for the labor constrained scheduling problem. In C.C. Ribeiro and P. Hansen, eds., *Essays and Surveys in Metaheuristics*. Kluwer, 2001. Dordrecht.

71. T.G. Crainic and M. Gendreau. Cooperative parallel tabu search for capacitated network design. *J. Heuristics*, **8**:601–627 (2002).

72. R.M. Aiex, S.L. Martins, C.C. Ribeiro, and N.R. Rodriguez. Cooperative multi-thread parallel tabu search with an application to circuit partitioning. *Lect. Notes Comput. Sci.* **1457**:310–331, 1998.

73. T.G. Crainic, M. Toulouse, and M. Gendreau. Parallel asynchronous tabu search in multicommodity location-allocation with balancing requirements. *Ann. Oper. Res.*, **63**:277–299 (1995).

74. G. Dahl and B. Johannessen. The 2-path network problem. *Networks*, **43**(3):190–199 (2004).

75. R.M. Aiex, M.G.C. Resende, and C.C. Ribeiro. Probability distribution of solution time in GRASP: An experimental investigation. *J. Heuristics*, **8**:343–373 (2002).

76. G.B. Dantzig and M.N. Thapa. *Linear Programming: Introduction*. Springer-Verlag, 1997. Secaucus, NJ, USA.

77. S.L. Martins, C.C. Ribeiro, and I. Rosseti. Applications and parallel implementations of metaheuristics in network design and routing. *Lect. Notes Comput. Sci.*, **3285**:205–213 (2004).

78. S.L. Martins and C.C. Ribeiro. Metaheuristics and applications to optimization problems in telecommunications. In P. Pardalos and M.G.C. Resende, eds., *Handbook of Optimization in Telecommunications*. Springer-Science+Businese Media, 2006. New York, chapter 4, pp. 103–128.

79. S.A. Canuto, M.G.C. Resende, and C.C. Ribeiro. Local search with perturbations for the prize-collecting Steiner tree problem in graphs. *Networks*, **38**:50–58 (2001).

80. A.C. Alvim and C.C. Ribeiro. Load balancing for the parallelization of the GRASP metaheuristic. *Proceedings of the X Brazilian Symposium on Computer Architecture*, SBC, Búzios. (In Portuguese). 1998, pp. 279–282.

81. L.S. Buriol, M.G.C. Resende, C.C. Ribeiro, and M. Thorup. A hybrid genetic algorithm for the weight setting problem in OSPF/IS-IS routing. *Networks*, **46**:36–56.

82. S. Watanabe, T. Hiroyasu, and M. Miki. Parallel evolutionary multicriterion optimization for mobile telecommunication networks optimization. *Proceedings of the EUROGEN 2001 Conference*, Athens, 2001, pp. 167–172.

83. L. Guo, C. Maple, and J. Zhang. Parallel genetic algorithms for third generation mobile network planning. *Proceedings of the International Conference on Parallel Computing in Electrical Engineering (PARELEC04)*, IEEE Computer Society, 2004, pp. 229–236.

84. E. Alba, C. Cotta, F. Chicano, and A.J. Nebro. Parallel evolutionary algorithms in telecommunications: Two case studies. *Proceedings of the CACIC02, 2002*, 2002.

85. E. Alba and F. Chicano. Solving the error correcting code problem with parallel hybrid heuristics. *Proceedings of the ACM Symposium on Applied Computing*, ACM, 2004, pp. 985–989. Nicosia, Lypues.

86. N. Melab, S. Cahon, and E.G. Talbi. Paradiseo: A framework for the reusable design of parallel and distributed metaheuristics. *J. Heuristics*, **10**:357–380 (2004).

87. S.M. Bhandarkar, J. Huang, and J. Arnold. A parallel genetic algorithm for physical mapping of chromosomes. *Proceedings of the 2nd IEEE Computer Society Bioinformatics Conference*, IEEE Computer Society, 2003, pp. 567–572.

88. L. Vermeulen-Jourdan, C. Dhaenens, and El-G. Talbi. A parallel adaptive GA for linkage disequilibrium in genomics. *Proceedings of the 18th International Parallel and Distributed Processing Symposium (IPDPS04)*. IEEE Computer Society, 2004. Sanla Le, MN, USA.

89. K.F. Lau and K.A. Dill. A lattice statistical mechanics model of the conformational and sequence spaces of proteins. *Macromolecules*, **22**:3986–3997 (1989).

90. E.E. Santos, L. Lu, and E. Santos Jr. Efficiency of parallel genetic algorithms for protein folding on the 2-D HP mode. *Proceedings of the Third International Workshop on Frontiers of Evolutionary Algorithms, 2000*, 2000, pp. 1094–1097. Atlantic city, NJ, USA.

91. D.E. Culler *et al.* LogP: A practical model of parallel computation. *Commun. ACM*, **39**:78–85 (1996).

92. H.D. Nguyen, K. Yamamori, I. Yoshihara, and M. Yasunaga. Aligning multiple protein sequences by parallel hybrid genetic algorithm. *Genome Informat.*, **13**:123–132 (2002).

93. R. Gras *et al.* Cooperative metaheuristics for exploring proteomic data. *Art. Intel. Rev.*, **20**:95–120 (2003).

94. M. Dorigo and T. Stützle. The ant colony optimization metaheuristic: Algorithms, applications and advances. In F. Glover and G. Kochenberger, eds., *Handbook of Metaheuristics*, Kluwer, 2003, pp. 251–285. Dordrecht.

95. M.J. Brauer *et al.* Genetic algorithms and parallel processing in maximum-likelihood phylogeny inference. *Mol. Biol. Evol.*, **19**:1717–1726 (2002).

INDEX